॥श्रीजी॥

Diamonds are Forever

[handwritten signature] Jay Ramsikh

08.03.23

My livelihood has revolved around diamonds—from polishing roughs to creating facilities to cut and polish them and trading them as gems. I treated diamonds as my God in the physical form—pure, unblemished, transparent and forever. From the hundreds of kilometres depth in the netherworld to the roughs and finally as glittering gems, as fireballs of trapped lights, by their multiple facets inside the pure carbon lattice structure, mounted on crowns and jewellery, diamonds never get altered, like the human soul, that remains untouched by any human act.

I took my chances and the odds favoured me. Good things kept happening and the chances I took turned out in my favour. Many things worked out as I planned them to, naturally and by destiny. Much might have been different had I been different. However, it was as if it had to be like that only. I have no judgment about my life and myself. There is nothing I am quite sure about, except that more than I was living my life, life was living through me. God is clear and only man's mind is clouded. I kept attending to the little responsibilities that came my way and God never failed me. You are nothing but you can do anything.

PRAISE FOR THE BOOK

It is a pleasure to learn about the publication of your autobiography titled, 'Diamonds are Forever, so are Morals'. The endeavor will surely serve as a source of inspiration for the coming generations. From the reminiscences and incidents of childhood, early education, to picking up life skills on the personal and professional front, nuggets of inspiring information are compiled in the book. The simile between morals and diamonds in the title of the book itself sets the tone. The emphasis on morals is particularly relevant to the modern times, especially for our youth. The reader gets swayed with the autobiography's flow of thoughts. May the publication receive the love and affection of the readers and motivate them to contribute for the larger good. I wish the publication all success.

Narendra Modi
Honourable Prime Minister of India

Now a leading tycoon in the global diamond industry, Govindbhai has risen from humble and rooted beginnings to make a mark for himself across the world. Since he hails from my district, I have witnessed the hard work, industriousness, and diligence with which he has conducted his business to reach tremendous heights. Along with his sharp business insights, Govindbhai has also been an epitome of kindness and generosity and has nurtured a culture of mutual respect amongst his people.

Dr. Mansukh Mandaviya
Union Minister for Health & Family Welfare and Chemicals & Fertilizers

Aptly titled, 'Diamonds are Forever, so are Morals', is Govind Kaka's autobiographical book depicting the various stages of his life. It tells the reader about the principles and values with which he lived till date. It is most befitting and exemplary that he has put the principles and ethics of life at the centre, valuing them as Diamonds.

Parshottam Rupala
Union Minister of Fisheries, Animal Husbandry & Dairying

Here is a life journey of an individual born in interior Gujarat around the time of Indian Independence, showcasing how the intrinsic value system present in the Indian ethos can result in the building of an enterprise starting from scratch and bring it to the level of global recognition. The journey brings out vividly the triumph of family values, honesty and integrity in business development and progress in life.

A. S. Kiran Kumar
Former Chairman of the Indian Space Research Organisation

Ever since I got to know him, I can say that [Govindbhai's] has been an untainted voyage. We do not have to merely go after physical pleasures or even have to become an accomplished ascetic. It is important to be just a seeker . . . The journey from zero to completeness looks not only successful but it *is* successful. Self-realisation, service to society and devotion to the Almighty are the three objectives of the seeker. As a monk, I feel that Govindkaka is a on a pilgrimage toward this triad.

Morari Bapu
Spiritual leader and renowned exponent of the Ramayan

I call 'life' an event, like a flower blossoming on a plant. Instead of trying to become something, blossoming is a just and fair experience. This is the difference between a diamond made by nature and a diamond made suitable for an ornament after cutting and polishing it . . . [Govindbhai's] life journey and experiences, will show readers their inner potential and inspire them.

Ramesh Oza - Bhaiji
Spiritual leader and preacher of Vedanta philosophy

Many people profess that the world is an illusion, and it is a place where one can easily get drowned. But Govindbhai's autobiography is an example that one can attain salvation even while remaining involved in worldly matters. His life is full of ceaseless activity, revolving around honesty, ethics, morality, and spirituality. The high point of his life is his spiritual outlook and Satsang with saints and noble persons.

Swami Sachchidanand
Social Reformer, Humanitarian and Philosopher

In business, employees come and go [but] morals endure . . . . [this] compelling autobiography perfectly captures . . . his life of servanthood, generosity, thoughtfulness, and kindness outside the office [that] have left – and continue to leave – an even greater mark . . . Diamonds endure, and so will his legacy.

Tom Moses, Sr. Vice-President
Gemological Institute of America (GIA)

It is full of unique insights and valuable experience.

Evgeny Agureev
Deputy CEO, ALROSA, Mirny, Russia

In many ways, [Govindkaka] has been a yardstick by which I have always measured my professional moves. He is the gold, rather, the diamond standard for all of us. [His] story is nothing short of a fairy tale.

Colin Shah
Chairman, Gems and Jewellery Exports Promotion Council (GJEPC)

[This] book is a story of the three most important institutions that weave through our lives—family, friends, and firms . . . In such a situation, relatives, friends and neighbours become partners and support each other through investments as well as in adversity . . . One can't help but conjecture that it is possible that the division reduced risks whilst at the same time provided a sense of comfort or insurance that the impact of failure, if it were to occur, would be limited. There are many interesting lessons for us all and for scholars of family business in this sublime book.

Prof. Errorl D'Souza
Director, Indian Institute of Management, Ahmedabad

DIAMONDS ARE FOREVER

So Are Morals

Autobiography of Govind Dholakia

As told to

ARUN TIWARI
KAMLESH YAGNIK

PENGUIN
ENTERPRISE

An imprint of Penguin Random House

PENGUIN ENTERPRISE

USA | Canada | UK | Ireland | Australia
New Zealand | India | South Africa | China

Penguin Enterprise is part of the Penguin Random House group of companies
whose addresses can be found at global.penguinrandomhouse.com

Published by Penguin Random House India Pvt. Ltd
4th Floor, Capital Tower 1, MG Road,
Gurugram 122 002, Haryana, India

First published in Penguin Enterprise by Penguin Random House India 2021

10 9 8 7 6 5 4 3 2

ISBN 9780670095728

Typeset in Adobe Caslon Pro
Printed at Thomson Press India Ltd, New Delhi

www.penguin.co.in

नष्टो मोहः स्मृतिर्लब्धा त्वत्प्रसादान्मयाच्युत l
स्थितोऽस्मि गतसन्देहः करिष्ये वचनं तव ll

(श्रीमद् भगवद् गीता, अध्याय 18, श्लोक 73)

O Achyuta, [my] delusion has been destroyed and memory has been retained by me through Your grace. I stand with my doubt removed; I shall follow Your instruction.

(Shreemad Bhagvad Gita, Chapter 18, Verse 73)

Contents

Foreword

Autobiography is a fascinating genre of writing. At one level, it is easy to write and within the reach of all. One knows oneself better than others do; one enjoys a privileged access to one's life and can talk about it without fear of contradiction. On another level, autobiography is one of the most demanding forms of writing, requiring a kind of moral discipline available only to a few. In writing about oneself, one is prone to the dangers of self-glorification and even narcissism. Since one inevitably writes about others who are part of one's life, one is also likely to invade their privacy and say things they may not wish to share with others or tell them in a manner they find hurtful. There is generally not any good reason why anyone should be interested in one's life and, therefore, the writer needs to show why his life is of importance and thus to exaggerate the importance and uniqueness of his life. Human life further has both fluidity and solidity, and an autobiographer needs to relate his experiences to his changing and constantly reconstituted sense of identity. An autobiography cannot be a mere narration of events and experiences. It must reflect on them, appropriate and assimilate them, and turn them into an integral part of a coherent story. Autobiography is in this respect quite different from biography with which it is often confused. It is not a species or form of biography, a story of one's life written by oneself, but rather an independent and unhyphenated form of writing.

Given these and other features, an autobiography is vulnerable to several dangers such as narcissism, boastfulness, moral insensitivity to one's family and friends, and so on. Not surprisingly, few autobiographies succeed in avoiding them. Mahatma Gandhi, one of the first Indians to attempt an autobiography, was acutely aware of this and expressed his dilemma in the foreword to his autobiography. He concluded that he would write not his own autobiography but that of his experiments in truthful living, and rightly entitled it 'Satyana Prayogo Athva Atmakatha,' putting the word autobiography not at the centre of the title as many believe but rather at the end.

In the light of what I have said so far, Govind Dholakia's autobiography is a remarkable piece of writing. Written in a story-telling style learned from Morari Bapu and Dongreji Maharaj, it is largely free from the characteristic vices of autobiography. He is rightly proud of his achievements, but I see no traces of self-glorification or boastfulness. He talks in detail about the various members of his family but never invades their privacy or says things they might find offensive. He is anxious that his children and brothers should not be spoiled by growing up in a privileged environment and sends them out to different places to fend for themselves for a few weeks. He narrates their experiences with kindness and good humour and brings out their individuality. He talks about Champa, his wife, with great affection, welcomes her criticisms and corrections, and displays a rare spirit of equality and comradeship.

Govind's life is held together by a guiding philosophy of life or what he calls the Triveni of life. This involves three basic beliefs, namely that honesty and ethics should inform all human activities, that there is a God or an unseen force that permeates everything, and finally that the family should be at the centre of one's life. 'I want to put God-centred devotion at the core of all my business activities,' says Govind. Work is a form of Bhakti, a way of serving God through serving one's fellow humans. This way of identifying God and humanity has been the defining feature of Vedantic humanism and forms the basis of Govind's approach to life as that of Vivekanand, Gandhi, and others.

This philosophy of life is supported by a body of insights harvested from sustained reflection on a wide range of human experiences. They regulate one's expectations and guide one through the varying circumstances that life throws up. Govind maintains that although pursuit of money is valuable and has a place in life, human relations far outweigh its value and are priceless. Money should therefore be made in such a way that the quality of human relations is not damaged. Like money, the pursuit of power, too, is valuable but tends to treat subordinates with contempt, to view one's own opinions as infallible, and needs to be disciplined and regulated. Life again never runs smoothly and along predictable lines. It is full of uncertainties, contingencies, and unanticipated challenges and these should be neither resented nor lamented but accepted as an invitation to fly high and to turn problems into a path to progress. These and other insights are summed up in five Sutras, which Govind with characteristic humility calls his 'final gift for posterity.'

An autobiography is meant to reveal the innermost springs of action and self-conception of the author. In this autobiography, we meet a fine human being, one who is warm-hearted, independently minded, thoughtful, decisive, concerned with those who are weak and vulnerable, proud of his workers whom he associates with the conduct of his business, committed to his extended family, and, surprising in a businessperson, a lover of Sanskrit. It is common to think that a successful businessperson is rarely a morally decent human being. This autobiography shows the opposite and affirms the old maxim *Yogah Karmasu Kaushalam* (Yoga is being successful at managing one's life).

No human being can be a model for another, both because no one is so perfect and because every human being is a unique author of his life. The most one can expect to learn from an autobiography is how the author wove the tapestry of his life, with the help of what resources, and what general lessons about the nature of human existence he learned and passed on to others. Judged by these and related standards Govind Dholakia's autobiography is an inspirational work and deserves a warm welcome.

London
October 2020

Professor Bhikhu Parekh
House of Lords

1

Activation

आप्तोक्तिं खननं तथोपरिशिलाद्युत्कर्षणं स्वीकृतिं ।
निक्षेपः समपेक्षते न हि बहिः शब्दैस्तु निर्गच्छति ॥

(विवेक चूडामणी, श्लोक 67, विभाग 1)

[Without] competent instruction, excavation, the removal of stones and other such things lying above it and grasping, a treasure hidden underground never comes out by being merely called out by its name.

(Vivek Chudamani, Shloka 67, Part 1)[1]

I do not qualify to write an autobiography, for I am neither a celebrity nor a public figure, nor have I done anything spectacular, except for the fact that I was born in a village in a farmer's family and could

---

[1] https://www.wisdomlib.org/hinduism/book/vivekachudamani/d/doc144513.html. Last accessed on date to October 10, 2021.

become a name in the Diamond Industry. Yes, it is true that I have come a long way from the conditions I was born into to where my family now is. Therefore, there has been a change and there must be reasons for that. How could a school dropout receive an Honorary Doctorate? How did a diamond polisher, who earned Rs 103[2] in his first month after a six-month apprenticeship without payment, become a billionaire employing 5000 people earning over a million dollars every month?

How did a farmer's son who would watch in disbelief at the aircraft occasionally flying in the sky over his village start an airline and connect towns in Saurashtra with other cities in mainland Gujarat? Was it fate or an unseen force? Was it hard work? Risk-taking? When I look back at my life, three things stand out of the mundane and routine that fills all lives: 1) the validity and efficacy of the straight path of honesty and ethics in achieving success in this world; 2) faith in God as an invisible force that runs this world and whatever lies beyond it; and 3) the essential role of the family system for the growth of individuals, communities, and society. I just played out the drama scripted on these three themes. Moved as if a puppet manipulated by the three strings in the agile fingers of the Master Puppeteer, who seemed to have a special fondness for this puppet, me—it was not without a reason. I am indeed a special puppet— more a person of the heart than the brain.

I was born in a small, tiled-roof house in the rugged and parched land of Kathiawar, where people looked at modernity as something dangerous and aggressive. Over 400 years ago, my ancestors travelled from Dholaka, which gave us our family name Dholakia, to Khambhada village and later in 1850 to Lathi. My grandfather Kanjidada owned land spread over three villages in Lathi. Kanjidada was very religious and generous by heart. He would act as an agro-advisor to King of Lathi, when in need. He divided his land amongst

---

[2] One US$ could be bought for Rs 4.76 in 1964.

his four sons with my father Laljidada owning a tract of land in Dudhala village. I was the fifth child in his family of five sons and two daughters.

I was born on the cusp between independence from the British and the making of the Indian Republic. The birth date mentioned in my school record is 7 November 1947, but in fact I was born on 1 November 1949, which was the eleventh day of the Kartik month of Vikram Samvat 2006 as per Indian calendar. I grew up in an atmosphere of change, where the generation of my father imbibed the ideals of Mahatma Gandhi and accepted the dream of a centralized socialistic economy of Jawaharlal Nehru in good faith but had been battered by many forces of the new times. I grew up in Dudhala, a village inhabited by about 700 people. My mother, Santokbaa, was the aperture of my consciousness. She was a great cook and I saw womenfolk cajoling her to learn culinary skills. My first childhood memory is that my mother would wake up well before dawn to begin her household chores. I also remember eating a rolled roti[3] with butter and locally made sugar and giving a ride to my four-month-old younger brother, Arjan, on a wooden rocking horse. My father was a well-built man, who was mostly out in the field. He owned forty acres of, not so fertile, land where cotton, groundnuts, bajara,[4] jowar,[5] wheat and sugarcane were grown depending upon the season. He was the embodiment of fearlessness, and he used to speak to the point without pretensions. My mother had patient ears and kind words for everyone. She was like God to me; I would always hang around her and even sleep next to her. In retrospect, I can say that I inherited compassion from my mother and fearlessness from my father as the basic building blocks of my personality.

There was a cow and a buffalo along with two pairs of oxen in our house. Besides, a cat and three dogs were de facto pets. We never

---

[3] रोटी, Indian Bread
[4] बाजरा, Pearl Millet
[5] ज्वार, Sweet Sorghum

owned them, and they never abandoned us. My mother would keep milk, butter, and curd, which were always in surplus in our house, in a clay enclosure, which acted as a rudimentary refrigerator. The cat somehow discovered the way to enter the enclosure and feast itself. It was normal for us to consume things tasted first by the cat. There were naturally many rats in our house to eat the grain stored in abundance and following them, to feast on rats, snakes would appear with regular frequency. My mother never felt scared by them, and we all would watch them come and go without any alarm. The dogs would escort the men to the fields and guard the lunchboxes from smaller animals. In the evening, they would return and sleep outside the house as self-appointed guards. When I was ten years old, another cow and buffalo were added to our family.

In great harmony with all the animals around, and in accordance with their simple habits and most predictable mannerisms. The first question that crossed my mind as a child, why our cow was revered as a divine mother and why the buffalo, despite giving more quantity of milk was discriminated against as some earthly creature. Once, we seven siblings had an assembly, headed by Bhimjibhai, the eldest child in the family, Nagjibhai, Shantaben, Parbatbhai, Devkuwarben, Arjanbhai and me speaking in that order of seniority on this issue. We almost decided that it is the colour of the buffalo's skin that made it inferior to the cow, but our mother overruled us citing that many cows also have black skin. The delegation then went to Umaiya Dada, the Brahmin-in-chief of the village and he declared the proximity of the cow with Lord Shree Krishna[6] as the reason for her special status.

Acting as a midwife, Manima, a tailor-woman in a village, would have conducted 300+ deliveries in our village. All seven of us were born in her presence. Until she died in 1975, she always took pride in mentioning that she was responsible for our birth. We respected

---

[6] भगवान श्री कृष्ण, Human incarnation of Supreme Creator God, Krishna

her just as everybody else did in the village. This was a time when births took place not in a hospital but at home.

Atmaram Bapu was a Bawaji[7] in our village taking care of a temple of Shree Ram.[8] His house was bereft of any article, and he would not keep any eatable in the house overnight. He would perform Puja[9] in the temple until evening and then only eat his single meal. He received food from village households and if there were any leftovers after his meal, he would feed it to the dogs with his own hands with utmost loving care, both for the food and the beast. We were told that in the year 1917, Atmaram Bapu had visited the Badrinath shrine in the Himalayas in his youth with my grandfather Kanjidada and a Sadhu[10] from a town called Lathi. They travelled by train until Haridwar and walked 300 kms from there to the Badrinath shrine located along the banks of the Alaknanda River at a height of more than 10,000 feet. They returned to the village after six months and received a heroic welcome.

There was a silent bond between our family and Atmaram Bapu. Whenever he needed some milk, curd, or anything else, he would visit us and my mother would give it to him, without him asking. It was an early lesson for me that thoughts can be read. Atmaram Bapu would simply say, 'Sita Ram,'[11] take whatever he needed, and leave saying 'Sita Ram' once again. Even otherwise, he hardly spoke anything other than 'Sita Ram' in all the years that I knew him.

Early childhood pains somehow are registered and never go away. When I look back at my childhood memories, they are all flagged by injuries and fevers, but each pain appears in conjunction with the loving care I received. When I was seven, one day whilst going to field with my brother Parbatbhai in our bullock cart loaded

---

[7] बावाजी, Person performing rituals in a temple
[8] भगवान श्री राम, Human incarnation of Supreme Creator God, Ram
[9] पूजा, a ritual in honour of the Gods, performed either at home or in the temple
[10] साधु, mendicant
[11] सीताराम, Chanting name of God Shree Ram and His wife Goddess Sita

with dried cow-dung cakes, I got my left index finger crushed under the cartwheel. As there was no doctor or dispensaries around, some crushed leaves of Moong[12] were applied to the wound. It must have prevented the sepsis but there was no relief from the pain. Entire day I remained in a make-shift cradle made between trees. In evening when I reached back home my mother realized gravity of my injury. My mother did not sleep a minute the whole night and the next morning, my father took me to doctor at Lathi boarding a bus.

The doctor cleaned up the wound and applied bandages. Lathi did not have X-Ray facility, it also lacked doctors with skills in surgery. It took some time for me to overcoming the pain involved with the procedure. Seeing my woes, my father bought four little Pedas[13] from a nearby shop as if to divert my attention. By the time I returned to Dhudhala, my sobbing stopped and when my mother asked me how I was feeling, I smiled at her and gave her one Peda that I had saved for her as a token of celebrating my first bus journey and maiden visit to Lathi.

Another time, I had a fever. My mother sponged my forehead with salty water to bring down the temperature. As there was no medical aid available, all parents could do was nurse me, try home remedies, and pray to God. I later learned that mother used to take a vow not to take certain food of her liking as a penance to invoke healing powers. I recovered after a few days but the way my mother doted upon me has remained with me forever.

During the rainy season of 1957, while playing Gilli-Danda[14] with my friends, I accidentally hit my mother's eyes. Hearing her painful scream, all my friends ran away but I stood frozen in guilt. How could I hit my beloved mother? Seeing blood oozing out of the wound, I almost involuntarily took a vow not to eat butter for a month so that my mother could recover quickly. The next day,

[12] मूंग, green chickpeas
[13] पेडा, sweet balls made up of concentrated boiled milk
[14] गिल्ली डंडा, street game played by hitting a smaller wooden stick with a bigger one.

seeing me refusing to have butter, my mother found out the reason. To remove my guilt she said, 'Indeliberate mistakes never incur sin, and no penance is therefore necessary.' She indeed gave me a double serving that I ate gleefully.

Once when I was playing with my friends in our verandah, boy from a nearby village Kerla on a speeding cycle hit me hard. I fell with the impact injuring my left ear. Our neighbour and my uncle came running to my rescue and put common tea powder on the wound to relieve my pain. I wondered how everyone knew little tricks that surprisingly worked. However, unfortunately, nothing worked to remove the pain of a scorpion bite. Hardly was there anyone in the village who had not been stung by a scorpion. A scorpion bit me twice. Both times my brothers took me to a local healer who treated scorpion bites practicing his own voodoo method. Nevertheless, the 'master healer' was my mother. As night approached, she would take me in her arms. She would move her fingers through my hair and all pain would recede in a secure sleep.

I remember how my mother, whilst going to the field with the cow and buffalo, taking lunch for my father and other menfolk, would wrap some Rotis in a cloth and give to our neighbour, whom we called Jamna Masi.[15] My younger sister, Devkuwarben and youngest brother, Arjan, who was hardly two years old, would play the whole day and when hungry, eat portions of the Rotis taken from Masi. In the afternoon, the three of us would sit near the rivulet, waiting for our mother to return from field. Then she would appear—cow, buffalo walking in the front, and she would be carrying a bundle on her head. It was forbidden for us to cross the narrow bridge. We would patiently wait for the cow, buffalo, and mother to reach our side. My mother would then take out from her folded scarf sugarcane pieces peeled by her mouth and cut for us. She used to lift Arjan as

---

[15] मासी, Mother's sister

if relieving us from the babysitting. If there was ever a time when I saw God, it was then and in the form of my mother.

One memory that envelops everything else about my childhood was a blind woman called Rajuma and her bond with my mother. A widow who had lost her son also to an early death, Rajuma used to live outside the village with her daughter, Jadi. They were destitute and their hut was bereft of any article, even a utensil. Rajuma would somehow walk to my mother who would fondly feed her and hear her heart. One day, my mother served her boiled sweet potatoes mashed in milk with sugar. In those days, sugar was a rare commodity. It used to come from Mauritius and was called 'Moras.'[16] Rajuma tasted it for the first time. Suddenly, she started sobbing and said, 'Ben,[17] your children and their children will enjoy abundance. The happiness you gave me—a blind lady with a wretched fate—today will return to your future generations and provide prosperity and peace.' These were the words from her heart. Later when her daughter grew up, Rajuma's relatives took her to live with them in Dhasa village for her safety and Rajuma became crippled.

Finally, she was shifted to an old age home at Satadhar as the winter was setting in. She met my mother before leaving the village. My mother fed her with love, packed some Sukhdi[18] for her. Both women were crying incessantly. That is the last time I saw her, but I can feel her presence even now when I close my eyes and enter her world without light.

I was tall and lanky and had a flavour for adventure. My first adventure was jumping in a well and learning in real-time how not to drown. When I was ten my elder brother tied a rope on my chest throwing me in a well ensuring that I start swimming. Once Nagjibhai, Parbatbhai and me suffered from Eczema, a common occurrence in villages those days. As no medical service was available,

---

[16] मोरस, Sugar in Gujarati
[17] बेन, Sister in Gujarati
[18] सुखड़ी, sweet made from wheat flour and jaggery in ghee.

we went to fish in the river for a cure. Sitting still in the Gagadiya river; fish in the river would eat away the itch mite creating scabies on the skin, a traditional remedy. I sat there still in water with my brothers, Nagjibhai and Parbatbhai, though the tickling sensation fish created made it difficult for us to remain quiet. But it worked and our eczema was gone for ever. It might be difficult for many in today's time to digest this treatment, but it was a success for us in the villages.

The school in Dudhala consisted of a thatched room and a large courtyard offering education up to class IV. All students would sit together and were taught by one of three teachers, Krupa Shankar, Kanubhai Jani and Bhanubhai. Kanubhai encouraged me to learn Hindi and with his efforts, I passed the first level exam of Hindi conducted by the Rashtrabhasha Prachar Samiti,[19] Wardha for non-Hindi speaking people. I was taught basic Gujarati and arithmetic. But while teaching the important topics, my generous teachers taught me something of science, something of geography and history, something about the Englishmen, something in fact, about everything. Once, our school building caved in during the rainy season and the school was shifted to the veranda of the Shree Ram Mandir in the village. Many times, goats and dogs would come and sit patiently as if attending classes with us.

I went to Toda, a village 3 kms away from ours, on a school picnic with our teacher, Kanubhai, as the guide. We went to see a Hanuman[20] temple constructed a century ago by the local king to ensure the safety and security of his people, on the borders of three villages. The king had also constructed a step-well for the provision of water to the people passed by. However, I remember this visit more for my first encounter with a Radio. The Toda Gram-Panchayat[21]

---

[19] राष्ट्रभाषा प्रचार समिति, National Language Promotion Commission

[20] हनुमान, divine companion of the Lord Ram in the form of a monkey in the Hindu epic, Ramayana.

[21] ग्राम पंचायत, village council is the grassroots-level of formalised local self-governance system in India.

was given a radio set by the government. The radio was switched on for us. How could we hear something that was said so far away that we could not even see that place? I tried to search if a pipeline was dug for the sound to travel such as in my 'piped telephone', which I would use for playing with my brother Arjanbhai.

Nothing comes free in the village. Everyone, right from childhood must contribute by one's labour. As a child, I too toiled. Even before I worked in our sugarcane field, I used to draw water from the well, take care of the oxen and assist in making jaggery. I would also help my brothers in cutting fodder. Later in the night, we would all sit, together singing Bhajans[22] and making bunches of fodder for the market. The jaggery was sold at 17 paise for a kilogram and 8 bundles of fodder went for a rupee. In a bullock-cart, I would go with my father to various villages to sell our produce. Thus, hard work, trade, and commerce, all three were ingrained in me in my childhood as my education.

There was a small makeshift Swaminarayan Mandir in a 10x10 Ft room in our village. Two Sadhus would visit the temple from Gadhada in Botad District every year and stay put for a few days. When I was 10 years old, they left some books in there while leaving. There were literally no books in Dudhala village, not even a newspaper. Out of curiosity, I browsed through the Shreemad Bhagvad Gita,[23] one of the books that came to my hand. I almost went into a trance when I touched this book for the first time. There were shlokas written with a commentary in Gujarati after every shloka. I was studying in the fourth standard and yet found no problem in reading the Gujarati text. In fact, sitting in the Mandir,[24] I completed the entire book in one sitting of some six hours. The next day, I returned to read the book once more. This was repeated many times and I got convinced

---

[22] भजन, hymns sung in praise of God
[23] श्रीमद् भगवद्गीता, a 700-verse Hindu scripture that is part of the Hindu epic, Mahabharata
[24] मंदिर, temple

that I had some connection with this book and that this connection was older than I was. What was written there looked so familiar and understandable, which was otherwise impossible for anyone my age to comprehend!

There was some magic that all the 700 Shlokas[25] in the book entered my system and at the age of sixteen I memorized all those shlokas in Gujarati without much effort. I could recite them fluently. Of course, this did not happen suddenly. It took me some time to learn how to recite every Gujarati shloka and then memorize it. I did not understand at the time the meaning of what was conveyed but I could connect with them. In one shloka, towards the end, Lord Shree Krishna says, 'Leave everything and come to me and I will take care of you. Do not fear.'

सर्वधर्मान्परित्यज्य मामेकं शरणं व्रज ।
अहंत्वासर्वपापेभ्योमोक्षयिष्यामिमाशुचः ॥

(श्रीमद् भगवद् गीता, अध्याय 18, श्लोक 66)

Abandon all varieties of dharma and simply surrender unto me alone. I shall liberate you from all sinful reactions; do not fear.

(Shreemad Bhagvad Gita, Chapter 18, Verse 66)

This one shloka captured my imagination. If I do God's work, God will take care of me. It never troubled my mind about finding out what God's work is. The power of 'do not fear' was indeed very empowering. God is taking responsibility of all my actions. All my actions righteous or unrighteous are accepted, if done for God. It was indeed a great deal—work for God, and God will take care of you!

---

[25] श्लोक, Sanskrit verses in a two line format.

In 1961, I joined a school in Lathi, a Taluka-level[26] town nearest to Dudhala village. It would take more than an hour to walk the six kilometers to the school barefoot. One of my teachers, Pranlal Dave, was very kind to me. When he came to know that I had already passed the first level exam of Hindi, called the Wardha exam, he motivated me to go for the second level. I found it rather difficult and requested him to teach me privately. He used to charge a fee of Rs 5 per month for such service but as I did not have the money, he most generously agreed to teach me free of cost. I did not pass the exam successfully because of my bad hand writings. Later, when my father came to know about it, he instructed his workers to deliver him fresh vegetables.

In the village it was a tradition to gamble on Janmashtami[27] day. When I was in class five, I saw young children gamble and make bets. That got me thinking about multiplying my savings by making some bets myself. After thinking for a while, I decided to gamble. Some boys were playing cards. I started playing with four Aana.[28] That day my luck was in full favour. After playing for about an hour or two, I won Rs 3. I was very happy as I had started with four aana and made that into Rs 3 clear win of Rs 2 and Paise seventy-five. Happily, I went home with the money, in the form of coins, in my hands and showed it to my brother Nagjibhai. He became furious and his eyes turned red. He slapped me so hard that all the money flew around. 'Don't you feel ashamed of gambling? We belong to the Swaminarayan[29] faith. We cannot gamble. Let others play! Sons of

---

[26] तालुका, an administrative division in some countries of the Indian subcontinent that is usually translated to 'township' also called Tehsil (तहसील).

[27] जन्माष्टमी, Birthday of Lord Krishna on the eighth day of the dark fortnight in Bhadrapad month of the Hindu calendar, which usually overlaps with August or September.

[28] आना, before the decimal system was introduced in 1957, a rupee had 16 aana and a coin of four anna was used as a quarter of the rupee.

[29] स्वामीनारायण, a yogi and ascetic whose life and teachings brought a revival of central Hindu practices of righteousness, non-violence and celibacy in Gujarat.

Patidars[30] do not gamble! They toil in the fields and earn money by sweating it out. Now gather all the money and put it in the temple. Tell God, I have committed a sin. I will not gamble again.' With tears rolling down, I followed my brother's instructions and put all the coins in the temple hundi along with my own four Aana. I vowed never to get into betting; in whatever subtle form it arrived to tempt me.

One day, in August 1961, the entire family was working in the field. My father was ploughing, mother was tending to the cows grazing nearby and we brothers were doing assorted tasks. Suddenly, we noticed a black snake. He appeared to be agitated and was sliding towards the cows. Apprehending it may bite the cows or calves, Nagjibhai picked up a spade to shoo it off, but in the process, the blade of spade cut the snake into two. The snake died instantly. In our village, snakes were a common sight, and we were conditioned not to be afraid of them. Only a few days ago, we had celebrated Nag Panchami, on the fifth day of the fading moon half, Krishna Paksha of Shravan month. Emotionally devastated, we brought the severed body of the snake back home. We prepared a platform with bricks, cow dung, and cremated the snake. The entire family mourned. It left a deep impression on my young mind. I have never eaten anything that has involved killing of a sentinel being. It is my firm belief that all living beings have the spark of the divine spiritual energy; therefore, to hurt another being is to hurt oneself. I also believe that any violence has karmic consequences. Why did that snake come to our field only at that instant? Why did Nagjibhai have a spade handy to charge at it? Why him, and not anybody else of us? Therefore, whatever had happened was indeed the closure of a loop. Alternatively, conversely stated, opening of a loop? I can feel the heaviness of this memory even now when I am writing it here.

---

[30] पाटीदार, an Indian landlord and agrarian caste found in Gujarat

Lathi town comes alive during festivals. On the day of Janmashtami, our village would turn into a small fair. I got this idea of bringing balloons, blowers, and whistles from Lathi and selling them in Dudhala. The problem was that I was not sure where I could get money to buy these things in the first place. Getting money from home for this venture was ruled out. With Shree Krishna's promise of 'do not fear' alive in my heart, I nevertheless approached Batukbhai, the shopkeeper in Lathi selling balloons, blowers, and whistles. Articles worth Rs 3 were taken as a loan, with the undertaking that Batukbhai would take back whatever remained unsold. I blew balloons until my throat started to hurt. I blew the whistle to attract customers. The first customer came and bought a balloon. He gave me 5 paisa in my hand—my first earnings! A wave of enthusiasm passed through my entire body. Everything was sold by evening. There was a total sale of Rs 6.5 with a clear profit of Rs 3.5 against the investment of Rs 3.

The next day, I returned Rs 3 to Batukbhai. 'You kept faith in me, and that is why I was able to do the business.' I said and offered him a share of the profit. Batukbhai refused. He told me that every man in the world has his first day in business. He further added that he had trusted me and given me the money because of his faith in Shree Krishna. Thus, Shree Krishna sent me money for my first business. He said, 'It is your money, and I will not take a paisa from it. Nevertheless, I would give you one free piece of advice—do not splurge this money. Consider your earnings as given by God and never use them on sensory pleasures and vagaries of the mind. If you save your money and use it properly, God will keep multiplying it. But if you use this money for pleasure and sin, he will take back everything.' Through Batukbhai, not only did Lord Shree Krishna became my investor but He also laid down my business policy for me.

My elder brother, Bhimjibhai, bought a new Hercules bicycle, priced at Rs 28 from Rajkot. At that time, he owned a general store in Dudhala. The experience of riding a bicycle for the first time was one of the most memorable moments of my life. Bhimjibhai assigned me to tilt a portion of the farmland before letting me enjoy my first ride. Next day I woke up at six in the morning to finish tilting with help from Parbatbhai. Came now a moment of joy, I had earned my first ride on a bicycle!

I rode to school. I was exhilarated but fell after going for some 60 feet. Undeterred, I got up and moved on. Till date the first experience with bicycle has remained intact within me. Later, in 1997, when in the function commemorating our DTC membership, a journalist asked me to share life's most exciting moment, I did not mention first air travel, or drive in my own Rolls Royce but my fall and rise with the bicycle.

During that period of my life bicycle was an inseparable part of me. I got a permission to ride bicycle when I came in class seven at Lathi. My friend circle grew with Devchandbhai Jodhani, Parshottambhai Malaviya, Manubhai Radadiya, Arjanbhai Kanani and Lajibhai Kanani in the centre. A little younger to me Nakubhai Jodhani and Ravjibhai Radadiya also joined the gang. My friend Devchandbhai Jodhani would pedal sitting on the back while I held on to handle in the front as if I am moving on a motorcycle. Such an exciting time I had during those days.

My father brought home pair of calves, Leriyo and Jeriyo. We showered incessant love on these young ones. Both needed no permission to go anywhere in our fields. As if to repay any debt of earlier births, this pair worked in our farm for over fifteen years. They understood everything as if they were humans. This pair of bullocks were tall and well built. There were no tractors then, and we would use bullock power in the field. One day, Leriyo fell seriously ill. A pall of gloom covered not only our family but also the entire village. None of us could see Leriyo suffering. I saw Parbatbhai whispering in the ear of Leriyo. I asked him what he was saying. Parbatbhai said, 'I am telling him to go away from this world and be in another world.' The next day, Leriyo died. I believe that whatever you are physically—male or female, strong or weak, ill or healthy, human or animal, bird or a reptile—all those things matter less than what your heart contains. If you have the soul of a warrior, you are a warrior. Parbatbhai's soul could speak to Leriyo's soul, and it willingly joined eternity. After Leriyo died, Jeriyo was left alone. The solace of a friend had gone. He lived for another year before leaving for Heaven.

My teacher Pranlal Dave gave me an old copy of Patan-ni-Prabhuta[31] written by Kanaiyalal Munshi. I loved it immensely and struck a chord with the character of Munjal Mehta, the Prime Minister of Patan. Then there was Minal Devi, the reigning queen of Patan. A Jain married to a Rajput king; she was the mastermind behind the politics of Patan. One day, when my father inquired if I had read the book, I asked him who the Jains were. Instead of answering my simple question, he told me to read the book carefully as everything was written there.

Gujarat had a lively tradition of Katha,[32] a community gathering to hear the story of Shree Ram from the Ramayan[33] or Shree Krishna from the Shreemad Bhagwat[34] by a saintly person called Kathakar.[35] The tradition always went through its journey with two vital aspects—'Bhajans'[36] and 'Bhojan Prasad.'[37] The son of Umaiya Dada, Dayashankarbhai was working in the Public Works Department at Rajkot. Once, he brought a Kathakar from there for the Bhagwat katha. He also brought a loudspeaker and a mike, called 'radio' and a great novelty in the village. People from nearby villages congregated for the 'grand' Katha and five guests stayed in

---

[31] पाटन नी प्रभुत्ता, The Glory of Patan—A Gujarati novel of K. M. Munshi

[32] कथा, a tale

[33] रामायण, Tale of Lord Ram

[34] भागवत पुराण, Ancient Stories of God Vishnu, the most-celebrated text of Hindu sacred literature in Sanskrit

[35] कथाकार, Story narrator

[36] भजन, hymns

[37] भोजन प्रसाद, God's blessings in the form of food

our house. One afternoon, when I was shelling peanuts for seeds in the field, I was sent to where the Katha was taking place to call one such guest. I heard the story of the liberation of an elephant named Gajendra being told.

Gajendra lived in a garden on Mount Trikuta, and he was a devotee of Lord Vishnu. One day, Gajendra went to quench his thirst in a nearby lake with his family. Suddenly, a crocodile living in the lake caught him by the leg. Gajendra tried hard to free himself from the crocodile's clutches but in vain. He trumpeted in pain and when Gajendra lost all his energy, he prayed to Lord Vishnu to save him from the clutches of the crocodile. On hearing his devotee's prayer, Lord Vishnu mounted on Garuda[38] and arrived on the scene carrying with him his Sudarshan Chakra[39] and killed the crocodile thus rescuing Gajendra and granting him Moksha.[40] I did not understand the meaning of Moksha but felt my body becoming light.

The guest, Ravibhai, to whom I was looking for, soon spotted me and broke my epiphany. I wondered if the Katha could be heard on 'radio' setup by my brother, so that I could continue to hear what happened next. I even reasoned out if was not possible to bring in 'pipeline' for transfer of sound for at that time I believed that sound could travel through a 'pipeline' like water.

Another problem bugging my mind was why our region was called Kathiawar. My father boasted that it is the country of the Kathi people, the Rajput warriors. Therefore, I asked him, 'Are we the Kathi people?' He was unsure but asked what else we could be. 'Is everyone living here a Kathi?' I asked. He replied that we are Patel, agriculturists, unlike the Bharvad and Rabari people involved in cattle grazing. Like the Koli, the Choudhary and Jat people who own lands and do farming. We are not warriors like the Thakor, Bhanushali, Kathi Darbars, Karadia, Nadoda, Dabhi, Chudasama,

---

[38] गरुड़, Eagle, vehicle of Lord Vishnu, the Sustainer aspect of the Supreme God.
[39] सुदर्शन चक्र, disc-like weapon having 108 serrated edges used by Lord Vishnu
[40] मोक्ष, *Salvation*

Ahir, Lohana and Maher. We are also not scholars like the Joshi, Anavil, Nagar and Modh. The world needs different people to do different kinds of work so that everything can be done efficiently. He further told me to focus on what we do and take it forward. Somehow, I was clear that I was not meant for doing farming in the village. However, I did not know what exactly I want to do and that meant leaving Dudhala.

Soon, the opportunity arrived. I was studying in class VII. My older brother Bhimjibhai had moved to Surat to work as diamond cutter, soon after his marriage a year earlier. Nevertheless, his wife was living in Dudhala, so that he could find his bearing in the city without being burdened. Now Bhimjibhai had come to take his wife with him. He asked me if I would like to join him at Surat. It was the last day of March 1964. I said, 'My exams start a week later. Can I join you after giving them?' My brother said, 'Govind, if you have to go to Surat and work, why do you want to study?' I made up my mind. As a courtesy, and more than that to express my gratitude, I went in the evening to Lathi and informed Pranlal Dave. I was expecting a rebuke, but he said nothing. He went inside his house and brought a book Saurashtra-ni-Rasdhar[41] written by Jhaverchand Meghani. 'Read this whenever you find free time in Surat.'

Going to Surat was not an easy affair. One must change trains at Viramgam Junction railway station. We were carrying a lot of luggage, kitchenware and even ration for a few months. It was 3.00 a.m. when we reached Viramgam, passengers on the train going to Ahmedabad had bolted the doors of the compartments from inside and there was no way we could enter. After banging the doors in vain, I decided to get into the train through the window, which did not have crossbars in those days, and opened the door for my brother and Bhabhi to board it just in time. The train arrived in Surat on 2 April 1964. There were horse carriages outside the railway station;

---

[41] सौराष्ट्रनी रसधार, a book written by Zaverchand Meghani

something I was seeing for the first time. We loaded our luggage on a carriage and sat atop. My brother had rented a house in Bhojabhai-ni-sheri (by lane) in Mahidharpura area which was once a stable for horses. After freshening up, I wanted to see the city. Ravjibhai Radadiya from our village, who had come to Surat six months prior, became my escort and guide. The city of Surat was big, grand and beyond my imagination. I had never seen before a building of the size of the Surat Fort. Its reflection in the Tapi River captivated my mind. This historical fort which was planned and built between 1540 and 1546 by Khudawand Khan, a General in the army of the King of Ahmedabad, Sultan Mahmood-III (1538-1554), is one of the chief ancient monuments of Surat. The fort defended the city from the pirates and from the Portuguese who arrived there by sea and who were attracted by the legends of India as a Golden Bird. At Chowk, the center of the city in those days, Ravjibhai bought me Khaman, a Gujarati delicacy made by steaming fermented gram flour and yogurt batter for 10 paisa, which we ate sitting in Gandhibaug. We reached Bhagal crossroads. There were so many three-wheeled rickshaws[42] moving around. I wondered how a three-wheeled vehicle could move so fast. It will fall. I stood there for more than an hour, waiting for one of them to tumble. However, none had toppled so far.

When I left Dudhala, my father bought fabric from a shop in Lathi to stitch a dress for me, white colored fabric for shirt and black for trouser. In Surat, I went with Bhimjibhai to a tiny tailoring shop in to Pipla Sheri locality. The stitching charges were Rs two for the shirt and Rs five for the trousers. Bhimjibhai informed the tailor that only a month ago he got his pajama for Rs 1.5. When the tailor highlighted the difference between pajama and trousers to justify the higher charges, Bhimjibhai asked him to stitch a pajama. Pitying us perhaps, tailor stitched a lengha.[43] It was after wearing it for a year I understood the meaning of a pair of nicely fitting trousers.

---

[42] रिक्शा, a mode of fuel powered transport by three-wheeled vehicle
[43] लेंघा, crudely tailored trouser

To put things in context for my young readers, Surat had been attracting migrants from the arid and impoverished peninsula of Saurashtra to work in Zardozdi[44] factories. Zari[45] is a very fine thread of gold or silver used as brocade for export and in saris. The metallic thread is woven into fabrics, primarily of silk, to make intricate patterns and elaborate designs of embroidery. Zari work is highly labour-intensive. Later, when diamond polish work started coming to Surat and Navsari in the early 1960s from Bombay and Rangoon, primarily for cost-cutting, as labour there was expensive, young men from Saurashtra also started coming to Surat to find their fortune. This newfound opportunity turned out to be better than zardozdi.

When I arrived in Surat in 1964, there were around 200 people in the diamond cutting and polishing factories and the population of the city was 300,000. Diamonds are the purest matter on earth. They are formed in the great depths of the earth, under intense heat and immense pressure for millions of years and come out through volcanic eruptions. They are rare and therefore, highly valued. Once the diamonds were cut to a good shape and polished, they became a bundle of light and then were acquired by the rich and powerful of the times. Antwerp in Belgium had been the epicentre of the diamond trade in the world.

After India became independent and wealth started coming to the industries and businesses, a market for diamonds was created in Bombay, Surat and Navsari. People started selling them to other places in India and even began exporting them. Some Indian businesspersons started buying rough diamonds in Antwerp and started making money by getting them polished in Bombay and re-exporting them at significantly higher prices. H. H. Zaveri, H. B. Shah and Mohandas Raichand were amongst the pioneers of the diamond business in India.

---

[44] जरदोशी, type of embroidery
[45] जरी, brocade

Surat is situated on the banks of the Tapi River, called Tapti in Hindi. The Tapi River is considered as the daughter of the Sun God, and hence known as Suryaputri Tapi. Even Surat was once upon a time known as Suryapur. I used to walk along the river, would sit on the riverbank and watch the patterns of reflecting lights in the water. I learnt that the Tapi River starts from the Aravalli Mountain range in the Betul district of Madhya Pradesh and flows between two spurs of the Satpura Hills, across the plateau of Khandesh, and then through the plain of Surat to the Arabian Sea. It has a total length of around 724 km and finally draining into the Gulf of Khambhat, an inlet of the Arabian Sea. The Tapi flows roughly parallel to the longer Narmada River to the North, from which it is separated by the main part of the Satpura Range. The two river valleys and the intervening range indeed form the natural barrier between northern and peninsular India.

Coming back to my story, I joined Gordhanbhai Khadsaliya's diamond factory at Daliya Sheri as an apprentice. Arvindbhai Dabhoiwala gave me a broken porcelain pot and taught me how to grind that to a shape. In two weeks, I acquired all necessary skills under his watchful eye. It was 20 April 1964, when Arvindbhai gave me a rough diamond to work with. An industrial-quality diamond is mounted at the end of the stick, and the stick is held by hand against the rough gem diamond, forcibly contacting the stone to slowly brute (scratch) the material away. Without getting nervous or overwhelmed by the difference in the value of a porcelain piece and a rough diamond, I polished it as per his instructions and to his satisfaction. It was very satisfying to see the lower-quality diamond scratching the gem diamond stroke by stroke to remove diamond dust and small fragments until the crude shape was accomplished. My apprenticeship with Arvindbhai lasted for two months; I spent the next four months with Ishvarbhai Dholakia for acquiring additional skills in cutting and polishing. There was no stipend whatsoever paid to the apprentice. My first job was in the factory of Hirabhai Vadiwala. I earned Rs 103 in my first month's work of polishing a rough diamond.

Curiosity has been a dominant force driving me. One day, I walked into the Dutch-Armenian cemetery in Gulam Falia (Street) near the main road leading to Katargam Gate. The grandiose mausoleum of Baron Adrian Van Reede bewildered me. I had never seen such a magnificent building. The Armenian cemetery is situated adjacent to the Dutch cemetery. I used to try to figure out what could have been written on the epitaphs. One tombstone of a woman named Marinas whose death was mentioned as 1028 of the Armenian Era (that would be the Christian year 1579, I later learnt) enchanted me. Where was Armenia? What could have brought these people here, thousands of miles away from their birthplace? Did they know they would never return?

An old person, fair complexioned, frail with a white beard and unkempt hair was watching me pensively wandering around the cemetery aimlessly. I also noticed his presence and overcoming my fear and hesitation, I greeted him. He did not respond and gave me a blank look. I asked him if I could sit by his side. He nodded. 'Why are you here?', I asked. 'Why are you here?', he questioned back. 'I have come to see this cemetery,' I answered. 'Any of your family members buried here?', he asked. I got little afraid. Can't you see that I am a Hindu? I thought of saying, but replied politely, 'No one, we are Hindus. We cremate our dead.'

'I know, but what brought you here?', that man asked. 'I am new in the city, and got curious to see this place,' I said. Then the man asked me to sit down. I sat on a stone platform. After waiting for a while for the man to speak, when he said nothing; I said, 'These tombs are very grand. People who are buried here must have been great people.' 'My great-grandmother is buried here,' the man finally said pointing out a tomb. I asked, 'And your great-grandfather?' 'He left for Armenia, and since then we are here, alienated,' he answered. That day was my first encounter with the force called history. Nothing remains new and beautiful forever. The people of Armenia came all the way to Surat as warriors in their heydays. They have gone back, and Armenia hardly had any connection with India and yet, traces survived like that poor recluse.

My inquisitiveness about Rani Minal Devi's religion, which was bugging me since childhood, took me to Chintamani Jain temple, in the Shahpore area. It was built in 12th century by a Solanki king, to honour his guru, Acharya Hemachandraji, a Jain preacher. The temple looked simple from the outside, but I was surprised by the intricately and beautifully carved designs on the wood inside. There were beautiful paintings made on the roof depicting Acharya Hemachandraji, King Kumarpal and other Solanki kings. Unlike Hindu temples full of noise and activity going on around, it was a clean, well-maintained, and peaceful temple. Nobody was there for me to ask any questions to, but I returned with a deep sense of peace inside as if no more questions existed.

I soon learnt how to work on a bruting machine and joined the factory of Laljibhai Kheni at Kumbhar Street, Galemandi. Though Bhimjibhai and Bhabhi supported me well, I started staying in a little portion of the common house meant for the workers. My impeccable habits and religious bent of mind made my colleagues and even the elders call me 'Govind Bhagat.' I did not protest. I secretly felt pleased about it. It was at Laljibhai's factory that I met Bhagwanbhai Patel and Virjibhai Godhani, ten years elder to me. I developed an unexpressed comfort zone with Bhagwanbhai and Virjibhai. It was a gradual process of mutual respect, affection, and appreciation, spread over many years.

However, everything was going well, my heart was yearning to start my own little business. I wanted to be a leader and not a follower. To my hormone-charged young mind, a leader was meant to stick his neck out on a bold course of action even as the rest of the world wondered in awe. The only way ahead for me was to stand out from the crowd and to stand for something special. Laljibhai Kheni blessed my aspirations but advised me to understand the business in depth before getting into it. 'Business is like a one-way street; you never return once you start,' he told me. Later, when I was reading Satyana-Prayoga Athva Atmakatha[46], I realized the soundness of Laljibhai's advice. Gandhiji was 46 years old when he returned to India. Gopal Krishna Gokhale, who Gandhi regarded as his political mentor, had advised him to remain silent for one year during which he was to try and visit as many parts of India as physically possible, and meet as many people as he could, and acquaint himself with their problems. This was what Laljibhai was telling me. I decided to obey him most sincerely. I developed a habit of walking long distances, mostly in the early morning. It was my own peculiar way of meditating. Later, I learnt that walking meditation is indeed a wholesome practice called Kinhin[47] in Buddhism. I used to follow different roads to walk without any purpose or design.

One day, my walk took me Chaprabhata, where Mahatma Gandhiji stayed during the Dandi March. In 1930, Mahatma Gandhi decided to protest the British Government's position of levying a staggering 2400 per cent tax on salt, an item of daily necessity. The noble path Mahatma chose was that of non-cooperation. Taking 80 marchers with him, he began walking from Sabarmati Ashram in Ahmedabad on 12 March 1930 to reach Dandi, a beach 245 miles away, where he picked up a handful of salt in defiance of the British. He arrived at Chaprabhata on 11 April 1930, addressed a public meeting in Surat and crossed the Tapi River. I wondered how sixty-one-year-old Gandhiji would have endured such a long walk. 'Why can't I walk the sixty-one kms from here to Dandi?' I thought.

After thinking for a few days, I decided to do it. I took some days off from my work and embarked on the journey on 30 September 1967, which was a Saturday, to trek the great man's march to Dandi.

---

[46] सत्य ना प्रयोग अथवा आत्मकथा, An Autobiography: The story of My Experiments with Truth by M. K. Gandhi

[47] किनहिन, Kinhin are Buddhist sermons spoken by the enlightened masters.

I took a halt at Dindoli in Vanz, Dhaman in Navsari, Vijalpur, and Matwad and reached Dandi on 2 October, on Gandhiji's ninety-ninth birthday. In Dandi, there was a shop selling memorabilia about Gandhiji. I bought Satyana-Prayogo Athva Atmakatha, Gandhiji's autobiography in Gujarati. After spending the afternoon there, I walked to Moriya Bapa temple in Karadi in Jalalpore and slept there at night. The next morning, I walked to Navsari and took a bus back to Surat. I was filled with determination to make full use of the freedom our ancestors achieved for us, not only for the betterment of self but society as well, after a great struggle.

In October 1968, during the Diwali[48] vacation, I boarded the train to Bombay with my friends Karamshibhai Malaviya, Mohanbhai Kakadiya and Bhurabhai Ballar. We were all fired up with dreams to make it big in life. Life in the village was no good; the city was good but only for the wealthy. The poor in the city were more miserable than the poor in the village. Our vision was that we must live in the city and be wealthy. Working hard was the only way we knew to success. Each ticket cost us Rs 2.50, the labour of half-a-day in the factory. Glued to the window seat of the train, I saw the skyline changing from lush green to hillocks and it was apparent that we were going to a different place. Moreover, what a place it was! It was a beautiful and unique world!

We were dumbfounded when we got down at the Bombay Central Railway Station. So many railway tracks ended into a perpendicular long corridor at the southern end. There were people everywhere moving in an orderly manner with a sense of business and purpose in the air. Everyone was wearing prim and proper clothes, and no one was barefoot. There was a big garden just outside the station's main building. We took a while to sit in the garden to be acclimatized before daring to come out of the station building. An old locomotive named 'Little Red Horse' was kept in the garden.

---

[48] दीवाली—the Indian festival of lights, usually lasting five days and celebrated during the Hindu Lunisolar month Kartika (between mid-October and mid-November).

We had been recommended the Hotel Thakar Nivas at C. P.
Tank; a water tank that must have been named after the philanthropist
Cowasjee Patel who built it. We got into a taxi and asked the driver
to take us to Thakar Nivas. The taxi driver realized that we were new
to the city and took a longer route to extract more fare. We knew
we had been 'taken for a ride' but we were enjoying the ride. Such
a big city! Tall buildings, trams running on roads and well-dressed
people. We were busy watching the city without even blinking our
eyes. The taxi driver took us to Thakar Club at Kalbadevi instead
of Thakar Nivas. At that time, we even did not have any idea that
there were many hotels and not just one. We decided to stay where
we had planned and walked to Thakar Nivas from Thakar Club on
foot. When one is enjoying, nothing seems difficult. When the heart
is filled with excitement and enthusiasm, everything seems easy and
simple.

Bubbling with excitement, like soda water in a bottle, we almost
immediately came out of the hotel after freshening up. There were
so many cars, mostly Fiats. We started walking on the beautiful
pavements following the signs towards Zaveri Bazar that was about
two kilometers away. I insisted that we visit the Mumba Devi
temple first before entering Zaveri Bazar. It was an ancient temple
dedicated to the Goddess in Her fisherwoman form, named Mumba.
'Aai'[49] is the word for mother in Marathi. Later in 1995, the city
would be renamed Mumbai from Bombay to honour Mumba Aai.
Zaveri Bazaar is a muddle of narrow lanes, dotted with hundreds of
jewellery shops that sell gems and jewels. It is said that two-thirds
of all gold trading and dealing in India originates here. During the
early nineteenth century, a jeweller named Ambalal Zaveri was
famous for the quality of his gold. We ate lunch at the B. Bhagat
Tarachand restaurant. A large photograph of Tarachand Chawla,
displayed behind the cash counter, captured my attention. Later, I

---

[49] आई, Mother in Marathi language, spoken in Maharashtra

came to know that Tarachand came to Bombay from Karachi in 1895. He was a generous and kindred spirit and would often allow customers to eat free if they could not afford meals. This justifiably earned him the title 'Bhagat.'[50] I got goosebumps upon hearing this.

In the evening, we walked on the road by the side of Azad Maidan. Then, I saw to my left the Forbes Building on Charanjit Rai Road where the office of the Consulate General of the Kingdom of the Netherlands was situated. I walked to the building and felt enchanted. There were large English words engraved on the building. I boldly asked a passerby what they read. To my surprise, he told me that the words were not English but Dutch. I was under the impression that all white-skinned people came from England and spoke English. Therefore, it was a great revelation that there are other countries where people of the white race live and speak languages other than English. For a long time, I stood motionless like a statue. I took a vow to enter the building someday sooner rather than later and go to the Netherlands, wherever it was.

I was awestruck standing in front of the Flora Fountain. Then I asked who the goddess whose statue adorned the top of the fountain was. A passerby told us that she is Flora, a Roman goddess of flowers and the season of spring. The four corners of the fountain are decorated with mythological figures. Even the locals did not know about them. Five roads converged at Flora Fountain. Unmindful of the busy traffic, there were so many birds, mostly pigeons, hovering around, many of them sitting atop the statue. Honestly, this mix of movement and stillness filled me with a profound sense of peace. Like we all have an eternal Atman alive in our ever-changing bodies, this statue on a buzzing junction of five roads crowded with people and traffic, was just like that.

After spending close to an hour there, we walked towards the Gateway of India and the mighty Arabian Sea greeted us. The sight

---

[50] भगत, a devotee of Lord

of the majestic arch, the Gateway of India, and the hustle around it was surreal. Ships moving in the sea and the Gateway of India made us feel as if we were in some other world. Such was our enchantment that we forgot that we were hungry. I spent many hours learning that the Gateway was built to welcome King George V and Queen Mary, the first British monarchs to visit India in December 1911. Later, it was called the 'jewel in the crown' and a symbol of conquest and the British Empire.

Then we noticed a huge building with a great dome. 'What must this be?' we wondered. Overhearing us, a local person told us that this was the Taj Mahal Hotel. 'It is a very big and splendid hotel. Dignitaries from the country and around the world come here to this hotel. A beautiful restaurant, a big salon, and many other things are there in the hotel,' he said with confidence. 'Can we go there, and see?' I asked him. 'You people cannot go there. Looking at your clothes, the watchman won't allow you to enter the premises of the hotel,' he said, sadistically enjoying our discomfort and walked away.

Curious and determined to see the hotel, I called a taxi and asked him to take us to Taj Mahal Hotel. The driver was laughing at our ignorance as the Hotel was just across the road where we were standing, but to make his money, he took us in the car, circled around the hotel block and dropped us in the portico. Saluting us guard opened taxi door to let us in. We entered in only to reach the exit door. However, the guard had his eyes on us. He approached us with a menacing look and escorted us out of the hotel. Humiliated and a little angry at the rudeness of the guard, we did not speak for some time. Later listening to our dialect, a Gujarati contractor working in the hotel building on some repairing project identified us as 'apnewala'[51] and encouraged us to enter the hotel from the back-door service lane.

---

[51] अपनेवाला, own people

Finally, we were inside the hotel lobby. Where do we go now? This question captivated our minds. Our eyes caught the direction of the restaurant, and we started walking towards it. A waiter dressed in a white uniform courteously approached us and made us take our seats. Speaking something in English, he presented the menu before us. None of us knew English but feigning our illiteracy, we asked him to get us tea. Sitting there, we felt like princes. Everything there—the furniture, the tablecloth, curtains, lights—was like of some palace we had never even imagined.

The waiter returned after quite some time and placed bowls of milk, sugar, and a kettle of hot water. He also served some biscuits. We added milk, then sugar in the cup. But where was the tea? We figured that the tea bags kept in a bowl were supposed to be used. So, we tore open the teabag, added it in the water, and added the milk in the cups. Without straining tea, we gulped it. It tasted awful. We knew that there was some mistake. The waiter came and gave us a bill of Rs 20. Looking at the condition of the cup, he must have realized our predicament, but he said nothing. He took the money, thanked us and departed graciously.

Once bitten, twice shy—we did not dare walk out from the restaurant using the lobby and quietly went out from the way we came in—service door in the backside. Upon reaching near Regal Cinema, Bhurabhai took out the tissue paper from his pocket he had got from the hotel. 'Ah! You picked this up?' I asked. 'Yes, obviously, it had to be taken. If we say that we had gone to the Taj Mahal Hotel, no one will believe us. This is the proof, and we can show it to the disbelievers that we had indeed gone there,' he said pointing out to 'Hotel Taj' printed on the tissue paper.

We spent four days in Bombay and met many people in the Zaveri Bazaar to understand the diamond business in our own little ways. Most of the traders came here during World War II from Palanpur State and were known as Palanpuri Jains. They established their offices and small manufacturing units, where small amounts of imported rough diamonds were cut, polished, and sold in the international market. Since most of them were traders, they would not do any work themselves but hired other people's services.

There was a good number of Bengalis working in the Bazaar, but mostly in making gold jewellery. Gujaratis were dominant in the cutting and polishing of diamonds. Personalised couriers called Angadias[52] did the transportation of rough and finished diamonds. The Angadia system works on mutual trust and is an unofficial courier cum banking service. They are the conduits to the transfer of crores of rupees belonging to traders and rich people.

Back in Surat, one day on a Sunday evening, I was loitering in Bhagal Chowk with my friends. A Katha was in progress there. Out of curiosity, I sat in the congregation. Shree Ramchandra Dongreji Maharaj, a renowned narrator of the Shreemad Bhagwat was giving his discourse. I was mesmerized by his voice and his trance-like way of talking. There was no preaching, except a gentle inducement in a loving, kind voice. I was so enchanted that I decided to attend this Katha for the rest of the seven days. That day's Katha concluded at 6.00 p.m. Morarji Kalidas and Kanaiyalal Modi had organized this Katha jointly along with other individuals. Shree Morarjibhai was one of the leading lights of the Jari industry of Surat. To give a perspective, Surat Jari commands a geographical indication (GI), an indication of the product's source and a certain quality standard. Kanaiyalal Modi was a known share broker and a renowned social worker during 1960s in South Gujarat. He was instrumental in ensuring the growth of Surat General Hospital that provided medical help to the poor and needy of this region in 60s and 70's. His son Sunil Modi is now looking after this hospital.

Deeply moved, I requested Laljibhai Kheni to grant me week-long leave from work so that I could attend the Katha of Dongreji Maharaj every day. Laljibhai did not like the idea and told me that

---

[52] आंगडिया, local courier service, unorganized but efficient and effective

such luxuries do not just exist for people working in the diamond polishing industry. Everyone is a part of a long chain and whatever is allotted to one link must be done and passed on to the next link. 'You have to polish your quota of twenty diamonds anyhow, Govind,' Laljibhai said with a tone of finality. I was in no position to argue. After some time, I asked Laljibhai if it was okay to attend the Katha during the day and work from 6.30 p.m. until midnight to complete my work. He agreed but told me that I was crazy for my age. The entire next week, I attended the Katha during the day and worked in the factory until midnight. I felt no fatigue or disorientation. On the contrary, I had a deep sense of satisfaction and happiness. I felt as if a strange power had entered my system enhancing both my stamina and resilience.

In the Katha, Dongreji Maharaj spoke about the importance of giving respect to others. He said that if you wish for respect, you must first respect the other person. He gave an example of the echoing mountains of the Himalayas. He said that if you go and shout, 'May God bless you,' then your voice will echo back the same words. If you shout, you are bad, you will hear 'you are bad' ten times. Similarly, in this world, whatever you send out comes back to you. Next day onwards, I started calling everyone with respect. Colleagues teased me, some thought that I lost my mind, but I responded only with a smile. And it was as if I experienced a miracle, from that day onwards, nobody ever humiliated me. Soon, I had earned a place next to the factory owner, Laljibhai Kheni. This was a taking-off moment of my life. I could see things unseen to others, like a satellite in orbit.

Virjibhai's younger brother, Hiralal, had a problem with his heart valve. He needed an operation that was possible in Bombay. I accompanied both the brothers to Bombay, and we stayed in the house of Mohanbhai in Mulund. Mohanbhai was 'Mama'[53] of Virjibhai's wife. I realized that everyone called Mohanbhai Mohan

---

[53] Uncle, Mother's brother

Mama. He had a fleet of taxis and hired a garage space, to repair taxis, at Raghav Wadi in the Opera House area near French Bridge where many diamond merchants had their offices. From Mulund, we took a local train to Victoria Terminus, walked to Mohan Mama's garage, and moved around. Without a second thought, Mohan Mama gave his taxi along with a driver and said, 'this taxi will be with you for entire day.'

Dr Nimesh Shah performed the surgery on Hiralal at Bombay Hospital, near the Churchgate station. The hospital, established by renowned industrialist Rameshwardas Birla as a public service, was modern and considered the best in the country. Hiralal recovered well. I was amazed to see the boundless love and selfless service in Mohan Mama. How can anyone be so willing to give his time, attention and help of every kind including his own house, food, logistics and even money? I was meeting him for the first time, and it made little difference to him. He made me feel no different from Virjibhai. I learnt from Mohan Mama that compassion is not about providing solutions to people's problems. Compassion is about giving all the love that you have, and problems are solved automatically. By the time, we returned to Surat after spending more than ten days in Bombay, it was certain that I would be working in this city. Whatever doubts were there in my mind, Mohan Mama had resolved them.

A day before we were to return to Surat, Mohan Mama took us to the Babulnath Temple, an ancient Shiva temple on a small hillock at Chowpatty, at the end of Marine Drive and South of Malabar Hill. Mohan Mama told me that the Gujarati community, who came to Bombay for business and sought the protection of Lord Shiva, had revered this temple. Maharaja Sayajirao Gaikwad in 1890 and the Gujarati merchants who found success and affluence in Bombay built the current temple. Standing nearly 500 feet above sea level, facing Arabian Sea, I was certain that I would be working in this city. Whatever doubts were there in my mind, Darshan of Babulnath, the Lord who lives under the Babul Tree, removed them.

Vashrambhai Narola, known as VB, who married my sister Shantaben on 8 February 1958, played a key role in my own marriage, and we would enjoy a life-long association in business. He is not only my brother-in-law but a great friend as well, so to say, and I used to enjoy his company. In 1969 I started a small unit of polishing diamonds. I struggled for about four months, but it was not working out. VB was a witness to my hardships. In October 1969, I had no funds to pay the monthly salary to my workers totaling Rs 300. I asked my friend Bhagwanbhai to accompany me to Nanalal Jewellers at Rajmarg to help me sell my gold chain. However, Bhagwanbhai refused to sell the chain, and handed me over all his savings of Rs 300 so that I could pay my workers.

By this time, I had become an ardent practitioner of Dongreji Maharaj. One day I recalled Maharaj saying, forget about the past. It is over. Whatever you could have done, you did. No amount of lament will change the situation. Do not worry about the future for no one can predict what all is there waiting to happen, and it will happen anyway. Live in the present and make your best effort. Your future is hidden in your present. If you are handling your present well, your future will always be good.

मन्मना भव मद्भक्तो मद्याजी मां नमस्कुरु ।
मामेवैष्यसि युक्त्वैवमात्मानं मत्परायणः ॥

(श्रीमद् भगवद् गीता, अध्याय 9, श्लोक 34)

Focus your mind on Me [Shree Krishna tells Arjuna], be My devotee, be my worshipper. Bow down to Me. Engaging your mind in this manner and regarding Me as the supreme goal, you will come to Me.

(Shreemad Bhagvad Gita, Chapter 9, Verse 34)

I was wonderstruck with this simple prescription. In the night, I heard a voice, clear and loud—You can do anything, give all your efforts to me, see me in everyone, and leave the rest to me. It was not a dream. It was not a hallucination. The next day, even before taking bath I wrote down on a piece of paper: 'I am nothing, but I can do anything.' I felt a great sense of peace inside. I started practicing working in God-consciousness and was amazed to see great benefits. It was so effectively neutralizing the vestiges of egotism in my personality.

2

Enterprise

सर्वं परवशं दुःखं सर्वमात्मवशं सुखम् ।
एतद् विद्यात् समासेन लक्षणं सुखदुःखयो ॥

(मनुस्मृति, अध्याय 4, श्लोक 160)

All that is dependent on others is painful; all that is dependent on oneself is pleasing; he shall know this to be, in short, the definition of pleasure and pain.

(Manusmiriti, Chapter 4, Verse 160)[1]

Whether I had some predisposition for an ascetic life dedicated to the larger public good as a teenager, I was unsure. Since childhood, I did not have an interest in dresses, luxuries, ate a minimum quantity of most simple food, and observed thrift with whatever little money

---

[1] https://www.wisdomlib.org/hinduism/book/manusmriti-with-the-commentary-of-medhatithi/d/doc200265.html. Last accessed on date to October 10, 2021.

I had. I also had the habit of spending time alone in reflection, cooking my own food and attending religious discourses. Dongreji Maharaj had become my idol and I even kept his photo in my 8 x 8 feet room. Maybe I was subconsciously role modelling him.

I got my own copies of the Shreemad Bhagvad Gita and Shree Ramcharit Manas and whenever I found some free time, I would read them aloud as if giving a public discourse. One day, I asked my imaginary audience, 'What is the role of a Sadhu in society?' I then read out these lines from Shree Ramcharit Manas.

साधु चरित सुभ चरित कपासू ।
निरस बिसद गुनमय फल जासू ॥
जो सहि दुख परछिद्र दुरावा ।
बंदनीय जेहिं जग जस पावा ॥

(श्रीरामचरितमानस, बालकांड, दोहा 2, चोपाई 5-6)

A saintly person, tasteless, stainless, indifferent, and yet useful, full of goodness,
A blossoming cotton plant, ginning, spinning, weaving—suffering, becoming cloth, covering defects of others, thus valued, and adored![2]

(Shree Ramcharitmanas, Balkand, Doha 2, Chopai 5-6)

The Supreme Creator, all-powerful, all-knowing God working out His will upon humanity, has also created Maya[3] and given us the illusion of power and control, our own space, which we refer to as free will and boast of our family, our property, our power, and our wealth. However, since we are morally free agents, able to make both

---

[2] Arun Tiwari, 'Modern Interpretation of Goswami Tulsidas's Ramcharitmanas', Pune: Sakal, 2018 p.

[3] माया, delusion of a human mind, unable to see the reality

good and bad decisions, we also carry the burden of great danger that comes along with this freedom. Therefore, we need saints in our society. Thus, I concluded that day.

This adage became my mantra for the rest of my life. This world is ever-changing. It has been created as a mix of good and bad, masculine, and feminine, yin and yang—always balancing between them. In the present Age of Kali,[4] however, bad is obviously abundant—but good is not absent.

Stepping aside from the normal path, I decided early in my life to pay my respects even to malicious and unkind people as I saw them as an integral and inseparable part of the world. Countless people are hostile without purpose even to those who are friendly with them, and they delight in others' anguish and defeats and whine over their success and prosperity. The presence of the bad is as real as the presence of the good. The challenge is to discern between them. Why should I be angry at these wretched souls?

It was the last Sunday of January 1970. Bhagwanbhai and I went to a Crystal Ball Reading shop. For a fee of Rs 10, one was allowed to ask three questions. I had only one question and it was about how to start my own business. As instructed, I sat in front of the crystal ball in a relaxed manner. Focusing on my breathing and observing it to calm down for few minutes, I placed my hands on the crystal ball and visualized my business office. Then I took my hands off the crystal and took a good look at the ball, allowing my eyes to relax and become unfocused. I could see some sort of mist forming inside of the crystal and converting into an image of three people sitting on a table and talking to each other.

There was no doubt in mind who these three persons were. I could see Virjibhai, Bhagwanbhai and me working in our own factory. We got one room in Nagoriwad for a monthly rent of Rs 45. It was a small room of 10 x 15 feet but big enough for our ambition at that

---

[4] कलि, Fourth and last stage of the world according to Hindu mythology

time. On Thursday, 12 March 1970, at 1.15 p.m., a time that was considered auspicious, we cracked a coconut, ate some sugar, and started the factory. Virjibhai's brother, Hiralal, and brother-in-law, Devshibhai, also joined the factory. Rameshbhai Pachchigar was our Tax Advisor and Prabhakarbhai Trivedi our first accountant. In fact, Rameshbhai's sons Rupin and Janak would later be associated with our business carrying forward their father's legacy.

We needed a good name for our company. Dongreji Maharaj had come to our rescue. Following his teaching that only God's grace leads to any accomplishment, hence, one must always start everything in God's name and keep God's share in the business that would be used for helping others in God's name. It was beyond doubt that our company's name would be in the name of God. Being Vaishnavas, we worship the incarnations of Lord Vishnu in human form—Shree Ram and Shree Krishna with equal zeal and reverence and 'Shree' meant the Hindu Goddess Laxmi, i.e., Goddess of Wealth. Hence, we registered the Shree Ramkrishna (SRK) Export Company in Surat with three of us as equal partners. In Bombay, Mohan Mama offered his motor garage at the Opera House for our office.

We started dealing with Hirabhai Vadiwala who received rough diamonds from P. D. Kothari, a Jain businessperson from Palanpur. Prevailing norms defined that the weight of the diamonds after polishing must be at least 28 per cent that of rough. The rest of the mass becomes dust, like powder of no worth. Working skillfully and with great caution, we consistently achieved 34 per cent of finished diamond product. It was an uncommon achievement. However, Hirabhai was not happy as 28 per cent was considered a normal yield during that period. He told us that this would not only create problems for other cutters and polishers but also create confusion in the industry. He advised me not to declare this additional yield and replace heavier diamonds with smaller diamonds to match the 28 per cent yield. 'This will also fetch you more money,' he said. I told him, 'No matter what, I shall never indulge in such unscrupulous activity, and neither would I ever move away from the path of honesty.' I refrained myself doing as he suggested and left the matter to his discretion. Later, I reasoned with myself, 'If six per cent more yield is possible, why should not I do this work on my own. I will get more profit. I should produce my own stuff.' Now, the question was, from where I could get rough diamonds.

As if guided by an unseen force, one day in April 1970 with Rs 500 in pocket I peddled my bicycle to Rameshbhai Shah's office. Rameshbhai was fondly called Raj Kapoor for his good looks and charming manners. I climbed the staircase and found Rameshbhai's brother Vasantbhai sitting there. He was of my age. 'I want to buy rough diamonds.' I said without beating around the bush. Vasantbhai looked at me for some time. Perhaps he was trying to assess if I had any money. He asked softly, 'Cash or on credit?' 'Cash' I said. 'We do not have any rough diamonds right now, but as you want to buy with cash, I will come with you. And you will have to give me one per cent brokerage.' I was determined, so I said yes without any hitch.

Vasantbhai took me to a few shops that were offering discounts. I wondered how there could be a discount on diamonds. After an hour of wandering, we landed at the office of Babubhai Rikhavchand Doshi and Bhanubhai Chandubhai Shah. They quoted Rs 91 as the price of one carat, but a minimum purchase of ten carats had to be made. That meant Rs 910 and a brokerage of Rs 10 had to be added. I said, 'Sir, I only have Rs 500.' 'It is not a problem. Give Rs 500 right now. The rest Rs 410 you can give after reaching your home. Vasantbhai will accompany you. Give the balance of money to him,' he said. The problem was that there was no money at home. Whatever I had with me was in my pocket. However, I did not want to miss the opportunity. Hence, I promptly made the payment of Rs 500. To make the remaining payment of Rs 410, I took Vasantbhai to my friend Virjibhai's house. Asking Vasantbhai to wait outside, I went inside the house. I told Virjibhai, 'Look brother, we will now do our own work. For that, we will have to take the risk of buying rough,' and then described what had happened. 'The problem is that there is a shortage of Rs 410, which has to be paid to the businessman and an additional Rs 10 as brokerage to the man standing outside,' I told Virjibhai. 'O Bhagat! What is the problem in that?' Virjibhai replied in his typical style. Nevertheless, there was a problem. Virjibhai called his wife, Shardaben, who was working in the kitchen. He told her to give me Rs 200 that she had for the household expenses. Then Virjibhai went to his neighbour Narsinhbhai Khalparwala and took Rs 200 on credit. He added then Rs 20 that he had in his wallet and said, 'Lo, Bhagat, the work is accomplished, Rs 420 done.' I went out, paid Vasantbhai the money, and made the first trade in my life. We sold the polished diamonds to Babubhai at 10 per cent profit after about a week. They were very happy with our work and started giving us as many roughs, as we wanted.

God's ways are beyond human comprehension. The moment you feel you are done; some strange thing happens pushing you for change. Babubhai Doshi had an associate from his village Vav, called Chinubhai Chamanlal Shah, who used to work in Bombay as a broker in the diamond market. In August 1970, he had some problems with his business. Hence, he came to live in Surat for a while. I met him at the office of Babubhai. One day, Chinubhai told me that my cutting was very good and that I must go to Bombay to get higher appreciation for my skills. God used Chinubhai to guide me on my path.

In September 1970, Yogiji Maharaj and BAPS Swaminarayan saints came to Surat. Hundreds of devotees thronged to see them, listen to them and I was one of them. Swaminarayan saints were closest to my heart since my childhood. They showed great manners, conducted themselves most graciously, and radiated purity of body, mind, and soul. They also made me understand that as an ordinary person, I could not save myself from the mire in which my human birth had cast me in without the help of someone who was outside and above this morass of the Maya. One essentially needs an emancipator who frees him from bondage. Yogiji Maharaj blessed me, placing his hands upon my head.

Yogiji Maharaj, as if reading my mind, patted on my back to sort out my confusion. I said, 'Maharaj, I want to be a Sadhu.' 'You are a Sadhu already.' Maharaj said. 'No, I am a worker in the diamond industry.' I protested. As if laughing upon my ignorance, Yogiji Maharaj said, 'There are millions of human hearts waiting to be polished and freed from their callousness. Go and polish these diamonds in the human flesh created by God. That is your mission. Moreover, you will need the support of your family, a wife, children, and other relatives. So, become a Grihastha.'[5] He gave me his signature blessing of a pat on my back, called Thappi.[6] There was no ambiguity. He was speaking in most clear words, looking straight into my eyes. I put my head on his feet. He gently lifted me and sent me off with his signature laughter.

My elder sister, Shantaben, got married and went to Nani Vavdi, a village in Bhavnagar District. In her new surroundings, there was a Patel family. A member of this family was working in a mill in Ahmedabad. Shantaben liked this man's elder daughter, Champa, and once she came to know that Champa's marriage was not fixed in the cradle as was the tradition in the Kathiawar village societies, there was no stopping Shantaben. She asked for Champa's hand for me. However, she was asked, 'How much wealth does your family possess?' A proud Shantaben retorted, 'We have 40 acres between five brothers. Is it not enough?' It was considered more than enough.

I was engaged to Champa in August 1964. Tradition of time did not allow Champa and me to meet before we were wedded. To catch her glance, I attempted many tricks. On the first occasion, I went with my friend Bhupatbhai Vavadiya on a bicycle to Nani Vavdi. No sooner had I reached the outskirts of the village than

---

[5] गृहस्थ, Family man
[6] थप्पी, pat on back

my sister Shantaben's father-in-law caught me. He asked me the purpose of my visit that I could not express. I lied to him, saying that I have come to take my sister to Dudhala. I had no choice but to go back to my village with Shantaben. I did not have money to travel back home on a bus, so I had to borrow it from my brother-in-law, Vashrambhai Narola. I left my bicycle at Nani Vavdi and headed back to Dudhala without having a glimpse of my beloved.

On another instance, disguised as farm labourers, myself and Vallabhbhai Narola, who worked with me when I set up my first diamond venture at Lathi, went to Champa's village. After waiting for an hour, we saw her outside playing with her sister. The thrill of seeing Champa for the first time after defying social norms still excites me.

After this successful attempt, I tried something different. I wrote a letter to Champa's parents in the name of my sister-in-law, Amritben, asking for Champa's photograph. This was unheard of. My in-laws did not approve of this idea, and they wanted to break our engagement. It is only after intervention from Champa's grandmother, Harima, that everything returned to normal. This is how the period between my engagement and subsequent wedding to Champa went.

My father was the happiest upon hearing of my consent to get married. The marriage took place in Vavdi Village on Vikram-Samvat[7] 2027 on the day of Vasant Panchami.[8] It was Sunday, 31 January 1971 as per the Gregorian calendar. Champa was 16 years old, I was 21, and yet our marriage was considered 'just-in-time' if not a little late. Champa was even deeper in tradition than I was. She effortlessly won everyone's heart. She remained veiled in front of the elderly male members of the family until I decided to get rid of this

---

[7] विक्रम संवत, Indian calendar starting in 57 BC
[8] वसंत पंचमी, A festival celebrated on the fifth day of the bright half of the Hindu lunisolar calendar month of Magha, which typically falls in late January or February, forty days before start of spring season marked by the Holi festival.

practice in my family members' meeting at Kosmada ten years after our wedding. We started staying at Surat in a rented house. I bought a Royal Enfield Bullet motorcycle with the pretext of managing my increasing workload but used it more to take my wife around in Surat. It was her first exposure to a city, and I was filled with pride to show her around as if I had created everything here. One day, her sari was entangled in the wheel, and she fell. I felt very bad and recalled my grandmother Motiba's words to my parents that money and the goddess of the house must never be flaunted.

My work was increasing, and more workers were required. It was easy to get workers, but where to make them sit was a question that bothered me. A bigger place was necessary to expand the business. We took a bigger rented place in Kadiya Sheri located at Saiyadpura in Surat. In no time, 100 workers were working in the factory. Our success increased our confidence. There is one specialty in the diamond industry. Nobody is a competitor here. Everyone is equal. There was no dearth of any work here, a person could earn as per his capabilities. Finally, we purchased a place of our own in Haatt Falia in Haripura. Our happiness knew no bounds after starting the factory in a place of our own. I also invited my younger brother Arjanbhai, who was studying in class V in the village to Surat for further schooling here. He joined V. T. Choksi School at Haripura.

On 28 November 1970, hearing the news of the demise of my cousin Valjibhai Ravjibhai Dholakia, I travelled from Mumbai to Bhavnagar by plane and then to Pratapgadh. Though a year elder, he was more a friend to me than a brother. At the young age of 22, he left behind his 18-months-toddler son, Paresh, and a twenty-year-old wife, Samjuben, who was also three months pregnant. A poisonous snake bit him while he was in the field in the afternoon. Before he could be taken to the Civil Hospital at Lathi, he collapsed in a bullock cart. No car was available in a village then. His wife later delivered a daughter. She raised both her children and took care of her in-laws.

Those were the days of Smt. Indira Gandhi. Between 1967 and 1971, Indiraji came to obtain near-absolute control over the Government and the Congress party, as well as a huge majority in the Parliament. The ascent of Indiraji was backed by her charismatic appeal among the masses aided by her near-leftward actions of nationalization of several major banks, and the abolition of the Privy Purse. I personally agreed to her former action but disagreed with the latter. To me, it seemed as if it was a breach of the commitment given to Maharajas of Princely States by the Indian Government in 1947. She took these major steps via ordinances, to the shock of her opponents, and was seen as being pro-poor. She was indeed adored by the disadvantaged sections—the poor, Dalits, women, and minorities. In the 1971 General Elections, people rallied behind Indiraji's populist slogan of Garibi-Hatao[9] and gave her a huge majority with 352 seats out of 518 in the Lok Sabha. I never believed in that slogan, as I knew poverty well. Later, in December 1971, Indiraji got Bangladesh liberated and was called Durga even by her fierce political opponent Atal Bihari Vajpayee.

In May 1972, my brothers Nagjibhai and Parbatbhai organized the Bhagwat Katha at Dudhala. I took my Bullet from Surat to Dudhala. The 500-kilometre ride took twelve hours and was quite an adventure. The one-way road was not only hazardous due to blinding by the traffic coming from the opposite direction but there were also potholes aplenty. After arriving in Dudhala like a hero, I decided to go around and invite relatives living in nearby villages for the Katha and went to Nani Vavdi, where my sister lived and of course, my in-laws. By the time I started my return journey, it was late in the afternoon. My brother-in-law, Premjibhai and my sister Shantaben's seven-year-old son, Dineshbhai, sat as pillions. We had typical Kathiawadi dinner at Ladu Fui's, (my father's sister), house at Rabhada village.

---

[9] गरीबी हटाओ, Remove Poverty, a political slogan given by Indira Gandhi

The Bullet was moving toward Dhasa from Damnagar. Near Dahithara village, over the bridge, was a sharp turn. I lost control of the Bullet and we fell into the dried rivulet. Fortunately, my nephew did not receive any serious injuries, but Premjibhai and I were badly injured, and I became unconscious. With the help of Amarshibhai Narola who was travelling in a public bus going to Damnagar, he took us to the government hospital in that bus. There was no service for X-rays or plaster in that hospital though. Both of us were then taken to Bhavnagar in a rented car somehow organized by Meghjibhai Meruliya and Ramjibhai Narola in the middle of the night. By the time we reached the private clinic of Dr Ramesh Patel, it was 3.00 a.m. The doctor attended to me and gave me proper treatment. My hand was broken, and the Doctor fixed a plaster. Later, we returned to our village where the Katha was in progress.

There were no mobile phones in those days, but news used to travel by word of mouth, the power of which should never be underestimated. The only thing was that the news would often be distorted when communicated by many mouths as many ears in the process heard it. People in Dudhala were told that I had died of a road accident. So, when I arrived alive, there was jubilation all around. Of course, my wife could not immediately see me, and her turn came only after 9.00 p.m. She affectionately cleaned my badly swollen face of the muck stuck on it with her Pallu[10] and I literally slept in her lap.

My relative, Meghjibhai, retrieved the Bullet from the accident site to Dudhala and carried out the police formalities. It took many weeks for me to be back on my feet and during this time Champa showed exemplary caring and concern. More than nursing me most efficiently, she drove my mind off the accident and worries in her simple ways. Lying on the bed, I used to wonder: How was romance

---

[10] पल्लु, the usually decorated end of a sari that hangs loose when worn.

and courtship possible in India with the seclusion of women? Rather, how did young people's love for one other lead to marriage?

When I involved Champa in my thoughts on this matter, her first reaction was that of surprise. She blushed over the mention of love. Then she rolled out the feminine aspect of the human soul for me that helped me in developing respect for women for the rest of my life. Champa said in her simple way, 'in youth, romance and love, the world is pretty much the same.' She further added, 'Only the emotional response differs because of social traditions. Secluded as women may be, no social force on earth has yet succeeded in shutting out love. Its tenor and complexion can however be altered. The gushing, overwhelming feeling in nature can become a small voice of the heart and thoughts. Civilization may transform love, but it never stifles it. A country like India has always celebrated Radha and Meerabai and they are most revered.'

In December 1973, a socio-political movement called Navnirman-Andolan[11] started by students and middle-class people in Gujarat, protesting the economic crisis and corruption in public life. Chimanbhai Patel was the Chief Minister and there were allegations of corruption against him. The urban middle class was facing economic crisis due to the high price of food grains. I was amazed to see the rise of the collective consciousness of the people. It was such a powerful force. A place near my residence, Rampura, was the epicenter of this movement in Surat. Thousands were injured, and the Chief Minister arrested tens of thousands during the movement that led to his resignation.

For the first time in Gujarat, a non-Congress government was formed headed by Babubhai Jashbhai Patel. Though Indiraji imposed emergency rule all over the country in June 1975 to save her government after her election, it was declared void by the Allahabad

---

[11] नवनिर्माण आंदोलन, a socio-political movement in 1974 in Gujarat by students and middle-class people against economic crisis and corruption in public life.

High Court. The Babubhai government continued for a few months. Many activists opposing Indiraji and her emergency rule had come and settled in Gujarat and the State became an island where people working for democracy could take refuge. The Centre would dismiss the government of Babubhai soon.

Our new business picked up well and we started seeing a little wealth. Respecting my father's emotions, I celebrated our success by contributing Rs 51,000 to Laljibhai Kanjibhai Dholakia Patel Wadi at Damnagar in 1975. This was the largest donation amongst Patidars in Saurashtra at that time. This meagre contribution in the service of community defined my future path. Wealth comes in a family by the grace of God. As family is a part of community, all receive support of people around in every little thing, including raising children, and therefore every rich man in society is duty-bound to give back to the community a good part of his/her wealth. It is never called charity; it is called duty.

As the business flourished, Bombay became my second home. Every week, for three days, I lived in Bombay. I was travelling by 'Flying Ranee' train and staying at Adarsh Hotel, Kalbadevi. Living in Bombay was a very different experience. Even though Surat was much different from life in the Dudhala village, it was a Gujarati city, nevertheless. Meanwhile, Bombay was full of South Indians and North Indians and of course Maharashtrians. I found them all very different people. Not only their physiques, but also their temperaments, their food and their habits were also very different. 'How come these all very different people were Indians?' I thought. What is it that binds them all? I must know that and for that, I must first go to the lands of these different people. Gokhaleji's advice to Gandhiji to undertake a tour of India that made Gandhiji broad base the fight for freedom from the Indian elite to the ordinary people of the country was buzzing in my head.

In early 1976, when Champa reminded me about our India tour, it was as if she had read my mind. We decided to undertake a month-

long tour during the Diwali vacation in November–December 1976.
My friends—Karshanbhai Paladiya, Ravjibhai Radadiya, Popatbhai
Kakadiya and Shivalal Shingala and their families joined us including
their four little children. We hired a Matador van, so that we could
follow any route and take breaks whenever we felt the need for it. It
cost us Re 1 per kilometer.

India is such a vast country that it cannot be seen in a month or
for that matter even in a year. For a week, we discussed where to go.
We, in Gujarat, saw the rest of India from a North-South orientation.
States that were north of the Vindhyachal Mountain range were in
North India. Gujarat and Maharashtra are two distinct cultures
but culturally closer to the North. Tamil Nadu, Andhra Pradesh,
Karnataka, and Kerala are considered mainly as South India. We
decided to head north with a resolve to go south the next year.

I personally identified places by their heroes. For me, Rajasthan
was Maharana Pratap, Maharashtra was Shivaji Maharaj, Punjab was
Guru Gobind Singhji, Delhi was Raj Pithora Prithviraj Chauhan,
Uttar Pradesh was Rani Lakshmibai, Madhya Pradesh was Rani
Ahalyabai, and Bihar was Samrat Ashoka and Chandragupta
Maurya.

Passing through Ahmedabad, we first reached Ambaji, the border
town between Gujarat and Rajasthan surrounded by the Aravalli
Mountain range, which would go all the way to Delhi running
approximately 500 miles in a Northeastern direction. In the holy
temple of Arasuri Ambaji, there is no image or statue of any goddess.
The holy Shree-Visa-Yantra[12] is worshiped as the main deity. No
one can see the Yantra with the naked eye. It is a Shakti Peeth[13] and
a pilgrimage destination in Shaktism, the goddess-focused Hindu
tradition. There are 51 Shakti Peeths by various accounts, of which
between four are named as Maha (major) in medieval Hindu texts.

---

[12] श्री वीसा यन्त्र, In the holy Hindu temple of 'Arasuri Ambaji,' there is no image or statue
of the goddess. The holy 'Shree Visa Yantra' is worshipped as the main deity.

[13] शक्ति पीठ, holy places where body parts of Goddess Sati fell

Most of these historic places of goddess worship are in India, but there are seven in Bangladesh, three in Pakistan, three in Nepal, and one each in China and Sri Lanka.

Shakti Peeths are based on the legend of the death of the Goddess Sati. Out of grief and sorrow, Lord Shiva carried Sati's body, reminiscing about their moments together as a couple, and roamed around the universe with it. To put an end to this macabre sight, Lord Vishnu cut Sati's body into 51 body parts, using His Sudarshan-Chakra.[14] The body parts fell on the Earth to become sacred sites where all the people can pay homage to the Goddess. To complete this massively long task, Lord Shiva took the form of Bhairav, His fierce manifestation associated with annihilation. We were told that the Heart of Sati Devi has fallen here at Ambaji.

Our next stop was Nathadwara, which was about a 4-hour drive into the Aravalli Mountains in the state of Rajasthan, on the banks of the Banas River in Rajsamand District. The temple of Shree Krishna houses the deity of Shreenathji, the Lord's 7-year-old infant form, when He lifted the Govardhan Parvat (hill), with His left hand and made a fist with his right hand and resting it at his waist. The image is in the form of a single black marble and a large diamond is placed beneath the lips. Vitthal Nathji (1516-1588), popularly known as Gusainji, the younger son of Acharya Vallabhacharya (1479-1531), institutionalized the worship of Shreenathji here. The temple, also known as 'Haveli of Shreenathji,' was built in the seventeenth century under the rule and protection of Maharana Raj Singh of Mewar. About three kilometers from Haveli was the Shreenathji Gaushala. The size of the Gaushala[15] and the way more than a thousand cows were served there was extraordinary.

The 350 kms road journey to Jaipur took about eight hours. It is one of the earliest planned cities of modern India based on

---

[14] सुदर्शन चक्र, Shree Krishna's weapon
[15] गौशाला, Cowshed or a place where healthy cows are kept and nurtured

the principles of Vastu Shastra and Shilpa Shastra, and we found it to be rightly so. There are three gates facing the East, the West, and the North. The Eastern gate is called Suraj pol or sun gate, the Western gate is called Chand pol or moon gate and the Northern gate faces the ancestral capital of Ajmer, Ajmer pol. Ladies would enjoy the Hawa Mahal, The Palace of Breeze, which was used as the chambers of the royal women. We performed puja at the Shree Govind Devji temple in the City Palace complex and at Shree Moti Dungri Ganesh Temple perched on a small hill. We took a stunning elephant ride up the hill to the main entrance of Amer Fort.

From Jaipur we went to Kurukshetra, it is also known as Dharmakshetra ('Holy Place') and as the 'Land of the Shreemad Bhagvad Gita.' According to the Puranas,[16] Kurukshetra is a region named after King Kuru, the ancestor of Kauravas and Pandavas,[17] as depicted in the epic Mahabharata. From here, we went to Chandigarh, the first planned city of independent India designed by French Architect Le Corbusier acting as a capital city for Haryana and Punjab. Later we reached Amritsar, the seat of Shree Harmandir Sahib, popularly known as Suvarna Mandir (the Golden Temple). A truly majestic shrine, the temple is built around a Sarovar (pool) that was completed by the fourth Sikh Guru Ram Das Devji in 1577. The fifth Guru, Arjan Devji, placed the Adi Granth here in 1604. Maharaja Ranjit Singh, after founding the Sikh Empire, rebuilt the Mandir in marble and copper in 1809, and overlaid the sanctum with gold foil in 1830 making it the Golden Temple.

We had a good time in the sprawling complex of the Mandir that housed several buildings around the sanctum and the pool. One of these is the Akal Takht, the chief centre of religious authority of Sikhism. There is a big clock and a museum. However, I was most impressed with the Langar—a free kitchen that serves a simple

---

[16] पुराण, Sanskrit sacred writings on Hindu mythology

[17] कौरव पांडव, Five brothers Pandavas and Hundred brothers Kauravas, characters in epic Mahabharata

vegetarian meal to over 1,00,000 visitors who visit the holy shrine daily for worship. Everybody in the kitchen was a volunteer doing service. It was heartening to see very rich and influential people in society serving in the kitchen and washing utensils.

After we came out of the Langar and were relaxing in the large marble compound of the Mandir watching the enchanting image of the Golden Temple in the Sarovar,[18] a white-bearded Sardarji engaged us in friendly conversation. When we told him that we were from Gujarat and had just visited the Shreenathji Mandir, he blessed us all and recited a verse in Punjabi:

एक क्रिसनं सरब देवा देव देवा त आतमा ॥
आतमा बासुदेवस्यि जे को जाणै भेउ ॥
नानकु ता का दासु है सोई निरंजन देउ ॥

(गुरु ग्रंथ साहिब, पृष्ठ 469, मेहला 2)

The One Lord Krishna is the Divine Lord of all; He is the Divinity of the individual soul. One who understands the mystery of all-pervading Lord; Nanak is a slave to him; He himself is the Immaculate Divine Lord.[19]

(Guru Granth Sahib, Pg 469, Mehla 2)

From the Mandir we walked to the nearby Jallianwala-Bagh.[20] On 13 April 1919, the traditional festival of Baisakhi,[21] thousands of Indians had gathered in the Jallianwala-Bagh, an open area of six to seven acres, roughly 200 yards by 200 yards in size. Acting Brigadier-

---

[18] सरोवर, pond
[19] https://www.sikhphilosophy.net/threads/can-sikhs-worship-bhagwan-sri-krishna.40966/ Last accessed on date to October 10, 2021.
[20] जलियाँवाला बाग, Place in Amritsar where massacre took place on 13 May 1919
[21] बैसाखी, first harvesting of crops celebrated in Punjab

General Reginald Dyer, Chief of British Army in Amritsar, ordered his troops to begin shooting toward the densest sections of the crowd in front of the available narrow exits, where panicked crowds were trying to leave the Bagh. The shooting continued for approximately ten minutes and stopped only after bullets were exhausted, after approximately 1,650 rounds were fired killing 379 innocent Indians. There is a memorial now erected there. I feel every Indian must visit this place once to understand what it meant to be a slave nation.

We then drove to the Mata Vaishno Devi shrine in Katra in Jammu and Kashmir on cold winter days. All vehicles must stop at the foothill and pilgrims have to trek nearly 12 km to a Holy Cave located in the folds of the three-peaked mountains at a height of 5200 feet. We hired mules for the women and children and all men trekked. The festive mood of the hundreds of people trekking was amazing. They were joyous and singing. From their appearances and dresses, one could easily make out they came from different and far away parts of India. It took us about four hours to reach the temple and during this time, we learnt by heart the different names of Mata Vaishno Devi. She was called Pahadawali,[22] the Goddess who lives upon a mountain; Jyotawali,[23] the Goddess who shines like an oil lamp and spreads light everywhere; Sherawali,[24] the Goddess who rides upon a lion or tiger; Latawali,[25] the Goddess with long locks of hair; and Meherawali,[26] the Goddess who is always merciful.

Inside the cave, there was no idol contrary to what we had expected but three small-sized rocks. After coming out, overhearing our disappointment, an elderly person explained to us without us asking, that in the Treta-Yuga,[27] when the Earth was overburdened

---

[22] पहाड़ावाली, Goddess residing in mountains
[23] ज्योतावाली, Goddess who shines like lamp
[24] शेरावाली, Goddess who rides upon tiger
[25] लतावाली, Goddess with long hair
[26] मेहरावाली, Goddess who is merciful
[27] त्रेता युग, second of the ages of mankind as per Hindu mythology

by the wicked and tyrannical rule of the demons, the three eternal Goddesses decided to combine their energies to rid the Earth of impending doom. The three natural rock formations called the Pindies are representative of Mahasaraswati, Mahalakshmi and Mahakali giving the shrine its name 'Vaishno Devi.'

At that time, Kashmir was not plagued by terrorism. There was happiness all around. There were no fears and no concern about security. How do I describe atmosphere of Kashmir? It was indeed a 'paradise' as called by both poets and commoners. Everywhere you look, enchanting beauty was in abundance. But then there were problems in Paradise. First, we were cheated by a 'guide' who took us to a very run-down hotel for a price that would get us to stay in an 'Houseboat'[28]. Then, the diesel tank of our vehicle got frozen, and the Matador refused to start. However, there was so much fun in Kashmir that such petty troubles did not come in a way. The view of Dal Lake was spectacular. We experienced snow in Pahelgaon and Gulmarg and all were thrilled. We played in the snow all day keeping burning coals in a pot and hung them around our neck. No one had ever seen this way of keeping oneself warm. Many people in Kashmir at that time could not afford warm clothes. Such fireplace was a blessing for those people.

We drove through Himachal Pradesh enjoying the fascinating sights of the mighty, snow-clad Himalayan peaks. Himachal Pradesh State derives its name from the father of Goddess Parvati. It is natural that the state has sacred temples of her various forms— Naina Devi, Jwalaji, Chintpurni Devi. Each temple has a unique character and touches a different chord in one's heart. I vividly remember, even after close to five decades, an ancient temple in a cave located in the Dhaulagiri Mountain range situated in Chakmoh village near Kasauli.

---

[28] 'Houseboats' are decorative wooden houses constructed on boats that moored around the lake and plugged in to the local plumbing and electricity.

This cave temple is the residing spot for Baba Balak Nath, an ardent devotee of Lord Shiva and all his pilgrims fast on every Sunday for their faith. We were told that couples who are unable to bear children and pray to Babaji there, are blessed with a child. However, women pilgrims were prohibited from entering the cave and had to worship the deity from outside the cave. I prayed to Baba Balak Nath with Champa standing by my side for blessing us from outer of the cave. We were offered rota, a sweet bread made of jaggery and wheat, as Prasad.

We also visited an ancient, Baijnath Temple, a temple of Lord Shiva in Kangra district. Lord Shiva is worshipped here as Vaidyanath, or the 'God of Healing'. We enjoyed the most enchanting view of the Shivalik Mountain range at the Jakhu Hanuman Mandir near Shimla atop a peak at an elevation of 8000 Ft. The legend is that Shree Hanuman stopped here to rest while searching for the Sanjeevani-Booti.[29] There were countless playful monkeys being fed by visitors. They were all most peaceful and harmless. On our way to the Shree Badrinath shrine, we stayed at Dehradun, Missouri and Haridwar.

Remembering Gagadiya River of Dudhala, I was tempted to take a swim in the almost freezing water of Ganga. Everyone else excused himself or herself of the idea. I went inside the knee-deep water and took my swim. Suddenly, a gush of water removed the sand underneath my feet. I lost my balance and almost drowned. Champa and others on the bank of the river could not do much except shouting for help. Suddenly, a miracle happened; a man approached me, held my hand, and brought me safely out of the water. Later, we performed Arti at Har-ki-podhi after offering prayers at Chandi Devi and Mansa Devi Temples before proceeding to Badrinath. On the way we stayed at Rishikesh. We bathed on

---

[29] संजीवनी बूटी, medicine that Lord hanuman brought from Sanjeevani Mountain for Laxman as described in epic Ramayan

the banks of Ganga. I recorded Vishnu-Sahastranaam-Shtotra[30] on a cassette recorder there. It is still played as a daily prayer at our workplace in year 2021 as a daily morning prayer. Switching over to state transport buses, we left for Badrinath in state transport bus. Roads were narrow with tall mountains and deep valley on its two sides. It was a very scary experience for us. We spent a night at the Joshimath. Day at Badrinath was full of snowing, raining and foggy. After offering prayer at the temple, we started back repeating a fifteen-hour ordeal.

I sat for a long time in the Badrinath temple. Lord Vishnu is called the husband of Badri (Goddess Lakshmi) and the idol is a self-manifested one of Shaligram stone. There are the idols of Uddhav, Narayan, Nar, Kuber, Garuda and Narada, in the sanctum sanctorum, all facing east. It is said that this temple was a Buddhist shrine until the eighth century and Adi Shankara converted it into a Hindu temple. As I found this temple quite different from any other Hindu temple, I felt inclined to this view, but then, was not Lord Buddha part of Hinduism? Such controversies are more to divide people by those who are ignorant of the great inclusive, non-dual nature of the Vedic civilization. On our return journey, we reached New Delhi.

New Delhi is a great city. We saw the Parliament House, Rashtrapati Bhavan and the entire Raj Path until India Gate. It was so different from the rest of India and one can make out easily that it represents the power of outsiders over the Indian civilization and its people. We stayed at Gujarat Bhavan. And to our great joy we got an opportunity to meet Prime Minister Indira Gandhi. About ten groups of tourists were taken to the lawns of Prime Minister's house. After an hour she came and accepted our greetings. We took our pictures with her. We were so pleased when she asked us, without

---

[30] The list of the thousand names of Lord Vishnu is referred to as Vishnu Sahastranaam Shtotra

any prompting by her staff, whether we were from Gujarat. That was the hallmark of a great leader connected with her people.

From Delhi, before going to Agra, we visited Vrindavan and Mathura. The Shree Bankey Bihari Mandir at Vrindavan was majestic. I felt drawn to the graceful threefold-bending form of Lord Shree Krishna. We went to the Gita Mandir, also known as Birla Mandir, which is located on the outskirts of Mathura, on the Vrindavan—Mathura Road. The presiding deity of the shrine is Lord Lakshmi Narayan. Shree Jugal KishoreBirla built Gita Mandir in memory of his parents. There is an incredible Gita Stambh,[31] built from red sandstone. On it is inscribed the entire Shreemad Bhagavad Gita. The verses have been inscribed with sharp precision, with each letter as discernible as others have. We also visited the Keshav Dev Mandir at the site of where Lord Krishna was born and offered our prayers at the sacred place.

We came to know that Aurangzeb attacked Mathura, destroyed the Keshav Dev temple in 1670, and built Shahi Eidgah in its place. In 1804, Mathura came under British control. When the East India Company auctioned this land, Raja Patnimal bought it. In 1935, the Allahabad High Court ruled in favour of Raj Krishna Das, descendant of Raja Patnimal. In 1944, Pandit Madan Mohan Malaviya acquired the land from Raj Krishna Das at the cost of Rs 13000 with financial help of Industrialist Jugal KishoreBirla. After the death of Malaviya in 1946, Jugal KishoreBirla formed, a trust named Shree Krishna Janmabhoomi Trust, later registered as the Shree Krishna Janmasthan Seva Sansthan and acquired the land. Jugal KishoreBirla entrusted the construction of the new temple with industrialist and philanthropist Jaidayal Dalmia. I would be coming here later for a deeper spiritual bonding.

From Mathura, we went to see seventh wonder of the world, the Taj Mahal, built on the bank of river Yamuna at Agra. From

---

[31] स्तंभ, Pillar

Agra, we went to visit Ram Janmabhoomi at Ayodhya. All of us had a bath in Sarayu River and offered prayers at Ram Lalla's Temple. Distance of 175 kms between Ayodhya and Prayagraj was covered in 5 hours. We took a holy dip at Triveni Sangam, the union of Ganga, Yamuna and Saraswati rivers. I remembered the saying, 'Surat nu jaman ane Kashi nu maran'[32] prevalent among Gujaratis on the way to Varanasi, which is also known as Kashi.

I found the adage that there is no other place on Earth like Varanasi to be true. The crowd and chaos of this city where both weddings and funerals take place simultaneously at the eighty-eight river front steps, Ghats, constructed by almost every major kingdom of India, namely, the Marathas, Scindias, Holkars, Bhonsles, and Peshwas. The great Vishwanath temple was inside a labyrinth of lanes, and I felt it could have been managed better. The ancient temple mentioned in the Puranas had braved several assaults of the invaders. The temple has been built and re-built several times over the past few centuries. Rani Ahalyabai Holkar of Indore built the present temple in the eighteenth century in the year 1780. In 1839, the two domes of the Temple were covered by one ton of gold offered by Maharaja Ranjit Singh. The third dome remains uncovered.

A simple glimpse of the Jyotirlinga[33] is a soul-cleansing experience that transforms life and puts it on the path of knowledge and bhakti. The Vishweshwara Jyotirlinga has a very special and unique significance in the spiritual history of India. Tradition has it that the merits earned by the Darshan of other Jyotirlinga scattered in various parts of India accrue to a devotee by a single visit to the Kashi Vishwanath Temple. I had been to the Somnath temple located in Prabhas Patan near Veraval in Saurashtra and at Nageshwar village near Dwarka and thus had Darshan of the two Jyotirlinga in Saurashtra. We took a route on our return, travelling

---

[32] Adage in Gujarati means 'For best cuisine go to Surat, to attain salvation go to Kashi'
[33] ज्योतिर्लिंग, a devotional representation of the Hindu God Shiva

through Fathepur, Jhansi, Kota and Banswara and entering Gujarat through Garadu, Godhra and Vadodara to Surat.

While working in the diamond business, I was intrigued by the energy that is stored inside diamonds. I learned from knowledgeable persons in the industry that diamonds are formed in the great depths of the Earth, 200 to 500 kilometers below the surface, by immense temperature and pressure, more than 1000 degree Celsius and 50,000 times the pressure of atmosphere, working on the carbon atoms, bringing them so close to each other that they become a crystal. The magma erupts out, taking the path with least resistance and forming a 'pipe' to the surface carrying the diamond along with it. Sometimes diamonds reach earth's surface with rocks, but most other times are frozen inside the 'pipes' in the rocks and have to be mined. Such 'pipes' carrying diamonds were first discovered in Kimberley town in South Africa and thereafter all such pipes are called Kimberlites. Only one in every 200 kimberlite pipes contains gem-quality diamonds and mining is therefore very expensive and involves significant luck factor. These diamonds even after they are found have to be cut and polished with great effort and skills to become gems, as people normally know them.

From the days I worked as a daily wage labourer in industry, I considered diamond as a God. I realized that harnessing a diamond's true potential was not only an art, but it was also a very precise and exact science. The skills needed to be a proficient diamond cutter and polisher would take years of training to acquire but the science part remained an enigma to most of the workers. When I went to Belgium, and more precisely, Antwerp—the global centre of diamond trade, I learnt lot of this science. Diamond cutting in Antwerp began in the sixteenth century, when masses of Jewish people who were expelled from Spain and Portugal settled in Belgium, bringing with them the knowledge of diamond trading. The time had come to make the dream I had formed standing in front of Forbes Building in Bombay in 1968 come true.

The diamond business works on reference. I had to go to Antwerp with a sound reference. I spoke to Rameshbhai 'Raj Kapoor.' He readily agreed to accompany me to Antwerp but demanded 3 per cent commission in the business. I saw no problem in that. Later, I discussed the matter with Shantibhai, and Navinbhai in Bombay and they not only endorsed my idea of starting a business in Antwerp but also offered 50 per cent partnership. I initially hesitated, as 50 per cent coming to us would be further divided into three. They told me, 'Let us start with this one-trip as equal partners. We will revisit it further based on the profitability.' Navinbhai deputed his younger brother Dilipbhai to accompany me to Antwerp.

A hundred people came from Surat in two buses to see me off at Bombay. Mohan Mama took care of all of them. In the wee hours of 16 January 1977, Dilipbhai and I travelled to Belgium. We flew on Sabena, the national Airlines of Belgium, from Bombay to Brussels. We would spend twenty-two days in Belgium. Without intending or even realizing so, I became the first person in my native district Amreli to go abroad. It was a thrill to experience the time lag. We were flying for eight hours and yet landed in Brussels at 6.00 a.m. 'We added many hours to our life.' I told Dilipbhai. He smiled and said, 'Enjoy, Govindbhai till you lose them when we fly in the opposite direction upon our return.'

It was a long walk to reach the main gate of the airport. I had never seen this kind of a busy airport. Every five minutes, a plane was landing or taking off. A chilling wave passed my entire body as I got off at the airport. Such cold weather! The temperature was three degrees. Suddenly, it started drizzling, making the cold even more biting. We took a taxi to Antwerp, about forty-five kilometers from there. My mind was going back to Surat. Brussels metropolitan had a population of hardly two million, but its airport was so huge and busy while Surat was not even connected by air.

Antwerp is a riverside city like Surat. The Scheldt River drains into the North Sea like the Tapi into the Bay of Khambhat. I lodged myself close-by to the Diamond Quarter, called Diamantkwartier locally. It is an area of about one square mile consisting of several square blocks where 1,500 companies operate from their small offices doing a turnover of twenty-five billion dollars every year. About 5,000 merchants, brokers and diamond cutters live around this area. The first question that crossed mind was how this place had become a centre of the diamond industry. Unless this question was answered, I would not enjoy the place. The answer came sooner than later over dinner with Rajeshbhai Mehta, who was running his company Super Gems there.

Antwerp is the undisputed capital of diamond trade and celebrated in the industry worldwide. 'Before it was known for its diamonds, Antwerp was the most important trading and financial centre in Western Europe. It is location on the River Scheldt connects the city to the North Sea, facilitating its trade success during the early fourteenth century. The world's first stock exchange was developed in Antwerp at this time, and traded valuable materials such as diamonds, gold, silver, and copper. The Antwerp diamond exchange was established around 1456. In the same year, Belgian Lodewyk van Berken invented the Scaif, a polishing wheel infused with a mixture of olive oil and diamond dust. For the first time, it was possible to polish all the facets of the diamond symmetrically at angles that reflected the light in ways never seen before. The Scaif revolutionised diamond polishing. This invention increased orders among the European aristocracy and attracted many diamond artisans. The discovery of diamonds in Kimberley, South Africa in 1871 also significantly increased the number of diamonds and established Antwerp as the diamond capital of the world.[34]

Back in the 14th and 15th centuries, India was mining diamonds, rough diamonds arriving from India were brought first to the city of

---

[34] http://www.sandersjewelers.net/articles/why-is-antwerp-the-diamond-capital-of-the-world. Last accessed on date to October 10, 2021.

Bruges and then to Antwerp in Belgium, where they were polished and set in jewellery for the rich and famous of the colonisers in Europe.

There were many Indians in the Diamond Quarter. Most of them, young Jains namely the Mehtas and Shahs from Palanpur in Gujarat, arrived there looking for better fortunes. They were working at the bottom of the business with low quality roughs, which offered very small margins of profit. They were sending these stones to family members back in India for cutting and polishing, where labour costs were a fraction of those prevailing in Antwerp.

Cheap labour, large families, and a willingness to work harder than the competition earned the Indians respect in the Antwerp business community and created a new business area for small stones. I found myself at perfect ease in this faraway land. We must invest our profits and begin to move up the value chain, I thought. And I started sending rough diamonds to India for processing.

Newly wedded Satishbhai Zaveri worked as the man-in-charge after Rajeshbhai Mehta at Super Gems, looking after customer development. He and his wife Smita Zaveri were my hosts at Antwerp, and I spent many weekends at their home. We went sightseeing in and around Antwerp many times. His contribution in my success is enormous. He died of cancer. I specially went to Antwerp to bid him a farewell and pay my respects. It was my first experience wearing a formal suit during cremation.

In Antwerp, I visited a weekly Paathshala[35] for the children from ages six onwards, run by mothers from the community, imparting them the values and knowledge of Jain scriptures. They had already bought land at Wilrijk, nearby Antwerp, for constructing a Jain temple and living there with owner's mentality. I was to ask about the Patan queen Minal Devi, my question that had been pending for

---

[35] पाठशाला, school

an answer since my childhood but held on for a better occasion in the future.

On a weekend, we travelled from Antwerp to London. India was still a British Commonwealth Country and Indians could enter the United Kingdom by Visa on Arrival. My surname on the passport was mentioned as 'Patel,' a generic surname of all Patidars then, and the immigration officer took his time to allow me in. Later, I officially changed my surname from Patel to Dholakia. London looked familiar. It was like Bombay. I was surprised to know that London's largest industry was finance, and its financial exports. I sat for a while in a public square in the City of London, an area of about one square mile. It was here that the finances of the British Empire 'on which the sun had never set, and whose bounds had never been ascertained' were handled. Before returning to Antwerp, we visited the northwestern boroughs of Harrow and Brent where many Hindu communities had settled. We also went to see 'Kohinoor' diamond at Tower of London.

On the night of my return, I had a dream. I saw Goddess Lakshmi smiling at me. I had seen a painting of Raja Ravi Varma and she was looking exactly like that, wearing a red sari. She asked me about my lakshya, or goal in life. I said, 'I don't know.'

'Then, who will know?' the Goddess asked. I was speechless. Then she said, 'My name is Lakshmi[36] and I look after those who have a Lakshya[37] in their lives. So, if you want my blessings, tell me your Lakshya, and you will have it, I promise.' Tears welled up in my eyes. I said in choked voice, 'O Mother, I am so ignorant, an idiot. I am running around without knowing my Lakshya. How do I correct myself? I am not intelligent; I am not educated.' Goddess Lakshmi said, 'You are honest, and pure, and that is enough for me to be with you. I am not particularly favorable towards the intelligent and

---

[36] लक्ष्मी, Goddess of Wealth
[37] लक्ष्य, aim.

knowledgeable. My sister Sarasvati[38] looks them after. I am pleased with you and so let me help you in having your Lakshya.'

I felt paralyzed lying in my bed. The dream continued. Goddess Lakshmi was saying, 'I have eight forms, Adi Lakshmi, Dhaanya Lakshmi, Vidya Lakshmi, Dhana Lakshmi, Sanatana Lakshmi, Gaja Lakshmi, Dhairya Lakshmi and Vijaya Lakshmi. Depending upon your goal—spiritual enlightenment, food, knowledge, resources, progeny, abundance, patience, and success, I support them with abundance and success. So, tell me son, what do you want?'

I said, 'O Mother, give me spiritual enlightenment.' The Goddess smiled and said, 'Had you asked for Dhana Lakshmi, I would have established you here controlling a quarter of the Diamond Quarter. Nevertheless, you asked for Adi Lakshmi, so go back home. I will always be with you, giving you enough for all your good works. Do whatever charity you want to do without any fear.' When I took the return flight to India the next day, I was a different person.

We bought rough diamonds of Rs 26 lakhs in that trip. After making gems out of them, we made a profit of Rs 9 lakhs,[39] getting Rs 4.5 lakhs for ourselves and rest for D. Navinchandra & Co. Since we started our firm in 1970, we had never seen a profit of more than Rs 5 lakhs. Seeing it doubling suddenly was indeed thrilling. We made another trip after a few months and bought Rs 39 lakhs worth of roughs, and then made another trip, and so on. We had finally become rich!

In the Shreemad Bhagvad Gita, Lord Shree Krishna reveals that He has created an eight-fold Prakriti[40] within which we all live. Interestingly, besides the five foundational materials—earth, water, fire, air, and space, God has also created intelligence that runs this world, the mind, and the sense of 'I.'

---

[38] सरस्वती, Goddess of Knowledge
[39] लाख, one hundred thousand
[40] प्रकृति, nature

भूमिरापोऽनलो वायुः खं मनो बुद्धिरेव च ।
अहँकार इतीयं मे भिन्ना प्रकृतिरष्टधा ॥

(श्रीमद् भगवद् गीता, अध्याय 7, श्लोक 4)

Earth, water, fire, air, ether, mind, intellect, and egoism thus is
My Nature divided eightfold.

(Shreemad Bhagvad Gita, Chapter 7, Verse 4)

After coming to Surat, I became a good friend of Karshanbhai
Paladiya and Vallabhbhai Dholakia. Around the same time when
I started Shree Ramkrishna Exports, they set up 'Krishna Export'
together as partners. Manjibhai Khakharia has been my third youth
friend. Manjibhai also had set up his company but later went to
the U.S. with two of his sons. They set up Motels in Dallas. His
third son carried forward his father's legacy of diamond business and
became the raison d'être for him visiting Surat every few months.

The diamond industry cannot enforce written contracts as
diamonds are easily portable, universally valuable, and virtually
untraceable, and state courts find impossible to enforce executory
contracts for diamond sales. The industry operates on credit, relies on
trust, and hence favours a tightly knit community and family-based
business networks. To ensure trust, Orthodox Jewish community in
Antwerp and Tel-Aviv had long relied on the effective social control
mechanisms of their community. With their reputation at stake,
no one dare to cheat. Gujarati business communities operate along
similar lines, with strong family networks and a high incidence of
marriage within their ethnic group. An additional source of cohesion,
support and solidarity comes from the caste community.

Initially when Palanpuri Jains entered the closed world of
Antwerp's diamond industry, they started to specialize in smaller,
lower-value roughs, and used the cheap labour and excellent skill of

Surat's diamond cutters and polishers to produce diamonds that had larger market potential. They bought from source and offered longer buying periods on credit to undercut the competition, enabled the Gujaratis to gain a foothold in Antwerp. Three of my friends in the diamond business, Mohanbhai Dhameliya, Nanubhai Surani, and Arvindbhai Mavani decided that it was time for people in Surat to take advantage of polishing and selling in dollars themselves and shifted to Antwerp.

Champa was naturally happy with our progress except for the fact that she was yet to have a child. During the Diwali vacation in November-December 1977, we decided to go to South India. Karshanbhai Paladiya, Ravjibhai Radadiya, Devchandbhai Jodhani and Shivalal Shingala along with their families joined us. We used the Matador van again like last year, but its rent had increased to Rs 1.25 per kilometer.

Honestly, I was unsure of the heroes in the South Indian history. Therefore, mythology plays a very important role in my identification system. Tirupati and Trivandrum were Lord Vishnu, Rameswaram was Lord Shiva, and Madurai was Goddess Meenakshi. We had little connection with the most powerful deity of South India, Shree Karthikeya, also known as Subramanian. It is with this mindset that we decided to explore the Southern part of our country.

We drove straight 235 kms to Nashik via Saputara. We visited Trimbakeshwar, the seat of a Jyotirlinga and the origin of the Godavari River, and Shirdi, the home of the late nineteenth century saint Shree Sai Baba, near Nashik. Our next stop was Apegaon, the birthplace of Sant Dynaneshwar. From Apegaon we went to see the Bhimashankar Temple in the Ghat region of the Sahyadri Mountains and the source of the River Bhima, which flows southeast and merges with the River Krishna near Raichur in Karnataka.

We visited Hyderabad passing through the famous Deccan Plateau and the Kingdom of the Nizam. I was keen to see Golkonda, a fortified citadel, and an early capital city of the Qutub Shahi dynasty, created to have control over the Kollur diamond mines, which were indeed gravel-clay pits on the South bank of the River Krishna. These mines were operated until the nineteenth century. This area would later in year 2013 make way for the Pulichinthala irrigation project and was submerged in 50 Ft of water.

Tirupati was truly majestic. The Temple surrounded by the Tirumala Hills is dedicated to Lord Venkateshwara, a form of Vishnu that had appeared here to save humanity from the trials and troubles of Kali-Yuga.[41] The temple architecture, built in the third century, was very different and we could see that we were in South India now. From here, we drove to Madras, the biggest cultural, economic, and educational center of southern India.

Madras was built as a major naval base, the central administrative center in South India, as Bombay was in the West, and Calcutta was in the East. Marina Beach, running six kms, was amazing. The entire stretch features numerous statues and monuments that have come up over the years along the beach promenade. I especially liked The Triumph of Labour statue of four men toiling to move a rock, depicting the hard work of the labour class. I was most pleased to see the statue of Mahatma Gandhiji in the 'Dandi March' stride.

We visited the Kapaleeshwarar Temple dedicated to Lord Shiva located in Mylapore and the Parthasarathy Temple dedicated to Lord Vishnu in Triplicane. Interestingly, one of the oldest structures in Madras, the Parthasarathy temple has five forms of Vishnu: Narasimha, Ram, Gajendra Varadaraja, Ranganatha and Krishna. I had heard Gajendra Moksha earlier in my childhood and had an epiphany. Later, I understood Gajendra as the man, the crocodile as sin, and the muddy water of the lake as Samsara. Materialistic

---

[41] कलियुग, the last of the four ages the world goes through in a cycle of four ages described in the Sanskrit scriptures.

desires, ignorance and sins create an endless chain of karma in this world and are like a crocodile preying upon a helpless elephant stuck in a muddy pond.

The prayer made by Gajendra on this occasion became a famous hymn in praise of Lord Vishnu.

शुक्लाम्बरधरं देवं शशिवर्णं चतुर्भुजम् ।
प्रसन्नवदनं ध्यायेत् सर्वविघ्नोपशान्तये ॥

(स्तोत्र रत्नावली, मङ्गलम् 1, श्लोक 5)

Wearing white clothes, all-pervading [Lord Vishnu], bright as the Moon with four arms. O compassionate and gracious Lord; ward off all my obstacles and give peace.

(Stotra Ratnavali, Mangalam 1, Verse 5)

From Madras, we drove to Tiruchirappalli to visit the Srirangam Temple of Lord Vishnu, in the resting posture, considered the biggest functioning Hindu temple in the world. Bound by the Kaveri on one side and its distributary Kollidam on the other side, it looks surreal. Shree Ramanujacharya made this temple his monastic home and wrote his famous commentaries on the Brahma-Sutra[42] here. Acharya's body is preserved at this temple. Sandalwood paste and saffron are used to preserve the body even now, open for Darshan, and no other chemicals are added.

We went 160 kms further south to Madurai. In Madurai, we went to the Shree Meenakshi Sundareswaran temple in Madurai on the southern bank of the Vaigai River. The temple has two separate shrines for the goddess Meenakshi Devi (the mother

---

[42] ब्रह्मसूत्र, a Sanskrit text summarising the philosophical and spiritual ideas in the Upanishads.

with the beautiful fisheyes), a form of Parvati Devi with Shree Sundareswaran, Lord Shiva, both open to the East. The temple also included Lakshmi Devi, flute-playing Shree Krishna, Rukmini Devi, Lord Brahma, Sarasvati Devi, and several other Vedic and Puranic deities. Unlike other temples, where Lord Shiva is the principal deity, Goddess Meenakshi is the principal deity here. We spent more than two hours in the sprawling temple complex, which is laid out based on the principles of symmetry and loci, called Mandala.[43] We heard several stories—the marriage of Meenakshi and Shiva was the biggest event here, with all gods, goddesses and living beings having gathered. Vishnu is believed to be the brother of Meenakshi. Vishnu gives her away to Shiva at the wedding. Here we saw elephants as casual visitors in temple.

A little tired, we were all sitting, waiting for the Aarti,[44] when I noticed Champa in trance-like situation. Tears were rolling out of her closed eyes. I was worried but did not want to disturb her. Her face was radiating, and she seemed to be in a higher state of consciousness. After some time, her tears stopped, she smiled to herself and opened her eyes. She became conscious of my concerned stare and gestured at me not to say anything. We all got up and participated in the most magnificent aarti I had ever seen. There were separate lines for men and women. After the aarti, an old Tamil woman put her hand on Champa's head and whispered मीनाक्षीं प्रणतोऽस्मि सन्ततमहं कारुण्यवारांनिधिम्[45] (Devi Meenakshi, who is an Ocean of Compassion will come to you). We had been married for seven years and had no child and there could be nothing more we could have asked for than this blessing that we got without asking that evening.

---

[43] मंडला, an esoteric diagram, A mandala is a geometric configuration of symbols.

[44] आरती, a Hindu ceremony in which lights with wicks soaked in ghee are lit and offered up to the deity.

[45] https://greenmesg.org/stotras/meenakshi/meenakshi_pancharatnam.php.   Last accessed on September 4, 2020.

We then turned east and driving 160 kms reached Mandapam. There was a road bridge connecting the Rameswaram Island and we boarded the train to cross over the Pamban sea bridge constructed during World War I by the British for military reasons. Interestingly, it was India's first sea bridge, and was the longest sea bridge in India until the opening of the Bandra-Worli Sea Link in 2010. Of course, now a road bridge has also been made. It runs parallel to the rail bridge. The majestic Shiva temple here is called Shree Ramanathaswamy Temple, famous Rameshwar, as it is believed that Shree Ram had established it and worshiped Lord Shiva before proceeding for war on Ravana in Lanka.

We drove almost along the seashore to reach Kanyakumari 325 kms from Rameswaram. It is the southernmost town in mainland India and the confluence of the Arabian Sea, the Bay of Bengal and the Indian Ocean. The British called it Cape Comorin after the Cape of Good Hope, a rocky headland on the Atlantic coast of the Cape Peninsula in South Africa. Swami Vivekananda is said to have attained enlightenment on the rock amidst waters here and a beautiful temple has been built here. We took a short ferry ride and visited the temple that was constructed out of the contributions made by the public by buying one-rupee folders throughout the nation.

On our return, we visited Thiruvananthapuram, the city of Lord Ananta. Lord Vishnu, called Padmanabhaswamy, has a lotus emerging out of His navel, and is enshrined in the eternal yogic sleep posture, Ananta Shayana, on the serpent Adi Shesha. It is believed that Lord Parasuram consecrated the idol in the Dvapara Yuga. It is said that the value of jewellery and diamonds in this temple chests exceeds 20 billion dollars.

On our way back, we passed through Cochin, an important spice trading center on the west coast of India from the 14th century onward, like Surat; Mysore, the capital city of the Kingdom of Mysore for nearly six centuries ruled by the Wadiyar dynasty; Goa, famous for the Full Moon parties and night-long concerts; Mahabaleshwar, the origin of the Krishna River; and finally, Mumbai, my second home by that time.

On 16 January 1978, the government said that high-value notes of Rs 1000, Rs 5,000 and Rs 10,000 would cease to be legal tender at the close of banking hours on that day and that all banks and treasuries of governments would remain closed for transactions. At places like Crawford Market and Zaveri Bazar in Bombay people were selling Rs 1,000 notes for as little as Rs 200. Businesspersons did not want to deposit their high denomination notes in banks, as they feared income tax problems. I had 60 notes with me and gave them away in charity. The Maganlal Dhanjibhai Shah Public Charitable Dispensary set up in Surat seventy-five years ago in 1866 was developed into a full-fledged General Hospital at that time, now known as Mahavir Hospital. Like many other businesspersons in Surat, I dropped the notes in a donation box kept there. Though Prime Minister Morarjibhai Desai inaugurated the renovated hospital on 11 October 1978, the hospital did not get anything for the money it received in high denomination notes. The wealth was just junked. The gold and commodity prices fell sharply. Incidentally, the Rs 1000 note did not return until the new millennium when the Atal Bihari Vajpayee government reintroduced it in November 2000 with the picture of Mahatma Gandhi.

After our return, Champa had a change in her disposition. She had always been a god-fearing person and now she had become God-involved. She told me that very soon, our child would come, and it would be a girl. I did not contest. However, I learnt from her simple devotion that God never leaves us, never abandons us and never gives up hope in us. God watches over us waiting when we would make a prayer for hope. It was during the Chaitra-Navaratri,[46] when we visited Dr Tijoriwala for Champa's routine checkup, she

---

[46] चैत्र नवरात्री, Chaitra Navratri is an auspicious nine-day long Hindu festival which begins on the first day and extends till the ninth day of the Shukla Paksha during the month of Chaitra falls in March or April

carried out a pregnancy test and confirmed the arrival of a child in our lives. Our first girl child was born on 28 October 1978. There was no confusion in our minds about who she was. We named her Meenakshi as if to complete a formality.

Our Antwerp business partnership with D. Navinchandra & Co. was flourishing. I had established my position in the diamond business and was making good money now and yet unsure about what exactly I was there for. The bigger sense of purpose was elusive. 'What can I as an individual do?' I asked myself. 'Where do I fit into this complex industry?' I thought not for hours but for days and weeks at an end. I was not getting any clear answers. One day, I recollected Dongreji Maharaj's words, 'He who does not see God in his brother cannot serve the country or serve God.' We are five brothers; the eldest Bhimjibhai had brought me to Surat with him. My second and third brothers, Nagjibhai and Parbatbhai, had been farming the land at Dudhala.

A thought germinated in my mind, 'Why shouldn't my brothers join me in Surat?' After patiently waiting for the right moment, I visited them and broached the topic with them. 'I wish that you both come to live in Surat.' I said presenting my idea softly. 'Why should we come to Surat? We do not have any problem here.' Nagjibhai instantly retorted. Before I could say anything further, he said, 'Do you know we have a good reputation here? Why should we come there and become dependent? Who knows us in Surat? Here, on just one call, the entire village gathers. In the whole village, only we have a motorcycle. If someone has an emergency, he runs down to us. If someone wants Rs 200-500 on credit, he comes to us without hesitation. We are the support of our village. Shall we get such respect in Surat? If I come to Surat, despite being the older brother, I will have to ask you for money to spend!' He had finally said what I had feared the most.

I knew that my brothers had lived their life with dignity. They would never ask anything from anyone. They used to do farming in the village and earned enough out of it. In addition, suppose even if they needed anything, they never gave the slightest hint about it even to any of the others. They were satisfied. They used to manage in whatever they had. They had their own definition of happiness. 'There is no question of asking me for any money. Is not all my money yours? I have arranged that you will never have to ask me for money. You just go to our Accounts Department and take as much money as you wish. Nobody will ask you anything. If you suggest, we can even arrange where you can get a fixed amount every month. A person will come and give you the money. You need not even come to take it.' I said trying to allay their fears, but in vain. The best was to keep the matter suspended. I said, 'Please think over it later and decide. What I have told you is my earnest request to you.'

After that, whenever I met my brothers, I always asked them whether they had thought about coming to Surat. Every time, my brothers answered in the negative. However, with my persistence, both my brothers understood that I was requesting them sincerely. They knew that their brother sincerely wanted them to live comfortably and that is why he was repeatedly asking them to come to Surat. It took nearly three years for me to persuade Nagjibhai and Parbatbhai to come to Surat.

Now the next question was how to keep my brothers engaged in Surat. I knew their natures. Sitting idle was impossible for them. I settled Nagjibhai in the real estate business and Parbatbhai in the diamond grading business. Gradually, both the brothers also started earning well. Now, they did not need to take any money from my company.

Once we five brothers joined hands, a sense of security developed in my mind. If I missed something, my brother was there to cover it up. Yet, I felt that something was amiss. I was not sure why I was doing all this hard work. Apparently, it was for more money, more work, and again more money. But what was to be done with that money? We were investing most of our earnings back into our business. We were contented to live in rented houses. None of us had a knack for pleasures of the flesh and the mind. As the business was growing, I needed a bigger purpose. I was looking for some signposts, some maps, some guides.

3

Edification

मनो हि द्विविधं प्रोक्तं शुद्धं चाशुद्धमेव च ।
अशुद्धं कामसंकल्पं शुद्धं कामविवर्जितम् ॥

(ब्रह्मबिन्दु उपनिषद्, श्लोक 1)

The mind is said to be twofold:
The pure and the impure.
Impure—by union with desire;
Pure—free from desire completely.

(Brahmabindu Upanishad, Shloka 1)

Surat is a very old city, and money had always been here. The city was originally established on the Southern bank of the Tapi River with a castle. The activities were concentrated within the inner wall. People came here primarily for business, lived their high times, and withered away. Portuguese, Mughals, Marathas, all came, conquered it, only to be defeated by another force. However, they all left their marks behind, some good, some scars I mentioned, the Dutch-Armenian Cemetery in Gulam Falia earlier. Could the Marinas really leave the city? When occupied by Mughal Empire, Surat became an outpost for travel to the Hajj pilgrimage. Thousands of Muslims gathered at the Mughal Sarai here every year waiting for the ship to take them to Saudi Arabia.

Every man, powerful in his time—local merchant princes and the establishments of Turkish, Armenian, English, French, and Dutch traders—made their mansions in Surat in their high times to their tastes. However, the labour that supported their trade and serve their pleasures lived in mud-and-bamboo tenements and crooked streets. These faceless, rootless people developed the crafts of silks, cottons, brocades, and objects of gold and silver in their small, unaired, and often dark homes. Indeed, Surat has always attracted wealth and power, labour and struggle, wisdom, and enlightenment. It had been a great crucible where different cultures and classes melt together making a unique temper and luster in the process.

In 1964, population of Surat was mainly concentrated in 'Fort Area,' The main streets were lighted with incandescent light bulbs installed on poles by the municipality. Very few cars moved on roads, with some 'auto rickshaws', scooters and horse carts. Cycles were widely used for commuting. I had successfully graduated from a diamond-polishing worker to a small factory owner with a steady clientele to not only earn for family and myself but also support the livelihood of many people working in our enterprise. However, I knew well in my heart that this was not enough, let alone adequate. Something was missing in all this. My heart had a yearning, my mind had a void. Moreover, this state of seeking something that you do not even know used to take me for long walks and visiting old and sacred places. Unfinished stories are always important. Those who are attuned to hear echoes of those who were speaking earlier before those in this world indeed enjoy the benefit of time travel.

One such place in Surat was the Anglican Church, now known as CNI Christ Church, in Chowk Bazar created by the British. It was constructed in 1824 and had ten feet long Cross-and a 300-year-old bible. I am a devout Hindu but secretly like the manners, decency, and decorum in the way Christians worship. One Sunday, I even sat through the mass service. I did not understand much of what the priest was talking in a rather dramatic and loud voice, but one thing struck me when he said, 'living a good life is like the building of a house.' Each one of us ought to be helping one another to become a better person by doing things that uplift people intellectually or morally and help them learn. Good literature, art, and music are edifying. That chance visit on an idle Sunday morning to the church in Chowk Bazar indeed gave me a great insight of edifying myself.

Business indeed grows in steps. You start doing something small, learn everything about everything involved. It takes two to three years' time, involves a lot of patience, focus and hard work. Many businesses go bankrupt because people failed to wait and complete their learning at this stage. Such people thought that they knew everything and tried to expand without gaining enough experience. The expansion would make them take risks and any one mistake would wipe them off completely. Spending countless hours studying and feeling the diamonds, talking to people at every level, travelling relentlessly and learning from every interaction, this was a way to carry on business.

In 1979, a recession struck the diamond industry. For thirty years following World War II, the diamond industry had enjoyed relative calm. Usually stable and growing, the market performed in an orderly manner, with goods supplied based on global demand. Prices rose steadily. The diamond market started changing drastically since the mid-1970s. By 1976, most world economies began to experience rising inflation. While this should have boded well for diamonds, but eventually led to a debacle that threatened the very core of the industry.

Israel was a relatively young but rapidly growing diamond center. The Israeli government was eager to promote the diamond trade because of its contribution to the country's overall gross national product. To make things move even more quickly, the government supplied several Israeli banks with huge amounts of money at very low interest rates to be passed on to diamond manufacturers and dealers so they could build their inventories. The government also set up a system whereby the dollars that were brought into the country through the sale of diamonds received a more favorable exchange rate, despite this global diamond markets including Israel faced recession.

During this period, experienced firms like D. Navinchandra & Co. evolved a smart strategy. Shantibhai told me, 'Govindbhai, let us keep polishing our roughs nevertheless and hold them in inventory as gems waiting for the market to turn. But as there would be no actual sale for some time, you have to bear the cost of polishing diamonds.'

It was tough and uncomfortable, however, it worked and when the market turned in less than a year's time, we made good money. During this turbulent period, one thing I realized that if I must grow further in the industry, I must understand the economic factors that altered the supply, demand, and value of diamonds.

To spread education in the mostly uneducated Saurashtra Patel community, we seven friends got together and formed a Trust 'Saurashtra Patel Kelavani Mandal', in which Vallabhbhai Savani, Kanubhai Mavani, Mavjibhai Mavani, K. D. Waghani made a very pioneer contribution. This was the first social Trust to spread education in Surat. The Trust currently runs a public library, which benefits thousands of students each year. Kanjibhai Bhalala, a young commerce graduate, used to come here to take books for his studies, and being very smart, this young man was liked by all the trustees very much, and gradually handed over the responsibility of the library to him and he handled that responsibility very diligently and continues to this day.

In another such social campaign, Shree Ramjibhai Italiya, a pioneer of diamond industry in Saurashtra, was organizing mass weddings with great enthusiasm and sincerity to curb the extravagance of weddings and extravagant expenses. He got the inspiration for mass marriage from a District Judge named J.R. Savani in the early 1980's. After the demise of Hon. Judge, the leaders of the society along with Ramjibhai made this work their personal mission. Initially, very few couples came forward for marriage, but with the help of leaders of society, in 1987 the number increased to fifty. Initial efforts were a bit lax, but more community leaders joined in and made mass-marriage their goal. Now people don't have to be persuaded, they just walk in front. People's perceptions have also changed that this is a better way to have a dignified marriage than to fall into the pit of seemingly wrong expenses.

One problem persisted was that of the marriages of migrant youth. In Surat, these people were away from their families and communities, and it was extremely difficult for them to find a suitable partner. Many went to their native places for their weddings and brought their spouses. However, these women faced immense difficulties in adapting to city life. Therefore, in 1980, I brought together like-minded people and created the Shree Saurashtra Patel Samaj Trust (SPS) to encourage 'Mass Marriages.' This Trust organized matrimonial counselling and provided logistical support to start a new family. K. D. Waghani was a founder President of this Trust. Kanji Bhalala later took over the reins of this Trust, as he had remained socially active since the days of his youth. To lead by example, he got married in a Mass Marriage himself. Keshubhai Patel regarded Kanjibhai as a master motivator and whenever he spoke in any meeting, he could easily raise funds from people for any public good. Kanjibhai later set up the Varachha Co-operative Bank along with P. B. Dhakecha, Narendra Kukadiya, Prabhudas Patel and others. It is one of the finest co-operative banks in Gujarat.

Once the industry buoyed out of the recession, I decided to go to Israel and know firsthand how the system worked there. In February 1982, I went there along with Dilipbhai with whom I went to Antwerp earlier. India did not have diplomatic relations with Israel then. Though India extended de-jure recognition to Israel in 1950 and allowed Israel to maintain a consulate in Bombay to facilitate the voluntary immigration of thousands of Indian Jews to Israel, relations between Jerusalem and New Delhi were not always warm. For nearly four decades—India as a leader of the Non-Alignment Movement maintained close relations with the Arab World and the Soviet Union; Israel meanwhile linked its future to close ties with the United States and Western Europe.

We travelled from Antwerp to Tel Aviv by Swiss Air. Israeli immigration gave us a paper visa and did not put any stamp on our passports, which would have made almost all Gulf countries out of bounds for us. We stayed at Hotel Armon Hayarkon, close by to the Embassy of the United States. From our hotel window, we could see the majestic view of the sun setting in the deep blue waters of the Mediterranean Sea.

The famous diamond market of Israel is in the Ramat Gan area. We took a taxi to reach Ramat Gan from our hotel, which was about 5 km away. We had been buying diamonds through Rupenbhai Bhanshali of Aarohi Diamonds. He could speak Hebrew fluently. Rupenbhai introduced us to Meir Anavi, Simon Barbi, and Dudi Siama. There were 13,000 workers engaged in diamond cutting and polishing in the Ramat Gan area. Diamond cutting had been the oldest industry in Israel, which was the most important global center for polishing and cutting diamonds at that time, taking a pole position in the world for large diamond manufacturing. I was told that there were over 400 firms doing cutting and polishing of diamonds. In the Tel Aviv area, the diamond exchange was also located, with the rest in the cities of Netanya and Jerusalem.

I had heard a lot about Kirtilal Manilal Mehta, who was considered as the doyen of the world diamond industry and the father of Indian diamond industry. In 1944, he founded Beautiful Diamonds in Bombay. In 1953, Kirtilal started Gembel European Sales (GES) NV in Antwerp. Later, Kirtilal established diamond companies in Hong Kong in 1956 and Tel Aviv in 1968. Kirtilal opened Occidental Gems, in New York in 1973. As goes the legend, when his wife Lilavati died in 1964 in Bombay, he built Bandra's Lilavati Hospital, where the Maximum City's rich and famous rush when they fall ill, in the loving memory of his wife. In 1970, Kirtilal handed over the global diamond trading company to his sons—Prabodh Mehta and Rashmi Mehta. In 1993, I attended a celebration in Bombay that commemorated the completion of his seventy-five years in business.

We first met his son Rashmibhai Mehta. He was very cordial and invited us home to meet his father. Kirtilal Mehta was a well-built man with a kingly aura. After his wife Lilavatiben died, he remarried an Israeli Jew woman Esther and made Tel Aviv his business headquarter. I asked him only one question, why did he prefer Tel Aviv for his home instead of Europe or North America. 'I like the weather here,' he said crisply. Then after a pause, he said, 'Kindness to the needy, benevolence, faith, compassion for the suffering, a peace-loving disposition, and a truly humble and contrite spirit, is abundant in Jewish society. I felt at home with Jews rather than Westerners.'

I found the Israeli diamond cutting and polishing industry to be one of the top and most advanced in the world. In general, about 20 per cent of the cut and polished diamonds of all sizes would pass through Israel, making Israel the world leader in both the manufacture and export of these stones. How much of this work could be taken to India? I wondered. 'A lot, actually most of it,' was the answer I got from my inner voice. Why would Israelis allow that? The Jews suffered through hell in the past and for them to trust outsiders was extremely difficult. I took a personal decision on that day that I would win their trust. I made business arrangements in Tel Aviv. Since then, we have excellent and mutually beneficial relations with the Israelis.

Immediately after my return, Meenakshi suffered from Jaundice. Champa took a while to notice a yellowish tint in her eyes but once Meenakshi got a high fever, she became intensely worried and inconsolable. We consulted Dr A. T. Desai. He said it was toxic jaundice. Generally, jaundice occurred due to temporary obstruction in the biliary ducts, or it may be due to a liver condition that is preventing the liver from processing the bilirubin appropriately. But toxic jaundice in a four-year-old child did not make any sense to me. Here was my beautiful child growing up with love and care, her mother doting over her every move. How could she have all these frightening things happening inside her tender body? Dr Desai explained to me that she must have had a viral infection. 'You already know. Right now, the entire city is under chaos,' Dr Desai said. He also alerted me about the possible threat to the life of my child and inquired if I could get Intravenous immunoglobulin (IVIg) from Europe though it would be very expensive, and six injections would be required. Some doctors in Bombay knew the sources. This medicine would help stop the breakdown of red blood cells in Meenakshi's body.

I called many of my friends in Bombay to get injections. One injection was worth Rs 1500. At that time, the price of 10 grams of gold was Rs 500 and obviously, injections worth Rs 9,000 were costly. A man boarded the train to Surat with the injections and it was administered in the morning. However, there was no immediate relief. Dr Desai asked me to have faith in God. Helpless and worried, I started doing Japa[1] on my rosary dipping it in the sacred water. How could the Creator have decided to grant only 4 years to my

---

[1] जप-Chanting silently name of God

little daughter? With such thoughts tormenting me, tears started rolling down my eyes. I felt some vibrations in the water. Perplexed, I sprinkled the water upon Meenakshi. She responded by opening her eyes and I knew that she would be all right. However, it was only after three injections, on the third day, Dr Desai told me that Meenakshi is out of danger. She took another month to be her normal self.

Feeling deeply grateful in my heart but shaken out of my comfort zone, I took three decisions. First, get a temple of Lord Shree Ram renovated in Dudhala village. Second, discard the prevailing practice of 'Parda' or 'veil' in family. Third, to set-up a Relief Center and Medical Center in Surat with the aim of supporting needy people with financial assistance to tide over unexpected hardships and providing almost free medical treatment. The 'Parda' custom was later discarded by our entire community.

I was surprised to see Champa taking interest in the welfare of the girl child. After Meenakshi's illness, she was shaken and developed compassion for the plight of poor women and children, especially girls. One day, she told me that if a family is poor, a son is the first to be fed only after that is the less valuable girl given leftover scraps to eat. Parents are more likely to seek medical help for sick sons rather than for daughters who are ill. She started distributing some sweet packets and giving them to the girls and their mothers at local health clinics. One day, Champa told me that she saw Goddess Sarasvati in a dream, and that I must open a school at the earliest opportunity, especially for the girls. It took some time but eventually happened.

Champa and I had our second child, a girl, on 12 October 1983. Recollecting Champa's dream, we named the child Shweta, after Goddess Swetambara[2]. We decided to celebrate Shweta's arrival by starting a self-study center for the growing number of our employees

---

[2] श्वेतांबरा, Name of Goddess Sarasvati

My father, Laljidada, owned a tract of land in Dudhala village of Amreli district in Gujarat. He worked hard, spending most of his time in the fields.

My mother, Santokbaa, was an embodiment of emotion. She used to manage the house with seven children, took care of our cattle, helped my father in the field and was available to anyone who needed help.

Family system is indeed God's greatest gift to humans – it gives life a purpose, discipline and meaning. This picture from 1995 shows our three children – my daughters Shweta and Meenakshi and son Shreyans.

The first Family Meeting at Kosmada village in March 1982 with my brothers and their spouses in presence of our parents for removal of the social ill of the veil tradition. Since then, we meet every month and have remained close-knit.

This is the picture of Laljidada's extended family taken on 15 January 2005 at Dholakia Farm on the wedding of my daughter, Shweta.

On my first visit to Antwerp, Santokbaa, Parbatbhai, Bhimjibhai and Laljidada came to bid farewell at Mumbai Airport on 16 January 1977 (From L to R)

I consider myself as twice blessed, first by being born to my mother and second being married to my wife, Champa.

As a young man, the Bullet used to be an extension of my person. This recent picture is to capture that old spirit of a 'knight'. My old Bullet is no more, and I have used a Rajdoot since.

Family system is all about guiding the next generation and forgiving the last.
With my son, Shreyans, and grandsons, Ish and Aan, in 2020.

President of India Shree Ramnath Kovind came to Surat to give away the Santokbaa Award on 29 May 2018 breaking government protocol.

'Grand Dholakia Family: Six Families, Six Generations,' now numbering more than 1,500 individuals, meet annually Navratri to commemorate our union. This picture is taken on 13 October 2019 with 1,269 members present.

Prime Minister Narendra Modi invited my family to his official residence on 29 September 2018.

Then Gujarat Chief Minister Narendra Modi attended Shreyans' wedding on 29 November 2009. We all dressed in traditional Kathiawar attire.

My two partners Virjibhai (centre) and Bhagwanbhai (right) were my alter egos. We together made a very successful 'trinity.' This picture is clicked in a studio in 1971 on Diwali with our spouses.

Went to Antwerp in 1977 on my maiden trip with Dilipbhai Mehta. This picture is taken at Bombay airport before our departure. Seen are partners of D. Navinchandra & Co. including Dilipbhai, Shantibhai, Shrenikbhai and Navinbhai (from left).

I laid down a very clear succession plan. Seen in the picture are Arjanbhai, Dineshbhai, Jayantibhai and Rahulbhai (from left) who were made partners at SRK in 1995. Sheryans, Akshay, Nirav, and Arpit make the third-generation leadership.

We connected Surat to various cities by air by starting Ventura Air Connect Airline. With Savjibhai Dholakia, Laljibhai Patel, Gujarat's Minister of Aviation Saurabh Patel and Lavjibhai Daliya ('Badshah') on the inauguration day in December 2014 at Surat airport.

I have two mentors: Shantibhai (left) and Navinbhai (right). This picture was taken during their visit to the inauguration of Shree Ramkrishna Complex on 18 April 1997.

I met Mahendrabhai Parikh at Antwerp in 1977. With him is the Doyen of Indian pharmaceutical industries, Shree Pankaj Patel of Zydus on 1 January 2015 in Surat.

Ashitbhai Mehta, lovingly called Munnabhai, encouraged me to venture into the higher league of polishing big diamonds in 1997 saying, 'If you do it, India will do it.'

On 2 May 2019, De Beers delegation under the leadership of Paul Rowley, Executive Vice President, Global Sight-Holder Sales visited us in Surat. Seen in the picture are SRK's first, second and third generation leaders.

At De Beers Jwaneng mine in South Central Botswana on 19 August 2014. Operational since August 1982, it is the richest diamond mine in the world by value.

I accompanied Prime Minister Narendra Modi and Chief Minister of Gujarat Anandiben Patel to Beijing in 2015. This picture is with Chinese Premier Li Keqiang.

I consider visit of Shree Ratan Tata to my home at Surat on 4 May 2018 as the acme of my good fortune.

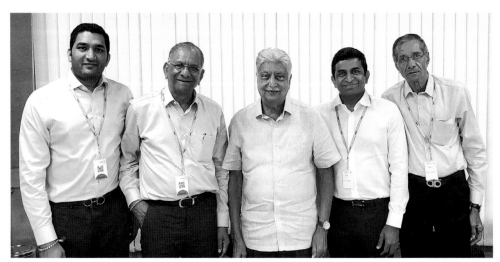

Shree Azim Premji is informally known as the Czar of the Indian IT Industry. Interacted with him along with Shreyans, Rahulbhai and VB at Bengaluru on 19 November 2019.

In 2015 'SRK Empire' became the first manufacturing building in country to acquire 'Green Rating' from USGBC, later enhanced to 'Platinum Rating' in 2018.

Immaculate craftsmanship and unmatched quality are on display at our recent manufacturing facility 'SRK House,' another Platinum LEED certified building built in 2018.

We envisioned the idea of Surat Diamond Bourse (SDB) at Diamond Research and Mercantile (DREAM) City. Once completed in 2022 SDB will play a vital role in economy of India.

and their family members. Though I had not met Pandurang Shastri 'Dada,' I had gotten very positive feedback about the self-study process Svadhyaya,[3] which he had developed based on the Shreemad Bhagvad Gita and which he was spreading across villages. I have attended many of his Satsangs[4] on Sundays in Madhavbagh in C.P. Tank in Mumbai. As a thanksgiving for Shweta's arrival in our lives, we established the Ramkrishna Svadhyaya Pariwar platform in Surat, which holds Satsang meeting every Saturday.

Svadhyaya, which closely translates to 'in-depth study of the self' is a process based upon Vedic philosophy. Pandurang 'Dada' has given many social projects. Yogeshwara Krishna is worshipped with Parvati, Ganesh and Shiva in a natural setting called Vriksha Mandir. The deity Surya is recognized in the form of sunlight. Community members participate in Bhava Bhakti (emotional devotion to the divine), Kruti Bhakti (actionable devotion by voluntary service to the divine in all of god's creation), and Bhakti Pheri (devotional travel to meet, work and help the well-being of the community partners). All men and women in the organization are treated as a Pariwar (family). I intended to put God-centric devotion at the core of all my business activities.

It soon led me to Indravadanbhai Choksi, one original Surti. One of my friends Harjibhai once said to me,' Govindbhai, will you join for a Satsang in Surat which will suit your temperament?' And in the same evening at 8.30 pm we went to Indravadanbhai who lived on Parsi Street in the Ranitalav area of Surat. He inherited Bharat Printing press from his father and worked as a printer. He was deeply spiritual. He started having Satsang at his modest residence. I shared with him my Church experience and he said that a teacher would always find a learner. He explained to me the concept of edification. 'Don't be good to please others, while

---

[3] स्वाध्याय, self-study
[4] सत्संग, gathering with like-minded, uplifting people, especially those on a spiritual path.

edifying ourselves, we put our life in order and build it. And the first lesson in edification is punctuality, which if practiced honestly, immensely improves the quality of whatever we do in our lives,' he said. The Satsang would start precisely at eight-thirty in the evening. There were hardly any people at 8.25 p.m. but within the next four minutes, everyone used to come. Satsang would get over at 9.30 p.m. Moreover, within five minutes everyone had gone. I acquired my lessons of time management from him.

Indravadanbhai told me, 'Punctuality is a wonderful trait of a person. It brings you admiration and respect. By being punctual you display your respect for people and time.' I asked him one day, rather offensively, 'Sir, you have sold your business, living a life without any pressure of work, why should you bother about time?' He smiled and said without taking any offence to my rude remark, 'You are taking for granted the gift of life, and you are given for free. Each breath we inhale comes with a responsibility, an obligation, to return something good in its exchange. Can you afford to live without breathing?' he asked. 'If not, how can you waste the time of others, by keeping them waiting by not arriving in time, or keep others waiting by not attending to them?' Several times I tried to involve him in some social work that I could sponsor and, in that way, take care of some comforts around Indravadanbhai but he gave me no such opportunity. He was contented with his small comforts and modest conveniences.

We never discussed any political, or should I say, worldly issue during Satsang. The discussion always centred on Shree Krishna, Shreemad Bhagvad Gita and Shreemad Bhagwat. At a rather early stage in my life, I started understanding God as all-pervading consciousness, present everywhere, every time, and available to everyone. It is ignorance of this simple fact that creates all sort of stupid, bad, and even harmful behaviour in the world and the Satsang at Indravadanbhai's place provided me this awareness and saved me from many errors, I would have committed otherwise.

I was drawn to Indravadanbhai's simple manners and the clarity of his thoughts and spent many evenings at his place. There was no dogma, no cult building, no push, and no agenda of any kind whatsoever. People were welcome to participate in the chanting of God's name, share their problems if any and return with some clarity in their mind and peace in their hearts. I found Indravadanbhai to be the embodiment of simplicity. I learnt from him that life is simply a collection of little lives, each lived one day at a time. Each day should be spent finding beauty in flowers and talking to animals. A day spent dreaming and watching sunsets and enjoying the cool, refreshing breeze cannot be bettered. It was such a selfless enterprise on part of Indravadanbhai.

Indravadanbhai's Satsang was indeed a congregation of some pious souls. There, I became acquainted with Narsinhbhai Sutaria, Manjibhai Navdawala, Hirjibhai, and Dani Dutt Jha, a teacher in the Sanskrit Paathshala in Surat. Manjibhai Navdawala lived like an ascetic. He hardly lived one or two months in Surat. Rest of the time he spent in Vrindavan, Haridwar, and in the Himalayas. Narsinhbhai joined my company for polishing diamonds and later became a working partner in Bhargovi Diamond Company. I invited Dani Dutt Jha to be my Sanskrit teacher and later his son, Hitnath Jha, would teach Shlokas to my children. Dani Dutt Jha introduced me to Shree N. Gopalaswami who acted as the Municipal Commissioner of Surat from 1977 to 1980 and later became the Chief Election Commissioner of India. I am still cherishing the friendship of Shree Gopalaswami even today.

In June 1984, I accompanied Indravadanbhai on his annual pilgrimage to Akhandanand Ashram in Vrindavan. We had Satsang with Swami Akhandanand, an exponent of the Bhagwat Purana and a scholar of diverse spiritual traditions including Vedanta, Bhakti, and Shastras, was ordained into Sanyasa by the Shankaracharya of Jyotishpeethadhishver, Brahmanand Sarasvati. Akhandanand Swami was called a moving library and his Pravachans (discourses) were transcribed as books. There were more than 300 such books. Shree Krishna Janmasthan Temple at Mathura was constructed under his eyes. The foundation stone of the temple was laid on 11 February 1965 while it was inaugurated on 12 February 1982. Later, his devotees erected his statue in the same place besides the statues of Madan Mohan Malaviya, Jugal Kishore Birla and Hanuman Prasad Poddar. Akhandanand Swami informed us that he visited Prempuri Ashram, near Babulnath, in Bombay every year. I instantly decided in my heart to meet Swamiji at Prempuri Ashram whenever he would come there. I have attended many of his discourses at Prempuri Ashram.

However, the most remarkable person I met around that time was not exactly in the Satsang, but through it—Atmendraji. An officer of Indian Administrative Service (IAS), Atmendraji had been posted as the Collector of Ahmedabad in the early 1950s but was sent to the Indian Embassy in Netherlands in Amsterdam by the political masters not happy with his stern ways of working. He was a celibate and withdrew from the worldly life after his mother passed away. He set up a cottage in Uttar Kashi in 1958 that functioned as his residence and Ashram.

He came to Surat to visit Indravadanbhai. Though he was there for five days, I could not meet him as I was in the welter of work. In a beautiful coincidence, I met him on the train to Bombay when he was leaving and spent about five hours with him. Atmendraji told me that we were all different streams of consciousness scattered in physicality with the ultimate destiny of merging into One Consciousness that had created this entire universe. Based on our purity, like that of light to become a laser, we were guided to interact towards a bigger purpose, no single stream could ever know. On reaching Bombay Central, I drove him to Victoria Terminus for a train to his next destination, Pune. On my insistence, he took Rs 100 for his sundry expenses during the trip. Same Rs 100 bill he returned to me through Indravadanbhai after almost six months saying that he did not need any money on a trip to Pune. Such was his simplicity and humility!

It was now time to build a bungalow. I had delayed it for many years, putting whatever money I was making back into the business. I had bought a plot on Katargam Road and now it was time to build a house there. As if to compensate for all the delay in my decision, I wanted to make a dream house. My quest of 'an engineer with taste' took me to Jayantbhai Makwana. He was a man of professional integrity and was brutally honest. He said that in Surat, there are three phases in house building—Harakhva, Barakva, and Hadakva -loosely translated in English as euphoric, practical, and acrimonious. In the euphoric phase, that comes first, the client wants the best in the world. This phase gradually wanes into practicalities and finally there is a fight over every issue when expenses start exceeding budget. He said, 'So far, I could complete all my projects within two phases and had never gone into the third phase.'

The bungalow took three years to complete. Jayantbhai came to the site every single day and put his heart and soul in the building. His blend of engineering accuracy and architectural imagination was peerless. On the land of Ramjibhai, opposite our site, some squatters were living. Jayantbhai suggested that those people be paid off else, after the property is ready, they would demand a very fancy amount to vacate the place. There were eleven huts. Jayantbhai offered everyone Rs 3000. Nine families accepted the offer readily and left by the noontime. However, two people not only hassled but also called for a local thug. Jayantbhai calmly told him 'One name' after hearing which the thug disappeared. He did not leave the site until he settled them for Rs 5,000 each by 11.00 p.m. The determination, steadfastness, and sense of purpose of Jayantbhai was incredible. The bungalow when ready was admired by everyone in Surat.

I had invited my younger brother-in-law Jerambhai Khokhariya, known popularly as JB, to Surat for training in diamond work. His dedication and friendship had been unique. Jerambhai helped me realize that a friend is someone who understands your past, believes in your future, and accepts you just the way you are. He also worked with me at Laljibhai Kheni's factory in 1969. Jerambhai made his own mark in the business. He worked as a partner with Savjibhai Dholakia in Hari Krishna Exports for 20 years and would establish his own company, Shree Krishna Exports in 2010.

By 1983, our factory was running successfully. All three of us had distributed the work of the factory in a seamless manner. I used to purchase rough diamonds, Virjibhai looked after manufacturing and Bhagwanbhai would manage the sale of polished diamonds. We were seen as an example of great partnership in Surat. Virjibhai was a bundle of energy, always working with enthusiasm. One day in August, around Janmashtami time, I saw tiredness on his face. He sat down suddenly. I took him to Dr Mukund Mehta. He ordered some tests and diagnosed a tumour in Virjibhai's stomach. 'It can be simple or cancerous. The best way is to get it checked in Bombay,' doctor advised.

Bhagwanbhai and I rushed to Bombay and met Shantibhai, our friend-philosopher and guide. He unhesitatingly took charge of the situation and took an appointment in Harkishan Hospital at Prarthna Samaj. The same hospital was later taken over by the Reliance Foundation in 2006. They added a twenty-two-floor building to the seven-floor old heritage building and transformed it into a world-class medical facility, now known as Sir H. N. Reliance Foundation Hospital and Research Centre. The next day, Virjibhai arrived. He was diagnosed with fourth stage adenocarcinoma. 'Whatever has to be done, needs to be done fast,' we were told. Shantibhai and Navinbhai handled all requirements, from smallest to most significant including hospital and doctors. The operation lasted for six hours. 'The cancer had spread more than our anticipation. We have given our best try. There is a need to provide radiation now. It all depends on how well the body responds,' said the doctor.

Virjibhai was kept in hospital for some days before taking him to Panchratna residence.

Virjibhai told me, 'O, Bhagat! You have been saying that the operation was successful then why do we need to take radiation. Are you hiding something? My children are very small. Vinod is just twelve years old; Ramesh is only eight years old. My daughters, Rasila and Rekha are even younger than they are. How many dreams I had seen for my kids?' I was finding it extremely difficult to lie about the cruel reality and keep it from him. When Virjibhai started recalling his youngest daughter, 'Rekha would be waiting when will her father come,' I started crying.

Later in the day, Shantibhai and Navinbhai sat with Bhagwanbhai and me on a sofa in the office. When I apologized for being emotional, Shantibhai said that pain is an inseparable part of life. Then he said something very important which I still remember, 'Govindbhai, your sensitivity is not a sign of weakness. To feel your pain intensely is not a symptom of feebleness, it is the trademark of a truly alive and compassionate heart. There is no shame in expressing your authentic feelings. Those who are at times described as being a 'hot mess' or having 'too many issues' are the very fabric of what keeps the dream alive for a more caring, humane world. Never be ashamed to let your tears shine a light in this world.'

Every two days, Bhagwanbhai and I took Virjibhai to the Bombay Hospital for radiation therapy. However, his health was deteriorating instead of improving. When we told this to the doctor, he said in cold words, 'Radiation not only kills or slows the growth of cancer cells, but it can also affect nearby healthy cells. Damage to healthy cells can cause side effects.' When we pressed further and wanted to know if there could be any relief, he said, 'Healthy cells that are damaged during radiation treatment usually recover within a few months after treatment is over. But sometimes people may have side effects that do not improve.' Then after about a week, the doctor told us, 'There are not many days left, and let the truth be told to the patient.' We knew the inevitable but when the decisive moment finally arrived, we did not know from where to start talking about it. I felt a ton of weight on my shoulders, and it felt like my feet were not ready to move ahead.

Overcoming the paralysis of our senses somehow, Bhagwanbhai and I went into Virjibhai's room at our residence in Panchratna on 15th floor. 'Virjibhai, our destiny is not long now. Our fates are ruined.' Saying this much, I started crying profusely. Bhagwanbhai also was very remorseful. Virjibhai too started crying but became normal after some time. He said, 'Do not cry now, you can cry later once I go away. You take care of yourselves. I had enough of this treatment. If I must die, let me die at home. Please take me to Surat.' We asked doctors and they said as there is nothing that could be done now, let Virjibhai go home. On our way back to Surat in the train, Virjibhai said philosophically, 'Govind and Bhagwan, both of you have been God-send to me. I would have been polishing roughs had you not met me. I am ten years older than you. Both of you gave me the madness of youth that had left me already. You changed my story but the ultimate meaning to which all stories refer has two faces: the continuity of life, the inevitability of death. No one can change that. So, let us be together till my end comes.'

Earlier, the three of us had visited Babulnath temple, knowing fully well that it would be the last time Virjibhai was there to pray to Lord Shiva. When we were sitting there after Darshan, we heard an old, Kannadiga man reciting a poem of Basaveshwara:

उल्लवारू शिवालायव माडूवारू ।
नानेनु माडली बादवानायया ॥
एनन् काले कम्भ देहवे देगुला ।
शिखे होन्ना कालाशवाईएया ॥
कूडाला संगमा देवा केलैया ।
स्थावारक्कालिवुंटू जांगंक्किल्लव्यया ॥

(वचना- 4, उल्लवारू शिवालय, मधुवरू)

Those who have wealth will construct Shivalaya.

What should I do? I am very poor.

Hence, my legs shall be the pillars and my body shall be the temple.

And my head shall be the kalasha of temple.

Please Listen . . . O lord of the meeting rivers [Shiva].

The physical structures can banish, but never your disciples.

(Vachana-4, Ullavuru Shivalaya, Madhuvaru)

After reaching his home in Surat, Virjibhai felt better. All our friends used to come home in the evening and chat. Bhagwanbhai and I used to stay there only. Champa would come every day and spend time with Virjibhai's wife Shardaben. One day, Champa and Laxmiben, Bhagwanbhai's wife suggested that before Virjibhai passed away, something be done to make him happy. What about the engagement of his daughter Rasila? When I broached this topic with Virjibhai, he immediately agreed. Rasila, though fourteen, was engaged with Paresh Golakiya who was working with us. They both liked each other. I could see the shine in his eyes when both the children took his blessings on 1 November 1983 when our three partners' families celebrated Diwali together.

Diwali is not merely a festival for businesspersons in Gujarat. We celebrate Diwali as the end of the year. Therefore, the next day is celebrated as Bestu Varas or New Year's Day. When we were taking stock of our business, we realized that in our absence from Surat for about four months, Shantibhai and Navinbhai ensured uninterrupted operations of our factory there and carried out the business seamlessly without making any show whatsoever of their profound acumen and support. It was hard to believe that people like them existed in our world. For them, business was a sacred Dharma, which was to be upheld with hard work and honest dealings. Further, it hardly mattered who owned the business; what truly mattered was everyone involved in the enterprise—partners, employees, dealers, and suppliers; that each was dealt with a fair hand in the best interest of the business and that no one was never favoured over another.

Virjibhai knew that it was his last Diwali. He told me, 'Govind, do you remember in the village we used to get salt collected from the evaporated ponds and taste it as 'Sabras[5]' to bring luck in the New Year. Get me that.' I fulfilled his wish. On the last Monday of the month, Virjibhai told me, 'O Bhagat, take me to Kantareshwar Mahadev Mandir.' I said, 'I will definitely do that, but you always said you are an atheist.' Virjibhai did not answer. After a while he said, 'I want to take a ride. I want to see Surat. This city has given me a reputation and provided me with friends like you. This city has fulfilled my dreams.'

We took him to the temple in Katargam area. He was in intense pain. With a lot of effort, he alighted from the car and sat on the floor for a while in deep contemplation. He folded his hands and bowed his head while returning. I could see that his last moments were near. Only in the final minutes of their life, would an atheist choose to worship. 'There is a pure white light behind the curtains of this world, all drama is only here.' Virjibhai said, in the car on our way back. I heard from him these last words. On the next day, on 29 November 1983, Virjibhai breathed his last. It was the evening, when in our village, the cows would return home. Virjibhai chose this time to return to his heavenly abode.

What was to be done with Virjibhai's 33 per cent partnership in the business? This question was staring at Bhagwanbhai and me. There are some rules in society and business. Even before the death certificate was issued, some things had to be worked out. Society forces you to make some decisions. The legislations too mandate finishing certain formalities before a specific time. Most of the people felt that after Virjibhai's death, his wife Shardaben must be paid Virjibhai's share and the matter be closed.

---

[5] सबरस, considered an omen

Bhagwanbhai and I sat alone in our office next evening. We were not comfortable in settling Virjibhai's legacy by paying off Shardaben. It was the easiest way, but we were not okay with that somehow. How is our society? After a person dies, many ties automatically are cut. In our community, it is also believed, that after the husband dies, the paternal side relations get over, and after a wife's demise, the maternal side already get over. After a person dies, even the blood relations get weaker. We were stuck trying to figure out how to keep a business partnership going after the death of our partner!

Both, Bhagwanbhai and I were clear that we were not going to end the partnership. Nevertheless, we were also acutely aware of the other side of the coin. Suppose we made Shardaben a partner in all earnest; however, if luck did not favour us, and business went in loss, people would say that both partners ruined Virjibhai's family. People would also say that we swindled away the money of Virjibhai. When you progress, there are jealous people, who are just waiting for a chance to ruin your name. It is the fate of businesspersons that they are constantly forced to choose between their desire to not be a bad person and their desire to be a good businessperson. We decided to consult Shantibhai and left for Bombay together.

Shantibhai heard us patiently. He was thoughtful. After some time, he told us that our decision to make Shardaben as partner did not seem correct. When we insisted that he must explain his rationale, Shantibhai said, 'Shardaben is a housewife. She does not have any understanding of the business. How could she be? She is still in shock of her husband's demise; she has the responsibility of four kids. Then there would be many around her to influence her. What will happen if she, as a partner, writes a letter to the bank that no transaction should be done without her signature?'

We were dumbfounded. This was how the world worked. Shantibhai was telling us the truth as he experienced it, not dispensing us some bookish knowledge. 'What do you really want to achieve by not just paying Shardaben off? Is that the way business is done?' he asked. I said, 'That will be too little a sum. Our intent is to see Virjibhai's money grow as ours and his children flourish as our children.' 'Very good, then keep both of his sons as partners,' said Shantibhai.

We had not even thought of this. We had always looked at Virjibhai's sons as little kids. Shantibhai was giving us a new idea, a solution that was truly 'out-of-the-box.' We heard him carefully. 'Virjibhai's partnership is 33 per cent, make both sons partner of 17 per cent each. Educate them until they are eighteen and make them ready for business. Their future will be built, and your wish will also turn true.' Shantibhai's advice touched our hearts. However, we had to know what Shardaben thought. We returned to Surat with our hearts and minds clear.

We went to Virjibhai's house first thing in the morning. Even before we could propose our point, Shardaben surprised us by telling, "Do you know what your brother told me before going to Heaven?' She continued without waiting for our reply. She said, 'You both are like God only. Keep faith in them. Never quarrel with them. Never create any inconvenience for them.' Then Shardaben folded her hands and said with tears running over her cheeks, 'Brothers, you can do anything that you feel okay for us. Whatever you do will be good for us only.'

Bhagwanbhai and I made Virjibhai's sons Vinod and Ramesh partners in the company. We invited our friends Vitthalbhai Limbachia and Manjibhai Khakharia to assess the company's Balance Sheet and to remain as witness so that in the future there would be no doubts about any misappropriation of Virjibhai's share in the future. We arranged the best education for both the children and provided them with practical training for handing our business. Once they were fully groomed, the elder son Vinod was sent to Bangkok to handle the business there. At times, it is essential to hand over responsibilities fully to sons. They should be allowed to take decisions by themselves. The real parents and guardians give their kids the right to make mistakes as well.

During October 1984, I, along with Virjibhai's family, went to Haridwar on the banks of the Ganges for the immersion of ashes of Virjibhai along with families of Popatbhai Monpara, Shivalal Shingala. It was 31 October 31 1984, as we were returning to Mangalashram we received news that Prime Minister Indira Gandhi had been assassinated by her own security guard. Riots and fires spreaded like wildfire. The looting of Sikh shops and places started, we had to stop at Haridwar as the trains to Delhi were canceled for twelve days. What a tragic fate for a mighty leader like Indiraji!

During this extended stay at Mangalashram, we saw with Shree Ram Swaroop Swami, a 400-year-old manuscript of Harivansh Purana written in Sanskrit in golden ink, worth about Rs 4 crores. Today, this invaluable book is in the custody of Swami Bhagwat Swarupji.

Back in Surat, I started taking my life as a threefold bhakti—I felt an emotional connection with the people who met me during my business, be it traders, partners, or workers, sensing a divine hand bringing all of us together and there was harmony all around me. I started looking at the work of diamond cutting and polishing as an art form and so many opportunities started appearing before me as if from thin air. In addition, a deep conviction had set in my heart that I must use the wealth that was coming my way not only for the good of people who were working with me but also for the general welfare of people.

With the moral strength I received from Indravadanbhai's satsang, one day I wrote a letter to him and told him to spend fifty thousand rupees. He did not say anything but wrote back saying, 'Do the needy people around you, or the children and parents of your artisans get proper treatment? Do their children get to drink milk? Do they get appropriate education? Check it all out, help them if they feel the need and then if any surplus remains, let me know.'

I understood the gist of it. Seeing the path of public service directed by Indravadanbhai and his own selfless instinct inspired me to ask, how people must suffer in their daily life, how much pain they have, what shortcomings people around us are living in? For them, we have to do something especially when we have money out of God's mercy.

With Indravadanbhai's inspiration, in memory of our dear friend and partner Virjibhai Nanjibhai Godhani, we established the V. N. Godhani School at Katargam and set up a medical center. For Champa, making a school and medical center was a dream come true. This created a unique model wherein children would get best education irrespective of their caste, religion and creed for a nominal fee and patients could get medical consultancy, treatment and diagnostics and physiotherapy services. We invited reputed medical consultants to the Center so that the needy patients could get the best of advice without paying high consultation fees of these doctors. The Medical Center on the ground floor of school was christened as the 'Nanduba Medical Center' in the name of Bhagwanbhai's mother, to provide medical investigation and therapeutic facilities at a token price to people at large. X-Ray, sonography, pathology laboratory was also started in the center. We opened a medicine store offering complete trade discount to the patients. Many needy people indeed flocked to avail these services.

Dr A. T. Desai, who treated Virjibhai for his ailment, was the Chairman of the Surat General Hospital. He mulled over the idea, while talking to me on telephone, of setting up a low-cost dialysis center for the people of Surat. I immediately agreed to his proposal and thus the 'V. N. Godhani Dialysis Center' was set up. Since its inception on 12 September 1999, the center has been running in the service of the people of Surat. Sachchidanand Swami, Kashirambhai Rana, Minister in Central Government and Hemantbhai Chapatwala, Minister in the Gujarat State Government inaugurated this center.

The discovery of diamonds in Australia around 1980 was a watershed event in the diamond industry. The Argyle Diamond Mine was in the East Kimberley region in the remote north of Western Australia. Argyle is the largest diamond producer in the world by volume. However, due to the low proportion of gem-quality diamonds, it was set to close by 2020. It is the only known significant source of pink and red diamonds, producing over 90 per cent of the world's supply. It additionally provides a large proportion of other naturally coloured diamonds, including champagne, cognac, and rare blue diamonds.[6] We were amongst the first to polish Australian roughs. We found them extremely hard. The worker, who could polish five diamonds in a day, would not succeed in doing more than two roughs of comparable size and shape.

The Indian diamond industry is indeed best equipped to polish these diamonds, which were mostly of low colour and clarity. Huge quantities of rough diamonds started pouring in, which required larger workshops. Our factory was quickly evolving into a leading diamond center, utilising the best technologies available in the market.

The goal in cutting a rough diamond is to maximise the market value of the faceted stone or stones produced from that piece of rough. This value is based on the well-known four Cs: Carat, Colour, Clarity, and the less easily evaluated Cut. As put nicely in an industry article, 'Before the diamond is mined, it has no value. When the original piece of rough is discovered in the mine, extracted from the host rock, and sorted, it rises on a value chain going further to jewellery manufacturer and then to the retail jeweller.'[7]

In 1990, we started ordering Australian rough diamonds. It was difficult to work on because of its hardness. About seventy per cent

[6] https://www.shreehk.com/argyle-mine-diamond/, Last accessed on date to October 10, 2021.
[7] Gems & Gemology, Vol. 33, No. 2, pp. 102–121 (https://www.gia.edu/doc/Modern-Diamond-Cutting-and-Polishing.pdf. Last accessed on date to October 10, 2021).

of raw diamonds were wasted in cutting and polishing. My cousin Manjibhai Dholakia was running his diamond factory in Bhavnagar under the name of Bhavani Gems. With his original ideas he showed 'diamond fraternity' how to get double the production from the available machinery. And at the same time, he taught us how to do business with minimal investment and resources. But unfortunately, this rising star of the diamond industry was eclipsed. His habit of chewing 'Gutka' tobacco caused cancer, which affected his business.

Mavjibhai Koshia of Bhavnagar was one of the first to work on Australian rough diamonds in India. He also had some difficulty in running his own business. Manjibhai introduced us to Mavjibhai with the guarantee that they would make our hard Australian diamonds. Mavjibhai sent his two younger brothers - Maganbhai and Kishorebhai, and nephew Mahendrabhai to me to Surat to train them in diamond industry. A new company called Jewel Star was formed, to work on Australian rough diamonds. With our business our relations also grew, we became relatives by giving two of our daughters in their family.

Later, I had an accident. I was going to Bhavnagar. We left Surat around 10.00 p.m. on 10 November 1992. My cousin nephew Virjibhai was sitting in the front seat and driver Kanjibhai Parmar was on the steering wheel. I was sitting in the rear seat. On our way, we stopped at a textile mill at Kim near Surat for some work and loaded a bundle of clothes, which was kept by my side. I removed my shirt and dozed off resting on the bundle only to be woken up with a thud. When we were hardly 30 km away from Bhavnagar, around 4.30 a.m. on the Kalubhar River Bridge, Kanjibhai lost control and the car fell breaking the parapet wall on the right side, somersaulting twice in the process. I escaped unhurt thanks to the bundle of clothes by my side. Virjibhai received minor injuries. However, the problem was that our driver Kanjibhai was not to be seen around. For the first time in my life, I felt panic.

We started looking around for him frantically and after an agonizing half-hour of wandering in the darkness, we found him some 30 meters away. The door of the car had opened with the impact of parapet wall and Kanjibhai had been tossed over. He was lying unconscious. We fetched a bed sheet from the car wreckage and used it as a stretcher to take Kanjibhai to the road, a climb of about 10 meters. I was barefoot, simply wearing a vest, yet profusely precipitating even in the cold. Many passing vehicles ignored our request for a lift. Finally, one bus stopped but it was not going to Bhavnagar. It dropped us off at Sihor. We arranged an ambulance and rushed Kanjibhai, still unconscious, to Bhavnagar. Fortunately, he was just under shock and after receiving treatment regained his consciousness. He told me, 'Sheth, I fell asleep with open eyes. I saw car going out of control but could not do anything as my body was paralyzed.' It was the worst three hours of my life. While lifting the heavily built Kanjibhai, I had a slip disc that troubles me even today.

Rains are considered one of the greatest life-giving forces and imbibed in culture and the expectations of its people. The monsoon season is incubated as heat in the subcontinent increases while the Indian Ocean to the South remains cool, thus unleashing a stormy mix of air that then pushes up from the South. In 1987, less than a third of the country received normal rainfall, with the hardest-hit areas receiving rainfall as low as 75 per cent below normal. Two-thirds of India's annual grain crop is supposed to be grown during the summer monsoon. The problem was especially acute in the 70 per cent of the country's farmlands that had no irrigation systems in place and depended entirely on rain. In these areas, fields that were normally iridescent-green with rice are bare, brown, or stunted. The drought had been most devastating in the sandy western regions of Gujarat and Rajasthan.

That year, drought struck Saurashtra. From 1984, Gujarat, and particularly the Saurashtra region had been facing continuous rainfall deficiency. In 1987, the rainfall deficit was 42 per cent in Gujarat and

74 per cent in Saurashtra and Kutch. Against a normal output of 2 million tons, Rabi[8] production fell by half, causing a loss of Rs 1000 crores to the farmers. There was a complete absence of surface water. Forty dams were completely dried up and another twenty dams were partially dried up. In Saurashtra alone, 5,000 cattle died. Amarsinh Chaudhary, the then Chief Minister of Gujarat who was an Adivasi[9], made a call seeking the help of people of Saurashtra living in Surat, to save the cattle. I decided to lead the effort, transported 2000 cattle, and housed them in a Gaushala[10] constructed at Jothan, 20 km north of Surat downtown.

Realizing the gravity of the situation, we approached our people in Antwerp. Dilipbhai Thakkar had tears in his eyes when we described to him the dire situation. He brought together Mahendrabhai Parikh of Diarough, Rashmibhai Mehta of Gembel, Dilipbhai Mehta of Rosy blue, and Rajeshbhai Mehta, Nanubhai Surani, Girdharbhai Gajera and Mohanbhai Dhameliya and other 30 persons together to pool Rs 2 crore.[11] We transported fodder from Maharashtra and Madhya Pradesh. We created the Prabhu Hruday Jivdaya Trust with twenty-one members from Saurashtra in Surat as Trustees to take care of birds and stray animals and cattle shed for cows.

Once the crisis was over, we publicly handed over a cheque of Rs 1 lakh to over 50 Gaushalas in Saurashtra. Chief Minister AmarsinhChaudhari called to thank Vallabhbhai Savani, Ramjibhai Italiya, Damjibhai Pavasiya and me for this mammoth effort. He said, 'My government was stuck up in this swamp, but for the Diamond Industry's help, it would have sunk.'

Champa gave birth to our third child—a boy, on 21 May 1987. It was Thursday, under the sign of Gemini. Our two daughters were

---

[8] Rabi crops or rabi harvest are agricultural crops that are sown in winter and harvested in the spring in India
[9] आदिवासी, Tribals, Aboriginal
[10] गौशाला, Cows Shelter
[11] करोड, 1 Crore, 10 million

the happiest people on earth that day. They were running around with joy, as if fairies floating in the air. After few days of his birth, I went to attend Satsang at Indravadanbhai's place. As was the practice, we were dispersing without any social talk immediately after the Satsang got over at 9.30 p.m. Nevertheless, making an exception that day, Indravadanbhai gestured me to stay back. Manjibhai Navdawala and Dani Dutt Jha also did not depart. Then, Indravadanbhai chanted one shloka:

श्रेयश्च प्रेयश्च मनुष्यमेतस्तौ सम्परीत्य विविनक्ति धीरः ।
श्रेयो हि धीरोऽभि प्रेयसो वृणीते प्रेयो मन्दो योगक्षेमाद् वृणीते ॥

(कठोपनिषद्, अध्याय 1, वल्ली 2, श्लोक 2)

The good and the pleasant come to a man and the thoughtful mind turns all around them and distinguishes. The wise chooses out the good from the pleasant, but the dull soul chooses the pleasant rather than the getting of his good and having it.

(Katha Upanishad, Chapter 1, Valli 2, Verse 2)

They gave their blessings to my son. Manjibhai said, 'Let your son inherit all your good deeds in life and multiply your goodness.' When I told Champa about it after reaching home, she said, 'Every son inherits his father's wealth. Manjibhai gave blessings to our son to inherit your good work. Why don't we name him Shreyans?' I was about to laugh at her sudden enlightenment but suddenly realized that our son had indeed been given to us by God to partake in all the good work that had been done through me and take it beyond me. There could be no better name for our son.

To rejuvenate after this exhaustive mission, on Champa's advice, I decided to visit Atmendraji in Uttarkashi with my infant son. My friends Shivalal Shingala and Mavjibhai Savani lapped up this idea and they decided to join with their families. All three families reached Uttar Kashi and stayed at Kailash Ashram on the banks of the Bhagirathi River. Atmendraji came to see us from his cottage 400 meter away on a high slope. I told him that we had come here for Satsang and would stay for ten days. He gave us the 2.00-3.00 p.m. slot every day. That day in the evening, leaving women and children behind, three of us friends walked five miles to the Maneri Dam. The dam was diverting water into a tunnel that was feeding the 90 megawatts Tiloth Power Plant.

The next morning, we woke up to a bright sunny day and decided to take bath in the river. Unlike in the plains, rivers in hills are narrow, move at great speed, and have powerful currents. That day, the flow was there but it was calm. The children were excited after entering the water and demanded to go near the submerged stones mid-way in the river. It did not seem hazardous, so all the three families walked deeper in the stream. Everyone was enjoying. Suddenly, the current of the river became stronger. Before we could understand anything, the stones we were walking on started being submerged. I thought everyone would be drowned in the river. Was this the end of life? Did fate have us here for this reason? Kids were too young, they had barely seen anything in life, was the foremost thought in my mind at that fleeting moment. I instructed everyone to hold each other firmly circling children with our bodies. Suddenly, there was a miracle. A strong gush came, and instead of carrying us away in the current, threw us back on the riverbank. Even today, decades later, I get shivers recalling that moment. When people tell me the stories of Sadhus walking on water or elevated in thin air, I do not get amused. I believe the real miracle is not to walk either on water or in thin air, but to walk on earth.

The ten days I spent in Uttar Kashi, especially the ten hours of Satsang with Atmendraji, deepened my spiritual understanding and strengthened my resolve to make a lot of money by excelling in my business and use it for the larger good of the people who crossed my path in life. I had seen many people in my business-owning many places where they go to hide and live multiple lives. I planned to always live with my family members and do nothing that would force me to hide from them. For I had realized that hiding never eliminates what one is hiding from.

I tried in various ways if I could do anything to support Atmendraji in his pious service, but he would not accept anything from anyone. Even the fruits I tried to give him; he returned the next day. Then I organized a community lunch, called Bhandara[12] there, expecting him to join. However, Atmendraji observed fast that day so as not to get into it. Was he puncturing my ego? Making me realize that there is nothing I can do for him or give to him. When I shared my frustration with him finally, he said, 'As you simplify your life Govindbhai, the laws of the universe start operating upon you; loneliness will not be loneliness, shortage will not be shortage, nor limitation will be limitation. Like a flower on a plant moving with the breeze, like a stone flowing in the river, like a cloud in the sky making and dispersing different shapes you are alone but become a part of the whole creation.'

In October 1990, we went for a family tour to Hong Kong and Singapore. It was my first exposure to the East. We had never seen anything like Hong Kong—tall buildings, narrow lanes filled with people, wealth and filth woven together. Of great military value, Hong Kong had seen a lot of war. In 1842, the British snatched away Hong Kong from China after winning the First Opium War. Later in 1898, China was made to lease Hong Kong together with 235 other islands to Great Britain for 99 years. During World War II, Japan briefly, occupied Hong Kong before it came back to the British after Japan's surrender in 1945. Post World War II, Hong Kong saw good times and by the 1970s, Hong Kong had been established as

---

[12] भंडारा, free food served to the community by an affluent person as an offering to the divine.

an Asian Tiger, one of the region's economic powerhouses, with a thriving economy based on high-technology industries.

An article summarised very well that the Hong Kong diamond market was the gateway to China's consumer market. Hong Kong's modern-day diamond trading history dates to the 1950s. At the time, the then-British colony was making its first strides as a modern trading center in the post-WWII era, neighbouring People's Republic of China was ruled strictly according to communist doctrine, and trade of luxury goods or providing manufacturing for other countries was far from how it viewed itself. Despite that, to the large traffic of businesspersons from the West, Hong Kong provided goods and services to international firms looking for low-cost labor. Quickly, the local services expanded from low-cost items to higher-end and luxury products. These included, among other things, diamond jewellery.[13]

The gradual opening of China to the global economy, specifically the development of factories in special industrial zones near the border with Hong Kong in the 1980s, brought great fortune for Hong Kong's diamond trade. By 1985, diamond manufacturing and trading was significant enough to establish the Hong Kong Diamond Bourse (HKDB). The Asia Pacific region emerged as an important market for diamonds and residents affluent enough to create an international hub in Hong Kong. In June 1987, the HKDB became the 20th member of the World Federation of Diamond Bourses (WFDB).

I found the consumption and trade of diamonds and jewellery through Hong Kong typical of their economy as the world's largest re-export center. With low taxation and free trade, Hong Kong was a magnet for companies seeking to trade with China while catering to Hong Kong's tourist traffic and affluent residents, and Hong

---

[13] https://www.ehudlaniado.com/home/index.php/news/entry/hong-kong-s-rise-to-diamond-fame. Last accessed on date to October 10, 2021.

Kong was a central trading location for the entire Far East. We had to establish ourselves in the Hong Kong market sooner rather than the later, I thought. Before leaving, we truly enjoyed our ride in the hundred-year-old Peak Tram that rose to about 400 meters and was so steep that the buildings we passed by all looked as if they were all leaning like Tower of Pisa in Italy.

We had heard a lot about Singapore as a land of civility, discipline, and perfection. The Changi Airport, opened in 1981, was fantastic. However, the size of Singapore disappointed us. It was as small as 40x25 sq. km and as artificial as a shopping mall. Singapore was indeed a City-state wedged between western Indonesia and peninsular Malaysia and derived its strength for being the independent financial hub in the region—a little bit of London and Switzerland in the East.

You could see Indians, mostly Tamil people, everywhere in Singapore. The very name Singapore comes from a combination of two Indian words—Singha and Pura (The City of Lions). However, once the British took control of Singapore, it appeared as if the Indians lost their influence forever. I felt good seeing a beautiful statue of Sang Nila Utama, considered as the original King of Singapore who had founded Singapore in 1299, erected at the prime spot at Boat Quay. It is pity that while we teach trivia about Mughal kings in our schools, there is no mention of great Indians who established kingdoms in Indonesia and Malaya.

Upon my return, I decided to expand the business. When I shared my vision with Bhagwanbhai, he was not enthusiastic. 'What is the need? This much we have done and even that it is not less. The business is flourishing well. We have good profits. Why should we take unnecessary and more hassles? I think we should not take more worries. I do not feel it necessary to increase production' he opined. In the diamond factory, we had employed 500 workers and I wanted to add 300 more, for which Bhagwanbhai was not agreeable.

Balance continues with a consideration of the way I dealt with my life. What I did not like about life in the village was the lack of power with its people. Villagers often lived at the mercy of the blows of outrageous fortune—climate, markets, lawlessness, etc. The only action I could take against that fate was to migrate to city. There was no way opposing them, but to escape. Many people from Saurashtra came to Surat as an act of empowerment, moving out as a way of defiance, rejecting the 'business-as-usual,'opposing and defeating the slings and arrows of outrageous fortune. Living in villages, a life of toil was a passive state whereas struggling in a city instead was an active state. To flourish in the city, one had to acquire wealth—charge fully armed against Fortune—so, the whole proposition is circular and hopeless because one does not have the power of action in life.

I really missed Virjibhai in those times. He used to intervene between Bhagwanbhai and me and would often find a mutually acceptable solution to move on. At times, based on the majority of two, decisions were taken. He had also believed that a good business ought to keep evolving. नदि: वेगेन शुद्ध्यति - 'If water were at a standstill, it would start smelling foul,' was the natural thought process of Virjibhai. Therefore, one day I confronted Bhagwanbhai. I said lovingly, 'Brother, our thoughts on how to proceed with our business are quite different. I feel we should consider that we separate courteously. Our businesses are going to run well. We should practically separate so that we may expand or hold our operations as per our wishes.' Bhagwanbhai agreed.

When news of our separation leaked in the diamond market, there was a lot of commotion. Most people were shocked. Why were Govindbhai and Bhagwanbhai separated? Some people started casting doubts on our business. Something fishy must be going on for a long time, otherwise how would this happen suddenly? One cannot stop people from expressing their opinion and therefore, I ignored the talk. There were also our well-wishers in the diamond market and in the Patel community. Valjibhai Kesari, Bachubhai Desai, and Vitthalbhai Limbachia did not like this storm in the teacup. They felt there was nothing wrong in ending the partnerships as in business it was common and even brothers could be separated. However, they wanted to know the reason for us parting ways.

They met us together. Bhagwanbhai and I said that there was no reason. 'There were no grudges nor any quarrel. There was no question of any fight. As such everything was going on well,' we both said without any hesitation. 'Very good,' Bachubhai said. 'If you now talk about separating, then we all will sit outside the office fasting in protest.' Valjibhai said. 'Give us some time.' Bhagwanbhai and I said, and everyone dispersed. After they left, the two of us sat in the room and made a list of our disagreements. 'Let us decide on what to hold on to and what to let go. 'It will be better that we understand everything by ourselves rather than someone else telling us,' we thought. I asked Bhagwanbhai to list five of my ways he disagreed with, and I listed five of his attitudes disagreeable with me. I also listed what could be tolerated, what could be changed, and what we could live with unresolved. After about an hour, we announced our decision that we will not separate for the next five years.

On 22 May 1989, the BAPS Swaminarayan Sanstha organized a Youth Convention at Vidyanagar, near Anand. I had been yearning to meet Shree Pramukh Swami Maharaj for a long time and found this a good opportunity to seek his blessings. I drove 200 km by myself. I was given an opportunity to spend some time with him. After Satsang with Pramukh Swami, I asked him what he felt about the dam on Narmada River near Navagam. He said, 'Yogiji Maharaj had blessed this project. So, it should be completed.' Pramukh Swamismiled and said, 'Let the opponents protest. Let us pray God to grant them wisdom.' Swamiji asked me to take up tree plantation. 'You live in Surat. People from entire country come there. Resolve any misunderstanding people have about the Narmada project.'

It so happened that I was in Bombay on 7 June 1990, when Pramukh Swamiaddressed a rally there. I attended the rally mainly to have his Darshan. Shedding his moderate manners Pramukh Swamideclared, 'We are Indians and Gujaratis. We have never fallen back anywhere and shall never march backwards. Moreover, the political parties and organizations of Gujarat and Maharashtra and abroad should with one voice say, 'the Narmada project will be completed.' The dam height should not be decreased even by one inch. Like Ganga River, the Narmada is holy and sacred. It is important that such sentiments should also prevail in us all. Let us prove that the proverbial saying—Gujarati's are brave only at the beginning—is false and show that our bravery shall endure till the end.'

Listening to Pramukh Swamithat day I realized that it was not right for the people to create hurdles in building Dam that would provide much needed water, for the parched lands, which was otherwise draining into the sea.

4

Power Plays

न कश्चित् कस्यचिन् मित्रं न कश्चित् कस्यचिद् रिपुः ।
व्यवहारेण मित्राणि जायन्ते रिपवस्तथा ॥

(हितोपदेश, मित्रलाभ 1, श्लोक 71)

No one [is] the friend of anyone, no one is the enemy of anyone;
by conduct friends are produced, so [are] enemies.

(Hitopadesha, Mitralabh 1, Shloka 71)

While the business was expanding, I started seeing the world—like
a complex gearbox, each wheel driving or being driven by another.
I saw nothing working independently. Households needed income,
which came from livelihoods, which in turn depended on markets,
which depended upon the economy, which operated at local and
global levels. A little tension between two warring nations in the
faraway Middle East would result in the local auto driver having
to pay more for petrol and be forced to charge more fare from the

passengers and face their irritation. The trucks bringing provisions to the city would increase their freight charges, affecting market prices and as a result, household budgets would get strained. Moreover, as if this economic interdependence was not enough, there were always political power plays in the background to control the levers of events.

The most unfortunate part of that era was the anarchism created by political leaders enticing college students to bring down an elected government. The Congress had 140 of 167 MLAs in the state assembly. Just to remove Chimanbhai from the Chief Minister's position in February 1974, his own party's MLAs resigned from the Assembly and took to the streets. Indira Gandhi was clearly paranoid with the developments that threatened her tenure as the Prime Minister of the country, despite having won the last Lok Sabha elections against all odds and earning the epithet of Goddess Durga after the 1971 war with Pakistan.

Morarjibhai Desai, who had lost out to Indira Gandhi in the race for Prime Ministership in 1967 and 1971 saw an opportunity in the students' anger. Always a man of establishment and a disciplinarian, Morarjibhai threw his weight behind the movement and launched a fast-unto-death agitation forcing out Chimanbhai's government before its term. It led Gujarat to come under President's Rule in February 1974. On 16 March, the state assembly was dissolved, ending the agitation. In that 'Nav Nirman' movement, more than 100 young men died, and thousands were injured, many crippled for the rest of their lives during the movement. I had seen 8 youths who had been shot dead by the police in the Rampura Road area. This was the first power-play I saw in my life. Young lives were lost even before they could get a chance to blossom. For whose benefit?

As if to take the game to the next level of complexity, a new theory, called KHAM was propounded. Veteran Congressmen Jhinabhai Darji and Madhavsingh Solanki were the chief architects of the theory. KHAM was an acronym for Kshatriya, Harijan,

Adivasi and Muslim and was meant to serve the purpose of creating a vote bank for the Indian National Congress. Ever since Sardar Patel, the Patel community had remained influential. Bhailal Patel further brought together the Patidars and the Kshatriyas. The KHAM theory alienated the Patel community permanently from the Congress.

As is now history, time's wheel turned and Indira Gandhi after running India under the Emergency Rule along with her young and ambitious son, Sanjay Gandhi, lost the general elections in 1977. Congress also lost the Gujarat elections and could win only seventy-five seats. Babubhai Patel, whose elected government had been dismissed during Emergency, became the Chief Minister again and led Gujarat till 1980, when the Janata Party imploded paving Indira Gandhi's way to return and the KHAM game was played to the hilt by Congress leader, Madhavsingh Solanki. The Congress won 149 seats in the 182-member Assembly. However, this landslide victory also came at a price—the powerful Patel community and the upper castes moved away from the Congress. However, it would take another decade before Chimanbhai could return to the top post in Gujarat in March 1990.

I had a great rapport with Dalsukhbhai Godhani, the Janata Party leader. He was the leader of the Opposition in the Gujarat Assembly (June 1980 to March 1985) when Madhavsingh Solanki was the Chief Minister and later became the revenue minister in the government led by Chimanbhai Patel and Chhabildas Mehta. He would always let me know in advance whenever he visited Surat and had at least one meal, lunch, or dinner, with me. Starting his career as a teacher at Lokbharati School in Sanosara, Bhavnagar, he was elected to the State legislature in 1967 as Independent Party (Swatantra Paksha) but later joined the Old Congress, headed by Hitendrabhai Desai in Gujarat and by Morarjibhai Desai nationally.

I never participated actively in politics but received my political bearings from Dalsukhbhai. He taught me that we could not deny or ignore our social history as people. Those who are powerful and affluent strive to keep things as they are; those who are impoverished and powerless strive to change the system. Politics is all about maintaining or changing the reality to placate your memory.

In August 1983, Dalsukhbhai Godhani took Mavjibhai Mavani and me to meet Morarjibhai Desai in Bombay. I was indeed curious to see the grand old man of Indian politics. Dalsukhbhai took me to a four-storied apartment called Oceana at Marine Drive. There was a police officer sitting at the entrance of the complex, but he did not bother about our entering inside. We went to the third floor. The door was open, and I was stunned to see Morarjibhai living with the bare minimal things. There were few chairs and newspapers on a table and many books around.

He was eighty-seven years old and to put things into perspective, he witnessed both World Wars, was a freedom fighter in the Indian Independence movement and was the only leader to be conferred with both, the Bharat Ratna, i.e., India's highest civilian award and the Nishan-e-Pakistan, i.e., Pakistan's highest civilian award. We spent almost two hours there. Dalsukhbhai appeared very close to Morarjibhai, as he was all ears to whatever he was telling him. I did not even try to hear their conversation and sat there enchanted in the presence of the tallest leader I had met in my life until then.

When we were leaving, I dared to ask him what one piece of advice he could give me was. He smiled and said softly, 'Material and physical comfort are sufficient only for well-fed domestic animals and birds. It is not so for men, who must live by their principles.' While walking out of the flat complex, Dalsukhbhai told me that even after serving as India's first non-Congress Prime Minister, Deputy Prime Minister, longest-serving Finance Minister, and the Chief Minister of Bombay State, he had about Rs 1,00,000 savings that he had made over the years which he donated to the Gujarat Vidhyapith along with earthly belongings. They are still preserved there so that they would be appreciated by the people he had worked for and not for his family to hold on to as trophies. Even the flat we visited was rented.

For a brief period of four months Hasmukh Adhia, came to Surat as Collector in mid-1990. He was a deeply spiritual person and a follower of Swami Visharadananda Sarasvati. I met him rather by chance in a meeting at The Southern Gujarat Chamber of Commerce & Industry where a discussion was going on the Karma Yoga. Hasmukhbhai called Chanakya a real Karma Yogi. He said, 'Karma Yoga means doing one's job without idleness, without selfishness and without ego. Chanakya always followed this in his life. He was never selfish. He always acted in the interest of the country. He played his role in a marvellous way, using all four means—Saam (encouragement to the right ones), Daam (giving one's dues), Bhed (distinction between good and bad) and Dand (Punishment to defaulters). He did not relax until he achieved his goal. But as soon as the goal was achieved, he stepped down from his position and went into seclusion.' Later Hasmukhbhai would rise to become the Union Finance Secretary and would be known as 'The Man behind Demonetisation.'

In those days there was no free television, the Central Government controlled Doordarshan and used it mostly for propaganda. People depended on talking to each other. Discussions and meetings like these mattered. Leaders used to meet people and organize mass movements and campaigns. So, when in September 1990, the Bhartiya Janata Party (BJP) President Shree Lal Krishna Advani decided to go for a padayatra[1] to inspire the people about the Ayodhya movement, I could understand what exactly he was doing. After the failure of both Congress and Janata Party, a new narrative had to be created. In 1990s, the Mandal Commission, Ram Mandir in Ayodhya and the Narmada Dam were unresolved power tussle. The Sardar Sarovar project was a vision of the first deputy

---

[1] पदयात्रा, walking parade

prime minister of India, Sardar Vallabhbhai Patel. By the time, the Planning Commission approved the project it was 1988 and then it caught the attention of social activists who contested that the dam did not meet the required environmental and social conditions as meted out by the Ministry of Environment and Forests.

During December 1990, peaceful marches were held under the leadership of Sachchidanand Swami in support of Narmada Dam project in Ferkuva, a site of one of the thirty dams planned on Narmada. Thousands of people turned up from different parts of Gujarat. I organized volunteers from Surat and created a free kitchen from 25 December 1990 until 1 January 1991. We prepared food packets every day and distributed to the marchers. Seeing the supporters of the dam, anti-dam group returned silently. It was a great victory of Ahimsa[2].

The Central Government in New Delhi was crumbling due to the constant bickering amongst the politicians. With India's foreign exchange reserves at $1.2 billion in January 1991 and depleted to half by June, barely enough to last for roughly three weeks of essential imports, India was only weeks away from defaulting on its external balance of payment obligations. The Reserve Bank of India had to airlift forty-seven tons of gold to the Bank of England and twenty tons of gold to the Union Bank of Switzerland to raise $600 million. National sentiments were outraged and there was public outcry when it was learned that the government had pledged the country's entire gold reserve against the loan.

During the 1980s, the competitive politics of populism, reinforced by the cynical politics of soft options, led governments into a spending spree. However, it was not possible for the government, or the economy, to live beyond its means year after year. Government finances became progressively unsustainable. The inevitable crunch came in the form of an acute economic crisis

---

[2] अहिंसा, non-violence

that was waiting to happen. The changes were dictated by the immediate economic compulsions of crisis management, combined with the stark political realization that the outside world was no longer willing to lend to India. International companies started coming in. India was very much benefited with the liberalization, privatization, and globalization policy the Government introduced in 1991. The Union Finance Minister, Shree Manmohan Singh, stood in Parliament to present a landmark budget that set India on a new economic path. During that period, the BJP announced the construction of a Ram Mandir on the land where they believed Lord Ram was born.

In early 1990s, Surat was notoriously dirty, and people were facing low quality of life in the city. Despite all its wealth, it was an expensive and dirty, garbage-strewn city to live in. Mounds of scarp and roaming livestock were a familiar sight. Illegal construction dotted every nook and corner, as did open-air eateries with leftovers carelessly thrown on the pavements. More than a quarter of the city had no sewage. Effluents from the industries were brazenly drained into the Tapi River. Almost a quarter of the people in the city were living in slums and during the rainy season, sewage water would overflow and stagnate around these houses. This was the norm and both people and officials accepted it as fait accompli.

One day, in 1991, I was sitting with my friend Parshottambhai Khadela, affectionately called Das Mama, at my home in the Vrundavandham Society at Katargam Road in North Surat. The society constructed its own approach road and maintained the cleanliness as well. We thought that instead of perennially lamenting about the pathetic state of sanitation in the city, why should we not do something. On the next Sunday, in the afternoon Das Mama and I, with our friends Popatbhai Monapara and Nanubhai Mayani, got a tractor fitted with a trailer and some simple equipment like brooms, shovels, and baskets and started removing garbage from the Katargam Main Road. Soon, about fifty people appeared to their disbelief, as they knew our status and a few of them even joined in our effort. We worked for an hour and dispersed after singing the National Anthem.

We organized ourselves as the 'Welcome Clearty Club.' There is no English word called 'Clearty' but we knew the meaning of 'clear' and 'ty' was entered after it to rhyme with 'society' perhaps. No one was named as an office bearer and all members were called 'commandos.' We would notify the locality to be cleaned a week in advance and never revisit a place, as our idea was to demonstrate that localities could be kept clean by voluntary efforts. In eight weeks, 250 members got involved in the cleaning work and the word spread all over Surat. Soon enough trolleys with five tractors arrived purely by volunteering effort. Each Sunday, we would start the work by singing the National Anthem at 3.29 p.m. and complete the work after singing National Anthem again at 4.30 p.m.

One day, two brothers—Janak and Utpal Mistry—came to see me. I knew their father Arvindbhai Mistry well, a gold medalist engineer, who continued the family business of machine tool manufacturing set up by his father Nanabhai Mistry in 1946. They both studied at NIT, Surat. They consulted me to diversify into the field of diamond processing machinery manufacturing and technology development. All such machines were imported from abroad and not easily available to most of the people in the industry. I told them two things. First, blessed are people who take their family business forward, and second, no industry can remain forever dependent on imported machinery if it really wants to flourish and become number one in the world. Therefore, I gave them my double blessings. Later, their younger brother Kamal Mistry also joined them. The only advice I offered to them was to aim to be the best in the world and for that collaborate with the best in the world. Merely copying another leader can never make you a leader. They aptly named their company Lexus, the name of the luxury car brand of the Japanese automaker Toyota.

Another facet of selfless service unfolded before me during that time. I have known Dineshbhai Upadhyay since the day he made my first rental agreement as lawyer in Surat. We have become like soul mates, and he was just around whenever I needed him. I bought a property in Varachha Road, emerging as River View Boulevard of Surat. Dineshbhai Upadhyay, a lawyer by profession negotiated the entire deal for me and closed it to my greatest satisfaction. In this process, he earned a commission of around Rs 1 lakh, which would be around Rs 1 crore in present terms (year 2021) but did not take. He said, 'I am not a real estate broker. I got into this as your friend, that deal is good for you.' It is indeed true that our most intense joy comes not from personal feats, but from helping other persons achieve their goals. We become more supple human beings when we find true joy in witnessing other people's successes and unabashedly share in their joyful accomplishments. Dineshbhai Upadhyay revealed upon me this secret by his action.

Shreyans had been growing as a cute boy under the care of his mother and two sisters. Acutely aware of my struggle with lack of education, especially when you deal with foreigners, I wanted my son to be properly educated and groomed. I shared it with my friend Dineshbhai Upadhyay. He told me, 'Govindbhai, it is not about knowing English, it is nurturing an all-round personality.' Within few days, Dineshbhai brought his friend Shashikantbhai Shah along. He was teaching in a college and was famous as a writer. Dineshbhai said Shashikantbhai would groom Shreyans.

Shashikantbhai used to live about 15 km away and would come on his scooter to spend an hour every day with Shreyans. He never put any pressure on Shreyans. There were days when Shreyans was not interested in learning. He just wanted to sleep or play. Shashikantbhai never felt any irritation. He would impart learning by telling stories to Shreyans. He sat for an hour, quietly reading a book, and left. Shashikantbhai seemed to possess an immutable sense of self-assurance that he bestowed upon Shreyans. In addition to that, he also impressed upon the child, the look of a man ensnared by what he perceived to be his own duty. For three years, this Karmayogi mentored Shreyans in a way that was a life demonstration of selfless work taught by Lord Shree Krishna in the Gita to me. He did not take even one rupee towards his time and effort.

First movers must make their own paths in a spirit of adventure and people from Gujarat had earned a great name in this regard. The advent of Europeans with their vast resources in the fields of trade and commerce was a heavy blow to the business classes who formed the backbone of the economy of Gujarat. Their governments supported the European merchants and naturally, they could win the Gujarati businesspersons into their comprador agencies as they lacked government support. Even after independence, things did not change. Political leaders looked at businesspersons as cows to be milched and government officials treated them as a goat for slaughter. To save themselves from this difficult situation and never-ending oppression, the merchants chose to shift their business activities to places that are more congenial rather than oppose them.

Going to Israel, for example, had never been easy. In 1990, like many Gulf countries, they started issuing the visa to boost Israel economy. Therefore, visa was made available from Mumbai itself. During those time 'EL AL' Israel airlines started its operation directly from Mumbai to Tel Aviv and I started taking that route rather than going from Antwerp. However, frequently flights were cancelled, sometimes for months altogether. During such times, I travelled through Egypt Airlines via Cairo. Immigration at Cairo had no system to manage the stamped passports. I was lucky but many travelers had lost their passports and suffered unimaginable anguish. Experience at Tel Aviv was far better than Cairo.

India and Israel established full diplomatic relations in 1992 during the regime of Prime Minister P. V. Narasimha Rao, as if legitimising the cultural connection and interpersonal relations that had been a significant element of the Indo-Israeli partnership. India is one of the few countries in the world where Jews have not faced persecution. Jews came to India in different waves over the past two thousand years and resided in different parts of the country without facing any discrimination.

Popular in Surat as 'Vallabh Topi'[3] because of the white cap he always wears, Vallabhbhai had been a Trustee to many social organisations I had been working with. Before the election in January 1990, Chimanbhai Patel, accompanied by his wife Urmilaben came to Surat. Chimanbhai knew my friend Vallabhbhai Savani. Haribhai Sarasiyawala invited me to his house along with Vallabhbhai Topi, Ramjibhai Italiya and Prabhudas Patel for breakfast with Chimanbhai. I was excited to meet Chimanbhai, as he was no ordinary man. He was highly educated, did his master's in economics and had been elected as the first president of the student union of the Maharaja Sayajirao University of Baroda in 1950. In the mid-1970s, Chimanbhai, as the Chief Minister of Gujarat, had resisted the authoritarianism of the all-powerful Indira Gandhi and sacrificed his position in the process. In 1974 he faced; a socio-political movement called 'Navnirman-Andolan'.

This was my first meeting with a high-level politician, I must say that it brought many surprises. Chimanbhai Patel's newly formed Janata Dal (Gujarat) was a party largely of upper castes with a concentration on urban centers where the BJP was putting up a challenge to the Congress. The Congress—Janata Dal (Gujarat) alliance was aimed at denting the BJP's urban vote-bank in the state. Chimanbhai asked Vallabhbhai to give him 'his whole-hearted support' in the forthcoming election. He said, 'Vallabhbhai, be clear that no matter what, even if the sky has to fall down, this time I have to form a government.' I was very astonished to feel his fierce ambition and confidence. I was wondering about his 'dependence' on

---

[3] वल्लभ टोपी, Mr Vallabhbhai Savani wears iconic cap known as Topi, hence Vallabh Topi

the 'whole-hearted support' of the local leaders. Perhaps this is how democracy operates, I thought. Later Chimanbhai won the election and formed the Government. Keshubhai Patel was appointed as Deputy Chief Minister.

Surat was ruled by Muslim nawabs in the seventeenth century and many Muslims live here in peace. A sizeable section of the local Muslims, mainly Memons, Patni, Dawoodi Bohras and Khojas, are traders and manufacturers in the artisan-based silk industry. The poorer ones are workers in the same industry. The recent migrant Muslims who have come to Surat over the past twenty years are employed mostly as weavers in the silk industry. In fact, Ismailbhai Cyclewala, a perfect Muslim man, owned my first factory premises that I rented. Among the local Hindus, the dominant groups are the middle castes—Kanabi, Khatri, Gola and Ghanchi, who have made their fortune after World War II.

What began as a Surat Bandh[4] on 7 December 1992 as a mark of protest for the demolition of the Babri Masjid in Ayodhya on 6 December 1992, swiftly degenerated into a free-for-all arson and looting when a small crowd tried to stop the traffic and compel some shop and factory owners to close their operations. Lumpen and communal elements stepped in to let loose a revelry of bloodletting and brutality that lasted for four long days. Over 150 men, women and infants were brutally killed.

On 10 December 1992, Chimanbhai sent Jivabhai Patel to Surat to get the exact situational report about the riots. I met Jivabhai with other members of the diamond community at the Circuit House. We told him the ground situation. The Muslims, infuriated by what happened in Ayodhya went onto the streets to protest and since the police were using considerable force against them, they felt even more indignant and clashed with migrant worker's crowds showing idiocy and cruelty that has ever been seen in the city.

---

[4] बंद,, public strike, refrain from doing any activities

On 28 January 1993, when a bomb blast took place near the Sadhana High School in Varachha, killing an eight-year-old girl, Alpa Patel, and injuring eleven people, I knew then that some sinister forces were at work to destroy the economy of Surat by creating fear amongst its large migrant population. Another grenade blast took place at Surat railway station on 22 April 1993. Migrants are an integral part of Surat's economy. Alienating them from locals is the surest way to remove prosperity out of Surat. I made sure that no one from our factory got involved in the violence and offered whatever help was possible to riot victims.

On 21 September 1994, the plague struck Surat. On hearing the news, I immediately returned from Bombay. There was panic everywhere. My first cousin, Ukabhai Paladiya ran away from Varachha Road without even informing his wife and children, carrying his cycle on a passing by truck to Zinzavadar village in Botad. He informed his family later that he was safe at his village and asked them to join him there. As a study later recorded, 'The people fleeing the affected zone are heading in all directions and taking the hysteria with them. With the discovery of three people afflicted with plague in a Bombay hospital, panic gripped that city as well. Tetracycline, an antibiotic for plague treatment, disappeared from chemist shops, not only in Bombay but also in Delhi. One-fourth of Surat residents (400,000 to 600,000 people) fled the city within four days of announcement of the epidemic. Among them were people still in the incubation phase of the plague infection. Broad-spectrum antibiotics required to curb the disease had been exhausted due to panic buying of medicines.'[5]

Trains running down a trunk line connecting Bombay to cities in the Indian interior had been ordered not to halt in Surat. Many airlines cancelled its flights to Mumbai. Surat and its residents

---

[5] https://www.montana.edu/historybug/yersiniaessays/godshen.html. Last accessed on September 29, 2020.

had become pariahs everywhere in the country after the city administration reported that a patient died of symptoms of the pneumonic plague—a highly contagious bacterial disease and the most virulent form that is invariably fatal unless treated early.

On 25 September 1994, the government brought in a Rapid Action Force of police to stem the exodus and to prevent frightened patients from abandoning the hospitals where they were being treated. A massive drive to kill rats and fleas helped in bringing the disease under control. After the confusion, the government recouped and stemmed the spread by identifying cases and giving antibiotics. It also fumigated cargo, cleared ports of rats and spread insecticides over vast areas. The Surat administration had controlled the outbreak in a week's time, but the city's reputation suffered. Businesses stopped and losses incurred amounted to around Rs 1000 crore. During that difficult period, the District Collector of Surat, Shree P. V. Trivedi, handled the grim situation in a decisive manner and with a firm hand.

The plague, however, proved to be a turning point for the city. With the blame being pinned on the Surat Municipal Corporation, the Keshubhai Patel's Government at Gandhinagar shook up the body in 1995, bringing S. R. Rao to Surat to clean up its act— from improving urban infrastructure to finding effective ways of responding to outbreaks. I spent many hours with Rao Saheb and saw him evolve a comprehensive plan for the municipal government to undertake a wide-ranging set of reforms to improve the urban environment. These reforms included the transformation of the water management system, with non-governmental agencies, civil society and the private sector working together to transform Surat as one of the cleanest cities through a broad approach to environmental management including smart initiatives in municipal sewage management. Later, when in 2010, Surat became the third cleanest city of India; I gratefully recalled Rao Saheb's zealous determination as the seed of this tree.

When Rao Saheb was to leave in 1997, he gave me an idea of constructing a garden in a Katargam area on an abandoned water body filled with filth and dirt. In a first of its kind in Surat, a beautification project was implemented on Public-Private Partnership (PPP) Model. He finished all the necessary formalities to set up this project in merely two days. Since then, we are maintaining 'Dholakia Garden' that is considered as a flagship garden in Surat. In one send-off public meeting, as a token of gratitude, I referred Rao Saheb as 'god of Surat' for the work he did for the city.

Later, when I met Shree P. V. Trivedi, the former Collector of Surat after a year at Gandhinagar, he was the Commissioner of Education. On reaching his office, his personal secretary refused to take my card inside as an important meeting of his with top officers was to last for at least another two hours. On my insistence, the personal secretary went inside to give my visiting card to Trivediji. Upon seeing the card, he rushed out, opening his cabin door to welcome me while keeping his meeting on hold. Such was the respect Trivediji held for me and I for him. He was one of the most scrupulous officers I have ever known. We are still enjoying each other's friendship after all these years.

On 6 February 1995, the Samuh-Lagan[6] movement attracted 650 couples for community-level wedding. Few of us friends thought that those who do not abide by their assertions, do not have the right to speak, so we should also marry our children in a mass marriage. Occasion of Rahulbhai's wedding was nearing. I proposed Rahulbhai's wedding be performed as part of a mass wedding. Everyone agreed, including Jinal, Rahulbhai's fiancée. The marriages were conducted in two shifts—325 in the forenoon and 325 in the afternoon. Arranged marriages and male domination are prevalent in Indian culture, especially in Saurashtra. Women were forced to a

---

[6] समूह लग्न, Group marriages or mass marriages

very restricted lifestyle that was gated by cultural stereotypes put up by society and the fear of what would happen if one went against them.

My brother-in-law Premjibhai's eldest son Nareshbhai was very close to Pramukh Swami, and he went to the temple every day to meet P. P. Swami, in charge of the Surat temple. Nareshbhai told him, 'I want to become a monk.' P.P. Swami called Premjibhai to the temple and told him that Naresh had an idea to become a monk. Premjibhai was inconsolable and he gave me the responsibility to persuade Naresh to change his decision.

I sat with Naresh in Swaminarayan Mandir at Rampura and reasoned out. 'Many have externally renounced the world and gone to the forests but have had either returned in the world more disillusioned or died in anonymity. It is not necessary to renounce everything that is external.' I spoke. 'And living in the world, surrounded by people, is even more difficult.' I argued. I also reasoned that I had wanted to renounce the world and become a Sadhu myself, but I stayed in Sansaar[7] and did not regret. However, I found Naresh's resolve as tough as a rough diamond.

Finally, the family conceded. There was a strong tradition of Patidar youth renouncing the world, especially in the Bochasanwasi Akshar Purushottam Swaminarayan Sanstha (BAPS), started by Shastriji Maharaj (1865-1951), who was born as Dungar Patel. He became a Swami within the Vadtal diocese of the Swaminarayan Sampradaya at the age of 17 where he was given the name Yagnapurushdas Swami. In 1907, he established BAPS after a doctrinal split from the Vadtal diocese, in Bochasan in the Anand district of Gujarat.

Naresh Narola took his Parshad Diksha in March 1995 at Sarangpur and Bhagwati Diksha on 4 December 1995 at Mumbai

---

[7] संसार, World and world matters. The world of people, relationships and transactions, controlled by money and power.

during Amruthmahotsava by Pramukh SwamiMaharaj and was given the name of Adhyatma Swarup Swami. Renouncing his family, he joined the world of monks. He would later become the Kothari of BAPS Swaminarayan Mandir by the side of Ghela River in Gadhada where Swaminarayan stayed for thirty years.

The year 1995 also marked the completion of twenty-five years of our partnership in the diamond business. We had organized the Silver Jubilee event at our River View Factory. We kept the event as a simple celebration of joy and invited Bhikhudan Gadhvi, a renowned folk singer and proponent of Dayro[8], a narrative singing tradition of Gujarat, to perform. A feast was hosted for everyone related to SRK in any way at any time. The next day, we had a gathering of the three partner families. We also invited Vitthalbhai Limbachia and Manjibhai Khakharia who had witnessed the entire journey of the company. No one in our family knew that we had decided to separate. The last five years were sort of a stopgap. Now the twenty-five years partnership would be ending. I broke the awkward silence and began the talk.

'Our company has progressed beyond our imagination in the past twenty-five years. The next generation of all three partners is now ready to handle the business. Virjibhai's sons Vinod and Ramesh are now capable of handling the business. The time has now arrived that we all lovingly and voluntarily conclude' I said. Now Bhagwanbhai got up. He elaborated, 'We all are united still in our relationships. Even after separation, we will still purchase rough diamonds together. Why don't you think like that, now instead of one, three companies will be working? Our hold will increase in the diamond industry. We are not separating because we are facing any problem; rather we are creating space for more growth.' Hearing us many members of our families became emotional, many started sobbing inconsolable. We consoled them all.

---

[8] डायरो, a folk art

Next day we sat for dissolution of partnership. When I offered River View Factory, the best of our assets to Virjibhai's sons, in a rare display of mutual respect and love, Bhagwanbhai immediately agreed. However, Vinod and Ramesh protested. They said in unison, 'We are still young, we can start a new business. Bhagwan Kaka is staying at Mumbai, to start a new company will be difficult for him, and so we must give the River View Factory to him.' Everyone's feelings were incredible, and they wanted to give the best to the other. This in itself was a very big earning. Otherwise, when a partnership dissolves, partners fight. They accuse each other that they did not get a fair share, and that there was an injustice. In this case, the situation was entirely the opposite. Everyone was ready to give the best to the other one.

Bhagwanbhai thus retained River View Factory. Vinod and Ramesh selected two factories at Pandole, Ved Road and Pajwa Falia, Gotalawadi. I kept the remaining two factories at Haat Falia and Katargam Road. With the division of the factories having completed, now came the question of the company's brand. Who would keep the name 'Shree Ramkrishna Export?' Everyone said, 'Let Govind kaka keep the brand.' I said, 'If you give this name to me, I will provide Rs 1 crore to both. If you want to use the name, you give fifty lakhs.' Bhagwanbhai did not find this reasonable. The fact was that nobody wanted anything. 'You keep the name, nothing related to money,' he said. We approached Shantibhai Mehta for a resolution. He ruled in favour of brand value but for Rs 50 lakhs and not Rs 1 crore that I intended to give.

On 5 April 1995, I attended the undivided company's office for the last time. Next day, I took charge of Shree Ramkrishna Export Company. Bhagwanbhai started his company in the name of Bhargovi (Bha-r-go-vi) Diamonds, indicating Bhagwanbhai, Govind and Virjibhai. Vinod and Ramesh began their company based on their surname, Godhani Gems, along with their cousins, Babubhai, Manojbhai, Hiteshbhai and Anilbhai.

Another star was rising on the horizon in the form of Savjibhai. My grandfather Kanjidada had four sons—my father Laljidada and his three elder bothers: Narandada, Ravjidada and Rudadada. Kanjidada divided his land giving tracts in Lathi to Rudadada, Pratpgadh village to Ravjidada and Dudhala to Narandada and my father. Narandada, having three sons, Veljibhai, Dayabhai and Dhanjibhai ensured that we read Vachanmrut[9] and Shreemad Bhagwat while at the temple regularly. Veljibhai had four sons, his eldest son Thakarshibhai expired in a motor accident while other three are settled well in Surat. Dayabhai's four sons are also settled in the diamond business in Surat. Dhanjibhai also had four sons. All his sons are settled in diamond business. As I came to Surat to work in the diamond cutting and polishing industry as an artisan, Dhanjibhai's son, Savjibhai, also came here discontinuing his school after the primary level to cut and polish diamonds. Before 1995, he had his own small unit. He joined our group of rough diamond buying along with Bhargovi and Godhani Gems, making a Unity Group of Four.

We used to buy roughs from Aarjav Diamond Company in Antwerp run by Ashitbhai Mehta, who was affectionately known as Munnabhai. During our one of trips in 1997 to Antwerp, Munnabhai had a friendly talk with us. 'Govindbhai, your Unity Group of Four is big and you are a master in smaller diamonds now. Few in the business can match your skill in making 10 to 100 diamonds from one carat of rough diamonds. No one has reached this stature before you,' he said. I was flattered. Such praise, coming from Munnabhai—the most credible voice in the global diamond industry, was no small matter. 'Why don't you try your hand on bigger size diamonds?' he asked.

And as per Munnabhai's advise we bought big sized stones from him and made bigger diamonds as per our understanding. We sold

---

[9] वचनामृत, Religious Teachings

two lots of bigger diamonds quickly and at a good profit. However, we were stuck with the third lot. A full week had passed without any buyer turning up. A lot of money was locked. We took the daring decision to sell the inventory at whatever price and unlock the investment. All four of us recovered but only after losing about Rs two crores in bigger diamonds. Would Munnabhai honour his 'profit will be yours, and loss will be mine' words? Would he be ready to sustain such a significant loss? Would he say that in the greed to get bigger diamonds, cutting was done poorly? There was also the possibility that Munnabhai could say, 'It was your mistake, why should I pay for it?'

Although it was our own responsibility, but we had to inform Munnabhai about the same. I took our Unity Group of Four, to Antwerp. Whatever happened, there was a lesson to be learnt from the entire episode. To our great surprise, Munnabhai picked up the entire loss of Rs two crores without even an iota of hesitation. He said that diamonds were a big game, and this kind of loss should not force us to leave the arena. If we quit now, bigger diamonds would never be manufactured in India and the industries in Belgium and Israel would have the power and influence to call all the shots forever. Munnabhai not only took the pressure off our head, but he also filled our heart with fire. He asked me, 'Tell me Govindbhai, does anyone else have bigger experience than you?'

Back in India, the entire group collectively decided to stop working on bigger diamonds concluding that it was not our piece of cake. However, I was not comfortable with that decision. If anything could be done in the diamond industry in Israel and Belgium, I should also be able to do it, or else I could not be considered a diamantaire.

The failure in working with bigger diamonds had made me restless. Why had this happened? Where did we go wrong? Not doing rough diamonds was not even an idea I allowed to settle on my consciousness even though our Unity Group of Four decided against it.

The more I analyzed, the more I realized. In Dudhala, who would have created a smooth path to walk, from the uneven and rough trail, from village to our farm? Who would have walked first on this path? Were they not hit by a stone, pricked by a thorn, or stumbled due to a pothole? Regardless of such difficulties, they had gotten up and walked again. Seeing their troubles did not deter from trying. I remembered Swami Vivekanand saying, 'Arise, awake and stop not till the goal is reached.'[10] I had stumbled and now, I had two ways. One was to leave the rough trail, and another was to create my own path. I had nothing when I started diamond business, but I had kept on moving. I needed to move on now as well.

The night of doubts had finally passed, and the golden rays of the sun filled my inner sky. I had decided within that I did not want to accept defeat. I wanted to test my nerves. I was in conversation with myself, challenging myself! I accepted the responsibility of manufacturing bigger diamonds in India. I refused to move away from this challenge. Just as Shree Krishna said to Arjuna—सुखदुःखे समे कृत्वा लाभालाभौ जयाजयौ ॥ (श्रीमद् भगवद् गीता, अध्याय 2, श्लोक 38)—Treating happiness and sorrow, gain and loss, and conquest and defeat with equanimity, then engage in battle[11]- I had to move on and master the art of cutting and polishing big diamonds.

Incessant thoughts did not let me sleep in the night. I listed down the top ten names of the businesspersons working in significant-sized diamonds in India. I knew most of them. Barring two or three, the rest all were novices in this business. If they all can do it, why cannot I? After reaching office the following day, I called for the meeting with Jayantibhai. Without beating around the bush,

---

[10] https://www.educationworld.in/arise-awake-and-stop-not-till-the-goal-is-reached—swami-vivekananda/. Last accessed on date to October 10, 2021.

[11] https://www.gitasupersite.iitk.ac.in/srimad?language=dv&field_chapter_value=2&field_nsutra_value=38&htrskd=1&etgb=1&setgb=1&choose=1. Last accessed on date to October 10, 2021.

I informed my desire to continue working in bigger diamonds. He was not in favour but did not stop me.

I picked up twenty to twenty-five selected workers and placed them under my direct supervision. Bigger diamonds were ready to be sent to Bombay for sales. I was still thinking about how to move further. Hearing about my resolve, a close friend of Jayantibhai, Laljibhai Patel of Dharmanandan Diamonds came to our factory, and watched closely the way our team was working. He was also working on bigger diamonds. He declared that one must demand 20 per cent margin on such diamonds. We have been selling at 5 per cent margin. Jayantibhai phoned Rahulbhai at Bombay office and asked him to increase the margin to 20 per cent. To our utter surprise, entire stock was sold in no time. Words that I was waiting to hear from Jayantibhai finally came. He said, 'Henceforth, I will take a responsibility for bigger diamonds.'

Jayantibhai called his close friend Arvind Shah of Ankit Gems who used to work in bigger diamonds. Jayantibhai went to him and told him to explain the best way to cut the bigger diamonds. Arvindbhai explained his theory in just one line. 'You just need to take care of two things,' he then explained beautifully, 'Firstly, while cutting and polishing the diamonds, care should be considered for perfection and proportion. If the height is more and the body of a person is fat, and the head and legs are small, will it be, okay? Alternatively, if the legs are long, and the head is big, but the chest and stomach are thin, will it be okay? In that way, in the diamonds also, the head, bottom and body everything must be in proper proportion. If the diamond is in proportion, then its beauty enhances.' Secondly, he added that proper facets of diamonds added to their magnificence.

Our inventory started moving fast. The enhanced price, along with surprise, brought happiness and hope. Everyone felt that we were on the right path. We decided to lead the market with bigger diamonds.

I was staying three days in Mumbai and four days in Surat. While having dinner with Rahulbhai one night, he said,' Diwali festivities are month and a half ahead. Big roughs are easily available in market. We must increase our production four times.' Later added, as if challenging me,' Kaka, you are a master cutter and polisher. It is a great opportunity to show your expertise. You produce diamonds and I will surely sell the finished goods quickly in the market. This is the most opportune time.' That night at 2 am he asked me not to stay at Mumbai for three days but to return immediately to Surat to take care of production.

And I decided to return to Surat taking the 6.00 a.m. Shatabdi Express instead of returning three days later as scheduled. The train reached Surat station at 9.30 a.m. I went straight to my office and called for a meeting of all the workers who used to work on bigger diamonds along with Jayantibhai. Some more workers who were working on smaller diamonds were added to the team on a volunteer basis. Working hours were changed to 12 hours from 8 hours.

Just a few days from Diwali, one stock of bigger diamonds was kept in the market for sale. All was purchased immediately. Never was such a fabulous response received. On Dhanteras[12], the calculations were done. In fifty days, how much work had been done? The work of bigger diamonds had increased by 8 times. The profit of those days had reached the gain of the entire year. Diwali is considered as the last day of the accounting year.

It was Diwali, and all the fireworks were illuminating the darkness. However, the real time is when a lamp is lit in our hearts. Whatever darkness has filled our hearts, it is removed, and light enters. A person must challenge himself and prove his worth to the time. Jayantibhai brought our company report. The excitement on his face was palpable. 'Our company is now on a way to become the number one company in bigger diamond cutting and polishing in

---

[12] धनतेरस, Day during Diwali people worship Goddess of Wealth

the world!' he said, almost shouting in excitement. I closed my eyes and prayed to God. I asked Jayantibhai, 'What time is it in Antwerp now? Let us call Munnabhai. He will be pleased'

My friend Dhirajlal Kotadiya introduced me to Dr Jitendra Adhia, pioneer of Mind Power and a Motivator. I immediately grabbed an opportunity to invite him to train our family members and SRK employees. Understanding the role of training, we never looked back in finishing our people well, just like a diamond, by inviting more such trainers to our factory. Veteran Dr B. N. Dastur joined us to show us a way forward in people management. A team of motivators, including Devrajbhai Chaudhari, Suresh Prajapati and Mrunal Shukla has been regular visitors at SRK. I firmly believe that lessons of motivation are necessary for members of any organisation. This tradition of training is still continued at SRK.

On 12 August 2009, the diamond industrialists of Surat gifted Dalsukhbhai Godhani Rs 75,00,000 on his seventy-fifth birthday so that he could use this money to live comfortably in his old age. However, he donated more than 50 per cent of that money off. For people like Dalsukhbhai, life was not a journey with the intention of arriving safely in a pretty and well-preserved body, but rather to skid in broadside in a cloud of smoke. His last ten years in the modest room in Sanosara, were like a battle returned soldier, thoroughly used up, totally worn out, but happy in his heart that he fought every battle well. He left this world on 23 January 2013, leaving behind a legacy of perhaps one of the last Gandhian leaders.

Leaders must not be confused with political parties in my opinion. They are all the same, regardless of whichever party they represent. The leaders I discussed with reverence here did not have a good time in their own parties because they were truer to the interests of the people they were representing and did not compromise on their personal convictions. In fact, all these leaders faced the financialization of politics in three different stages—local financing, high command financing, and now corporate financing. One must be an ostrich, and bury one's head in the sand, not to see the sign of corporate financing ruling the roost of politics today. Across the world, deals are cut with power dynamics of the country in mind.

However, before I close this chapter and move on with my story further, it is important that I share the negative side of power. Powerful people are prone to take risky, inappropriate, or unethical decisions and often overstep their boundaries. They tend to generate negative emotional reactions amongst their subordinates, particularly when there is a conflict in the group. When individuals gain power, their self-evaluation became more positive, while their evaluations of others become more negative. Power tends to weaken one's social attentiveness, which leads to difficulty in understanding other people's points of view. Powerful people also spend less time collecting and processing information about their subordinates and often perceive them in a stereotypical fashion. Finally, people with power tend to use more coercive tactics, increase social distance between themselves and their subordinates, believe that non-powerful individuals are untrustworthy and devalue the work and ability of less powerful individual.

Decorum forbids me to name the examples of negative power amongst the leaders. However, many of our leaders are suffering from these side effects of power and you can see them everywhere. It is indeed the biggest hypocrisy of our society that we do not like to talk about power but want to have it by whatever means.

I never found power scary, or evil, or having any negative moral valence. Power is the engine of progress and the more it is diffused and distributed, society becomes equal, peaceful and prosperous.

5

Ascend

नाभिषेको न संस्कार: सिंहस्य क्रियते मृगैः ।
विक्रमार्जितराज्यस्य स्वयमेव मृगेन्द्रता ॥

(हितोपदेश, सुहृदयभेद भाग 2, श्लोक 19)

There is no official coronation ceremony held or ritual performed
to declare that Lion is the king of jungle. He becomes king by his
own attributes and heroism.

(Hitopadesha, Suhridaybheda Part 2, Verse 19)

With Bhagwanbhai and Virjibhai's next generation proceeding on
their independent trajectories, the task ahead of me was to foresee
the global trends and work for India's advantage. Every successful
entrepreneur who ever lived started with nothing more than an idea,
knowing that motivation to explore new ways of doing things and
forging new partnerships were the two fundamental forces behind
success in business. Self-made entrepreneurs are built to tolerate and

withstand great risk. They know that hundreds if not thousands of people have already walked in their shoes, and they never complain when it pinches. After some time when the shoe stops pinching, as it always does, most of the people stop walking further. I was not going to let that happen. Internally illuminated by the Satsang, clean in mind and body by the habit of discipline, that involved everyday physical exercise including swimming, cycling and yoga and having understood the nuances of the diamond industry, it would have been great pity if I did not walk the whole track when there was a track. It was not the ideas of money or powerful and influential connections that drove me anymore, it was the willingness to outwork and outlearn everyone in the industry.

I expanded my business by setting up a new four-story factory building at Pajawa Falia, Katargam Road and upgraded the technology with laser machines and computer-based management systems. The factory could now accommodate 1200 crafts-persons and 500 staff members. We named the new building 'Shree Ramkrishna Complex.' We inaugurated the new complex on Ram Navami, on 16 April 1997 and in the esteemed presence of DTC[1] broker Mark Boston, Shantibhai Mehta, Navinbhai Mehta, Anup Mehta and Rupen Bhansali of Arohi Diamonds from Tel Aviv. More than 50 guests from the Mumbai diamond industry and 200 local diamond leaders joined this event. We hosted a gala dinner and cultural program where Commissioner of Police of Surat, Shree P. C. Pandey and many other officials joined us.

I had developed a habit of spending time with my employees in my attempt to create a sort of learning organization. We created a nice room as a learning center. My younger brother, Arjanbhai, my nephews, Rahulbhai and Jayantibhai, joined me by merging their own business into SRK. For businesspersons to come together, the

---

[1] The Diamond Trading Company (DTC) is the rough diamond sales and distribution arm of the De Beers family of companies.

excitement is usually about where they are going—that is, their strategy for gaining greater growth and productivity. It is never easy to lose your focus on this grandiose mission you established for yourself as an independent company. No one in a business can ever be independent, not only our roots but also even the branches are all enjoined like in a giant banyan tree.

I always believed that everyone wants to be innovative. If this idea is expressed, examined, nurtured, and allowed to develop, it will change the world, disrupt an industry, or set the company apart as a business success. Nevertheless, the truth is that few ideas are unique or new. Some of the most successful ideas are just iterative improvements on successful ventures that have come before but were ignored or not applied properly. It is here that a mix of old and new, of enthusiasm and experience, of excitement and restraint work. I told my team members not to be caught up in market saturation or competition. No matter what you do in life, you will face stiff competition. Use your closest competition. Evaluate their strengths and weaknesses and improve your business positioning, brand message, and pricing and marketing strategy to get an edge. Have a healthy competition but do not pull-down competitor using unfair means.

As Meenakshi grew young Champa started feeling anxious. One day, Vitthalbhai Limbachia proposed about Anil, son of Mathurbhai Sojitra. I knew Mathurbhai since before Meenakshi was even born. Mathurbhai Sojitra came to Surat from Saurashtra in 1968 with his three brothers, Nagjibhai, Kantibhai and Balubhai. Mathurbhai and Nagjibhai established Mani Exports in 1988. Anil and his brothers, Alpesh and Chetan, had been working with their father. My only concern was that after marriage, Meenakshi, the apple of my eye, should not go away in some other town, even Bombay and hence, this alliance looked excellent. On 25 March 1996, when Meenakshi was still a teenager, we got her engaged to Anil. It was decided that their marriage would take place in due course. One of Meenakshi's friends asked her, 'Do you know the boy you have been engaged to by your father?' She said, 'Had my father known my mother before their marriage? He had never even spoken with her. I always admired their marriage and if I can be as blessed as they are, what else do I need?'

The time for Meenakshi's wedding had arrived. We organized the Sangeet Sandhya at Dholakia Farm. The marriage took place on 4 December 1998. We built a Dudhala village at Surat. The excited brother of the bride, Shreyans, insisted that I must invite musical artist, Kishore Manraja, and the Bamboo Beats orchestra from Mumbai for the Garba Dance Party. His sister, Shweta, endorsed his idea immediately. I did not object to this little fun show that the children wanted. This was the first time Bamboo Beats came to Surat. The marriage function was organized at Sprawling Lawns in Athwalines. Swati Snacks from Mumbai were commissioned for catering. All invitees enjoyed this event thoroughly.

Amidst this pomp and spectacle, I felt empty and scared inside. For years, Meenakshi's laughter had cheered up the entire household. Now that she would be gone tomorrow, it was hard to imagine life without her. No matter how strong a person is this one thought is enough to make every father's heart heavy.

Another manner of celebrating Meenakshi's wedding was to do something beyond education and health. It was indeed not practical to compartmentalise problems into these two brackets. Miseries come in myriad forms to the poor. We founded Relief Center through our Shree Ramkrishna Welfare Trust in 1999 to provide whatever relief people might require. I also made a rule for myself that when in Surat, I would spend every day between 9.30 a.m. and 10.30 a.m. at the Relief Center. Beginning from 3 October 1999, I started listening to people—their problems, pains, and woes. Whatever I had, I had to share, most importantly, my time. There was no going back now.

As if to celebrate victory in this small battle, I got this quote of the French poet, Victor Marie Hugo, 'No power on earth can stop an idea, whose time has come.' The Relief Center was fully functional now. I trained a team of compassionate volunteers to coordinate the large influx of people and organize them in a manner so that the neediest was benefitted. I not only started giving money but also giving my time as a part of my own life that I would never get back. I consistently spend Rs 4 to 5 crores annually as my 'giving back.' Many heart-touching tales passed in front of my eyes and tears roll down my cheeks as I recall them now as if washing my soul.

I consider family business as the ultimate test for the goodness of people. Respect from your elders forms the core of a family business. What I have found is that, in a family business structure, sometimes what is needed more is a sense of discipline rather than creativity. You have to take everyone's ideas and make them work. When you are dealing with money, there is a limitation on how creative you can be. I decided to further embed philanthropy in our business so that it became an obligation for my future generations and not an option. There was an additional need in South Gujarat for computer and scientific education. We supported the management of the Sarvajanik Education Society established in Surat in 1912 to set up such a college. About 109 years ago, Chunilal Ghelabhai Shah, the spirited son of a teacher, founded the Sarvajanik Education Society with the management of just one school. I gave donation to set up the college for imparting computer and bio-technology education. I did not put any conditions, especially involvement in the management, and simply asked that the best people in the city run the institution.

Coming back to diamonds, Russian diamonds had been talked about for a while. Russia is a vast landmass with enormous geological diversity, and it was only a matter of time that they entered the diamond market. In 1949, rough diamonds were found in the Western Yakutia region of Siberia. By 1954, the first kimberlite pipe, Zarnitsa ('heat lightning' in Russian) was discovered. From that point, Russian diamonds made their way into world markets under a contract agreement with De Beers Corporation. However, it was not until the collapse of the Soviet Union in 1991 that Russians started doing business in the open market and emerged as the world's largest producer of diamonds by volume.

In February 1992, Alrosa was established as a closed joint-stock company by the decree of the President of Russia. I met Alrosa officials when they opened their office in Antwerp. I was impressed with the audacity of their vision. In December 1996, I went to Moscow with Praful Patel, a trader from Los Angles flying out of Delhi by an Aeroflot flight. We were received at Moscow by Eduard 'Edik' Vadimovich Ragulin, who would take us to Alrosa. Edik had Armenian ancestry, coming from the Southern Caucasus Mountain region and is the smallest state of the former Soviet republics. He knew only Russian. A Russian woman was translating what Edik was telling Praful Patel in English and he was communicating with me in Gujarati and vice versa. It was not a comfortable way to discuss business, but I was patiently handling it. However, after some time Edik got irritated. However, since he was sincere in business, we made a deal and he agreed to be our man in Moscow in dealing with Alrosa.

As if to release his own pressure, Edik engaged us in some small talk. He told us, 'Every Russian is born with three names: First is the given name, the middle is patronymic, and the last is surname. The given name is unique to the individual and chosen by their parents. The middle name is the father's name mentioned as *ovich/evich* (son of) or *ovna/evna* (daughter of). The surname is typically passed down from father to children, and a woman adopts the feminine form of her husband's surname upon marriage.' After this tutorial, Edik came to the point of explaining to us the meaning of Edik as 'a/the rich protector.' Edik was living in Moscow city itself and invited us to his home for dinner. I only said, 'Same in India. I also have three names. First is Govind, my given name; second is Laljibhai my father and Dholakia, my family name.'

Edik introduced his wife as the queen in a palace—Olga Konstiantinivna. I was wise enough to know now that this very gracious woman was the daughter of Mr Konstantin. 'Olga means holy, blessed.' Edik told us in a soft gentle voice, almost cooing like a pigeon. Knowing that we do not take meat, his wife had been learning to cook vegetarian food from a cookbook for a week. She served us a seven-course dinner. Not knowing the system, we took the 'starter' as the dinner itself and filled ourselves. After the starter, alcohol was served. As I did not take alcohol, I had Coca-Cola and made a toast. After that one by one, we had a seven-course meal, on a filled stomach. Looking at his wife, enthusiastically serving us, I suddenly remembered Lady Marinas, whose tomb I had seen in the Dutch-Armenian cemetery in Gulam Falia, years ago. Was this her? A chill went through my spine.

After every course, there was a toast. You must stand up from your seat, say some story, or a joke, or whatever, and cheer up. It lasted for about three hours. At 11.00 p.m., a high Edik insisted that we watch, most popular among Russians, Raj Kapoor's film Mera Naam Joker[2] on his home theatre. He had a collection of Raj Kapoor's movies. Edik's wife somehow conveyed to us with her expressions, 'To be a good guest—please be hungry, when you visit us. Nothing can make us more upset than a guest, who does not have a good appetite. We will think that you did not like the food.' Coming out of their home politely that day turned out to be a very difficult task. I was feeling a little scared. Why was Edik putting on such a sumptuous feast for us? Were we being set up? I had heard about a Russian fairytale where the sorcerer Baba Yaga provided a warm welcome to the fine youth she planned to eat later.

The next day, we had an appointment with Alrosa at 11.00 a.m. to deal in roughs. Later we all went to see the famous, Red Square. The cobblestone square was surrounded by beautiful architecture, of

---

[2] मेरा नाम जोकर, My Name is Joker, Raj Kapoor's Hindi film released in 1970.

such a great size and beauty that I had never seen before. There were commercial photographers taking pictures of tourists. These pictures were priced at 50,000 Ruble, equivalent to $8. Edik leaned over to the side of the photographer and placed a 50,000 Ruble bill in the photographer's coat from his pocket stealthily. When I objected to him paying for us and in that manner, Edik said, 'Currently Russians are having bad times, if anyone sees you with money in your pockets, we would be robbed. Money must not be shown in public here.'

The whole thing seemed like a deep mystery to me. The grandeur of Red Square and the desperate poverty of people on streets were not adding up. I used to hear that in Soviet Russia, the chauffeur and the boss sitting on the back seat of the car were making equal money except that the boss enjoyed more privileges and powers. In the Soviet Union, the average income in the top 1 percent was only four-five times higher than that of society. Nevertheless, after the Soviet Union collapsed in 1990, a new class of oligarchs grabbed Russian resources. Edik told me that between 1990 and 1996, prices rose nearly 5000 times. Salaries that were often paid late or not at all, did not keep up, becoming one-third in real terms. The result was a catastrophic drop in the living standards of people.

That day, we decided to have dinner in the hotel we were staying. It was service à la russe dinner, which means service in Russian Style, so many types of foods were presented decorated in silver platters, but we could not even eat anything except fruits. However, we were charged $325 a person. While seeing us off the next day, Edik put his hand on my shoulder and said something in a whisper. Later it was translated as, 'Welcome to Russia dear friend. However, beware, business here is a one-way street. It will not be possible for you to sell any polished diamonds back in Russia. Russians have no use of jewellery. We are earning, drinking, and eating type of people.' God has created a world full of very different people indeed. Even though some people dominate over others, the wheel of time raises the suppressed.

I decided to go to Hong Kong to witness the ceremony marking the transfer of its sovereignty from the United Kingdom to the People's Republic of China, ending 156 years of British rule, on the night of 30 June 1997. I was not born when Britishers left India in 1947 but I did not want to miss witnessing them depart from Hong Kong. A proud China reclaimed control over the prosperous city of Hong Kong marked by the bagpipers and Chinese lion dancers, all-night parties, and brilliant fireworks over the harbour.

As widely reported, 'After the ceremony, which lasted less than an hour, Prince Charles, and Chris Patten, the 28th and last British Governor of Hong Kong, left the hall and boarded the royal yacht 'Britannia', moored at Victoria Harbor. The British had arrived by sea and departed by sea, sailing away into history, and opening a new chapter in Hong Kong's turbulent history.'[3]

Every time we feel we know everything, something new arrives on the scene. Throughout the twentieth century, most people would never have thought about Canada being a producer of diamonds. Most people's knowledge of diamonds, including us in the industry, was fixed on mining operations in the Sun scorched Africa and finding diamonds in a country with a permanent winter had never crossed anyone's mind. All of this started to change in 1991 when two geologists, Chuck Fipke and Stewart Blusson, found evidence of diamond-bearing kimberlite pipes about 200 miles north of Yellowknife, Northwest Territories. One of these pipes was developed by BHP Billiton into the EKATI Diamond Mine, which produced Canada's first commercial diamonds in 1998.[4]

My eldest brother, Bhimjibhai, left this mortal world on 1 May 1999. I came to Surat with him in 1964 and lived with him for a while before finding my bearings. There is no other love like the

---

[3] https://www.washingtonpost.com/wp-srv/inatl/longterm/china/stories/hongkong. htm. Last accessed on date to October 10, 2021.

[4] https://geology.com/articles/canada-diamond-mines/. Last accessed on date to October 10, 2021.

love from a brother. Added to that, I had a tinge of indebtedness towards Bhimjibhai. With him around, all of us siblings could run through the fields and feel quite safe. He was the happiness of the happiest days of my childhood. His gift of a Hercules bicycle to me, which was the first gift I ever received in my life, forever remains a cherished memory in my heart. My parents felt a great loss. My mother did not speak a word for several days.

My brothers are caring, positive, strong, helpful, awesome, and reliable. Because I have my brothers, I will always have friends. However, I found another brother in a friend through Mathurbhai Savani. He was about fifteen years younger than me, and I saw in him the better version of my younger days. Born in the small village of Khopala, Gadhada Taluka, Saurashtra, he came to Surat and joined the diamond industry. His family had close links with the Bhartiya Janata Party (BJP) and Prime Minister Atal Bihari Vajpayee visited his home at Surat for dinner in 1996. A path to be elected for the legislative assembly was waiting for him but he did not opt for that. Concerned with the perennial water problem in Saurashtra, he asked me if I would join the community mobilization for rainwater conservation. Later he went to Rajendra Singh Rana[5] to Alwar, Rajasthan, for advice.

I came to know that 'Alwar district, which once had a grain market, was at the time largely dry and barren, as years of deforestation and mining had led to a dwindling water table, minimal rainfall followed by floods.' Rajendra Singh watched how the slow abandoning of traditional water conservation techniques, as building check dams, called Johad[6] locally, had further contributed to this problem. There was a race to dig a borewell and pull the groundwater up. As few years passed, these bored wells had to be dug deeper and deeper,

---

[5] https://en.wikipedia.org/wiki/Rajendra_Singh. Last accessed on date to October 10, 2021.

[6] जोहड़ community-owned traditional harvested rainwater storage wetland

pushing underground water table further down each time, till they finally went dry in the ecologically fragile Aravalli Mountain Range.

Rajendra Singh closely studied the Johads abandoned in previous decades. With the help of a few local youths, Rajendra Singh started desilting the Gopalpura Johad, lying neglected after years of disuse. When the monsoon arrived that year, the Johad filled up and soon wells that had been dry for years had water. Villagers pitched in and in the next three years, made it 15 feet deep. As a result, the area that had no groundwater for the past five years and was officially declared a 'dark zone' now had year-round water supply.

Rajendra Singh has said that the entire issue hinged on creating social awareness. Until people kept looking at others, especially the government to solve their problems, their lives would never improve. He undertook padayatra (walkathon) through the villages of the area starting in 1986, educating the population to rebuild the villages' old check dams. By bringing about 400 tiny earthen dams and a 244-meter-long and 7-meter-high concrete dam, they could revive the Aravri River in 1990, which was dried and dead for over sixty years. For Rajendra Singh 'Mining is a curse. People dig stones and take them away to the construction sites in cities, and rainwater flows through these cuts to waste.' Rajendra Singh fought the legal battle to get mining banned in the Aravalli Mountain Range altogether in 1992 and by 1995; the Aravri became a perennial river.

Rajendra Singh guided about the work in progress to revive rivers like Ruparel, Sarsa, Bhagani and Jahajwali, all of which had been dry for decades. Abandoned villages in the areas were being populated now and farming activities had resumed once again in hundreds of drought-prone villages in the neighbouring districts of Jaipur, Dausa, Sawai Madhopur, Bharatpur and Karauli. Later, Mathurbhai spent one month with Rajendra Singh, understood his work and philosophy in detail, returned with a conviction, and resolve to recreate Rajendra Singh's success in Rajasthan in Saurashtra.

Mathurbhai Savani now established the Saurashtra Jaldhara Trust. He invited others and me in the diamond industry to join the Trust to make it a collective effort so that it did not remain a one-man show. We decided to stick to a single agenda of rainwater harvesting and solving problems of drinking water, irrigation, and water for other uses. Mathurbhai used his political influence to involve then-Chief Minister of Gujarat, Shree Keshubhai Patel, in the project and got the entire red tape cut out of the administrative process for release of the requisite funds. With just two signatures, including one of the District Collector, 60 per cent cost of making a check dam would come as subsidy paid in front of the entire village by cheque. After Keshubhai got replaced by Shree Narendrabhai Modi as Chief Minister, Mathurbhai won his trust as well and invited him eighteen times to inaugurate check dams at various villages. We were instrumental in constructing around 1,25,000 check dams over a period of seven years wherein the Government of Gujarat spent almost Rs 7000 crores and more than Rs 4000 crores had come from NGOs and people at large.

In Dudhala, I along with my nephew Savjibhai constructed 110 channels of check dams with the support of local villagers and some villagers of Dudhala residing in Surat. Dhirubhai Malaviya and Mavjibhai Jodhani actively participated in this project.

Many times, things do not move the way we want them to. Shreyans was studying in class 6th at Fellowship School while my brother Arjanbhai's son Akshay was a student at Mithibai College in Mumbai. One time, during the middle of 1999, upon being asked about his semester result, Shreyans told Rahulbhai that he had cleared the exam with good grades. Shweta, however, knew the truth that Shreyans was lying. Rahulbhai informed me about this incidence on the telephone. Failure is acceptable but dishonesty cannot be condoned. I immediately rushed to Mumbai to teach the lesson of fearlessness and uprightness to my son. Upon reaching Rahulbhai's home, I learnt that although Akshay was supposed to be attending college, even he was bunking classes and skipping college. As a part of strategy to show these young ones the right path, after dinner that night, I invited Shreyans into my room and greeted him with the only slap I ever gave him. My sudden outburst was new to him. Akshay also could not tolerate my scolding. The entire family except the two boys were a part of the drama to tell them that, 'Better to be slapped with the truth than kissed with a lie.' After two hours of this play, both realized their wrongdoings. It is my experience that the truth always comes out in the end, no matter how hard anyone tries to hide it. Lies are just a temporary delay to the inevitable. I was at peace when I spoke with Shreyans and Akshay again. I looked into their eyes, and I was certain that it was the last time they would ever resort to lies. People resort to lying for the most common motives for telling lies, avoiding punishment. Since then, such an incidence has not occurred in our family.

Something very interesting happened in those days. A problem in the coding of computerised systems was projected to create havoc in computers and computer networks around the world at the beginning of the year 2000. It was smartly called Y2K bug, as in metric measurements K stands for the thousand. Most of the computer programs were designed to abbreviate four-digit years as two digits to save memory space.

As later explained by the Britannica, 'These computers could recognize '98' as '1998' but would be unable to recognize '00' as '2000', perhaps interpreting it to mean 1900. Many feared that when the clocks struck midnight on 31 December 1999, the computers would be using an incorrect date and thus fail to operate properly unless the computers' software was repaired or replaced before that date.

The US and the UK worked around the globe to fix the issue. The Australian government invested millions of dollars with the goal of checking systems and fixing software before the end of December 1999. India tapped the opportunity to provide the biggest pool of engineers. As the US utilized the services offered by the nation, many Indian companies like TCS, Infosys and WIPRO strengthened their base in the industry. Later, when I met Shree RatanTata, Smt. Sudha Murthy and Shree Azim Premji, I made it a point to tell them that this transformation of India's reputation in the world is because of their companies.

It is interesting to know that Russia ignored the issue and suffered no major disruption. It was reported that 'After the collective sigh of relief in the first few days of January 2000, however, Y2K morphed into a punch line, as relief gave way to derision—as is so often the case when warnings appear unnecessary after they are heeded. It was called a big hoax; the effort to fix it a waste of time.'[7] A youth in the computer business chuckled mischievously and told me, 'It is a problem hyped to make revenues by the software companies.'

One day while in Dudhala, I was walking through the place where Rajuma used to live. A flood of memories inundated my consciousness and I stood frozen for a while. I inquired about her and was told that she died many years back. Then I sent one person to Dhasa village to find out about her daughter, Jadi. The person returned with the news that Jadi was married off and was living in Surat. He gave me the name of a locality in Surat as her address. I felt this news was even better.

After reaching Surat, I sent my staff to locate Jadi, who was now called Kantaben. Her husband was working as a security guard. I invited her entire family at home and ate food with them. I invited her to come on every Rakhi day and sent gifts for the family every Diwali. I organized the necessary treatment for her son when he met with an accident. The peace that I feel by doing these small acts was deeper and profound than the happiness that had come from my commercial success in business. I attribute my today's success to Rajuma's never uttered blessing showered on my mother and

---

[7] https://time.com/5752129/y2k-bug-history/. Last accessed on date to October 10, 2021.

believe that my prodigy would continue to live under that protective umbrella of Rajuma's boon.

On 24 December 1999, members of the Harkat-ul-Mujahideen, Pakistan-based terror group, brought India to its knees by hijacking Indian Airlines Flight 814, commonly known as IC 814, in Indian airspace. There were 176 passengers and fifteen crew members on board. A sordid drama saw the plane going to Amritsar, Lahore, and Dubai before finally landing in Taliban-ruled Kandahar in Afghanistan. To end the hostage crisis, the Indian government had to release three dreaded militants. Millions of people watched in complete disbelief at the powerful Indian government operating through a gamut of indecision, chaos, inaction, knee-jerk reactions, and confusion creating a sort of 'what not to do when faced with a crisis' manual. The nation has long suffered the effects of this incident, unfortunately forcing the terrorists to leave.

While moving around in New York in June 2000, I entered an Armani showroom with Champa. I liked one tee shirt. Champa said it was beautiful and that I ought to take it. Before I could say anything, she kept it in the basket and I just checked the price, which was the sum equivalent of Rs 3,00,000. I recalled the second-hand shirt of Rs 2 and trousers of Rs 3 I used to purchase from the roadside market in my early days at Ruwala Tekra. Time not only changes people, it also changes the entire world around them. I put back the tee shirt on the shelf.

That day, I visited my earlier days in New York mall. Suddenly, it was August 1965. I was in Surat for almost sixteen months, and it was time to go back to the village. I packed my newly purchased tee shirt and pant worth Rs 5 in my bag. I had to return to Dudhala wearing new clothes. If I wore new clothes while boarding the train, they would be crumpled by the time I reached Dudhala. I put on my white pajama and shirt and kept new clothes in my bag. Many of my friends, up to fifteen or twenty, had come to bid me farewell at Surat railway station. My friends were thinking I was very lucky, as I was able to go back to the village. I too was counting my self as lucky since I had 'new' clothes in my bag.

Fast forward went my thoughts. As I had to get down at Lathi village, I changed my clothes in the toilet at Dhasa, one station before Lathi. Looking in the mirror, I felt great. Afraid of spoiling the new dress I decided not to sit while wearing them. I remained standing until the train arrived at Lathi. I had to take a horse-cart from Lathi railway station to reach my village. From there I rented a bicycle to Dudhala. My bag was secured on the carrier of the back wheel, and I rode straight to Dudhala.

Upon reaching home, I rested the bicycle against a wall and ran inside. Santokbaa was home. She did not know that I was coming. Surprised with joy, she hugged me with affection. Tears were rolling down her eyes. She said nothing while moving her hands on my head. She was very happy at seeing me well dressed. Others in the family were away in the fields. Therefore, I removed my clothes and hung them up so that I could wear them again in the evening when my father arrived home. I could hear my father arriving and I rushed to change my clothes. What if my father enquired about the money spent on the clothes? I put it on nevertheless, nervously, and touched his feet. He did not speak much but was happy that I was healthy and dressed well. My brothers were hugging me, looking at the new tee shirt with curiosity. In Armani Showroom in New York, Champa asked me, 'where are you lost?', I said, 'in bylanes of past.'

In October 2000, I received the 'Best Businessperson' Award by The Southern Gujarat Chamber of Commerce and Industries (SGCCI) from then Union Home Minister Shree Lal Krishna Advani. Shree Bharat Gandhi and Shree Praful Shah were President and Vice-President of the SGCCI. Shree Rajnikant Marfatia, Chairman, SGCCI Golden Jubilee Memorial Trust remained present on the occasion. In addition, present in the function were Shree Kashiram Rana, Shree Hemant Chapatwala, Shree Narottam Patel, Shree Ajay Choksi and CII's Chairman Shree Arun Bharat Ram.

Established in the year 1940, the SGCCI was the oldest and apex body of Gujarat, with a focus on growth and development of trade and industries of the Southern Gujarat region, spread from Bharuch to Vapi, 'Golden Corridor' of Gujarat. It was the fastest growing and one of the most prosperous parts of the state. The SGCCI had mastered the art of trade fairs and industry-specific exhibitions highlighting products to wider markets and establishing 'Brand Surat.'

A very dramatic thing happened on 7 November 2000. There was a diamond exhibition by De-Beers going on in the newly constructed Millennium Dome in Southeast London. Several jewels were on display, including the Millennium Star, a flawless 203 carat gem with an estimated worth of £200 million and considered one of the perfect gems in the world. The police laid a trap to let the four robbers, disguised as workers. Later the judge said, 'This was a wicked, professional plan and one which was carried out with the minutest attention to detail. Mercifully, the police were on to it.'[8] If the thieves had successfully carried out their plan, it would have been one of the biggest thefts in the history of the world.

On 26 January 2001, just as India was all set to celebrate the occasion of Republic Day, at 8.46 a.m., a powerful earthquake measuring 6.9 on the Richter scale shook Gujarat and hit Kutch the hardest. Even we in Surat felt the tremors and realized it was a huge earthquake. Surat had dropped out of the power grid and the telecom network. Many people came out on roads in areas like Varachha Road, Katargam and Athwalines. In Kutch, thousands of people who had invested their lives' saving to build their homes, saw them crashing like a house of cards. The houses which they thought were their own suddenly turned into heaps

---

[8] https://en.wikipedia.org/wiki/Millennium_Dome_raid. Last accessed on date to October 10, 2021.

of debris. I tried to call up people living in Bhuj to know how they were, what they were doing and what the conditions were like. However, it was not possible as communication lines were snapped.

The newsreaders on TV started saying that Kutch had been flattened. I did not like people speaking mindless things on TV about the tragedy. I wondered that whenever tragedy strikes, one is left either to die or with a plethora of ifs and buts to ponder over. Luckily, there were people working on ground reality. Braveheart volunteers reached the site in an incredibly quick manner and were helping people come out of debris and organizing medical help for the injured. By evening, thousands of funeral rites were conducted, and they distributed food to every single person in the towns and villages of Kutch. The way relief material was brought to Kutch was like magic. Shree Keshubhai Patel was the Chief Minister of Gujarat at that time. He saw the devastation of Kutch and carried out relief work on a war footing.

RSS deputed Narendrabhai Modi who reached the disaster site and camped there. He somehow got help from Railway engineers in cutting through jumbled steel bars and rescuing trapped people. The death of 20,000 people and injuries to more than 1,50,000 others due to the earthquake left hundreds of thousands homeless and destroyed or damaged more than 3,00,000 buildings. A large majority of the local crops were ruined as well. Thousands of livestock died. The Gujarat State Electricity Board pulled off a minor miracle when it laid a 165 km line from near Morbi to Bhuj to bring power to a region where every other piece of the grid had collapsed.

Along with the members of the Surat business community, we mobilized twenty-two truckloads of relief kits comprising kitchenware, rations, and blankets and reached there by 30 January. By that time, over 10,000 volunteers were deployed in Kutch district, many of them from Vishwa Hindu Parishad (VHP), RSS, and Swaminarayan Sanstha, saved the day for the people. Now the mammoth task of rehabilitation was ahead. We were aghast, watching a narrow street in Bhuj, which was filled with the debris of buildings collapsed from both sides under which 225 students who were conducting traditional 'Prabhat Pheri' on the Republic Day were crushed to death.

In the rural areas alone, the individuals who needed materials for temporary shelters exceeded 15 lakhs. The majority were in the partially destroyed categories. Urban renters suffered the most. 1,50,000 people were in Bhuj. Shelters for families of these people had to be built either in situ or on alternative sites. Apart from the damage to residential property, commercial establishments, roads, power substations, railway tracks, telephone exchanges, water supply systems, educational institutions, hospitals, dispensaries, and other public buildings were either destroyed or badly damaged, putting them out of use.

Reliance Industries announced a large donation and adopted the town of Anjar. Essar adopted Surendranagar. Adani Group started a community shelter that provided food and shelter to 4000 affected people. Others, like L&T and some PSUs, made similar plans. Gems and Jewellery Export Promotion Council (GJEPC) constructed a renewed Amran village for 500 families at an estimated cost of Rs 15 crores. A handsome donation was received from Antwerp Diamond Traders by GJEPC for this cause.

We also constructed two new villages, for 100 families each, with all the necessary amenities. We named them Godhani Gram, after my partner, Virjibhai, and Nanduba, after the name of Bhagwanbhai's mother. Our Shree Ramkrishna Charitable Trust constructed these villages.

Post-quake in October 2001, Chief Minister Keshubhai Patel was made to resign in the state. Narendrabhai Modi, never having faced an election until that time, took over as Chief Minister of Gujarat. He displayed an adeptness at post-disaster administration and acquired immense political capital from the success of the reconstruction work. Narendrabhai saw in this challenge a great opportunity for social reconstruction.

In rural Gujarat, each new or reconstructed village was to be given access to roads and community buildings and supplied with water and electricity. New houses, built on public-private partnership models, were to be registered in the names of husband and wife, a measure intended to promote gender parity in relation to property. All payments to individuals for the reconstruction of a damaged house were to be made through the banking system. The stated rationale behind this was to ensure transparency.

Over 3,65,000 new bank accounts were created within three months. The payments were pegged against the various stages of construction to ensure that new and stricter building regulations were followed. Finally, there was a mandatory policy to insure houses against future natural calamities. In this manner, the reconstruction programme connected the citizenry to the financial institutions and ensured that the state was no longer the primary underwriter of property damage caused by natural disasters.

Numerous community participation programmes were held in affected areas with local involvement so that they might get benefits like housing assistance and access to public services. Volumes of printed information and instruction were produced, and countless workshops, meetings and presentations were held in hundreds of villages. Such programmes were pushed hardest in rural areas, where liberal ideas of responsibility and decision-making came face to face with caste hierarchies and other entrenched forms of power and inequality. It was as if Gandhiji's dream of local development had finally come true.

Hope is a very powerful force. It was during these two years, starting with the earthquake, the upheaval caused by the 9/11 attacks on the World Trade Towers in New York, and the communal riots in Gujarat, that I realized the power of passion over knowledge, the power of myth over history and the power of beliefs over facts. Yet, hope always triumphs over any calamity. Life is under no obligation to give us what we expect and yet we expect and succeed in getting what we desire. There is a beautiful Shloka, I had learnt from Dani Dutt Jha:

आशा नाम मनुष्याणां काश्चिदाश्चर्यशृङ्खला ।
यया बद्धाःप्रधावन्ति मुक्तास् तिष्ठन्ति पङ्गुवत् ॥

(महा सुभाषित संग्रह, श्लोक 5429)

Desire is the name of a strange binding for man. Those tied keep running, but those free sit as if ensnared.

(Maha Subhashit Collection, Verse 5429)

Tragedy was waiting to happen. My mother had a fall in 1998 and became immobile after the accident. She very resolutely said no to surgery that could perhaps have gotten her limited mobility. We respected her wish. However, it resulted in atrophy of her limbs. From the beginning of 2002, her situation started deteriorating. Champa acted like a 24x7 nurse for her. The entire family supported Champa in her work. We could see her end coming. I stopped going out of the house fearing that she should not breathe her last in my absence.

I recited Kapila Gita to my mother and she heard every word of it with full attention.

Devahuti asked her son Kapila, who is indeed God-incarnated:

निर्विण्णा नितरां भूमन्नसदिन्द्रियतर्षणात् ।
येन सम्भाव्यमानेन प्रपन्नान्धं तमः प्रभो ॥

(श्रीमद् भागवतम् पुराण, स्कन्ध 3, अध्याय 25, श्लोक 7)

I am very sick of the disturbance caused by my material senses, for because of this sense disturbance, my Lord, I have fallen into the abyss of ignorance.

(Shreemad Bhagavatam Purana,
Skandha 3, Chapter 25, Verse 7)

The word *asadindriya-tarshnat* is significant. *Asat* means impermanent, temporary, *indriya* means senses, and *tarashanat* refers to agitation. Devahuti is expressing that she is tired. She wanted to get relief by hearing the instructions of Lord Kapila.

तस्य त्वं तमसोऽन्धस्य दुष्पारस्याद्य पारगम् ।
सच्चक्षुर्जन्मनामन्ते लब्धं मे त्वदनुग्रहात् ॥

(श्रीमद् भागवतम् पुराण, स्कन्ध 3, अध्याय 25, श्लोक 8)

You are my only means of getting out of this darkest region of ignorance because You are my transcendental eye, which, by Your mercy only, I have attained after many, many births.

(Shreemad Bhagavatam Purana,
Skandha 3, Chapter 25, Verse 8)

The word *paragam* is very significant. Paragam,[9] refers to one who can take you to the other side. This side is the conditioned life; the other side is the life of freedom. We are suffering simply because of ignorance. By the instruction of the spiritual master, the darkness of ignorance is removed, and thus the disciple is enabled to go to the side of freedom.

On Wednesday, 10 April 2002, my mother departed around midnight surrounded by the family. Us four brothers, our two sisters,

---

[9] परागम, an outcome

our families, all were around her. Everyone offered her a sip of water of the Ganges as a mark of love and respect and their final service. My father watched all this sitting in silence.

The next day morning, my father spoke to me saying, 'Your mother worked very hard.' This led to my elder sister Shantaben to recall how mother would get up at 3.00 a.m., attend to livestock, prepare food, that included hand-grinding wheat flour, attending to the children, go to field with lunch, take the cattle to graze and later return home in the evening to milch them and cook dinner. This kind of toil is beyond the imagination of modern people. 'During delivery of all her seven children, she was working in the field till the final day and returned in few days' time,' my father reminisced.

After performing all rites, I visited the relief center after a gap of few days. A thirty-two-year-old woman, Kumudben Jivalal Nayak,[10] very tired and exhausted, came. She said, 'I want to meet Govind Kaka,' I said. 'Ben, I am Govind. Please tell me.' Tears started rolling out of her eyes and she could not speak for a while. I offered her water and waited for her to regain composure. Then she said, 'I do not want to die. I want to live for my seven-year-old son and marry my three daughters off.' Then, she shared her medical reports. She had a severely damaged heart valve and needed surgery and valve replacement. I supported her with all the expenses. She was successfully operated at Mahaveer Hospital. Two months later, she came with her husband, a street vendor, and four children to the relief center and told me, 'I have never seen God before, but I am seeing one in you now, who saved me from death.' I told her all of us are the reflection of one God. Kumudben was later employed at SRK kitchen.

On 30 August 2002, water from the Narmada entered Saurashtra through the 70 km long Kadi Dhanki Lilapur-Saurashtra canal system. When I told it to my father, he doubted first if it was true

---

[10] Name changed to protect her privacy

but later called it God's work. Narmada water had reached Kadi having travelled a 264 km journey from Sardar Sarovar Dam through the Kevadia Kadi main canal system. Narendrabhai announced that about 200 cusecs[11] of water would be pumped out of the Saurashtra canal and poured into 110 km long Vallabhipur branch canal system from 30 August to irrigate 1.36 lakhs hectare of land. 'The water supply from Narmada to water-starved regions would approximately save about 150 MW of power by way of saving electricity bills on drawing water from tube wells,' he said.

During the weekend of 15–16 February 2003, a big drama unfolded in Antwerp. A ring of thieves broke into a vault two floors beneath the Antwerp Diamond Centre, thought to be among the world's most fortified business premises, and made off with at least $100 million worth of loose diamonds and gold jewellery. Entry into the centre's vault required a building access card, a two-story descent underground to a guard-controlled gate, and both a key and one of 100 million possible combinations. If a person somehow entered the vault unauthorised a broken magnetic seal on the vault door, a motion detector, infrared detector, and light detector would detect him. If he tried to tunnel in, seismic sensors would detect him. With a police station not more than 200 feet from the Diamond Centre's front entrance—and a police kiosk even closer—any detected thief would be captured in minutes. Since all the detectors activated silent alarms, the thief would not know he had been detected until he was already surrounded. Nevertheless, somehow the Antwerp thieves defeated all these measures. The loot was never found.

Nevertheless, the real turning point in Gujarat came with Global Investors Summit held from 28 September to 2 October 2003 at Ahmedabad, Gandhinagar, and Surat. Union Finance Minister, Shree Jaswant Singhinaugurated the Surat Summit. A former officer of the Indian Army, he was royalty personified. Narendrabhai

---

[11] unit of flow equal to one cubic foot per second (especially of water).

rolled out red carpet welcome to corporates from India and abroad. About 125 foreign delegates, 200 Non-Resident Indians, 200 leading dignitaries and other participants from about 45 countries participated in the summit held during Navratri. At the end of the event, 76 memorandums of understanding worth $14 billion for investment were signed. Nothing of this sort had ever been achieved anywhere in India. Vibrant Gujarat is organised biennially.

Following the global trend, we took the decision to expand and diversify into the jewellery segment and set up a jewellery-manufacturing unit in Santacruz Electronics Export Processing Zone (SEEPZ), a Special Economic Zone in Andheri East area of Mumbai.

One evening, I took Rahulbhai and Shreyans to Prempuri Ashram with the idea of making them know that while this world was busy in doing what it was doing, certain extraordinary things kept happening as if by some unseen force. Prempuri Maharaj was the Peethadhishwar of Kailash Ashram in Rishikesh. It was the same Gurukul where Swami Dayanandawas moulded as a teacher. Prempuri Maharaj started teaching in Mumbai in the early 1960s. The Prempuri Ashram Trust is functional since it was set up in 1967.

It was a five-storey building founded in 1967 by devoted followers of Swami Shree Prempuri Maharaj. There are three floors dedicated as Pravachan[12] Halls, one floor is a Yoga Hall, and one floor for the Sanyasis' Quarters, Ashram Office, and a small Canteen. The terrace can be used to conduct Homas[13], as I recently discovered. We found it a unique center of spiritual activity right in the heart of the bustling commercial city. However, for me, it became necessary place to visit in Mumbai ever since then.

People know Mumbai for films, for business, money, and for hundred other attractions. But it is no less ordinary a fact that since

---

[12] प्रवचन, religious discourse
[13] होमम्, ritual offering to God

the very first time the Ashram premises were activated in 1975, there has not been a single day when a Pravachan and Svadhyaya session has been skipped—not even weekends/holidays—such was the tremendous power of resolve of Prempuri Maharaj with the backing of Akhandanand Swami. Also, of course, the students, many of whom started as young men and women, are now past retirement age, and still committed as ever.

While I was ensuring that my next generation learn these fundamental truths of life, I was also cautious in creating enough space so that the new generation could spread their wings as they liked and fly as high and far as they dared. Maybe as a sign of grown up or conditioned by things happening unexpectedly even after best planning and effort, I stopped bothering much about the future. I developed a liking for uncertainty. I realized that too much certainty, conformity and rigidity take away the natural joy of experiencing life as it arrives. We may not know what exactly will happen tomorrow and to be ready to accept with an open heart and mind is the hallmark of a happy man. I liked the idea of flying in sky over walking on road for going through life. In fact, I made Dr A. P. J. Abdul Kalam's autobiography, Wings of Fire, a compulsory read for everyone in the company. Multiple copies of English original and Gujarati translation AganPankh[14] were kept in our library, as there is something that everybody can extract from this book.

Back to business, while diamonds are cut, polished, and processed in nearly thirty countries, India, Israel and Belgium have dominated the world diamond cutting and manufacturing industry. Other centres include the Northwestern Territories of Canada, China, and Thailand. African countries having diamond mines like South Africa, Botswana, Namibia, and Angola also joined. Because of its international competitiveness arising out of low-cost and skilled diamond processing, India has emerged as the world's

---

[14] अगनपंख, 'Wings of Fire'

leading diamond cutting and polishing center, accounting for 92 per cent share in terms of pieces in global production.

I invited my entire team, now three generations working together, for a daylong vision meeting. We drove to Daman, about 120 km south of Surat. For more than 400 years, Daman was a significant part of the Portuguese empire in India along with Diu, Goa and Dadra Nagar Haveli, the influence of which could still be observed here. The blissful atmosphere of this place was indeed refreshing. We shared our thoughts and articulated that future growth in diamond jewellery was likely to be largely driven by the cutting and polishing of medium and large stones, currently dominated by Belgium and Israel, with higher realizations.

A gradual shift in Indian exports to higher-value segments, reflected in higher per carat realization. Bulk buyers from the US and the European Union were increasingly buying Indian diamond-studded jewellery, because of its affordability. Trends in the US market were also expected to favour Indian exporters. The long-term outlook for the Indian gem and jewellery industry looked positive. However, we felt that India's competitive advantage centered on skilled labour had to be combined with a ready adoption of leading-edge technology.

President Kalam came to Surat on 15 October 2003 on the invitation of Acharya Mahapragya, the Jain seer camping in the city then. It was Dr Kalam's seventy-second birthday. I stood at Terapanth Bhavan in the City Light Area with a bunch of flowers to greet him. There was no interaction, but a divine connect was made. The spiritual energy shared in the simple act of seeing and being seen has the tremendous power to transform lives. A great soul is always giving Darshan to help people in their evolution, changes patterns in their life by cleaning up areas of their subconscious mind.

By this time, we were seen as a major player in the Diamond industry. The De Beers group gave us sight holder's status. I sought this status in 2003, had been denied but got it ultimately. We were the authorised bulk purchasers of De Beers rough diamonds under a regular contract. Sight holders' sales happened in London. Rough diamonds would arrive there from De Beers' operations in Botswana, Namibia, South Africa, and Canada, after being sorted into more than 5,000 categories. De Beers hosts sales ten times a year, known as 'Sights' because, during the sales period, customers are able to inspect the rough diamonds offered to them before deciding what to buy. Sight holders operate from diamond centres around the world, including New York, Antwerp, Tel Aviv, Mumbai, South Africa, and Hong Kong.

India is making nine out of every ten polished diamonds in the world and eight are done in Surat. The remaining gems are processed in the hubs like Navsari, Amreli, Visnagar, Bhavnagar and Ahmadabad. There are almost 4,000 cutting and polishing enterprises in Surat, employing 700,000 people. We are one of the leading manufacturers of diamonds in India.

Having worked at all tiers, it was time to position SRK from where it could position itself into the global orbit. Sevantibhai Shah gave me a Guru Mantra in my early years in the industry. He said, 'Govindbhai, others may copy your systems, but they cannot copy your heart, put your heart in your work, it would make it difficult to compete with you.' I never drifted away from his advice. He also advised me to refrain from taking financial debt of any kind.

Sometime during July 2003, the President of Surat Diamond Association, Nanubhai Vanani put up an idea of moving up in the diamond value chain by establishing a Jewellery Park in Surat. Convinced by his thought, Sevantibhai Shah, Chandrakantbhai Sanghavi, Parag Shah, Pravin Nanavati, Devshibhai Bhadiyadra, Dinesh Navadiya, Chunibhai Gajera, Mavjibhai Mavani, Nanubhai Vanani and I met Narendrabhai Modi and his Chief Secretary P. K. Laheriat Hotel Gateway in Surat on 30 September 2003. The idea of setting up India's largest jewellery park, measuring 20,00,000 square meters, was well received by them. The initial offer of Rs 600 per square meter with discount of 50 per cent was put to us. Not happy with the price of Rs 300, and unsure whether Government will heed to our request of lowering the price of land, we parted with a promise to meet again. Late in the night, Nanubhai received a call from P. K. Laheri asking us to join him for breakfast at circuit house at 8.00 a.m. to sign the MoU. The clause of price was kept open. The government knew about the firmness of our intent of establishing a world-class Jewellery Park in Surat, and we put our trust in the government's intent not to overcharge us for the land.

Few months passed by without any further progress. On 9 February 2004, Shree Chandrakantbhai Sanghavi, Shree Jivrajbhai Surani, Shree Nanubhai Vanani and I went to Ahmadabad and met Industries Minister Shree Anil Patel, Energy Minister Shree Saurabh Patel along with Chief Secretary Shree P. K. Laheri. Principal Secretary Industries Shree Raj Gopal, Industries Commissioner Shree Arvind Agrawal, and Managing Director Gujarat Industrial Development Corporation (GIDC) Shree Haribhai Patel were also present. Respecting our discomfort with Rs 300 per square meter price, the Government lowered it to Rs 225. I spontaneously uttered, 'What a clean deal it is involving no red tape tactics. No one can stop the progress of the state with such a visionary at its helm.'

The swift and firm decision that was followed by action had become the hallmark of Gujarat administration. On the foundation-laying day, 20 December 2004 of Gujarat Hira Bourse (GHB), Chairman of Gem Jewellery Export Promotion Council (GJEPC) Shree Bakul Mehta came to Surat to express gratitude to Shree Narendrabhai. Shree Chandrakant Sanghavi took over as the first Chairman of GHB. Shree Navinbhai Mehta and I joined as the Vice-Chairmen with Shree Nanubhai Vanani as the Secretary. In good faith GHB would later return 10,00,000 square meters of land to Government without any premium. GIDC would set up Textile Park on that land additionally benefitting the people of Surat.

I was honoured on 7 November 2015 as I visited Prime Minister Modi at PMO.

I attended Independence Day on 15 August 2018 'with the President of India at Home' with my wife.

Sweet memory of meeting with President Pranab Mukherjee along with then-Union Minister Mansukhbhai Mandaviya at Rashtrapati Bhavan on 22 March 2017.

Missile-Man and President Dr APJ Abdul Kalam visited SRK on 8 August 2013. He was impressed with utilization of technology in diamond processing and with our social commitment.

On 19 June 2016 with Border Security Forces (BSF) at Indo-Pak border on Nadabet, Union Minister Rajnath Singh felicitated me with his own garland expressing gratitude on behalf of our brave soldiers. Minister of State Haribhai Chaudhari also remained present.

With the then BJP President Amit Shah at his residence on 7 November 2015 in Delhi.

With my close friend Mansukhbhai Mandaviya, Minister of Health and Family Welfare of India.

At Umiya Mandir, Unjha in North Gujarat 'Laksha Chandi Yagna' with Ministers Shree Parshottam Rupala, Shree Bhupendrasinh Chudasama, and Shree Saurabhbhai Patel on 18 December 2019.

Well-regarded as 'Veer Bala', Chief Minister Anandiben Patel is a role model for millions of young girls in Gujarat. I joined her in a business delegation to Beijing in 2015.

Chief Minister Vijaybhai Rupani brought in a new style of leadership based on partnership. During his visit to SRK in 2016 with his spouse Smt. Anjaliben and Shree Mansukhbhai Mandaviya.

I was very close to Shree Keshubhai Patel, the tallest Patidar leader in Gujarat.

I had a great rapport with Shree Dalsukhbhai Godhani, leader of the Opposition in the Gujarat Assembly in 1980.

In October 2000, I received the 'Best Businessperson' Award by The Southern Gujarat Chamber of Commerce and Industries (SGCCI) from then Union Home Minister Shree Lal Krishna Advani.

I met President Bill Clinton at the U.S. Green Building Council's meeting where I received an award in Boston in November 2017.

Saint Shree Ramchandra Dongreji Maharaj, a renowned narrator of the Shrimad Bhagwat made me feel the divine essence inside the human body. But for his presence in my formative years, I would never become what I have become.

Revered Saint Shree Morari Bapu and I come from the same land in Saurashtra. On a 'lamp lighting' ceremony on the first day of Ram Katha, 'Manas RamKrishna Hari' organised by SRK in 2015. With him is Shree Rameshbhai Oza.

Revered Saint Shree Morari Bapu and I come from the same land in Saurashtra. On a 'lamp lighting' ceremony on the first day of Ram Katha, 'Manas RamKrishna Hari' organised by SRK in 2015.

SRK organised 'Shree Ramkrishna Bhagwat Pravaah' Katha by Bhaishree Rameshbhai Oza in January 2020.

Bhaishree Rameshbhai Oza lead by camaraderie, visited my residence in January 2020.

Swami Chidanand Saraswati is instrumental in taking live 'Ganga Arti' across the globe using technology. This picture is taken in January 2020 during his visit to Surat.

Baba Ramdev has been a great friend and spiritual benefactor to our family since 1990. I visited his Ashram at Haridwar on 31 October 2016 with family.

I have been a part of the mission of Saint Shree Swami Sachchidanand Maharaj having Ashram at Dantali in Gujarat.

On the first day of year 2015, HH Dalai Lama was conferred with Santokbaa Award

On 9 October 2019 we met Shree Sadguru Jaggi Vasudev at his Isha Foundation towards plantation of 42 lakh trees on advice of Shri Kirankumar of ISRO.

I interacted with Sri Sri Ravishankar, Indian spiritual leader on Transcendental Meditation on 13 February 2007 during his visit to Surat.

In 1989 Shree Pramukh Swami Maharaj, spiritual head of Shree BAPS Swaminarayan Sanstha visited our residence at Panchratna, Mumbai.

Had a meeting with Indian lifestyle coach, motivational speaker, and engineer, Shree Gaur Gopal Das, 22 January 2021, at ISKON Mandir, Girgaon Chopati Mumbai.

Daily Satsang at Shree Indravadanbhai's place between 1982 and 1994 helped me profoundly. This picture taken on 10 February 2015, shows Shree Indravadanbhai in the corner and mutual friend Manjibhai Navdawala in the centre.

Shree Atmendraji has been my 'Light House' whenever I ventured out in the unknown waters. This picture is from our visit to his Ashram on 10 April 2006 at Mysore.

While traveling with P. P. Swami to one village at Dang in August 2017 we found an ancient looking idol of Hanuman lying deserted under a tree. We decided to construct 300 temples with place for social gathering.

Nagaland's first 'Sibrai (Shiv) Temple' was inaugurated at Dhansiripar near Dimapur on 17 June 2019 by Shri P B Acharya, Governor of Nagaland with the idol we provided.

Shweta was married on 16 January 2005 in Surat to Piyush, son of Popatbhai Kevadia of Bhavnagar and my acquaintance for twenty years. Bhavnagar stands second in the diamond cutting and polishing industry after Surat, with 1,000 units operating from the district and employing more than 1,00,000 people. Some of them made big in ship-breaking work. The Alang ship-breaking yard at Bhavnagar is the biggest in the world, recycling about 50 per cent of the salvaged ships of the world. Of course, Bhavnagar is the major salt-producing districts in the state. British used salt for their profits. It was only after independence that salt making became an industry. Now, (in 2021) India is the third-largest producer of salt in the world after China and the United States and exports it to Japan and countries in the Indo-China region. It was a great pleasure to host these highly successful businesspersons. Piyush was running Unique Gems, engaged in the manufacturing and trading of cut and polished diamonds (CPDs). Baraat[15] came to Surat and stayed for two days.

A tragedy struck us on 28 March 2006. Popatbhai Kevadia was driving alone his Opel car from Surat to Bhavnagar. After completing the entire journey, while he was entering Bhavnagar, his car was hit by a public transport bus. The passersby pulled him out of the smashed car and rushed him to the hospital. This incident confirmed my belief that the unseen forces are acting upon all of us. Since the morning that day, Popatbhai's wife, Vasantaben was having anxiety attacks. She called many times Popatbhai and my daughter Shweta, living in Mumbai, about their well-being. Her other son Dilipbhai pacified her fears and went to work, however. Still anxious, she decided to go to Swaminarayan Mandir and sat there in prayer. When the accident happened, it was as if she already knew about it.

Vasantaben's intense prayers indeed saved Popatbhai's life but he entered into a coma. The family came under tremendous stress. The

---

[15] बारात,groom side procession in Indian wedding

family showed exemplary courage. Popatbhai's parents, as if doing a penance, used to sit by the side of their son throughout the night, taking six-hour turns between them. However, Popatbhai would not know and feel when his wife Vasantaben would make him sit on a wheelchair and take him around the housing society. Later they sold off their bungalow in Bhavnagar and started living in Surat.

I do not know what it is like to be in coma. I cannot even say that I know what it is like to be sleeping. If there are no dreams during my sleep, then I presume the sleep would be like a coma. We might say of such a life that it is not like being anything. The family was protecting Popatbhai's empty life on the assumption that come the morning its normal functions will be restored. I visited them on every important day and sat by the side of Popatbhai as if talking to him.

To mark the seventy-fifth anniversary re-enactment of the Dandi March, on 14 August 2005 we organized a Gandhiji Antevasi Sammelan to felicitate persons who worked closely with Gandhiji at Surat's Sardar Patel Auditorium. People, including women and children, turned up in large numbers to meet Shree Narayanbhai Desai, Shree Chunibhai Vaidya, Shree Jayant Pandya, Smt. Nilamben Parikh, Smt. Dashriben, Shree Ghelubhai Nayak and Shree Parbhubhai Patel. What was fascinating for me was that even after Gandhiji's death, some of his ideas were taken much further by the people. This means you need not relate to the historical Gandhi but try to experiment in many ways to explore changes without wearing Khadi, and yet be successful.

Two Gandhian principles I imbibed were Truth and Peace. People say that being in business makes it challenging to talk the truth. However, the kind of person I am, I always want to find the underlying cause of an issue—be it social, personal, or political. It was indeed difficult, but I continue to be the way I am. I did not look for short-term gains but over time, I held peace talks with warring people and eventually settled issues amicably. I continue to stick to these principles, which makes me what I am now. These ideologies can be passed on to our next generation who can also learn how to become better citizens of the country.

I visited China in September 2005, as part of the delegation of Gem Jewellery Export Promotion Council (GJEPC), India's apex body supported by the Ministry of commerce and industry. Nareshbhai Mehta of Chennai led the delegation that included Vishal Bhansali, Ravibhai and C. V. Ravindranath from the diamond industry. We visited Shenzhen, Panyu and Shanghai in China and Hong Kong. The visit gave us tremendous information on the market, trends, consumption, retailing pattern in China. Visiting the Shenzhen and Hong Kong fair gave an extremely comprehensive view of the delegation.

The most important accomplishment of the trip was observing the factory setups particularly in cubic zirconia (CZ) synthetic stones industry at Wuzhou. Wuzhou is a prefecture-level city having 1,00,000 people working in CZ cutting and polishing out of the total population of 7,00,000. The new-age machinery and equipment, the advantage of the disciplined labour and the very high productivity levels of labour were a revelation.

I was fascinated by seeing hundreds of thirty-two-seater buses being used for transportation. At each bus station, a bus would carry passengers from point A to point B with the frequency of every two minutes. I wrote to Dr Kanubhai Mavani, the Mayor of Surat, to introduce such a transportation system in Surat, which was practically devoid of any public connectivity. Kanubhai has been a self-made man of grit and determination. While working as a diamond cutter, he had acquired BAMS degree and practiced as an Ayurvedic Doctor. He also obtained degrees in Law and Journalism and rose to become the Vice-Chancellor of Saurashtra University, Rajkot, and Mayor of Surat. He took my idea to his heart and in 2007; Surat introduced city buses for mass transportation.

The Chinese have a fancy for coloured diamonds, unlike in India where colour-free diamonds are valued more. As goes the industry perception, 'A chemically pure and structurally perfect diamond has no hue, like a drop of pure water, and consequently, a higher value. The D-to-Z diamond colour-grading system measures the degree of colourlessness by comparing a stone under controlled lighting and precise viewing conditions to master-stones of established colour value. Many of these diamond colour distinctions are so subtle that they are invisible to the untrained eye; however, these distinctions make a very big difference in diamond quality and price.'[16] The scale starts with D as the absolute colourless, excluding letters A, B and C that had been used earlier to designate colour in the diamonds.

Coloured diamonds have a noticeable body-colour when viewed in the face-up position. Brown and yellow are the most common colours in natural-coloured diamonds. Diamonds with natural pink, blue, orange, green, red, and violet body-colour are extremely rare. It is believed in diamond industry parlance that out of 100,000 diamonds, only a few will have the colour as colour diamonds are formed when just one speck of an atom that is not carbon gets trapped in the diamond.

The most affordable coloured diamonds have a brown, grey, or black colour. Attractive diamonds in these colours often sell for a few thousand dollars per carat. Yellow diamonds are next in rarity. Many people consider yellow diamonds to be the most beautiful yellow gem because of their brightness, fire, and exceptional lustre. Blue, green, and pink diamonds are much rarer than yellow diamonds. Another step up in rarity are orange, violet, and red diamonds. Those of finest colour and quality will sell for very high price per carat. Red diamonds are the rarest coloured diamond.[17]

---

[16] https://www.kasturidiamond.com/know-your-diamond. Last accessed on date to October 10, 2021.

[17] https://geology.com/diamond/coloured-diamonds/. Last accessed on date to October 10, 2021.

Interestingly, one of the all-time greatest sources of diamonds, and the source of many of the legendary coloured diamonds, are the diamond mines of the Golconda near Hyderabad. These mines were the source of many important coloured diamonds including 'the Nassak (43.8 carats, blue), Sancy (55.23 carats, yellow), Daria-i-Noor (182 carats, pink), Hope (67 carats, blue), Dresden Green (41 carats, green), Princie (34.65 carats, pink), Wittelsbach-Graff (31 carats, blue), Idol's Eye (70.21 carats, blue), Agra (31.41 carats, pink), and Noor-ul-Ain (60 carats, pink).'[18]

The world's largest faceted diamond is a yellowish-brown weighing 545.67 carats. Named Golden Jubilee, it was cut from a 755.5 carat piece of rough found at the Premier Mine in South Africa in 1986.[19] The famous Koh-I-Noor (Mount of Light) diamond, originally with the Kakatiya dynasty, present-day Warangal, and now on public display in the Jewel House at the Tower of London, is one of the oldest diamonds in the world and is believed to be more than 5000 years old. As the original 191 carats Koh-i-noor failed to impress viewers, it was ordered to be re-cut as a brilliant oval by Prince Albert, husband of Queen Victoria. The Koh-i-noor now weighs 105.6 carats. 'Brilliant-cut diamonds usually have fifty-seven facets, but the Koh-I-Noor has eight additional 'star' facets around the culet, making a total of sixty-five facets.'

Interestingly, the Koh-I-Noor diamond is said to carry a curse. Queen Victoria wore the Koh-i-noor not in her crown but as a brooch on her dress. After her death, the Koh-i-noor was set in the crown of her daughter-in-law, Queen Alexandra, the wife of Edward VII, at their coronation in 1902. 'He who owns this diamond will own the world; but will also know all its misfortunes. Only God or a woman can wear it with impunity,' is the widely spoken curse of the Koh-i-

---

[18] https://en.wikipedia.org/wiki/Golconda_diamonds. Last accessed on date to October 10, 2021.

[19] https://en.wikipedia.org/wiki/Golden_Jubilee_Diamond. Last accessed on date to October 10, 2021.

noor. Victoria therefore willed that a female Monarch should only wear Koh-i-noor. If the head of State was a male, his wife wears it.[20]

As I briefly mentioned earlier, the EKATI Diamond Mine discovery in Canada in 1998 led to thousands of prospectors travelling to Northern Canada. By 2006, three major mines were producing over 13 million carats of gem-quality diamonds per year. This placed Canada as the third-largest producer of diamonds in the world. The activity associated with the production of diamonds brought billions of dollars in commerce to the economy of Northern Canada.

Compared to roughs produced in other parts of the world, the diamonds produced from Canadian mines are very high quality that supported a high average price per carat. A small number of coloured diamonds are found in Canada. Occasional yellow diamonds are found at Diavik, located about 200 miles north of Yellowknife, Northwest Territories and about 120 miles south of the Arctic Circle, and a few rare pinks have been found at Victor, in the James Bay Lowlands of Northern Ontario, about 50 miles west of Attawapiskat. Although exploration for new deposits continues, the pace has dropped dramatically from the original boom.

On 9 October 2005, I was given the Suryapur Ratna Award by the Surat Municipal Corporation (SMC) along with Dr Nimesh Vashi, an environmentalist. I received the plaque from my old friend and Union Cabinet Minister for textiles in the Atal Bihari Vajpayee government, Kashiram Rana along with Rs 1,00,000 in the presence of Rajya Sabha Member Shree Pravin Naik, Mayor Snehlata Chauhan, Dy. Mayor Dhirubhai Savani, Municipal Commissioner Pankaj Joshi and other elites of Surat. Surat got prominence as a safe place to do business. First, the textile industry and then, the diamond cutting, and polishing industry brought immense wealth to

---

[20] https://www.thehindu.com/features/friday-review/Kohinoor-the-mountain-of-light/article14475983.ece. Last accessed on date to October 10, 2021.

the city. In fact, Surat has averaged 11.5 per cent annualized growth since 2001-02, which is the highest in the country. I returned the money making it Rs 7,50,000 to Surat Municipal Corporation as Corpus to organize an annual lecture series.

During 1999 a young Sadhu, Ramdev arrived in Surat. Quite early in his life, Ramdevji chose the path of celibacy and asceticism. He used to come frequently to our residence at Surat for meals. Since those days we have close family ties with him. He convened special ten days Yog Shibir at our farm for the benefit of my family. He invited me to join his newly formed Trust as one of its Trustees, which I gently declined, saying, 'Swamiji, our paths are different. I will not be able to do justice to the work.' He gave his signature smile and said nothing.

One day, I had the pleasant surprise of watching Ramdevji on TV. The millions of people now called him 'Baba Ramdev' conveying esteem, courtesy, or respect for him. The Aastha TV channel began featuring him in its morning yoga slot. Established in 2000, as a spiritual TV network, the Aastha Broadcasting Network Ltd. was established by Kolkata-based Santosh Kumar Jain and Prabhat Kumar Jain and listed on the Bombay Stock Exchange (BSE). Parbatbhai was especially happy to see his friend and he would attend his show every day. Many children also joined him. In Baba Ramdev, I could see a star was born. Soon, Aastha channel and Baba Ramdev were broadcasting yoga shows through its UK affiliate and in the USA. By 2006, it would be reaching 160 countries around the world. Besides yoga, Aastha channel featured spiritual discourses, socio-cultural ceremonies, and religious events, accompanied by meditation techniques and devotional music, and even astrology, crystal therapy and aromatherapy. India was really rocking!

On 30 October 2005, I took 500 members of SRK family to Haridwar in a chartered AC train to celebrate Diwali vacations. It was a novel idea and created both excitement and happiness. Around this time, Baba Ramdev finally launched his herbal medicine business he discussed with me in 1998, with his aide Balkrishna, born in Haridwar to Nepalese immigrant parents. In 1995, Baba Ramdev founded Divya Yoga Pharmacy in Haridwar, and in 2006, they founded Patanjali Ayurveda, a fast-moving consumer goods (FMCG) company involved in the manufacturing and trading of FMCG, herbal, and Ayurvedic products. Baba Ramdev did not hold a stake in Patanjali Ayurveda and Balkrishna owns 98.6 per cent of the company. However, Baba Ramdev became not only the face of the firm and endorsed its products to his followers across his yoga camps and television programmes.

Shreyans and his cousin brothers were completing their teens. One day, I was discussing with my nephews, Rahulbhai Dholakia and Jayantibhai Narola, how to ensure that these young scions of our business know the real world. I went through tough experiential learning, which was not possible for the next generation as they had been born and brought up amidst abundance, care, and conveniences. After deliberation of few days, we worked out a novel way of sending them to unknown cities for a month to live all by themselves. During mid-April to mid-May 2005, Shreyans and his other cousins, Akshay Dholakia, Nirav Narola, Brijesh Narola and Mitesh Bhatia went to Hyderabad, Bangalore, Jaipur, Indore, and Chandigarh respectively. No one else in a family was given any knowledge about their whereabouts. I gave each young man Rs 7,000. All returned with their stories.

Shreyans came back with interesting experiences from Hyderabad. He stayed in a dormitory where he was accused by fellow residents of stealing a mobile phone that was later found out by the hotel manager. They called him the 'Son of a Thief.' He was refused a job as a salesperson in a shoe showroom as the manager of the store thought him to be someone who had run away from home or a thief, though he was wearing Nike shoes worth thousands. Later, he worked as a cleaner in a hotel where he picked dishes and leftover non-vegetarian food, which he left after three days.

Shreyans shared with me the arrogance of the sons of the neo-rich. While he was working as a door-to-door salesman-selling encyclopedias and science-fact-books, he somehow convinced a guard of a bungalow to allow him to enter inside and sell the books. A young boy opened the door. Seeing a salesperson at the doorstep, he humiliated him and rudely asked Shreyans to go away. While coming out of the bungalow Shreyans saw a C-class Mercedes parked. He thought, 'O, boy! Your head is pumped up with a C-Class Mercedes while I have several E-Class cars in my house.'

Such lessons are not taught in university. Only life teaches them through situations and people. We must not unnecessarily protect our children in our bubbles but allow them to encounter life and learn. Later, I went to places where Shreyans had worked incognito. One woman selflessly took care of Shreyans. I employed her son at our Bombay office, and he flourished there as a diamond trader. This tradition of learning continues in our family.

Coming back to diamonds, a basket of technologies started arriving in the market, especially from Israel. Earlier in 1994, we acquired Laser Diamond Cutting machines from TLT, Antwerp. We had already bought a measuring machine from Sarine in 2001. Kantibhai Dharamsibhai Narola, popularly known as K. D. Bhai took charge of manufacturing operations. He was already managing human resources with a deft hand and started taking keen interest in the new technology arriving in the diamond cutting and polishing field.

Dhirajlal Kotadiya represented the Israeli company, Sarine Technology, in India. He revered me as his 'God Father' and considered me receptive to new ideas. Dhirubhai advised me to take a trial of new technology developed by Sarine and I found significant improvement in the quality of work we had been doing with the new machines. We ordered the first 100 machines of Sarine and became the first in the world to use the new machines.

At SRK in 2005, we installed a mapping and planning 'Helium' machine of Lexus Softmac, Surat. There was a talk in the market that soon 'X-Ray, Sonography machines' would arrive looking inside the diamond rough to plan a cut. In 2010, we bought Galaxy Machine from Sarine, an 'X-ray Machine' for diamonds that would detect any kind of fracture in a stone.

At that time, there was no sign of CRM (customer relationship management) system in the diamond industry, though it was practiced vigorously elsewhere in the market. The main reason for this impediment was a far more humane level of communication between the organization and the customer—internal and external. No outside system was able to capture it, even tangentially.

I told in our partners' meeting that good communication was always based on honesty, openness, trust, and respect. If all companies applied such an approach, this positive 'aura' would soon have an impact on society, resulting in a reduction of stress, uncertainty, and destructive conflict, in short: a better life for all and a healthy business too! In Mumbai, Rahulbhai and Shreyans made a great team envisioning expansion.

Together they analyzed that they had four customer cabins in their office and were attending not more than a dozen of them in a day. Out of curiosity, Shreyans asked a few of them why they spend so much time in examining a diamond. Besides lustre, they said inclusions would draw their attention. This made Shreyans consider making an automated system for grading a diamond based on what customers considered to be of value.

When Shreyans discussed this idea with me, I immediately concurred. The only caution I offered was that to not be confined only to 4C chart, which was an excellent guideline but did not fully explain what would catch a customer's interest. Once a diamond is graded, as truly as possible, its price must be fixed, irrespective to whether a customer takes it or not. As a seller, we must know what the right price for our product is. The aim should be that entire marketing process becomes transparent and measurable. Rahulbhai and Shreyans made this conviction of mine the cornerstone of their journey to develop our own grading and selling system that would become a billion-dollar online sale engine a decade later.

6

Human Gems

शतेषु जायते शूरः सहस्रेषु च पण्डितः ।
वक्ता शतसहस्रेषु दाता भवति वा न वा ॥

(व्याससृति, अध्याय 4, श्लोक 58)

One in hundred is born a hero.
One in thousand a scholar.
A good orator one in ten thousand,
but a generous giver may or may not be born.

(Vyasa Smriti, Chapter 4, Shloka 58)

The 2001 Census had revealed an overall drop in gender ratio from 928 to 883 in Gujarat over the past ten years. Gender imbalance in a society is like a creeping process. It occurs very slowly. It does not look like a serious problem for a long time but when it reaches a critical mass, the social order is disturbed, and it cannot be corrected easily. Gujarat was acutely suffering from this malice. How to prevent female foeticide and cultivate an attitude of equality amongst boys and girls? I sat with Mathurbhai Savani and Laljibhai Patel and after many hours of deliberation, identified it as an attitudinal problem. The solution to this problem lied in the awakening of the common person. Hence, we decided to club the hugely successful Water Conservation project with the 'Save the daughter' campaign and like Saurashtra Jaldhara evolved the Beti Bachao campaign. The program would be organized under the banner of Samasta Patidar Samaj.

The success of a campaign depends on invoking the people's emotional involvement with the campaign. We distributed two lakhs postcards to the representatives of more than 1500 schools of Surat. The girl students at these schools, aged 13 to 17, would write messages on the postcards and send them to different schools in other talukas.

Mathurbhai came up with another brilliant idea of adding Laddu with it and designed it as 'Beti Bachao Maha Laddu' program. The launch date of the program was fixed as the first day of 2006 well in advance. Thirty-five thousand volunteers contacted 2,52,000 families asking two simple questions: How many female children were there in the family? How many male children were there in the family? Of course, they also captured other details like education, livelihood, income status, social identity, and so on.

The volunteers collected a handful of grain, sugar, and a bottle of water from every family. From these collected items, a very big Laddu of 15000 Mann (a local unit of weight equal to 20 kg) was prepared. This Laddu was 35 feet high with a diameter of 65 feet, looking like a hill. It was kept at a place near Kamrej, a Satellite Town of Surat on National Highway 8 from Mumbai to Delhi. This Laddu entered the Limca Book of Records and was called the Beti Bachao Maha Laddu.

The volume of traffic that day was such that it became impossible to drive any vehicle on the 200 feet wide Surat—Kamrej road. People who wanted to attend the program were compelled to walk long distances to participate in the event. More than 12,00,000 people attended the program. Seven stages were prepared, each being big enough to accommodate more than 200 people. More than 1600 leading persons from all over the state and from across India turned up. Sachchidanand Swamiji was the main speaker at the event. He was the most revered living saint in the Patidar community. He performed the Arti and administered the oath: 'We will never let female foeticide take place in our family; we will cultivate an attitude of equality amongst boys and girls, and we will prevent others from committing the sin of female foeticide.' Former Chief Minister Keshubhai presided over the function.

This was for the first time in the world that such a huge program was organized against female foeticide. The Laddu was divided into small portions as Prasad[1] and was placed in thirty-five lakhs boxes, which were distributed in all the cities and villages of Gujarat. The emotional connect was palpable. As the food and water were collected from each family, everyone felt 'This is my program.'

The 2006 Surat flood occurred from 7-10 August 2006, affecting about 80 per cent of the city. The sudden release of a large amount of water into the Tapti River from the Ukai Dam caused the flood. The Government of Gujarat described the flood as a natural calamity, while certain reports described it as a manmade disaster. Surat, the industrial city, remained marooned three days after water from the raging Tapti River flooded it. The total loss to the city was estimated to be around US$ 2 billion. Though SRK Company and people suffered losses, we reconciled ourselves to help other, more agonised people. Renowned administrator and long-standing friend, Shree S. R. Rao came as Officer on Special Duty to control the situation. Another distinguished officer, Shree Guru Prasad Mahapatra also joined the recovery efforts. More than 50 JCBs were provided by the Saurashtra Jaldhara Trust and 8000 volunteers worked round the

---

[1] प्रसाद, Holy offering

clock. We were given 1000 trucks and eight mobile-tyre-puncture repair-vans went around fixing stranded vehicles. Clearing the muck off the Surat Municipal Corporation (SMC) land was a gigantic effort. Round-the-clock kitchen service was set up for the eight thousand volunteers.

Shree S. R. Rao reminded me of the work we had carried out at 'Welcome Clearty Club' (WCC). In the third week of August 2006, more than 800 'commandos' joined to wash the roads of the city with the support of the fire brigade for water. Along with Rao Saheb and Shree Guru Prasad Mohapatra, other officials, notably, SMC Commissioner Shree Pankaj Joshi, Shree Amarjeet Singh, Shree Ros Manju, Shree Raj Kumar, Shree Manisha Chanda, Shree Shekhar Vidhyarthi, and Shree Rahul Gupta, eight IAS officers, also joined our campaign. Shree S R Rao camped at Vidya Bharti School at Bhatar Road to oversee relief operations. Like the legendary phoenix, Surat resurrected itself showing once again its resilience character after the 1994 plague.

That year, between 24 and 30 October 2006, we decided to take 130 members of SRK family to Sri Lanka, during Diwali vacations. We flew Mumbai-Colombo. Though Sri Lanka is part of our collective consciousness due to Ramayana, somehow not many people go there, identifying it with Ravana. We were indeed surprised to see Colombo and Greater Colombo Resort Region, spread along Mount Lavinia, south to Negombo in the north. It was full of international tourists. There was no sign of the golden fort of Ravana. In fact, we found Sri Lanka a predominantly Buddhist country. Their link with India is more with King Ashoka,[2] whose children came and settled here, than for the Ramayan.

---

[2] Ashoka, last major emperor in the Mauryan dynasty of India. Following his successful but bloody conquest of the Kalinga country on the east coast, Ashoka renounced armed conquest and adopted a policy that he called 'conquest by dharma' (i.e., by principles of right life). His vigorous patronage of Buddhism during his reign (265–238 BCE) furthered the expansion of that religion throughout India.

On 21 December 2006, revered Shree Rameshbhai Oza inaugurated Bharat Cancer Hospital at Surat. In 2003, Mahendra Katargamwala, Rasikbhai Hansoti, Dr Bipin Desai, Sevantibhai Shah and I had met Chandrikaben, the Managing Trustee of Bharti Maiya Trust to discuss a proposal of Thakorbhai Saroliwala who was ready to give away his building for cancer hospital at Saroli Village near Surat. Later in this same hospital, Nirali Radiation Center would be set up in September 2009 with the aid of Shree Anil Naik of L&T, who had lost his four-year granddaughter to this disease. This cancer hospital is a great boon to people of Surat suffering from this dreaded disease.

I was very keen to institutionalize the memory of my mother. I consulted many people on this issue. If I started a school or hospital, it would be known in the city. If we created a University, maybe it would be known throughout the state. What is that which would spread my mother's name throughout the country and the world? Finally, we decided to constitute a Humanitarian Award in her name to 'honour the greatness of spirit and transformative leadership' by giving the award to those personalities who would positively impact society, permeated powerful values, and encouraged the youth into spreading compassion and competing ideologies. The award would celebrate selfless service and inspire others to follow their paths. Based on wide-ranging consultations, we decided to confer the first 'Santokbaa Humanitarian Award' for the year 2006 to Satya Narayan Gangaram 'Sam' Pitroda.

Pitrodaji had travelled to Chicago in 1964 to study electrical engineering. Born in Orissa in 1942 in a small village to Gujarati parents, since early childhood he had nurtured dreams of living in the exciting world of cities and faraway lands. After going to the USA and then succeeding there, he had experienced the agony of disconnection that those living away from their Indian families experienced in those times. The lack of availability of telephones in India meant he could not even talk to his parents during their illnesses. Moreover, when he would visit them, he would be mostly unable to contact his family in Chicago.

Until the 1980s, the Indian telephone network functioned on an electromechanical switch system. Telephones were a privilege of the rich. There were barely 2.5 million telephones in the country, and almost all of them belonged to businesspersons and government officials and leaders living in urban centers. The service was truly appalling. With no foreign exchange in the treasury to import digital switches from the US, Japan or Europe, the Indian government was helplessly looking for ways to modernize the nation's telecommunications.

Indigenisation was the answer. A Swadeshi[3] approach had worked wonders in aerospace, and it would do so in telecommunications. In 1984, Prime Minister Indira Gandhi invited Pitrodaji to return to India. She asked him to develop a digital switching system suited to the Indian network. Pitrodaji suggested establishing a Centre for Development of Telematics that would be called C-DOT. Prime Minister Gandhi was firm with her support. C-DOT was promptly registered as a non-profit society, funded by the government but enjoying complete autonomy. By this time, Pitrodaji was a naturalised US citizen. Nevertheless, he renounced his US citizenship and resumed his Indian nationality to work in the Indian government. There was no looking back. Pitrodaji extended digital telecommunications to every corner of the country, including his village in Orissa.

The Governor of Gujarat, Shree Nawal Kishore Sharmaji, awarded the first Santokbaa Humanitarian Award to Pitrodaji on 19 January 2007 in a function held in Sardar Smriti Bhavan on Varachha Road. A former speaker of the Rajasthan Assembly Governor Sharmaji called the work of Pitrodaji in transforming the Indian telecom system a long walk to freedom.

---

[3] स्वदेशी, indigenous

Pitrodaji said in his acceptance speech, 'In my personal advancement, technology gave me the tools to fight poverty, cut across caste and community barriers and bring pride in performance. Technology was helpful in not only generating personal wealth but also generating ideas and exploring new concepts related to products, services, markets, growth, developments, values, and work. Technology taught me a great deal of discipline, good interpersonal relations, teamwork, management and a systematic approach to problem-solving with a focus on clear objectives, measurable milestones and commitment to reach fruition.'

My training of diamonds was progressing well. By this time, I had all necessary practical knowledge of the Diamond business. I conceptualised the ideal workspace of a modern diamond cutting and polishing factory. We were doing well in business and the next generation had found their bearings. To give them the space they needed and seeing my ideal factory, I decided to create a new facility for the company. It would be a greenfield project, built from scratch. Once this idea was captured, we spent close to a year to research the top facilities of the world for reference. Shortly thereafter, for expansion, we decided to purchase eight textile factories, located on Vastadevadi Road in the Katargam area, a short distance from our present factory, but closed. This legal process lasted for about a year.

Later for a year we researched on world class and latest facilities for our factory. We knew our requirements and also the latest technology and materials that were readily available; we combined both of them and came up with the unique idea to build a one of its kind diamond factory in the industry and the world. People play an important role in any enterprise, especially if the vision is bigger than an individual is. I never allowed my ego any claim upon my vision and invited the best people to collaborate, even though most of them were younger than me. It is what you know, and what you can do, that matters and not your age and your inheritance

My young friend Parag Shah, the Chairman of diamond company K. Girdharlal & Co., is a thinker and the visionary. I asked him for ideas on our factory. He has established International Board school in Surat. He created 'Fountainhead School' jointly with Vardan Kabra, an IIM-A alumnus and introduced Snehal Shah to me. We engaged Snehal Shah of Ess Team Design Services LLP as an architect, to design the factory. He specialized in the design of diamond factories in India. They were supported by Pankaj Dharkar Associates, Ahmedabad for HVAC, Apoorva Parikh, Ahmedabad for Electrical and Aqua Design Consultants, Ahmedabad for Plumbing design and execution. Rajesh Makwana, son of my friend, Shree Jayant Makwana who built my bungalow in 1984, now an Interior Designer, acted as a key support during the entire tenure of the project. Another person introduced to me by Parag Shah was Chartered Accountant Nirav Jogani, a partner at Suresh Surana & Associates. Brilliant Nirav Jogani is acting as our financial advisor and is a ready reckoner for any fiscal matters. Thus, with the guidance and cooperation of all the experts, the dream of our new factory building 'SRK Empire' began to come true.

It was during this time that Tanishq, the first and the most famous jewellery brand of India, approached us. It is a division of Titan, promoted by the Tata Group in collaboration with the Tamil Nadu Industrial Development Corporation (TIDCO) to make watches in India. The idea of a jewellery company sprouted out regulatory necessity in the mind of Xerxes Desai, an old Tata hat and the first managing director of Titan. Watches and jewellery businesses indeed go together in Switzerland. As goes the history, 'By the end of the 1980s, the Titan Company launched Tanishq to earn its own foreign exchange to buy quartz for the watches, focused largely on exports of jewellery as no one would ever buy watches made in India. But after the liberalization of 1991, when the exchange issue was fixed, Titan decided to use the brand in the

Indian market. The first production plant launched in August 1992, and Tanishq's first store opened in 1996 in Bangalore.[4]

When a meeting was set up with Bhaskar Bhat, the next managing director handpicked by Xerxes Desai, the first question I asked him was the meaning of Tanishq. Bhaskar's face beamed up with a glow of reverence. He said this name was the creation of his guru, Desai Sir. He joined the two Sanskrit words Tan (body) and Nishk (gold ornament), a name synonymous to superior artisans or absolute design. Very subtly, their parent company, Tata also was reflected, for those who are good in reading between the lines. I liked both the man and the answer he gave.

Brilliant people surrounded Bhaskar. The whole Tanishq team was like a proverbial Naulakha-Haar.[5] I met C. K. Venkataraman, who studied at IIM-Ahmedabad, Ajoy Chawla, who studied at IIM-Calcutta, Sandeep Kulhalli, who studied at Symbiosis Institute of Management Studies, a multi-faceted executive L. R. Natarajan, Sanjay Ranawade, and young Revathi Kant a bundle of creative energy. The first thing Bhaskar told us was that 5-6 per cent loss of gold was unacceptable to them. Could we bring it down to 1 per cent? It was a challenge no one would take in those times. However, I told my grandnephew, Nirav Narola, son of Dineshbhai Narola that it was the opportunity of a lifetime to meet these great people and associate our names with the Tatas. 'I am nothing, but I can do anything'—both the lock and the key are in the mind.

There were many grounds for me to say so. Let me narrate one experience here. When Nirav was ten-year-old, he was playing with a top. Suddenly, the pointed metal edge of the top pierced through his left eye, damaging the cornea. At the hospital of the best eye specialist in Surat, Dr Upendra Kligar, other two eye specialists Dr Suresh Sonani and Dr Arvind Chitale joined, but they all expressed

---

[4] https://en.wikipedia.org/wiki/Tanishq. Last accessed on date to October 10, 2021.
[5] नौलखा हार, high priced necklace

their helplessness. They said that Nirav's eye is completely damaged. It was clear to me that treatment was not available anywhere to undo this damage. I asked them, 'what if we take him to USA?' They said take him anywhere, but the result would be null. I knew the consequences. I told doctors not to remove his damaged eye from the socket, it will be impossible to bear for the family. One month after the incident, to the satisfaction of his grandmother and my sister, Shantaben, I took Nirav to Ahmedabad to consult Dr P. N. Nagpal. He said no medicine would work on him. Shantaben said, 'Now, my God will restore his vision. Let God do his work.' To the utter surprise of everybody, including the medical fraternity, after three years Nirav got 85 per cent of his vision back. He now commands our jewellery unit in Mumbai.

Coming back to our tryst with Tanishq, our team was made of brilliant artisans, but they had no idea of quality as a process. The Tanishq team gave our people the example of a single-line necklace. As any imperfect joint out of hundreds in the chain will create a torque, it is natural that the chain is twisted. The example and the message were absorbed well and a mutually value addition enterprise was created that would give the 'Illusion Setting' technique of putting a diamond with a gold ring patterned so that it mimicked the facets of the diamond to make it appear bigger. With their advice, suggestions, and guidance, we moved on and gained skills. And to this day, our business relationship has continued to grow.

With other members of the diamond industry, I contributed towards the R. B. Shah Super Specialty Hospital as an extension of the Mahavir Cardiac Hospital. Chief Minister Narendrabhai and Health Minister Jay Narayan Vyas came for the inauguration on 23 March 2008. While on the stage, I used this opportunity to brief our Chief Minister about the need of an outer ring road in Surat. For more than a million people living in Udhna and Varachha areas, the only way to be connected was a road via the railway station, which would choke every traffic junction along the way. A new ring road would ease the traffic and reduce the ordeal to people. Somehow, Narendrabhai appeared convinced.

I had been an admirer of Sachchidanand Swamiji, a profound thinker and spiritual teacher, living an ascetic life. Born in North Gujarat, he left his home at the age of twenty-one seeking moksha. Wandering on foot, walking along the railway tracks for thousands of miles; he reached Varanasi, studied Sanskrit for seven years there, and earned the degree of 'Vedantacharya' (equivalent to a PhD) from Banaras University. From there, he travelled to Belur Math and stayed there for a while but did not join the Ramkrishna order. He stayed in Vrindavan for few years and finally returned to Gujarat after forty years. He lives in Dantali, close to the birthplace of Sardar Vallabhbhai Patel. Swamiji is a master orator. His language is simple though it lashes at the hypocrisy of society. It penetrates the hearts of every class and creed of society. He has written more than 140 books and is awarded by the Gujarat Sahitya Academy and Gujarat Sahitya Parishad. I saw him as a revolutionary saint.

In May 2008, I joined Sachchidanand Swami on a twenty-day tour of Eastern Europe covering seven countries. There were forty persons, ten were from Surat, twenty from other parts of Gujarat, while ten from USA joined us in Athens. This tour was not for enjoyment; rather, the purpose of the tour was to explore the historic significance of this part of the world. History of people who lived thousands of years ago was explored. Recent history of World War II and the bifurcation of East and West Germany was introduced to us. We studied circumstances in which the world's largest genocide was carried out by Hitler. Jews were brought in thousands of trains to various concentration camps killing millions of them. We were aghast listening to these stories of annihilation.

Swamiji told me that Moksha is not as easy as it appears. The two biggest snares of physicality are attraction towards women and money. Though Swamiji quit both, he did not feel liberated. He does not want salvation. Swamiji said Goswami Tulsidas was indeed very wise in praying to Lord Shree Ram in the final verses of Ramcharit Manas, never leave his heart, just as the desire for women and money never leaves the heart of a man.

कामिहि नारि पिआरि जिमि लोभिहि प्रिय जिमि दाम ।
तिमि रघुनाथ निरंतर प्रिय लागहु मोहि राम ॥

(श्रीरामचरितमानस, उत्तरकांड, दोहा 130 ख)

May You be ever so dear to me, Ram, as woman is dear to a lustful man, and as lucre is dear to the greedy, O Lord of the Raghus.

(Shree Ramcharitmanas, Uttarkand, Doha 130 kh)

What I learned from Sachchidanand Swamiji was that very few beings seek knowledge in this world. Most people take the conditions of their lives as they are. Very few people indeed ask questions. Even fewer people seek answers and rarely do people venture out to get them. Why is it so? Because status quo is like an addiction. People are afraid of changing it. They stick to familiarity; however unpleasant it may be. Asking questions is like opening the window of a closed room. Sometimes a whirlwind may enter, blowing away everything. We were indeed doing that. At Turkey airport, Swamiji gave us a parting gift. He said, 'God is an unforeseen power which runs the world around us. We may only propose, let Him do the next.'

On 15 August 2008, Chief Minister Narendrabhai inaugurated the swanky new building of Shree Ramkrishna Institute of Computer Education and Applied Sciences at the Sarvajanik Education Society. About 20 years back when we got involved, only one course named B.Sc. Computer Science could be started. We started new courses by utilizing space of an adjacent college managed by the same management but for providing postgraduate courses, namely M.Sc. Microbiology and M.Sc. Biotechnology, we required a new

building and equipments. Therefore, a completely new three-storey
building was constructed and equipped fully.

In September 2008, I, accompanied by Mathurbhai and
other members of Beti Bachao movement met Surat Municipal
Commissioner Ku. S. Aparnaji, along with Vice-Chancellor of
Veer Narmad South Gujarat University, President of Chamber of
Commerce and District Education Officer at Saurashtra Samaj Hall
at Varachha Road. Mathurbhai Savani explained how the people of
Saurashtra staying in the Varachha area had organized a programme
against female foeticide two years ago, and it was time to rekindle
the spirit. It was decided to organize a Yatra on the Beti Bachao
Abhiyan from Surat to the Somnath Temple immediately after
Diwali on 28 October.

The rally began on October 31, 2008, at Surat such that it would
end on 5 November 2008 at Somnath, covering 226 talukas between
the two centers. Water collected from the different talukas would
then be handed over to the priest of the Somnath Temple. A bottle
containing this water would be sent to the then President of India,
Smt. Pratibha Patil. The route of the rally included Ankleshwar,
Vadodara, Ahmedabad, Mahesana, Unja, Surendranagar, Rajkot and
Junagadh. Over 300 cars turned up flashing banners of Beti Bachao
Abhiyan. More than 1200 leading citizens belonging to different
sections of society joined the rally. Chief Minister Narendrabhai
Modi came to Surat to flag off the rally. He declared, 'Gujarat state
will have a balanced male-female birth ratio by its golden jubilee
year in 2010.' Narendrabhai added, 'Daughters are the pride of our
country and the glory of our society. It is wrong to believe that only
sons will take care of you in old age. There are instances where sons
have spoiled the dreams of their parents and daughters have nursed
their aged parents.' He joined the rally again in Ahmedabad.

Twelve programmes were held on the way. Two luminaries of
our times, Swami Sachchidanandji and Rameshbhai Oza, both born
in Saurashtra, graced many of these meetings attended by lakhs of

people and invoked the spirit of removing the evil social practice of female foeticide.

We, as businesspersons, do a lot of planning, discuss many aspects, take risks at times, hedge them on other occasions, and yet most unexpected things can happen wiping out all our plans as a tide takes away sandcastles made by children on the beach. On 15 September 2008 Lehman Brothers, the fourth-largest investment bank in the United States, behind Goldman Sachs, Morgan Stanley, and Merrill Lynch, collapsed. The New York Times reported, 'After Lehman filed for bankruptcy, and great swaths of the markets froze, it looked as if many other major financial institutions would also collapse.'[6]

To me, two things were very clear. Firstly, self-regulation was a myth. Secondly, whenever the financial sector outpaces the manufacturing sector, such problems recur. It is very important that financial sector remains rooted in the real economic activities and people do not try to make money out of money itself. I saw it happening in Israel earlier when banks were loaning huge amounts for rough diamonds that had never been cut and polished into gems, but the loans were used to buy more roughs leading to a market crash.

Initially, India escaped the direct adverse impact of the upheaval, since its financial sector, particularly its banking, was very weakly integrated with global markets and practically unexposed to mortgage-backed securities. However, the Indian diamond industry was not so lucky. We in India, especially the business community know to live with doubt and uncertainty and without knowing everything. So much so that I have now come to believe that it is much more interesting to live not knowing than to have answers that might be wrong. After the Lehmann Brothers crisis died down

---

[6] https://www.newyorker.com/magazine/2018/09/17/the-real-cost-of-the-2008-financial-crisis. Last accessed on date to October 10, 2021.

and recovery started, businesspersons quickly forgot the lessons and took hefty loans. The problems of non-performing assets the Indian economy is now facing (in 2021) were all born in that period of false euphoria.

Behaviour that may be ideal for an individual, for example, saving more during adverse economic conditions, can be detrimental for the business if too many individuals pursue the same behaviour, as ultimately one person's consumption is another person's income. Too many consumers attempting to save simultaneously can cause or deepen a recession. The consumption in our major export markets, primarily the United States, dipped. As rightly analyzed by a business magazine, '. . . to compound matters, the price of diamonds plummeted, and the industry was left holding huge amounts of inventory that it simply could not sell.'[7]

A shining woman star of that time, Varda Shine, Managing Director, Diamond Trading Company (DTC), the parent company of De Beers, and that way the most powerful person in the global diamond fraternity, came to India. The Indian diamond industry planned a 'Meet and Greet with Varda Shine' event to figure out the way ahead in the global recession. It was scheduled for 28 November 2008 at the Emerald / Jade Room at the Taj Mahal hotel, Mumbai. I planned to meet her on the occasion and take her time to inaugurate SRK Empire building under good progress in the next year. On 26 November, she left the hotel for a dinner outside, just moments before terrorists besieged the hotel. And by the grace of God all the members of the DTC delegation survived, 'God's blessing.'

After November 2008, the situation in business started getting worse. The diamond market quivered a little. In the market, news spread that many people would now be let go; many factories would close; there would be the reduction in diamonds cutting and polishing

---

[7] http://solitaireinternational.com/images/1703104922covery_story.pdf. Last accessed on date to October 10, 2021.

as there would be less export; payments would not be received in time and there would be a money crisis in the market. Slowly, all these things started getting true. I was worried. How could I come out of this? I am a farmer's son. When there was a drought, what my father and ancestors did was known to me. When there is a crisis, then it is necessary to withdraw from action as a tortoise takes its limbs inside. What and how much to reconcile, I based on my native knowledge. I knew that I had to think differently. Herd mentality usually leads to disaster. When the roads are straight, everyone can accelerate, it is only while going on an uneven road that the real exam begins. At that time, I remembered the verse of the Gita,

तेषां सततयुक्तानां भजतां प्रीतिपूर्वकम् ।
ददामि बुद्धियोगं तं येन मामुपयान्ति ते ॥

(श्रीमद् भगवद् गीता, अध्याय 10, श्लोक 10)

To those whose minds are always united with me in loving devotion,
I give the divine knowledge by which they can attain me.

(Shreemad Bhagavad Gita, Chapter 10, Verse 10)

Mostly during bad times, we make decisions based on the rumours that are prevalent in the market. You do not see the market, but you see your business. Seeing the demand, increase or decrease the stock. I measured our stock. It was more. I talked with Rahulbhai who handled marketing in Mumbai and suggested an increase in sales. Before the recession aggregates, reduce the inventory. I suggested to sell our inventory for what prices we could get and book our losses. By Diwali time we sold off majority of our stock.

I wrote a letter to 6000 of my staff members. The letter was kept on the notice board. 'The coming days are not suitable for our industry. Remember one thing: we are going to take care of you.

However, you all also need to be alert. Use money wisely in Diwali. If there are plans to go on trips, cancel it. If you have plans to buy a new house or a land plot, even if you are getting at cheapest rates, right now do not purchase. Do not lend money to anyone, and do not borrow money too. Do not do unnecessary expenditures. Guard your savings. Do not worry unnecessarily. The time changes. The sun does not shine full day. There are evenings, and then there are nights too. This time, how long the night prolongs, is not sure. We do not want our lamps to extinguish, hence use the oil wisely.'

Diwali vacation got over in three weeks. The market was still down. The talks that the diamond industry will never stand back were widespread. The workers feared and started going back to their native places. Some owners also decided to wrap up their businesses. The atmosphere was getting tense day by day. Most of the companies in the industry removed 25 to 75 per cent of their employees. I was advised by my partners to remove 30 per cent of our staff. 'That means, 1800 people will have to be fired, is it?' I asked. 'Yes Govindkaka, that many must be fired.' I got the answer. 'We will not fire anyone; I have always hired. I have never fired anyone,' I said. We reduced the number of working hours from eight to six. Even if the workers would get lesser wages, their houses could be managed. It is better to give everyone a little less instead of taking away everything from one and giving to another.

In January 2009, while this put us all in the red, it freed us up to start buying rough again at new, 50% lower prices and sell the polished diamonds that came out of it at the correspondingly low prices, 70%, that prevailed then, taking our profit at 40%. It indeed not only saved the industry but also helped it grow. We were now able to buy and process the rough that other centres were not buying because they were still trying to unload old inventories in 2008's high prices. Demand also increased along with profit. 'Let the workers work now for twelve hours instead of eight hours.' I spoke. I wanted to recover the loss that was incurred to the workers and the company during the recession. The production rose 150 per cent. The profit also increased one and a half times. The company that was on 25th rank in 2007 rose to 5th rank in 2009 after the recession. We entered the top five club in the Indian diamond industry.

Back to business, post the global financial crisis, India grabbed the lion's share of the market and there seemed to be no stopping the Indian behemoth. Indians were willing to book their losses and move on. Nobody else had taken on the kind of business risk the Indians had. The Indian diamond industry demonstrated self-belief and we put our money down with our belief. Not just the Indian diamond industry, but also the entire Indian industry as a whole—garments, pharmaceuticals, software—came out much better because of some fundamental differences in the way Indians do business.

Indian businesspersons do not speculate as much as others do. We never really had a debt culture. If you look at most Indian enterprises, the debt-equity ratio is usually in favour of equity. That is how we have always done business in this country and that is our greatest heritage. This helped us stay steady in the storm because our roots were strong. We had never seen such an economic crisis as we saw in 2008, but most Indians did not close shop. They sought solutions instead.

The real mood lifter, however, was the introduction of fully indigenous and patented Inclusion & Value Based Diamond Planning Machine (M-Box Machine) in the market by Lexus Softmac of Mistry brothers. We had been perennially dependent on import and this situation was hurting like an old shoe for a growing child. The planning of a polished stone inside the rough diamond had been recently taken over by computerized machines. The size of the diamond (weight in carat), the cut was well analyzed by the machines, but purity judgment had been most complicated. This could make a drastic value jump in the profit. I visited Janakbhai Mistry and congratulated him and his team for this brilliant achievement. Janakbhai showed me his library and shared that he read for two hours every night for the last twenty years, whatever be the time before going to bed.

This was a matter of professional success, but for our social commitment, we have established the Santokbaa Humanitarian Award. We announced the Santokbaa Humanitarian Award for the year 2007 for Narayanbhai Desai, the renowned Gandhian thinker and propagator of 'Gandhi Katha.' Like all true Gandhians, Narayanbhai Desai was living a life of simplicity and dedication in his native village, Vedchi. He was the son of Mahadev Desai, Gandhiji's legendary personal secretary. The Mohan-Mahadev relationship was so special that after the latter's sudden death on 15 August 1942, during their imprisonment at Aga Khan Palace in Poona in the wake of the Quit India Movement, Gandhiji remarked 'The whole life of Mahadev was a poem of devotion . . . Remaining the disciple, Mahadev became my Guru.' As such, Gandhiji showered his love, affection, and attention on young Narayan, who spent his early years in Sabarmati and Sewagram ashrams.

Narayanbhai himself became a widely respected proponent of Gandhiji's life, philosophy, and mission through his performances of 'Gandhi Katha,' which were week-long discourses in Gujarati, Hindi and English, conducted in the traditional Bhagwat Katha style with music and songs. He rendered more than 100 such programmes in India and abroad. In the words of Gandhiji's grandson, Rajmohan Gandhi, 'No one can take you closer to Gandhi than 86-year-old Narayanbhai Desai. He lived longer with Gandhi than anyone else living today. He understood Gandhi better than anyone else has. He has an amazing memory. He has a gift for telling stories; he is a poet, too.' Narayanbhai wrote forty books, including 'My Life is My Message', an epic four-volume biography of Mahatma Gandhi.

Narayanbhai was also a close associate of Vinoba Bhave in the Bhoodan Movement, and of Jayaprakash Narayan in his Sampoorna Kranti campaign. He called his residence in Vedchi 'Sampoorna Kranti Vidyalaya,' where he experimented with Gandhiji's ideas about 'Nai-Talim.[8] When I went to meet Narayanbhai, he told me, 'Waking up before Gandhi in pre-dawn darkness, and going to sleep long after his Master, my father lived Gandhi's day thrice over—first in an attempt to anticipate it, next by spending it alongside Gandhi, and finally by recording it into his diary.' We presented the Santokbaa Humanitarian Award to the son of such a Gandhi-dedicated nationalist for spreading Gandhian ideology.

On the societal front, we announced the Santokbaa Humanitarian Awards for 2008. The award was to be given to Dr Verghese Kurien, the father of the 'Milk Revolution' in India, for his work towards the empowerment of marginal farmers and landless labourers by uniting them in a formidable dairy cooperative. The Milk Revolution greatly affected the lives of millions of people in Gujarat socially, politically, and most importantly, economically. I went to meet Dr Kurien at his home in Anand with Champa to the delight of Dr Kurien's wife Smt. Susan Molly Peter. The house was simple, functionally furnished, and devoid of any luxury. It was a true Gandhian way of living, without even saying so.

I was surprised at his child-like simplicity. The first question he asked me was whether I had seen the film, he had produced. I was taken aback. I had no idea what he was talking about. As if pitying my ignorance, he talked about Amul's movie, 'Manthan,' and how the farmers of GCMMF (the Gujarat Co-operative Milk Marketing Federation) were its producers. He went on about how he picked up 'The Taste of India' concept and put it out. 'Between these two themes—women empowerment Manthan theme and Taste of India—I made an excellent brand.' Dr Kurien said with pride. 'Did you know that Amul is the only brand that works on 15 per cent commission?' he asked me.

Dr Kurien made me feel so at ease that I completely forgot my mission of making him accept the Santokbaa Award. He had already

---

[8] नयी तालिम, Inclusive Training

received the Padma Shree (1965), the Padma Bhushan (1966), the Krishi Ratna Award (1986), the World Food prize (1989) and the Padma Vibhushan (1999) and my idea was not to honour him but honour the Santokbaa Award if he accepts to take it. But here he was telling me stories.

Finally, the moment came when I submitted my request and he so graciously accepted without hesitation. 'You are giving me an award in your mother's name. I don't know if I am a Manav Ratna, as many people call me so many names, but as the award is in the name of your mother, I will accept it.' Then he fell silent. After some time, Dr Kurien said, 'My mother was a highly educated woman as well an exceptional piano player. I am what I am because of her. You know, there is a story behind everything. How a picture got on a wall. How a scar got on your face. Sometimes the stories are simple, and sometimes they are hard and heartbreaking. However, behind all my stories is always my mother's story, because hers is where mine begins. When should I come to Surat?' Unfortunately, he could not attend the Award function because of his ill health, but his daughter Nirmala attended the same.

The 2009 Award went to Dr Hargovind Laxmishanker (H. L.) Trivedi, a legendary nephrologist, immunologist, transplant surgeon and stem cell researcher. Dr Trivedi pioneered kidney transplantation in India, a procedure done though surgery to replace a diseased kidney with a healthy kidney from a live or deceased donor. Dr Trivedi was a founding director of the Institute of Kidney Diseases & Research Centre and Institute of Transplantation Sciences in Ahmedabad. By that time (in 2008), his team had performed more than 5000 kidney transplantations out of about 20,000 transplants done in India. Dr Trivedi told me, 'The annual requirement for kidneys is around 2 lakhs with a mere 6,000 transplants occurring.' Dr Trivedi further told me, 'As of now, kidney transplant costs around Rs 10 lakhs in private hospitals of the country. And post-treatment, life-long monthly cost is around Rs 15,000.'

We organized a function on 28 December 2009 at Sardar Smriti Bhavan, Surat to confer awards on Narayanbhai Desai, Dr Kurien and Dr Trivedi for the years 2007, 2008 and 2009. I was indeed waiting for an opportunity to invite Morari Bapu and approached him if he could present the award. Morari Bapu accepted my invitation with loving grace. Born on 25 September 1946, which was the Shivaratri[9] day in Talgajarda village near Mahuva, Saurashtra, he was a child prodigy. He learnt Ramcharit Manas from his grandfather, Tribhovandas Hariyani, and started giving discourses from the age of 20, attracting large crowds. Morari Bapu says that it is his motive to make Ram Katha accessible to the neglected, exploited, and marginalized segments of society, just as Ram himself went to the Shabris, Nishads and Sugareevas of that time.

In the award function, Dr Kurien's daughter Nirmala came with her son, Siddhartha, to receive the award on his behalf. Renowned Gandhian, Maheshbhai Kothari also remained present for the event. Maheshbhai remained unmarried and dedicated his life to serving children having mental retardation[10] by creating an Ashram in Navsari. Dr Trivedi received the award with his wife, Dr Sunita.

Speaking at the award function, Morari Bapu mentioned his deep bond with Dongreji Maharaj and the historic importance of him bringing the Shreemad Bhagwat Katha out of private homes to the public forum, thereby generating powerful bhakti bhava amongst people. Morari Bapu said that the purpose of human life was to serve others and giving awards to these great benefactors of people made him feel blessed. He mentioned my devotion to Dongreji Maharaj and said jokingly that he wished he were my Guru-Bhai[11]. Morari Bapu elevated the award function to another level when he cited

---

[9] शिवरात्रि, a Hindu festival celebrated annually in honour of Lord Shiva

[10] A disorder characterized by cognitive delays, mostly in poor families where pregnant mothers do not receive proper nutrition

[11] गुरु-भाई, peers, studied with same teacher

from Ramcharit Manas, equating the awardees as human forms of God:

जब जब होइ धरम कै हानी ।
बाढहिं असुर अधम अभिमानी ॥
तब तब प्रभु धरि बिबिध सरीरा ।
हरहिं कृपानिधि सज्जन पीरा ॥

(श्रीरामचरितमानस, बालकांड, दोहा 121, चौपाई 6 और 8)

Whenever righteous gets a beating and wicked people flourish, God takes different forms to alleviate pain and sufferings of the poor and good people.

(Shree Ramcharitmanas, Balkand, Doha 121, Chaupai 6 and 8)

Shreyans got married on 29 November 2009 in Surat to Sweety, the daughter of Pathologist Dr Nagjibhai D. Jivani and Hansaben of Surat. Shreyans' wedding was celebrated at Dholakia Farm and since that day, families of all four brothers made this farm their permanent home. Chief Minister Narendrabhai Modi, former Chief Minister Keshubhai Patel and former Chief Minister Chimanbhai Patel's wife Urmilaben Patel attended their wedding. It was as if a galaxy of stars descended upon our house. A host of Ministers—Union Ministers Shree Kashiram Rana, Shree Vallabhbhai Kathiria, State Cabinet Ministers Smt. Anandiben Patel, Shree Nitinbhai Patel, Shree Ashokbhai Bhatt, Shree Bhupendrasinh Chudasama, Shree Parshottam Rupala, Shree Jay Narayan Vyas, Shree Saurabh Patel, Shree Mangubhai Patel, Shree Narottambhai Patel, Shree Gordhanbhai Zadafia, Smt. Jasuben Korat and Shree Becharbhai Bhadani, many Members of Parliament and more than fifty state legislators came. Prominent Congress leaders, Shree Shaktisinh Gohil, Shree Arjun Modhvadia, Shree Tushar Chaudhari, Shree

Madhubhai Bhuva, and Shree Raghavjibhai Patel also graced the occasion. I was deeply touched by seeing Shree Dalsukhbhai Godhani attending the wedding despite his advanced age and ill health.

My long-standing friends in the government, 42 in number, CBI Director Shree Ashwani Kumar, Director General of Gujarat Police, Shree P. C. Pandey, Shree Kuldeep Sharma, Shree R. M. S. Brar, Shree Chitranjan Singh, Shree G. C. Raigar, Shree V. M. Parghi, Shree T. S. Bisht, Shree Nityanand, Shree Harikrishna Patel, Former Chief Secretary, Shree P. K. Laheri, Shree P. V. Trivedi, Shree H. V. Patel, Shree P. R. Sompura, Shree Pankaj Joshi, Shree J. B. Vora, Shree J. B. Patel, Shree C. J. Patel, Shree R. J. Makadiya, Shree A. J. Shah, Shree S. Jagdishan and Shree S. Golakiya, among others, came somehow managing their schedules. The Hon'ble Justice Shree R. M. Chhaya of the High Court of Gujarat and District Court Judge Shree Jagdish Raiyani also attended. I am writing all these names as a mark of respect to these great souls who did not judge me as a person from the business community but as part of the society, trying to make things a little better for the people at the community level. The presence of these guests strengthened my belief in God as an ultimate planner and executioner, without His blessings nothing ever moves. My father, donning his Kathiawadi turban was pride-personified that day.

I missed my mother Santokbaa the most that day. In my eyes, a mother is Goddess, the greatest power in the universe. Both my sisters, Shantaben and Devkuwarben, read my emotions well. They both came near me and held my hands as if to proxy our mother. I felt at that moment that we all were basically the extension of our mother's story. It was from her story that our stories had begun.

A heart-wrenching experience was waiting for me. On 8 March 2010, I was at Prannath Hospital interacting with patients and attending to their little needs, as had been my routine. There I met Damyantiben Chaurasia[12] who had tried to commit suicide

---

[12] Name changed to protect her privacy

by consuming acid after an altercation with her family. She was staying with her husband; four children, brother-in-law, in astute poverty, and the hardship of never-ending house chores broke her mental balance. Her trachea and esophagus were almost burnt by acid. She was not able to gulp water. I could not even bear the sight of Damyantiben in severe pain. No one was offering help; the treatment would be very expensive. Untreated, she would die of infection and starvation. I thought no, this could not be the fate of this unfortunate woman. I sat with the doctors and planned the complex surgery committing to all the expenses. The surgery went off well and she responded well to the treatment. Several months later, she came to our relief center and said, 'Govind Kaka, you are like my father, never shall I be able to pay back this debt.' I told her, 'To be alive is such a gift, never think of harming it. We all live under the debt of being alive and it can only be returned by serving and helping others.'

I have a great friend in Purushottam Prakashdas Swami (P.P. Swami), a Sadhu in the Dangs. He had played a key role in the construction of the BAPS Swaminarayan Mandir in Surat but later left the organization and set up a trust called 'Pra-yo-sha Pratisthan' named so by taking up letters from the names of Pramukh Swami, Yogiji Maharaj and Shastriji Maharaj. He thus dedicated himself to working with the tribal for social development. P.P. Swami was instrumental in igniting the spirit of my nephew, Naresh Narola who later joined BAPS as Swami Adhyatma Swarup. P.P. Swami told me that serving people amidst them, like them, elevating their living conditions by providing medicines, food and education was not charity but a service. P.P. Swami was telling Dangis to no longer see or identify themselves solely as members of a tribe, but as citizens of a nation of one people working toward a common purpose.

Earlier in 2005, I had supported P.P. Swami in setting up a free-of-charge secondary and higher secondary school for tribal students with hostel facilities at Malegaon, five kms from Saputara in the name of my mother, Santokbaa. Today (in 2021) the school has around 500 students. So far, twenty students have gone for their medical studies and more than 125 students have passed various engineering degrees. Last year in 2019, one student cleared the IIT JEE Mains and was enrolled at IIT-Delhi, which is unprecedented for P.P. Swami's school. Another student of P.P. Swami recently completed his doctorate from Navsari Agricultural University. Thirty-one students have opted to take up teaching as their profession. Twice, in 2015-16 and in 2019-20, the school was adjudged as the best school in the district, winning Rs 1,00,000 in prize money on both occasions. P.P. Swami's students have also excelled in sports and other extracurricular activities earning, Rs 300,000 in award money in the year 2016-17 during Khel-Mahakumbh[13]. Inspired by this success, Keshavbhai Goti took up renovation of tribal student hostels in Dang District with the close support from P.P. Swami and people at large.

On 22 May 2011, 120 members of the SRK family went to Switzerland. We flew to Zürich from Mumbai. Zürich is amongst the world's largest financial centers despite having a relatively small population. We visited Interlaken, which is surrounded by the Alps but is not actually in the mountains. The town is situated in between two beautiful lakes. The street connecting both lakes is the main shopping street. We took a train to go to Jungfraujoch, Europe's highest train station. Even in the month of May, the temperature was just 5 degrees Celsius.

On 18 January 2013, Chief Minister Narendrabhai Modi inaugurated the closed-circuit television (CCTV) camera surveillance network—'Safe City Surat'—of the Surat police, a brainchild of the then Commissioner of Police, Shree Rakesh Asthana. In a first of its kind collaboration, citizens of Surat initiated a unique project under the guidance of Shree Rakesh Asthana. The interesting thing

---

[13] खेल-महाकुंभ, State level sports

about this project was the way Asthanaji mobilized funding for it. About a year back, he came to SRK, spent four hours, and explained to me his idea. I involved some 20 diamond businesspersons and we committed Rs 5 crores by each one individually putting Rs 25,00,000. Later, the textile industry and Hazira Port companies also joined, and contribution also was raised to Rs 25 lakhs—equally given by all involved, mobilizing Rs 75 crores for this first-ever project in India, equipped with the latest technology in the world.

Instead of forming a new entity, this project was carried out under 'Traffic Education Trust' formed earlier for the welfare of city Police and for supporting traffic police. The Trust hired a 'Traffic Brigade.' I acted as a Founder Trustee of this Trust with textile businessperson, ShreeJ. P. Agrawal as the first President, and social worker Geeta Shroff as the Secretary. Shree Laljibhai Patel and Shree Ashok Kanungo are acting as its current (in 2021) President and Secretary who spearheaded this project. The project was supported by local Municipal Corporation and Government of Gujarat, which included citywide high-definition cameras, world class command and control center. Local technocrats provided their support in identifying the technology and its subsequent implementation.

Inaugurating this unique public safety project based on public private partnership (PPP) model, Chief Minister Narendrabhai exuded faith that the project will show the path to the nation in establishing a reliable vigilance network for crime detection. Narendrabhai said, 'with people having criminal intent misusing the latest technology, the use of the same by police for the security of common people was a necessity'.[14] 'Gujarat police force is the youngest in India in average age. The state government's approach is to recruit IT-trained youths in all cadres of police from constable to

---

[14] https://www.narendramodi.in/te/shri-modi-inaugurates-cctv-surveillance-network-of-surat-police-5060. Last accessed on date to October 10, 2021.

Police Inspector' he said. There was an apparent reduction of crime in the city as compared to earlier years.

Later, I met Rakesh Asthana few more times and bothered him with my queries about how he could succeed in filing a charge sheet against Lalu Prasad Yadav in 1996 leading to his arrest in 1997 and conviction after a prolonged legal battle. Rakesh Asthana had also caught the Directorate General of Mines Safety taking bribes in Dhanbad. 'By that time, this was the first case of its kind in the whole country, when the officers of the Director-General had come under arrest.'[15] Of course, in Gujarat he was a hero who had settled the 26 July 2008 Ahmedabad bomb-blast case within twenty-two days. Rakesh Asthana had also brought Asharam Bapu and his son Narayan Sai to book.

Biju Pattnaik, a banker with a difference, is a close friend of more than 25 years who guided us during rough weather. Before joining Indus Ind Bank, he managed the Gems and Jewellery portfolio as the Head of Asia for the Royal Bank of Scotland (RBS). He also acted as the India Head of the erstwhile bank, ABN Amro. In the year 1999, we were yet to become 'sight holders' of De Beers. Roughs were not easily available because of severe restrictions imposed by De Beers on their members. I went for advice to Mr Biju Pattnaik in a meeting planned with him at Hotel Oberoi, Nariman Point, Mumbai. The meeting, which was initially supposed to be a very short meeting, lasted instead for four hours. A person with immense knowledge about the global diamond business, Mr Patnaik asked us not to panic. His philosophy of economy centered on liquidity and skills. He knew about the kind of skill possessed by SRK. He advised us to slow down which we did. To me, he was a ready reckoner. He had a resource to provide the reference of each diamond company across the world, including details of individuals owning a company.

---

[15] https://www.afternoonvoice.com/cbi-vs-cbi-not-a-game-of-caged-parrot.html. Last accessed on date to October 10, 2021.

His valuable support to SRK can never be matched. Today Indus Ind Bank has the highest exposure in diamond industry. During his tenure as banker, there had not been any NPA, an incredible record indeed!

The 2010 Santokbaa Award was given to Smt. Poornimaben Arvindbhai Pakvasa, popularly known as the Didi of the Dangs and the mother of the renowned classical dancer, Sonal Mansingh. To put things in perspective, 'the Dang District has part of a forest that includes Purna Wildlife Sanctuary, which is shared between the districts of Dang and Tapi in Gujarat and Nandurbar District in Maharashtra, and Vansda National Park in Navsari District, which shares a continuous tract of forest with Valsad District. With just 2 lakhs people living in this 2000 square km area, Dang is the least populous district of Gujarat.

Born in 1913, in Ranpur near Limbdi State, Saurashtra, Poornimaben first met Mahatma Gandhi at Ranpur as an 8-year-old child. It was an epiphanic moment that defined the rest of her life. Poornimaben participated in the Dandi March when she was 18-year-old and got arrested. She was jailed in Rajkot in the same prison cell where Kasturba Gandhi, Maniben Patel and Mridula Sarabhai were also incarcerated. Poornimaben spent her time teaching writing skills to Kasturba and other prison inmates. Over time, their relationship grew close and intimate. Poornimaben lost her mother when she was 16, she treated Kasturba like her mother and received from her the love, tenderness, and care that every daughter covets. Mahatma Gandhi was appreciative of this act and gave Poornimaben his blessings to continue the path of education.

Poornimaben participated in the fifty-first session of the Indian National Congress at Haripura in 1938. This session was significant because it was headed by Subhas Chandra Bose as president and threw open the differences between Gandhiji and Netaji. Poornimaben had married Arvind Pakvasa the same year; Poornimaben stepped into another very important political family. Her father-in-law Mangaldas Pakvasa was a close confidante of Gandhiji.

Poornimaben's passion for social issues brought her to centre stage again in 1954. For many years worked as the chief of a military school in Nashik bringing an incredible, incandescent energy to her work. Her commitment to a lifetime's struggle to improve the lives of tribal girls led to the establishment of the Ritambhara Vishwa Vidhyapith in the Saputara region of the Dang district of Gujarat in 1974. Poornimaben's work at Ritambhara had an unstoppable momentum. Poornimaben received the Padma Bhushan in 2004. When we approached her for Santokbaa Award, she lovingly exclaimed, 'Why not!'

The 2011 Santokbaa Award was given to legendary agriculture scientist Dr M. S. Swaminathan, aptly called 'Father of Green Revolution in India,' for his role in introducing and further developing high-yielding varieties of wheat in India. I travelled to Chennai with my team to seek his acceptance of the award. We met at the M. S. Swaminathan Research Foundation (MSSRF), a nonprofit NGO trust Dr Swaminathan created after receiving the World Food Prize in 1998 and using $2,00,000 that came along with the prize. Swaminathan Sir met us for a long time and personally took us around the Foundation.

He told us that the thought of starting an independent organization to develop his ideas came to him in 1970, when Nobel Laureate physicist, Dr C.V. Raman told him to start an autonomous research center to realize his goals of sustainable development, which he now termed as the 'Evergreen Revolution.' Swaminathan Sir said, 'Both business and governments work within the framework of their priorities and their approach is naturally compartmentalized, whereas the biggest problem of the farmers is the sustainability of agriculture that unfortunately is not captured by anyone and remain neglected.' Elaborating further he said, 'MSSRF operates in five major program areas—Coastal Systems Research, Biodiversity and

Biotechnology, Eco technology and Food security, Gender Equality and Development, and Informatics.' He gladly accepted the award after finding my hands rough enough as that of a farmer.

On June 17, 2013, Swami Sachchidanandji presented the Santokbaa Manav Ratna awards in a ceremony held at Sardar Smriti Bhavan. P.K. Laheri, Former Chief Secretary of Gujarat and Prof Anil Gupta, Director, Indian Institute of Management, Ahmedabad (IIMA) and Rakesh Asthana, Surat Commissioner of Police came to the function. Smt Induben Ghelubhai Nayak received an Award on behalf of Poornimaben, later I went to her along with Champa to give an Award in person at Ritambhara Vishwa Vidhyapith in the Saputara. Swaminathan Sir was a superstar anyway! He received a standing ovation for his grace and agility.

Dr Swaminathan in his speech further explained his idea of 'Evergreen Revolution.' Quoting from his earlier speech at the 55th Indian Science Congress held in Banaras Hindu University, Varanasi in 1968, Dr Swaminathan said, 'The rapid replacement of numerous locally-adapted varieties with one or two high-yielding strains in large contiguous areas would result in the spread of serious diseases capable of wiping out entire crops, as happened before the Irish potato famine of 1854 and the Bengal rice famine in 1942.

Therefore, the initiation of exploitive agriculture without a proper understanding of the various consequences of every one of the changes introduced into traditional agriculture, and without first building up a proper scientific and training base to sustain it, may only lead us, in the long run, into an era of agricultural disaster rather than one of agricultural prosperity.[16] He summed up his speech with a clear warning: 'If farm ecology and economics go wrong, nothing else will go right in agriculture; and if agriculture goes wrong, nothing else will have a chance to go right in our country.'

---

[16] https://frontline.thehindu.com/other/letters/letters/article4935247.ece.   Last accessed on November 26, 2020.

After the award ceremony, I requested Dr Swaminathan if I could have some quiet time with him. He graciously nodded and sat with me for close to an hour. Swaminathan Sir told me that his father, Dr M. K. Sambasivan, was a famous medical doctor. Unfortunately, he died in 1936 when Swaminathanji was very young. He had built a big hospital in Kumbakonam, in the Thanjavur district of Tamil Nadu. Everyone wanted him to become a doctor and manage his father's hospital but the famine of Bengal in 1942–1943 motivated him to study plant genetics and develop new varieties of crops and breeding. It was not very well received in his family, but he went to the agricultural college at Coimbatore. Swaminathan Sir told me, 'I am saying all this to you because I could see that you love your family so well. They were all present in the function brimming with joy. But when it comes to the higher purpose of life, you must go against even your family, as Gandhiji and many others have done.'

I asked Swaminathan Sir how he felt when people call him the father of the Indian Green Revolution. He said, 'Not very good.' As if enjoying my discomfort, he kept silent for few moments and then said, 'In those days, for the first time, the Government was buying crops at a reasonable price. Therefore, if you are a farmer, you want to get as much money as possible. Punjab farmers, who were producing 4 tons, wanted to produce 6 tons, so they had to put in more chemical fertilizers. Small farmers wanted to maximize their income. That is the problem of sustainable development—the balance between today and tomorrow; whatever you do today should not be at the cost of tomorrow's prospects. My green revolution became a greed revolution.'

The next day, we organized interactions with more than 1000 farmers at Ramkrishna Hall of Samasta Patidar Wadi. When Swaminathanji got down at the portico, he expressed his surprise at finding more than 400 cars parked at the venue. I told him all these cars belong to the farmers of South Gujarat. They can own cars thanks to the science that you gave them. Later, while seeing

Dr Swaminathan off, I told him, 'Sir, by coming here to receive an Award in my mother's name, you did a great honour to me.' He said, 'Govindbhai, Earth is the supreme mother of us all. Always remember she even gives you diamonds. Consider your wealth not as 'property' but as a 'blessing.' Just leave what is enough for your children and spend the rest of your wealth in improving the conditions of the poor. It will not hurt your children; in fact, it will make them stronger, and they will have even bigger business success than you.'

Shreyans was diving deeper into online business. He studied the Justdial[17] model and found out how they managed the feedback data. This led him to develop a unique CRM for diamond sales. Following the proverbial two roads diverging in the deep woods, he took the road less travelled. Anyone else in his place would have outsourced the work, but he was convinced that unless you put all your insights about the quality of the diamond and how it was valued in full view of the customer, you would never win his confidence and once you make the customer feel like a winner by making a good purchase using his own confidence, he would never leave you and go elsewhere to buy. Shreyans told me, 'Papa, I am taking a hard path. Do I have your blessings?' I told him, 'Brave people are born for battles. The only advice I can give you is to never go alone in the battlefield unarmed.' He took my advice to heart and organized more than 100 departmental meetings. Not to create interruptions in routine work, which itself was hectic and quite taxing, he started spending time after office hours for these meetings. The best part was no one complained. Somehow, everyone was convinced about what Shreyans was doing.

Together, these young people, Shreyans and his team, entered the customers' minds. Therefore, there is a G grade of colour. However,

---

[17] Founded in 1996 Justdial is a company that provides local search for different services in India over the phone, website and mobile apps.

what about G+ and G-, a little bit of, micro grading? Working with Java and MongoDB, a cross-platform document-oriented database program, they were indeed developing the world's first diamond enterprise resource planning (ERP) system.

One day, I watched Shreyans and K.D. Bhai in a deep discussion at the 'shop floor' in our factory. When I invited both to my cabin, they said that it was not a business discussion but a technical one and that they were fine where they were. Later in the evening, when I asked Shreyans at home what they had discussed, he surprised me by saying that 'Every work must have a proper name.' He further said that when a customer buys a diamond, he has many thoughts, he has many doubts, and he naturally wants to make the best deal for him without even knowing what is best for him. Shreyans was learning words from K. D. Bhai as food for our customer's thoughts and lamps to clear any doubts. I was indeed glad. However, just to put Shreyans to the test, I asked him, rather cunningly, so what word he learnt that day and he silenced me by telling me something that was new, even for an old hat like me. He told me that he had observed his customers holding a diamond in their hands and rotating it as if enjoying the light of the diamond. He had spoken with many of them and picked up two words from them—'fire' and 'brilliance.' So, he was learning from K.D. Bhai where this 'fire' and 'brilliance' in the diamond was and how was it played? 'And what did you learn?' I asked. 'As the internal reflection of the light rays bounce back from facet to facet before returning the eye of the observer, a mirror finish optimises the dispersion, called fire in the industry parlance, of the brightness of the diamond, called brilliance.', Shreyans said. He was indeed right and was smartly blending industry vocabulary with scientific understanding.

I was very pleased with the way Shreyans was picking up the finer aspects of business and gelling with not only partners, but with other people in the company. Learning must not bring pride. I have seen many people succeeding without much individual intelligence but with their strong teams. Shreyans further told us in a partner meeting what he was doing, 'Polish and symmetry are the two factors of finish that are mostly felt but difficult to assess. A diamond graded as having ideal polish indicates that each facet on the diamond has a mirror finish. I am trying to develop a system if I can have grading report for my software.' He then asked me if twenty-five people working with him could be taken into a new IT company for in-house development. Without hesitation, I agreed and thus was born our captive IT Company, Peacock Technologies that later turned into SRKay Consulting, a full-fledged software and technology company.

For the new building that we had been constructing for our company, we solicited suggestions from major players of the Diamond Industry at various stages of construction. Meenakshi came to see the construction site one day. There was a discussion in progress on the elevation façade. I invited her to join and she, as if it was fated, selected maroon Indian granite in polished and flamed finish. In our culture, daughters are considered Laxmi since the Goddess Laxmi is the harbinger of fortune and prosperity. Meenakshi's chance visit that day made me feel that the new factory had indeed been blessed.

By this time, I had seen the best diamond factories in the world and captured the nuances of their design. Why should our building be second to anyone? I decided to pursue the LEED (Leadership in Energy and Environmental Design) certification for green building. A project earns one of four LEED rating levels: Certified, Silver, Gold or Platinum. In this pursuit, I met a wonderful person Mahesh Ramanujam. A native of Chennai, he graduated from Annamalai University in Computer Engineering. While working with Lenovo, which acquired IBM's personal computer business in 2005, Mahesh was involved in building healthier communities and democratising sustainable living as his life's goal.

We decided to go for Gold Rating certification, earned on the Green building criteria and became the pioneers in the Indian diamond industry in this regard. With further improvements, we would later achieve the highest Platinum Rating. In 2015 SRK Empire became a first building to acquire 'Green Rating' from USGBC which was later enhanced to 'Platinum Rating' in 2018. Our pursuit of excellence continues even today.

Varda Shine, Director, De Beers, fittingly inaugurated SRK Empire on 12 April 2011. As the first woman to be awarded the honorary lifetime membership of the Israel Diamond Exchange (IDE) recently, she was at the pinnacle of her illustrious career. 'India has become the fastest-growing market for De Beers. It's now a priority market for us.' she declared. 'It's also the most extravagant market in terms of its diamond designs. Women wear such extraordinary pieces. You wouldn't see that in Europe unless you were having dinner with the Queen.' she added. Declaring the 2010s as 'The Diamond Decade', she said, 'Growth in China and India was projected to drive demand, while the US would take small steps out of recession.'

After the function, Varda Shine freely interacted with the women of our family. Shweta spontaneously assumed the role of interpreter. Varda asked Shweta about the nose rings all senior women were wearing, 'Were they symbols of joy and fulfilment? Or were they symbols of submission?' Shweta surprised her by calling a nose ring a 'status symbol.' Shweta told her that Indian women are the bedrock of Indian society. However, the economic conditions and social attitudes have changed, and the traditional view of family life was being challenged from every side, being a wife and a mother was both the highest aspiration and biggest status of a woman in India. The choice between family life and education was not an either-or choice in India. Varda admired Shweta's thought clarity and expression. Varda affectionately held her hand on Shewa's shoulder said, 'For the sake of our own happiness and stability, for our families, for the businesses, and for a better society, we need both domestic and educational skills.'

My mentor, Ashitbhai 'Munnabhai', came to bless the occasion. After all the guests left, we sat quietly. Munnabhai said, 'Govindbhai, I am very happy for you. Generally, people, upon making money, start creating bubbles around them. They hide themselves in big mansions, move around in big cars and create a wall of personal staff around them, which at times stops even their family members from approaching them, forget about old friends. However, you are different. You are taking care of your extended family so very well, your employees, and your old-time friends. I am indeed very happy.'

I held Munnabhai's hands and for a while was at a loss of words. Then, to change the topic I asked him what his take on the changing times was. Munnabhai said, 'When was the time not changing? Times are always changing. However, there are always trends. There are always signs. The wise see that early, prepare themselves well. Those who made them blinded by enjoying their wealth in pleasures and seeking power, miss these signs and cry when reality bites them. It is indeed very important for businesspersons to stay away from cronies and sycophants, lead simple lives and spend time in solitude, preferably in natural surroundings.'

He took a long pause and then said, 'Who does not know that when gold prices go up, usually India is a seller and Western Europe is a buyer. When gold goes down, India is a buyer. However, they get it right over there, and we get it wrong here. Almost regardless of what is happening in the economy, if there is a wedding, they pull out all the stops. They save from the day the girl is born, and jewellery does not seem to be compromised. The difference is that now, like never before, 'pulling out all the stops' means more diamonds. I can see many hundred young billionaires rising with the rise of the Indian economy. The day is not very far away when you would be selling diamonds more to your own people than to the Chinese and the American rich.'

7

Higher Orbits

विद्यां ददाति विनयं विनयाद्याति पात्रताम् ।
पात्रत्वात् धनमाप्नोति धनात् धर्मं ततः सुखम् ॥

(हितोपदेश, मित्रलाभ 1 श्लोक 6)

Knowledge gives discipline, from discipline comes worthiness,
from worthiness one gets wealth, from wealth one can do good
deeds, from that comes bliss.

(Hitopadesha, Mitralabh 1, Shloka 6)

Kartikeya Sarabhai, the son of the legendary scientist, Vikram
Sarabhai, came to see me. The grandson of industrialist, Shree
Ambalal Sarabhai, his mother, Mrinalini Sarabhai and his sister,
Mallika Sarabhai, were both renowned Bharatanatyam dancers and
social activists. He truly represented modern Gujarat's first family.
He congratulated me for SRK Empire building earning the LEED

211

(Leadership in Energy and Environmental Design) Gold rating and our sustained support for improving the environment.

I told Kartikeyabhai that while I understood the need to support the environment and had participated to the best of my ability with my time and resources in water projects in Saurashtra, cleaning Surat and helping whoever approached me for help in saving the environment and livestock, I had no idea about his work. I told him, 'Please forgive me for my ignorance, but I am sure being the son of the great Vikram Sarabhai, you must be doing something of high value to the world and I would take it as God's blessing to hear from you about your work.'

Kartikeyabhai beamed up with positive energy and said, 'Govindbhai, for last many decades, let us say after World War II, in their pursuit to generate wealth, humans are consuming the natural resources faster than they can be renewed. The capacity of the earth to give materials for our consumption and more than that to receive back the waste is not infinite and it is indeed reaching a stage when any more activity is bound to create irreparable damage. There is no point in creating political noise and blaming industries for they do it for their profits. The better way is to stop consuming things to bring down the demand for materials as well as reduce the waste and take away the profit impetus from the companies. I have decided to educate children about this important idea so that when they grow up, they live by a better lifestyle.'

I was taken aback by the simplicity and honesty of Kartikeyabhai, almost my contemporary. I told him, 'Bhai, I could not study beyond Class VII, but you have been educated at Cambridge University in England and at the Massachusetts Institute of Technology (MIT) in America. You then took over as Chairman of Ambalal Sarabhai Enterprises Ltd., a pharmaceutical company set up by your legendary grandfather.'

Kartikeyabhai told me, 'My father took India into Space. Whatever I do, I can never match the grandeur of his enterprise.

I decided to give all my property and life to work towards cause of environment protection.'

I recollected Indravadanbhai's words when I gave him the news of my son's birth in 1987. He had told me, 'The good and the pleasant come to a man and the thoughtful mind turns all around them and distinguishes. The wise choose the good from the pleasant, but the dull soul chooses the pleasant rather than the getting of his good and having it.' Here was sitting in front of me a true embodiment of that principle. I got up and hugged Kartikeyabhai. He invited me to his home turned institute in Ahmedabad and I later went there after few years.

My father had turned 100 years, but he did not know exactly when he was born as there was no record, except that he remembered as a childhood memory that the World War I started, which was in 1914. After my mother departed in 2002, he used to remain silent most of times and in a contemplative mood. He was a disciple of Gadhada Gopinathji of Vadtal Swaminarayan and fond of organizing Satsang. He never complained about anything. Once he was served food without salt by mistake, but he had eaten it without saying a word. Later when others came to know the mistake, they realized the stoic attitude of the grand old man; he could endure any pain or hardship without showing his feelings or complaints.

My father's stay in the mortal world was going to end soon. Remembering the last days of my mother, I read aloud portions of Kapila Gita to my father.

ज्ञानवैराग्ययुक्तेन भक्तियुक्तेन चात्मना।
परिपश्यत्युदासीनं प्रकृतिं च हतौजसम्॥

(श्रीमद् भागवतम् पुराण, स्कन्ध 3, अध्याय 25, श्लोक 18)

People, equipped with transcendental knowledge and renunciation and engaged in devotional service for their eternal benefit, take

shelter at my lotus feet, and since I am the Lord, they are thus
eligible to enter the kingdom of Godhead without fear.

(Shreemad Bhagwat Purana,
Skandha 3, Chapter 25, Shloka 18)

Us four brothers—Nagjibhai, Parbatbhai, Arjanbhai and I—used to
sit near his bed in the evening. The only question he would ask us was
whether we were not doing anything wrong or illegal while earning
our wealth. Upon getting our assurance that we were following
the right path, he used to feel happy. One day, he said, 'Old age is
difficult. Even passing urine in the night becomes a huge ordeal.' On
1 April 2012, it was Swaminarayan Jayanti. All of us brothers were
sitting around him. Both of my sisters were also around. My father
said, 'I have no desire left. I will be going soon as a clean soul. There
is no fear of any questioning for I did nothing wrong or unjust ever
in my life.' He passed away a few days later the evening of 5 April
2012. When he breathed his last, we were chanting Swaminarayan
Dhun.[1] It was such a peaceful exit. He passed into eternity as if
walking through an open door.

On 16 May 2012, I went to attend the inauguration of Rameshbhai
Oza's Devka Vidyapeeth, near Rajula, founded on 20 acres plot
allotted by Chief Minister Narendrabhai Modi. The new campus
was created on the lines of the ancient Gurukul system of education,
with donations from people living in nearby areas. Speaking on the
occasion, Narendrabhai recounted an anecdote from the life of Field
Marshal K.M. 'Kipper' Cariappa, the first Indian Commander-in-
Chief of the Indian Army. Narendrabhai said that Field Marshal
Cariappa had all the respect and fame in the world, but he felt most
overwhelmed when his own native village in Coorg honored him.
'When our own people do something for us, the feeling is different.

---

[1] धुन, spiritual chanting,

Today would be very a different day for Bhaishree Rameshbhai Oza as he is among his own people.' Narendrabhai said.

Earlier, I had visited Porbander in 2008, Rameshbhai bestowed upon me the Rajarshi[2] Award. While conversing with Rameshbhai that evening, he reminisced, 'I realized that Porbandar is also the birthplace of Sudama, a dear friend of Lord Krishna. He had said,' At the request of the locals, I accepted the trusteeship of local school and started infusing funds into the school, which very soon gained recognition and the number of applicants to it increased.' In 1991, the Government of Gujarat allotted 85 acres of land for developing the school into a full-fledged learning center of Indian cultural heritage to house 500 students. The center would be called 'Rishikul' and the teaching would be given as per the ancient Vedic Tapovan[3] system.

In February 2013, Rameshbhai Oza organized a weeklong Ram Katha of Shree Morari Bapu at Sandipani Sanskrit University, Porbandar. I attended this Katha with my family. During Morari Bapu's Katha, I was pleasantly surprised to find Kokilaben Ambani with her son Anil Ambani and daughter-in-law, Tina Ambani. Film star Amitabh Bachchan also came during this Katha with his wife. In another surprise, Kokilaben's birthday was celebrated on 24 February 2013. The gracious woman, speaking in Gujarati said, 'Faith is a very powerful force. Faithful people are indeed healthy and seek education to emerge out of poverty. It is important that we support faith in people's hearts and Katha is the best medium for that.' Later, in 2020, when a Katha was organized to celebrate Kokilaben's birthday, Champa took the bahus[4] of the family—Jinal Dholakia, Rinal Dholakia, Rupal Narola and our daughter Shweta Kevadia with Dharmistha Ukani—to Anilbhai Ambani's Pali Hills Bungalow in Mumbai and met Kokilaben Ambani.

---

[2] राजर्षि, a sage who assists a king in governance
[3] तपोवन, forest monastery
[4] बहू, daughter-in-law

In September 2013, I stayed with Rameshbhai Oza on the bank of Narmada River at Dhyani Dhyan Ashram in Nikora village in Bharuch district with hundreds of his followers for four days. Universal in appeal, Rameshbhai was accessible to everybody. Time knew no limits with him and when one met him, one felt that Rameshbhai had all the time for them in the world. Logical in his presentation, he issued no commandments; he would speak so little yet would mean so much. His messages were inspiring and thought-provoking, helping people to transform themselves radically into better human beings.

Rameshbhai told me, 'Govindbhai, it gives a tremendous insight, a profound vision, and an entirely new perspective to the person who hears the narrative of Bhagwat. On hearing the Bhagwat, a person is never the same. The moment words of Bhagwat enter your system, you are changed. Bhagwat left no topic untouched—social, political, and economic systems, all these have been covered in this epic. It is, therefore, an important guide especially for the conduct of youth of our Nation in all their personal and social affairs.' The next day we all visited the 'Narmada Bat'[5] developed by my nephew Savjibhai. There we all had wonderful pleasure to bathe in Narmada River with Bhaishree. And then took pleasure in distributing children's clothes, biscuits, and chocolates as well as saris and other household items for the women and children in the surrounding hinterland villages.

I became a grandfather on the auspicious day of Shree Ram Navami on 19 April 2013 when a son was born to Shreyans and Sweety. We had no confusion in naming him as Ish as he arrived in the world on the birthday of Lord Himself. I consider having grandchildren a true blessing. The feeling of love you have when your own child gives birth to a new life is amazing. A grandchild can bring so much happiness into your life. When Sweety's father Dr N. D. Jivani met me, looking at my happiness he said, 'they say

---

[5] नर्मदा बेट, Narmada Island

genes skip a generation. Maybe that's why grandparents find their grandchildren so likeable.'

On 4 June 2012, I met Dr A. P. J. Abdul Kalam at his home, 10 Rajaji Marg in Delhi, with Dr Vallabhbhai Kathiria, Union Minister of State for Heavy Industries and Public Enterprises in Prime Minister Vajpayee's Ministry, Dr Ashwinbhai Desai, and Nikhil Contractor. Dr Kalam's young assistant Srijan Pal Singh, who studied at IIM, Ahmedabad was also there. I started cautiously saying, 'We have come here to give you an invitation, with a request, to visit Surat and experience our little world of diamonds.' Dr Kalam tersely said, 'What shall I do by seeing a diamond factory? I do not need to buy diamonds.' I said, 'No Sir, you do not come to buy diamonds, but you come to see the immense technological intervention in diamond manufacturing and actually see in person how the sophisticated technology is used efficiently and effectively by people having a rural background and almost no formal education. This is a very formidable combination of technology and its user.'

Dr Kalam did not answer and got involved in some small talk with Vallabhbhai. Then I said, 'Sir, we are also farmers, and, for generations, we are carrying out farming in our villages. We have a special affinity and love towards rural India. Sir, as said earlier, you also have a humble, rural background. Hence, we will have perfect tuning in our understanding. We will be able to think in unison.' Now I could see he was getting interested. Therefore, I raised my pitch and shared our experience of organizing medical camps in tribal-dominated areas of Dangs, Ahwa and Narmada districts. We also narrated details about water recharging and water conservation projects of Saurashtra Jaldhara Trust and its work in rain-starved areas of Gujarat. We shared details about our experience of setting up rural schools. Dr Kalam smiled and said, 'Now, I shall surely visit Surat. I am keenly interested in knowing about work being done in rural areas.' However, it took another one year before it could happen.

Dr A.P.J. Abdul Kalam kept his promise visiting SRK-Empire on 8 August 2013. He was at SRK Empire in his bandgala[6] with long white hair, a true embodiment of a 'wise old man' of India.

I took him around our facility. He was radiating positive energy. Everyone was so comfortable in his presence. He effortlessly mingled with the workers and asked the right questions about their work. 'I had an erroneous perception about your business. What I am seeing is a very high caliber work involving very fine engineering techniques and artistic skills.' Dr Kalam said. He was very impressed to see our dining hall and especially the chapati-making machine to have Gujarati style thin variety. He told me, 'You should have invited me during lunchtime!'

We organized a formal speech so that everyone got a chance to hear him. Dr Kalam spoke on the 'Culture of Excellence.' He said, 'Any institution is judged by the level and extent of research work it accomplishes which in turn, results in the development of technology. Technology is linked to the economy and environment through manufacturing of knowledge products. This, in turn, promotes prosperity in society.'

Like a good teacher, Dr Kalam gave an equation: Creativity + Courage + Purity of Character = Knowledge and said that 'I could see all three attributes in all the business processes of SRK through which I went. I could see creativity in the use of technology along with the head, courage in the ability to take risks and purity of heart in management. And this is what we encourage to other corporate houses.' While leaving he said, 'Govindbhai, you have changed my impression about the diamond industry. SRK is a temple of skill. Ensure that the knowledge generated here is shared with everyone.' I remembered Mani Iyer who visited me with Shree Arun Tiwari in March 2013. When I expressed my wish then that Kalam Saheb should come to SRK, Arunji had uttered 'He will surely come.' and

---

[6] बंदगला, high neck attire

he came indeed. Arun Tiwariji has been instrumental in arranging today's visit of Kalam Saheb. He served with Kalam Saheb as Scientist for more than three decades.

A slew of activities had been organized by my partners and family members in SRK to celebrate in a meaningful manner 50 years of my having come to Surat as a daily wage earner in the diamond industry. Once this news spread amongst friends and well-wishers, it gained momentum and fifty different ways were evolved for the celebration. Each week carried a special motto to benefit society, including traffic awareness, a deaddiction oath ceremony, training sessions for police fraternity, municipal councilors, and teachers in the community of Surat and other such activities. On 8 April 2014, a grand finale was held at the Surat Exhibition Centre in Sarsana in presence of 1500 guests. Dozens of diamond industrialists from Belgium, Israel, Hong Kong, Russia, China along with the Consuls of Malawi, South Africa, Namibia, Lesotho, Thailand, Russia, Canada, and Belgium remained present. On this occasion, I acknowledged the contribution of the 6,000 associates who were the engine of SRK and helped the company reach its fiftieth year in business. I remembered my old partners—Bhagwanbhai Patel and the late Virjibhai Godhani who were also integral to SRK's success.

On this occasion, Nirupa Bhatt, Managing Director (India and Middle East) of Gemological Institute of America (GIA), said, 'Govindbhai is a Karmayogi. The theory of Karma is his guiding principle. Will power and confidence are his inner strength. He is a gem of society.' Before joining GIA, Nirupaben worked as the India representative for Argyle. She knew the pulse of the Indian diamond business. She had a live contact with everyone in the business, be it a small manufacturer or a big diamond unit. She has always been more like a sister to me. My children address her as their aunt. She advised us to improve quality in jewellery unit to expand our exports. The Indian diamond industry has greatly benefitted from the establishment of GIA's office in Mumbai. Earlier, for a GIA certification, diamonds had to be sent to USA and brought back to India. The opening of GIA's office in India resulted in us saving a lot in terms of time, freight charges, and insurance and more importantly, we could afford business with a reduced inventory.

My mentors Shantibhai and Navinbhai had come from Mumbai to attend the occasion. Navinbhai Mehta said, 'Govindbhai is a person who has never lied or gave any false promise to earn business all his life.' Shantibhai gave his blessings, saying I am like a Yudhishthira who saw no evil in anyone. It was indeed heartening to listen to the industry leaders at this event. Sevantibhai Shah of Venus Jewels greeted our friendship and said, 'Govindbhai, who came from the village as a farmer, still remains a farmer, but he cultivates relationships with love.' He further said that the respect he commands in society is because of his inherent virtues. Sanjay Kothari, former Chairman of Gem Jewelry Export Promotion Council (GJEPC) showered lavish praise for my work. He said, 'Diamond fraternity is proud of Govindbhai as he is the regular visitor to IIMA for his dialogue with students.' My nephew, Savjibhai Dholakia of Hari Krishna Exports cited Saint Kabir,

'गुरु गोविन्द दोऊ खड़े, काके लागू पाय ।
बलिहारी गुरु आपने, गोविन्द दियो बताय ॥'

(कबीरवाणी से, 'बीजक' ग्रंथ)

'When Guru and Govind (God) meet standing together, who should I worship.
Guru has introduced Govind, Guru is higher than Govind.'

(Kabirwani, Bijak Granth)

He further said, 'I remember my mother telling me to be just like Govindkaka. He is the visionary of our family. He was instrumental in setting up my own company, Hari Krishna Exports. We started our work in Antwerp with his reference. He believed in me before anyone did. I do not have enough words to express my gratitude towards him. Govindkaka is an example of generosity, humanity and sportsmanship.' Professor Mani Iyer who represented a delegation from IIMA said, 'Govind Dholakia is a living legend of good business, worth emulating by any business executive.'

In a very meticulously guarded secret, my family surprised me by gifting me a white Rolls Royce Phantom. On this occasion my family members announced the creation of the SRK Knowledge Foundation with the purpose of giving back to society. My nephews, Rahulbhai and Jayantibhai, and entire young generation at SRK played the lead role in celebrations. Jayantibhai said, 'The completion of fifty years of SRK is an extremely special occasion for us as this day marks the importance of zeal, passion, determination and hard work of one man who sowed the seed of this landmark company, my Mama Govindbhai Dholakia. He is the torchbearer of Indian entrepreneurship and an example of the new shining India.' When my turn came, I expressed my gratitude to people who have played a special role in my journey of the last fifty years, most notably, Babubhai Doshi, Shantibhai Mehta, Navinbhai Mehta, Satishbhai and Smitaben Zaveri, Mahendrabhai Parikh, Ashitbhai Mehta, Mohan Mama, Nirupa Bhatt and Biju Pattnaik. Dineshbhai and Shreyans felicitated the diplomats from fourteen countries who attended our celebration.

Film star Boman Irani compered. Musical maestros Pandit Hari Prasad Chaurasia, Pandit Shivkumar Sharma, and Pandit Bhavani Shankar mesmerized the audiences with their performance. Poet-lyrist Javed Akhtar recited an ode for me.

जिधर जाते हैं सब जाना उधर अच्छा नहीं लगता l
मुझे पामाल रस्तों का सफ़र अच्छा नहीं लगता ll
ग़लत बातों को ख़ामोशी से सुनना हामी भर लेना l

बहुत हैं फ़ाएदे इस में मगर अच्छा नहीं लगता ll
ये सताइश की तमन्ना ये सिले की परवाह l
कहाँ लाए हैं ये अरमान ज़रा देख तो लो ll

(जावेद अख्तर रचित, ग़ज़ल)

Later, Javedji translated his poem for me in simple words. He said, 'There is no merit in moving ahead in a herd and walking on the beaten paths. Obeying the orders even if those are unfair and making deals that are wrong may be advantageous, but not good.' To commemorate the occasion, a book covering my life and achievements, 'Nothing to Everything—a Divine Journey', was launched by lead diamond merchants including Ashitbhai Mehta, Manjibhai Dholakia, Kishorbhai Virani, Anupbhai Mehta, Navratanji Kothari, Mahendrabhai Parikh, Govindbhai Kakadiya, Laljibhai Patel and V. S. Lakhani.

I have mentioned Ashitbhai Mehta, Manjibhai Dholakia and Laljibhai Patel earlier in a book, but there are many other 'diamond personalities' in the business. A technocrat, Kishor 'Maldar' Virani set up the first company equipped with latest technological interventions in diamond cutting and polishing. Anupbhai is Chairman of Bharat Diamond Bourse (BDB) in Mumbai and India's face in the global diamond market. Navratanji Kothari, Chairman of KGK Group in Jaipur, is considered as a doyen in the industry. Our offices were on the fifteenth floor at Pancharatna, Mumbai, once a famous address in the diamond business. He has been our well-wisher and acted as friend, philosopher, and guide. He and his wife Anila Kothari run a world-class, 400 bedded Bhagwan Mahavir Cancer Hospital and Research Center at Jaipur.

I met Mahendrabhai Parikh at Antwerp in 1977. To me, Mahendrabhai and his wife, Ramilaben resembled like Lakshmi-Narayana. I had a good time at their home whenever I visited Antwerp. He started his company, Mahendra Brothers, in Navsari.

Our Unity Group of Four was buying roughs from him. No prices were ever negotiated with him. Once, after confirming an order for 1,00,000 carats rough, while having tea at his office, I casually mentioned about the loss incurred by us on our earlier purchase through him, not as a complaint but as information, and this never happened in last thirty years we are dealing with each other. Without a second thought, he asked his son, Sonu, to reduce the price by two dollars per carat, amounting to 200,000 dollars, such was his generosity. For him, it was important that his customer should not make losses, especially when the customer puts total faith in him. No wonder that, third generations of SRK and Diarough are still working together with the same trust. My friends Govindbhai Kakadiya, owner of Shital Gems and V S Lakhani of Kiran Gems have been always there to support any collective good project.

I fondly remembered my old friend Mahendrabhai Kanchanbhai Shah. He was in partnership with Anandbhai Hirabhai. We started trading with him in 1971 in a very small way. Sometime in 2005, we met at his Mumbai office. Our hunger for growth was not yet extinguished. He said, 'Govind, in 1971 even if God had asked, we could not have asked Him more than what all we are enjoying today, and still we want more. Such is the fate of man; he is never satisfied.'

During this period, on 12 May 2014, the general elections were held in India. Hailed as the largest election in the world. The BJP-led National Democratic Alliance (NDA) won 336 Lok Sabha seats. I have been watching Narendrabhai Modi transforming Gujarat and watching him becoming the Prime Minister of India was such a great feeling. On 22 May 2014 when he was leaving for Delhi, I drove to Ahmedabad to bid him farewell at the airport. To everyone's delight, Narendrabhai suddenly turned back while walking towards the aircraft, took out the fountain pen from his pocket, walked towards Anandiben Patel, who took over as the new Chief Minister of Gujarat, and gifted that to her. She of course broke into tears at this affectionate gesture.

In August 2014, I visited Botswana. My brother Arjanbhai's son, Akshay, and my nephew, Jayantibhai's son, Arpit, accompanied me. It was indeed a very satisfying feeling to travel as three generations together. Botswana gained its independence from Great Britain in 1966. Within a year, a huge diamond mine was discovered in a remote area called Orapa, about 250 miles from the capital city of Gaborone by De Beers, the dominant seller of 'rough stones' in the world. In the early years of its nationhood, Botswana was one of the poorest countries in the world, with a per capita income of about $80 a year. In a matter of a few decades, diamonds made Botswana one of the most prosperous countries in Africa, with a real middle class, and a per capita income approaching $6,000 a year.

We took South African Airways direct flight from Mumbai to Johannesburg in a Boeing 767 and changed aircraft there to go to Gaborone. In fact, that service was later cancelled, and one must go to either Dubai or Frankfurt, or London to reach there. De Beers give 'sight' of the diamonds to more than 80 registered buyers as per a quota system that keeps on varying who buy how much and makes around $5 billion in sales every year in a building owned and constructed by them matching world's best standards. Earlier DTC was selling rough from London which now takes place from Gaborone.

I took some time off to see a little bit of rural Botswana only to find there was nothing there except large tracts of sand, hardly any population, or any other building. After a drive of about an hour, we stopped at a hutment. There was no crop except some muskmelons grown in a haphazard manner. Then we saw a small room where many pigs were cramped to be sold in market. I realized that the rural areas are not attractive to entrepreneurs who were keen to make profits because of factors such as the distances from the main centers, poor road networks, low population density and a market that was characterized by most customers who had no regular income and were highly dependent on these money transfers. Interestingly, many aged heavily built womenfolk were huddled together in idle chatter.

We also visited a school catering to about 500 students. There were five teachers. Students were disciplined and classes were in progress. They said education was compulsory over an age range starting between five and eight and ending somewhere between ages sixteen and eighteen. Girls and boys there had equal access to education. I was told that, 'All students were guaranteed ten years of basic education, leading to a Junior Certificate qualification. Approximately half of the school population attends a further two years of secondary schooling leading to the award of the Botswana General Certificate of Education. I was surprised to know that Botswana Government's expenditure on education, as percentage of GDP was 10 per cent. In India, it was 3 per cent.[7] I gave the teachers my business card and invited them to visit India as my guests, but they never turned up.

I commend the selfless service of many eminent dignitaries of the diamond industry of Surat who have contributed to this fifty years journey, notable being Sevantibhai Shah, Valjibhai Kesari, Jivrajbhai Surani, Kishorebhai Maldar, Babubhai Sanghvi, Lalitbhai Adani, Chandrakantbhai Sanghavi and others. Coming from North Gujarat in 1970, Sevantibhai Shah started 'Venus Jewel'. Known by the nickname 'SP', he is a social worker and a deep thinker. The credit for making big diamonds in India goes to Sevantibhai. Previously, such diamonds were made only in Israel and Belgium. Today, Sevantibhai's name is held in high esteem in the diamond industry. He has also built a multispeciality 'Venus Hospital' in Surat.

Shree Valjibhai Kesari, like the brightness of diamonds, started various processes of this industry in Surat. He has also played an important role in laying the foundation of BJP in Gujarat. He was

---

[7] National Education Policy 2020, India have allocated 6 per cent GDP in Education

the first 'sight holder' of Dee Beers in Surat. Jivarajbhai Surani, another 'sight holder' is a very fearless person. Jivrajbhai, who is also very active in politics, along with Valjibhai Kesari, has laid the foundation of the Saffron Party in Gujarat. Babubhai is a pioneer of KP Sanghvi & Co. He has started a 'Shelter for Cows' in Pavapuri, Sirohi, Rajasthan with more than five thousand cows. Lalitbhai Adani, founder of M. Sureshkumar & Co., which has grown tremendously in the last fifty years and is today doing business nationally and internationally. When Chandrakantbhai Sanghavi was the Chief of GJEPC's Western Zone, he also acted as the President of the Indian Diamond Institute, established by the Ministry of Commerce of India, which trains students in various aspects of diamond production and jewellery design.

Among the existing emerging diamond companies of Surat with growth potential are S. Vinodkumar & Co., H. Vinodkumar & Co., Star Rays, Ankit James, Kapu James, Shivam Exports, Narola Brothers, Unique James, Shree Krishna Export and Jodhani Brothers.

That year, I decided to take the entire SRK family to Haridwar during Diwali vacations, a repeat of our 2005 excursion. We chartered a special air-conditioned train for our travel and celebrated Diwali in Haridwar. On 24 October 2014, Baba Ramdev hosted our contingent of more than a thousand people in his Ashram and provided a sumptuous lunch. He personally took me around his vast factory making herbal medicines. Acharya Balkrishna met with the young business leaders of SRK and interacted with them answering candidly how an enterprise of Rs 20,000 crores came up in some 10 years' time. Remembering his days giving yoga training to our family members, almost twenty years ago, Baba Ramdev sat with us for lunch. He said, 'I never take lunch, but today I want to break that vow and share a meal with you out of my happiness.' I offered him a check of Rs 11 lakhs towards the excellent arrangements made for us, but he firmly declined saying,

'Lakshmi-Mata[8] has been very kind upon us, let me share Her blessings with all of you today.'

Travelling in Gujarat, especially to Saurashtra, was very arduous. Surat had an airport but would operate merely two flights during the entire day—one in the morning and another in the evening. The airport would be functional only for a few hours every day. Why not start an airline? Batukbhai in Lathi village came to mind who helped me sell balloons on Janmashtami. Having realized a need, it was against my grain not to do anything about it. Hundreds of my fellow businesspersons were watching the idle Surat airport in dismay. Something had to be done. More than anything, I aspired to become a man of value. It should not be a big deal—rent a plane, invest about 15-20 crores and the airline can be started, I reasoned in my mind. Surat had given me a lot. So, what was my duty in return?

I called up my business colleagues—Savjibhai, Lavjibhai and Laljibhai to pitch this idea before them. 'If each of us invests Rs 5,00,00,000, we will be able to start an airline. It will not be a commercial venture. We are sure to make a loss in this proposition. Surat has given a lot; it is time to repay the debt. We want our airport to remain functionally active. We start with a nine-sitter plane. If we do so, our airport can remain open throughout the day,' I said. Savjibhai's face lit up, 'Your idea is really very nice. But if we want to carry forward your idea, we must do it in a proper way. Why only five crores? What if we contribute ten crores?' That was incredible. Everyone welcomed the airline idea wholeheartedly. The next question was from where we get a plane.

We found out about Ventura Air Connect, an airline with two American utility aircraft Cessna 208 Caravan, a single Pratt & Whitney Canada PT6A tractor turboprop engine and fixed tricycle landing gear. The airline was operating flights within Madhya Pradesh but had been grounded for a while. I got great help on technical

---

[8] लक्ष्मी-माता, Goddess of Wealth

matters from Dr Nagesh Bhandari during this period. Nageshji was a medical doctor by profession, specializing in spinal surgery. He studied at Academic Teaching Hospital, University of Heidelberg, Germany under the guidance of the world-famous spine surgeon Dr Jürgen Harms. However, his passion had been flying. He established Ahmedabad Aviation Aeronautics Ltd & Western India Institute of Aeronautics at Ahmedabad, which would later metamorphosize into Indus University.

Four of us in the Surat business community –Savjibhai Dholakia of Hari Krishna Exports, realtor Lavjibhai Daliya the 'Badshah' of Avadh Group, Laljibhai Patel of Dharmanandan Diamond and I— made a consortium Diamond Aeronautics and purchased the entire company for Rs 26.5 crores. Out of these two planes, one would be kept for passengers and other for chartered services. We would join the entire Gujarat through airways. When the people of Surat came to know about this news, they were happy and commented that this is a true love of the city. However, a few businesspersons criticized us too, stating that this venture was not profitable and that it would be loss-making. 'Yes, we know that, but we have not started this airline to earn money. We accept the loss incurred. With the grace of God, we earn well from our businesses. We are happy to be part of Surat's development. We cannot count profits everywhere. At times, we must do things that give peace to our hearts also.'

The new airline commenced operations on 13 December 2014 with a flight from Surat to Bhavnagar. Nine passengers, left Surat in the nine-seater aircraft at 7:30 a.m. and landed at Bhavnagar in less than 30 minutes. This journey would otherwise take eight hours by road. We soon added Amreli, my native district. For a migrant labourer who came to Surat from there, it was like a dream come true!

On Republic Day 2015, my old friend N. Gopalaswami was awarded the Padma Bhushan. A 1966 batch Indian Administrative Services officer belonging to the Gujarat cadre, I had first met him when he was the Municipal Commissioner of Surat, during 1977 and 1980. He used to come to Sanskrit Paathshala to meet Sanskrit teacher Dani Dutt Jha. Later, he took over the charge of Chief Election Commissioner of India on 30 June 2006 and retired in April 2009. He is currently the President of Vivekananda Educational Society, which runs a group of schools in and around Chennai. He is also the Chairman of Kalakshetra Foundation, an arts and cultural academy founded in 1936 by Rukmini Devi Arundale. He was appointed by the Government of India as the Chairperson of the Empowered Expert Committee (EEC), a final authority to select twenty 'institutes of eminence' in India that would have complete academic and administrative autonomy. He is also guiding the SRK Knowledge Foundation and acting as a Jury member for selecting future Santokbaa Humanitarian Awardees. I called him over the phone, and he recited this beautiful shloka, an anonymous (स्फुट) saying:

हस्तस्य भूषणं दानं, सत्यं कण्ठस्य भूषणम् ।
श्रोत्रस्य भूषणं शास्त्रं, भूषणैः किं प्रयोजनम् ॥

(सुभाषित रत्न, भांडा गारम, भाग 159, श्लोक 291)

Giving away wealth as charity is the real embellishment of hands, and always speaking the truth is the embellishment of one's voice and listening to the scriptures and treatises of literature is the embellishment of the ears. Then where is the need of ornaments for embellishing the hands, neck, and ears?

(Subhashit Ratna, Bhanda Garam, Part 159, Verse 291)

On 14 May 2015, Chief Minister of Gujarat Anandiben Patel joined Prime Minister Narendra Modi with a twenty-six-member delegation of industry leaders and officials on the first day of his state visit to China. The delegation included top officials from Gujarat such as Arvind Agrawal, Additional Chief Secretary, Ms S. Aparnaji, Ms Mamta Verma, Mrs Minaxiben Patel, Ahmedabad Mayor, and representatives of major industries, including Shree Parimal Nathwani and Shree Hemant Desai of Reliance, Shree Sudhir Mehta of Torrent Group, Shree Nitin Shukla of Shell, Shree Shankar Kaka of Unique DyeChem, Shree Rajendra Shah of Harsha Engineers and my friend Mathurbhai Savani. Young businesspersons such as Karan Gautam Adani of Adani Group, B. K. Goenka and Chintan Thakar of Welspun, Jakshay Shah of CREDAI, Yatindra Sharma of KHS Machines and Harish Mehta of Suzlon and representatives of Tata Chemicals, Essar Group, and L&T joined us in China. I represented the diamond industry in the delegation. I had been an avid traveler, giving up no opportunity to see the new places but this was a different opportunity, travelling with Prime Minister and his delegation.

It would be my first visit as a part of state delegation, and I felt both good and elated. The world is deeply interconnected. The decisions taken by business leaders and governments eventually affect the life of ordinary people in factories, fields, and offices in a significant manner. Nothing, whether good or bad, happens without human decisions triggering it first. While I got proper business suits packed for the occasion, Champa made a bundle of Thepla and Sukhdi for me. Despite having all the glitter and gold of the outside world, we both remain simple, Kathiawadi people of the land at the end of the day.

On 17 May 2015, we arrived in Guangdong, formerly known as Canton. Guangzhou is the capital of Guangdong. Along with the neighbouring cities of Foshan, Dongguan, Zhongshan and Shenzhen, Guangzhou forms one of the largest urban agglomerations on Earth and is the heart of the Chinese manufacturing industry. I took some time off to visit the temple of the City God of Guangzhou. I was curious, as I knew China as an atheist country, so how come this temple? Which God is worshipped there? I found out that the Chinese traditionally believed that Guardian Gods watched over their cities. Every major city has its own City God to whom locals would appeal to during hard times. I found it quite an interesting concept. What if there was a God of Surat as a mediator to settle local issues?

We drove to Shenzhen across the Pearl River, on 19 May 2015. Shenzhen is the financial hub of China. Due to Shenzhen's proximity to Hong Kong, every multinational company doing business in China is headquartered here. It was here that Deng Xiaoping opened up the Chinese economy in May 1980 and converted Shenzhen as an SEZ, almost like Hong Kong on mainland China. We visited Hong Kong on 19 May 2015. The Gujarati Samaj in Hong Kong hosted a Grand Dinner at the Holiday Inn Hotel. Next day we landed at Ahmedabad in our Chartered flight from Hong Kong.

To succeed a great leader has never been easy throughout history. The burden of high expectations and the reality of internal strife presents a deadly combination before each successor of a legend as a rule almost every time. The business communities had benefitted from the Gujarat Model, but the businesspersons constituted around 10 per cent of the population. Fifteen per cent of the people are Adivasis; more than 15 per cent constitute fishing communities, pastoral and other peasants and artisan communities and Dalits. They were all rallying behind Narendrabhai but now conflicts between some of the communities around economic and social issues started coming to the forefront.

The seventh Santokbaa Humanitarian Award for the year 2012 had been announced for His Holiness the Dalai Lama, the foremost spiritual leader of Tibetans and believed to be the incarnation of Avalokiteshvara, a Bodhisattva of Compassion. I along with my family members met His Holiness on New Year's Day of 2015 upon his arrival in the city to everyone's joy. When I told him about my farmer background, he beamed with enthusiasm and said, 'I am a farmer's son from north-east Tibet. So nice to meet a farmer's son from Gujarat.'

The next day, at the Sanjeev Kumar auditorium, a packed crowd enthusiastically welcomed His Holiness' arrival to receive the Santokbaa Award. The Indian government accorded His Holiness the Dalai Lama, the Head of State honour, as the king of Tibet. The Governor of Gujarat, Shree O.P. Kohli conferred upon His Holiness the Award. Pankaj Patel, the Chairman of Cadila Healthcare and President of FICCI was the Chief Guest.

In his acceptance speech, His Holiness said, 'I have three commitments: as a human being to the promotion of human values in the interest of general happiness, as a Buddhist monk to encourage harmony and mutual respect among religious traditions, which all convey a common message of love, compassion, tolerance, contentment and self-discipline; and finally, as a Tibetan, to preserve the knowledge of the mind that is rich and deep and, while most accurately expressed in the Tibetan language, which is most useful and relevant today.'

I met His Holiness for the third time the next day morning when he departed for Nashik. I took some fruits for him that he politely declined. He said, 'As a Buddhist Monk, I eat only once in a day. It is good for health and helps in the meditation practice.' Then he laughed loudly and said, 'But I am very fond of sleep.' After a pause, he said, 'Even at the age of nearly eighty, I continue to read and study.' His Holiness gave me a very kind hug and said, 'Our hearts are now connected.'

On 8 February 2015 we held another function at Sanjeev Kumar Auditorium to confer the eighth 'Santokbaa Humanitarian Award' upon well-known philanthropist Smt. Sudha Murthy for the year 2013, ninth award upon political philosopher and scholar Lord Bhikhu Parekh for the year 2014 and tenth award upon nonagenarian Jesuit priest and mathematician Father Carlos Valles for the year 2015. As the title of this chapter suggests, these are the people, who transcended the limitations of this world of 'I' and 'mine' and even 'place' and 'time.' The three awardees have been living for humanity as beacons of knowledge, compassion, and service.

In her acceptance speech, Smt. Sudha Murthy, Chairperson of Infosys Foundation, and a teacher, said, 'To give, you must have. To donate you must first create wealth. My husband, an engineer, learned very early in his life that if he wants our country to progress, he must become an entrepreneur. Even before we saw wealth in our life, Murthy used to dream about how he would use it to build an excellent company. However, once he achieved his goal, he started using a good part of his earnings for the good of society. He handed over that responsibility to me and never interfered.'

Sudha Murthy was born in Shiggaon, Haveri in Karnataka in the family of the surgeon, Dr R. H. Kulkarni, and his wife Vimla Kulkarni. She graduated in Electrical and Electronics Engineering from the B.V.B. College of Engineering & Technology, now known as KLE Technological University, and completed her post-graduate in computer science from the Indian Institute of Science. She topped both the examinations. Sudha Murthy famously wrote a postcard to J. R. D. Tata to do something about the gender bias his company TELCO was promoting through its recruitment procedure. She later worked as the first lady employee there. She later joined Walchand Group of Industries at Pune.

Bhikhubhai Parekh was born in Amalsad, a small town on the Mumbai-Vadodara line. His father was a goldsmith and determined to give his son the best education. Bhikhubhai was admitted to the University of Bombay where he earned his bachelor's degree there in 1954 and his Master's in 1956. He then went to study at the prestigious London School of Economics in 1959, where he received his PhD in 1966. Bhikhubhai taught at the University of Hull for about ten years. He was invited as the Vice-Chancellor at the Maharaja Sayajirao University of Baroda and held the position for three years, between 1981 and 1984. After his return to London, Bhikhubhai was recognized as a man of immense understanding of human society and served on various bodies dealing with the issues of racial equality and multiculturalism. Bhikhubhai was appointed as the Chairman of the Commission on the Future of Multi-Ethnic Britain from 1998 to 2000. The report of this body is called the 'Parekh Report' and has been the basis for much debate on multiculturalism in the UK in the early 21st century. In May 2000, Bhikhubhai was bestowed the Royal title of Baron of Kingston upon Hull in the East Riding of Yorkshire and since then he sits in the Lords as a Labour Party peer. Reverend Morari Bapu presented these awards.

In his acceptance speech, Lord Bhikhu Parekh said, 'Every child is born with a great destiny including those born in poverty. This destiny is reflected in the early childhood and good primary teachers and parents can read the signs.' He fondly remembered how he was supported by all to go to London and become what he had later become. He also remembered his three years as the Vice Chancellor of Baroda University in 1980s and lamented that India does not have even one world-class University.

A Jesuit priest born in Spain, Father Valles, had lived in India for five decades and wrote extensively in Gujarati and on mathematics. In 1949, when he was fifteen, he was sent to India as a Jesuit novitiate. In India, Father Valles studied Mathematics at Madras University and completed his Masters in 1953. He was asked to teach mathematics at the newly opened St Xavier's College in Ahmedabad, where he had to learn Gujarati. After four-year theological studies at Pune, he was ordained priesthood in 1955.

The then ninety-year-old Father Carlos Valles drew thunderous applause when he stood up to speak. Father Valles said, 'I came to India when I was just fifteen-year-old from Spain. My father died when I was ten and my mother and I had tough times.' He then surprised everyone by switching over to fluent Gujarati and said, 'In

1960, I wrote a Gujarati book titled Sadachar.[9] Since nobody agreed to publish it, my mother published it. As the book became popular, I was invited to write in the Kumar[10] regularly. Later, I was writing in Sunday supplement of Gujarat Samachar a column titled 'Navi Pedhine', to the new generation.' There are more than fifty books written by Father Valles in Gujarati.

In the evening, Sudhaji visited our home and interacted with the women in the house. I decided to stay away from a 'ladies alone' meeting that was planned as an exchange of pleasantries but lasted for more than two hours in a well-articulated discussion. She shared her experience of rehabilitation of over 3000 prostitutes forced into trafficking by ensuring that they are married off to suitable grooms after providing them skills for their livelihood. She also said about the constant danger looming over her by touts and how she was provided with round-the-clock security. She told me that as she needed to travel to Gujarat, a safe place, she fled her security and travelled alone. We felt very proud of Gujarat state. The youngsters of our family were astonished when I informed them that Sudha Murthy, who annually donates a sum equivalent to our net worth, used a 'Santro Car' to move around in her city. Such a simplicity and humility she possessed.

Morari Bapu graced Ram Katha 'Manas Ramkrishna Hari' on the SRK Sports Complex, in Katargam, between 7-15 February 2015, we created to provide our young employees and associates an avenue for doing physical exercise and sports in the evening time. Morari Bapu was coming to Surat for Ram Katha after twelve years. We formed seventy different committees towards its preparations. About 5500 volunteers registered themselves, making it a truly social event. We made it a convergence of our entire societal mission. Bapu also agreed to make Beti Bachao, Vyasan Mukti, Cleanliness,

---

[9] सदाचार, good conduct
[10] कुमार, monthly Gujarati magazine

Environmental Awareness, Water Conservation, Organ Donation, Personal Hygiene, and even Traffic Awareness as daily themes in the Katha. Popular folk singers Sairam Dave, Osman Mir, Mayabhai Ahir and Ghanshyam Lakhani gave their performance. Eight lakhs people visited and were served meals as Prasad after the Katha.

On 24 April 2015, Dr Kalam visited Care Hospital in Surat. His office contacted me a day before and informed me that Dr Kalam wanted to meet me at the hospital. When I reached there at the appointed time, I realized that Dr Kalam invited me for a tête-à-tête before the event. Upon seeing me, Dr Kalam said, 'True Diamond has come.' We both sat together in a room alone. When I recall this private conversation of about 15 minutes, a shiver travels through my spine, as it was the last time that I saw Dr Kalam. He departed three months later, on 27 July 2015. That he sent a word to speak to me fills me with great joy. I feel duty-bound to share what Dr Kalam told me. It was like the parting advice of a great soul for posterity.

Dr Kalam told me, 'You know what I liked the most at your factory, when I visited it, the care you were taking to teach young men skills. I realized in your factory that diamond cutting, and polishing cannot be learned without working on diamonds. It is very important. I feel that every successful person owes a debt that can only be repaid by teaching others what you know. So, you create an institution where young people can work fearlessly under the watchful eyes of old masters, who convey to them what is wrong with the youngsters and simplify a complicated matter to explain it to them.' He also acknowledged the receipt of my letter expressing my support for his work for the rural development and promised to come to Dudhala.

Then Dr Kalam turned nostalgic. He said, 'I have worked in two great organizations, ISRO and DRDO. The biggest challenge is to make young people realize the importance of their work. What more can be done. India must not only be world-class; we must lead the world, and this is possible only if our young people feel that responsibility in their hearts.' Dr Kalam concluded with his thoughts about giving, 'I feel good about what I can give if I meet a person. You have earned enough money. Your children will earn even more than you will. You must ensure that they also practice your values. Teach them to use their wealth for the overall good of the people.'

I sat through the event. It was a large gathering of doctors. They were discussing drug-resistant pathogens and how indiscriminate use of antibiotics had created superbugs that are very difficult to treat. Dr Kalam said, 'Indiscriminate use of anything is forbidden by nature. Moderation and prudence are the two feet on which human life should move forward.' After the event, he departed with folded hands. He accepted lovingly the Sukhdi that Champa had especially made for him. Who knew that it was the last time we were meeting? Dr Kalam passed away a few months later, but my meeting with Dr Kalam that day gave birth to India's first population health project, which we will discuss later. When I recall that day, I wonder how foolish it is to want what never was or will never be, to lament the passage of time, and live with fear of an uncertain future. God always tell you what is to be done, in clear and definite terms. Men do not listen and waste their lives in futile pursuits.

When I first met Shree Mohan Bhagwatji, the RSS chief, on the inauguration of the Vidyabharati School-Hostel run by the Zadafia Trust in the Dediapada tribal area on 28 June 2014, I had the privilege of sitting on the stage with him. I was impressed by his brilliant talent and patriotism, during the discussion with him he promised to visit my home in Surat. Bhagwatji fulfilled that promise after a year.

On 15 August 2015, I met RSS Sarasanghachalak Shree Mohan Bhagwat and attended his function. It was hoisting of the national flag during the Independence Day ceremony held at Dr Ambedkar Vanavasi Kalyan Trust, Rander Road. Explaining the significance of the tricolour, Bhagwatji said, 'There are three colours in our national flag and there is a dharma chakra in between. This dharma chakra tells us that we all should live for the enforcement of religion in our country and that we must bring back the lost religion in the world. The saffron colour is positioned at the top of the flag. It is the colour of sacrifice, credibility, and knowledge. Our kings and saints had made great sacrifices for others; the colour of that sacrifice was saffron. The clothes they wore were saffron. At the time of daybreak, this saffron colour of the sun clears the darkness of night. It is the colour of knowledge. While white symbolizes piety and purity of life, green is the colour of prosperity in the world.' he said. At leisure he had 'Kathiawari' dinner with our family at our residence.

My brother Parbatbhai was not keeping well. He had a liver problem for many years. Four years elder to me, Parbatbhai was a staunch believer in God right from childhood. He told me after we moved to live in Dholakia Farm, 'Govind, living here on the bank of Tapi River all of us together is indeed heaven. But my disease will take me away from here.' And it did so on 22 September 2015. He had a brain hemorrhage. We rushed him to Mahavir Hospital but as the end was inevitable and near, we brought him home on a ventilator. He breathed his last at 12.15 p.m. in front of his entire family, including his wife, son and three daughters, us siblings, and close to 200 other family members who had gathered after hearing about his imminent departure from this mortal world.

On 6 November 2015, on Parbatbhai's birthday, I wrote a nine-page letter to my departed brother. 'You never fought with anyone in your life span of 70 years. You were tolerant to each situation and person. Like Arjuna, you were an enemy to none and a friend to all. Anyone who comes says the same thing that Parbatbhai was our friend. I used to say to them that he was everyone's friend. When I wanted to take you to Surat almost whole Dudhala told to take anyone but not Parbatbhai. Do not take him to Surat because he used to do Satsang, and he is our friend. Where will we go? With whom we will talk?' I concluded the letter expressing my anguish, 'The Soul and God, Birth and Death, Cohesion and Separation,

Karma Yoga, Gyan Yoga, Raj Yoga are rule of Universe. But this is the separation of births. We don't know when, where, and how we will meet? Everything is in darkness. We don't know how ignorant we are.'

Social problems are never easy to solve. When the 2011 census returned the much improved but still skewed sex ratio in Gujarat at 918 females per 1,000 males, Ramjibhai Italiya, Laljibhai Patel, and Mathurbhai Savani discussed with me the problem that for the boys born after 1970, there are 25 lakhs less women than men in the state. The idea of approaching Patidar communities in other states cropped up. Patidars are essentially a cultivator caste is known by the name of Kurmi, Jaat, Patil, and Choudhary, depending upon the language and state. There are 27 crores Patidars in India, we were told. In many states, the marriage of a girl involved dowry and a great financial burden for the parents.

In 2013, the Surat wing of the Samasta Patidar Samaj (SPS) began to organise marriages of Odiya girls with the Patels in Surat. In the first year, seven such marriages happened. In the second year, it rose to 22. We decided to evolve a system wherein girls from Patidar families could be brought into Gujarat and married to matching grooms here. Two problems, one of not taking non-vegetarian food and language, were seen but considered not unsurmountable. On 16 October 2015, 42 girls from Odisha's Kurmi community tied the knot with Patidar boys at a mass marriage ceremony in Surat. The selection of the eligible Patel bachelors was done at a seven-day interaction organized by the SPS in Katargam area of Surat in the earlier week.

We were keenly observing the results of the Laser Micro Jet (LMJ) technology developed by Swiss company Synova around 2010. It was a hybrid method of machining, which combined a laser with a 'hair-thin' water jet that precisely guided the laser beam by means of total internal reflection in a manner like conventional optical fibers. The water jet would continually cool the cutting zone and efficiently remove debris. Synova successfully entered the gem diamond cutting business after proving the value of this technology in the semiconductors industry. We ordered two machines for a million dollars.

I met Ajay Tomar the Inspector General of the Border Security Force (BSF) more as a matter of chance during one of his visits to Surat. Tomar Saheb briefed me about the tough job on his hands. He said, 'There's no border fencing on the marshland that acts as the natural boundary between Gujarat and Pakistan's Sindh province. The Border Security Force (BSF) personnel, who guard the 85-km-long creek coastline, use all-terrain vehicles (ATVs)— ones that function like boats in water—and deploy Creek Crocodile Commandos specially trained for patrolling the difficult to-maneuver place. On full moon days, the entire creek area is submerged in the high tide, forcing the BSF personnel to take refuge in the Sawalapur border outpost (BOP)—the only highland amid the creeks.'

I never knew of this harsh reality our soldiers have been enduring so that we people can live without fear and peacefully carry out our businesses. When Ajay Tomar became the Inspector General of BSF's Gujarat frontier, he presented me an opportunity to contribute towards the welfare of BSF soldiers and their families. Ajay Tomar, a native of Haryana, and having served in various districts of Gujarat had also been previously appointed as the Joint Commissioner of Police in Ahmedabad besides being the Chief of Gujarat Anti-Terrorist Squad. On 3 August 2020, he was posted as Commissioner of Police of Surat. His wife, Sunaina Tomar, an IAS officer, served as District Development Officer (DDO) in Amreli and was the Principal Secretary in the Education and Energy departments of the Government of Gujarat.

I involved our leaders Mansukhbhai Mandaviya, Vijaybhai Rupani, Rajnibhai Patel and Shankarsinh Chaudhary. I sent my team there to find out what was needed. Based on the ground report, we decided to provide medical equipment in a mobile clinic equipped with sonography, X-ray, and blood cell counting machines. We also gave 11,000 specially crafted goggles, Reverse Osmosis (R.O.) water plants and 7,000 mattresses. Families of martyred jawans were also given monetary assistance. With the help of the Union Home Minister Shree Rajnath Singh, BSF Director General K.K. Sharma, accompanied by Minister of State for Home Shree Haribhai Chaudhary, and Minister of State for Defence Rao Shree Inderjit Singh, came to Gujarat and attended a programme 'Hum Chale to Hindustan Chale,' at Nadabet, a border village in Banaskantha district, on 19 June 2016.

I developed an instant rapport with Shree Rajnath Singh. I told him that 'Union Home Minister is Sardar Patel for us, and, in you, I was seeing the Iron Man of India.' Rajnathji smiling declined my compliments. He put his hand on my shoulder and said that he was very happy to see that I was creating awareness among the 'First Line of Defence' but it was our 'First Wall of Defence.' While discharging their responsibility to watch over our borders, their own responsibilities have no borders. From curbing smuggling and fake currency notes across the borders to human and livestock trafficking, the BSF must do a very complex mix of operations. Rajnathji called me to stage and offered me a garland in a rare demonstration of his loving kindness.

While travelling with P.P. Swami to one village in August 2017 at Dang, I found an ancient-looking idol of Hanuman lying deserted under a tree. Shree Hanuman's birth is divine. The Valmiki Ramayana mentions Punjikasthala, a cursed celestial being sent to earth. She took up the name Anjana and married a monkey called Kesari. The Wind god Pavan impregnates her in a super-sensory manner, causing the birth of Hanuman, and relieves her of the curse.

अप्सराऽप्सरसां श्रेष्ठा विख्याता पुँजिकस्थला ।
अँजनेति परिख्याता पत्नी केसरिणो हरेः ॥

(वाल्मीकि रामायण, किष्किंधा कांड 4, सर्ग 66, श्लोक 8)

Punjikasthala, nice Apsara cursed and exiled to earth Assumed name of Anjana, wife of Kesari, the monkey. But she can still change her form by wish!

(Valmiki Ramayana, Kishkindha Kand 4, Canto 66, Verse 8)

मनसास्मि गतो यत् त्वां परिष्वज्य यशस्विनि ।
वीर्यवान् बुद्धिसंपन्नस्तव पुत्रो: तव भविष्यति ॥

(वाल्मीकि रामायण, किष्किंधा कांड 4, सर्ग 66, श्लोक 18)

Air god embraced her in manner transcending senses Impregnating Anjana, giving her a son; Brave, blessed with intelligence!

(Valmiki Ramayana, Kishkindha Kand 4, Canto 66, Verse 18)

I asked P.P. Swami why nothing was being done for our revered God. Swamiji said, 'Govindbhai, a lot is needed to be done in Dang. But who will do it?' Spontaneously words came out from my mouth, 'I shall do it.' Swamiji informed me that there were 300 villages having the same situation. I resolved to work on 300 temples. On second thoughts, and to avoid any ego-trap, I invited 50 per cent partnership from people at large in whose name the temple would be built. There was no public place in any of the villages, which were having merely 500 to 1500 people, to assemble. Designs were prepared for multi-purpose temples to support the community halls in these villages. On 17 April 2018 in presence of Morari Bapu, we handed over five temples to villagers. Later, on 24 March 2019 Dev Prasadji Maharaj of Anand Ashram, Jamnagar presented 11 temples and on 11 June 2019 Rameshbhai Oza gave 11 temples to villages, The process and the progress are in place for the construction and commissioning of the remaining temples. The SRK family will be happy if social utility is preserved along with religion and social harmony between us and religion is strengthened.

8

Rainbow People

द्यूतं छलयतामस्मि तेजस्तेजस्विनामहम् |
जयोऽस्मि व्यवसायोऽस्मि सत्त्वं सत्त्ववतामहम् ||

(श्रीमद् भगवद् गीता, अध्याय 10, श्लोक 36)

I am the gambling of the cheats and the splendor of the splendid.
I am the victory of the victorious, the resolve of the resolute, and
the virtue of the virtuous.[1]

(Shreemad Bhagavad Gita, Chapter 10, Verse 36)

Right from my childhood, I had deep bonding with Shreemad
Bhagvad Gita, or at times, I felt I was with Gita embedded in
my system. The ease with which I chant its Shlokas and imbibe
their meanings without any formal education in Sanskrit can only

---

[1] https://www.gitasupersite.iitk.ac.in/srimad?language=dv&field_chapter_value=10&field_nsutra_value=36. Last accessed on date to October 10, 2021.

be explained by the principle of Sukshma Sharira[2]—with which the Shreemad Bhagvad Gita came with me in this birth. Since childhood, I had understood and accepted the conditions of my life as 'given for a purpose' and not some random existence. The Shloka I used to begin this chapter has governed my thinking since then. Whatever happens, whoever does it, is all allowed and powered by God. Humans are the most advanced creatures on Earth for they are also given a God particle in their heart that makes them the instrument of God if accessed and followed.

Had I lived as a farmer in Dudhala, I would have done something else there. Since I came to Surat, I did something else than agriculture. Had I settled in Mumbai, or abroad in Europe, some other things would have happened through me. There are so many things, so many types of works, and so many types of people— in temperament, abilities, and dispositions—what grades them superior, or inferior is the degree of excellence in whatever they do. Lord Krishna told Arjuna that even if someone kills another person on the battlefield, both, the killer and the killed, are God Himself.

य एनं वेत्ति हन्तारं यश्चैनं मन्यते हतम् ।
उभौ तौ न विजानीतो नायं हन्ति न हन्यते ॥

(श्रीमद् भगवद् गीता, अध्याय 2, श्लोक 19)

He who deems It [the Self] a slayer and he who thinks of It as slain—both are ignorant. For, the self does neither slay nor is slain.[3]

(Shreemad Bhagavad Gita, Chapter 2, Verse 19)

---

[2] सूक्ष्म शरीर, a series of psycho-spiritual constituents of living beings, believed to carry on with transmigration.

[3] https://www.gitasupersite.iitk.ac.in/srimad?language=dv&field_chapter_value=2&field_nsutra_value=19&etsiva=1&etgb=1&etssa=1&etradi=1&etadi=1. Last accessed on date to October 10, 2021.

The important point, as explained by Lord Shree Krishna, was the purpose for which someone was killing, and someone was killed. Was this purpose selfish? For personal grandiose, sensory pleasures, egoistic obsessions? Alternatively, was it done in the sense of making the best use of one's life by attending to one's duties and giving the best effort possible? We saw the idea of Surat Diamond Bourse (SDB) at Diamond Research and Mercantile (DREAM) City as one of the reasons for which we were brought to Surat and showered with success, stature, wealth and above all imagination. People in the Diamond industry at Surat who lived before us did not have this great infrastructure coming up here. Those who would come after us would find it already existing. It is me and other people like me who are responsible to see that this great enterprise is created in such a way that a decade from now, Surat will be recognized as global diamond hub.

We saw a great opportunity in Prime Minister Narendrabhai Modi's concept of building 100 smart cities in the country, a great opportunity. Surat was now making 90 per cent of the world's diamonds and had a large presence of diamond processors and traders and yet sales were done in Mumbai. Every Monday, 5000 people travel to work in Mumbai. The real estate was costing Rs 50,000 per square feet there, while we could make a better working place here in Surat at the rate of Rs 10,000 per square feet. We met Chief Minister Anandiben Patel and she understood our point and the idea. A 700-hectare site in the southern part of Surat, adjacent to the village Khajod, the Outer Ring Road and close to the Dumas beach was finalized. A Special Purpose Vehicle, Diamond Research and Mercantile (DREAM) City Limited was formed for the implementation.

Citing Gujarat's efforts in creating smart cities, namely GIFT (Gujarat International Finance Tec-City) and Dholera Special Investment Region (SIR), Chief Minister Anandiben Patel said with growing urbanization, such initiatives in urban development and planning were needed to tackle the pressure on existing cities. She cautioned that already 42 per cent of people in Gujarat lived in urban areas. By 2030, this could go up to 60 per cent. Our cities would be unable to handle the pressing demands of urban infrastructure and civic amenities. We needed to build smart cities in response to these needs. The Gujarat Infrastructure Development Board (GIDB) assigned the consultant team comprising of HaskoningDHV Consulting Pvt Ltd in consortium with HaskoningDHV Nederland BV and Knight & Frank India Pvt Ltd for this project.

The DREAM City would mainly house an international diamond-trading hub, Surat Diamond Bourse (SDB), spread out over about 40 acres of land. The SDB was planned to be constructed on an area measuring 6 million square feet, at the estimated cost of Rs 10,000 crores. It would house around 4200 offices for diamond traders from India and abroad. The twin groundbreaking ceremonies of the two projects took place on 15 February 2015 at Khajod site in presence of representatives from diamond mining and trading nations South Africa, Botswana, Lesotho, Zimbabwe, Ghana, Namibia, Russia, Australia, and Canada. Interestingly, on the occasion, diamond merchants from Surat and Mumbai had done an extempore token transaction of polished and rough diamonds worth Rs 5 crore, the payment of which was done in the presence of the Hon'ble Chief Minister to her great delight.

The commencement of the work in DREAM City depended heavily on the administrative approvals and clearances. On 21 January 2016, the members of the Surat Diamond Bourse met the new Chief Secretary Shree G. R. Aloria, IAS, who was earlier the Municipal Commissioner at Surat, and followed it up with another meeting on 18 March 2016. Although the intentions behind the meetings were positive, the momentum that had been created under Anandiben's administration was missing. We decided to apprise the Chief Minister, Shree Vijaybhai Rupani, of the situation and on 31 January 2018 travelled to Gandhinagar by special Scania Bus. After a long time, I enjoyed the company of Mathurbhai Savani, Laljibhai Patel, Vallabhbhai Lakhani, Ravjibhai Monapara, Arvindbhai Ajbani and Kishorebhai Koshia.

We told the Chief Minister that right from the Chief Secretary to the Commissioner of Surat, every official in the chain of command had been replaced. It would be very difficult to brief every official afresh and requested his intervention to set things straight. Vijaybhai did not disappoint. He took a meeting with all the officials involved and declared in clear terms that DREAM City was the future of Gujarat and that he wanted to see it not only as the embodiment of the business spirit of Gujaratis but as a center of excellence. Whatever decisions had been taken by Anandiben's administration stood valid and were to be taken forward. In fact, he ensured that the best officials were involved with the DREAM City project.

When we later met Shree Anil Mukim, Chief Secretary, Government of Gujarat and Banchhanidhi Pani, Municipal Commissioner of Surat, both of whom took charge as Chairman and Managing Directors of DREAM City Board respectively, we realized that the spirit of pursuit of excellence possessed them. All other directors—Shree Pankaj Kumar, Shree Mukesh Puri, Ms Mamta Verma, Shree Ashwini Kumar, Shree Milind Torawane, Shree Rakesh Shankar, Shree Mahendra Patel, Shree Dhaval Patel and Shree C. P. Nema—made an incredible team which was rare to find anywhere in the government. They impressed us all at SDB. Architect Morphogenesis, New Delhi designed the project and responsibility of construction work entrusted to Ahmedabad-based construction company PSP Projects Pvt. Ltd. To ensure speedy implementation of the project various committees were formed. Kishorebhai Koshia, Asheshbhai Doshi, Manekbhai Lathiya, Ishvarbhai Navadiya, Rajendrabhai Shah, Dahyabhai Jivani, Manharbhai Saanspara and Tulshibhai Monapara have contributed immensely to development of SDB. Once completed in 2022 SDB will play a vital role in economy of Gujarat.

In his visit to SRK Empire Surat Municipal Commissioner Shree Banchhanidhi Pani asked me, 'Kakaji, what mantra do you follow? I am very pleased to see a building of class in Surat!' I told him, 'It is all about dealing with the narrow-minded people, which most of the people you meet and come to work with you actually are. There is no point in fighting with them. Instead, I compel them to change their mindsets about who they stand to be, not by arguments, but by focusing on what is to be done. I make them know the importance of the work they are here to do. If they change themselves, it is fine; if they do not, they leave that is also fine. The good news is that we all are pursuing excellence!'

Chief Minister of Uttar Pradesh Yogi Adityanath visited Surat in January 2018 for the promotion of forthcoming UP Investors Summit 2018 along with his team of officers and industrialists. I shared a stage with him in a program organized by The Southern Gujarat Chamber of Commerce & Industry. The Principal Secretary, Industries Alok Sinha was a key person of an event later invited me to his hometown Meerut on 8 September 2018 to begin a citywide cleaning campaign after hearing about our 'Welcome Clearty Club.' He acted as a Municipal Commissioner of Meerut between 2015 and 2017. During his tenure as a Chairman of Airport Authority of India between May 2009 and August 2014, he was instrumental in the development of Surat airport. He is considered as 'S. R. Rao' of Meerut. Young Alok Kumar Pandey, a Gujarat cadre officer now on deputation in U. P. also worked in organizing UP Summit.

What I found truly incredible and peerless was the ashram of Sadhvi Ritambhara, 'Vatsalya Gram' in Vrindavan. Here, there was support for destitute women who did not have their own family. There were three different age groups. The first group was of children whose parents left them destitute. The second category was middle-aged women, and the third category was elderly women, those whose families considered too old and had been kicked out of their own homes. All women here 'form' separate families. There are

7-8 children in every family and there are some middle-aged women and elderly women. Women and children, they both share a loving bond. I met in Vatsalya Gram, a woman named Amy, now known as Amrita, whose parents live in London, but seeing the atmosphere here, she left her family and started living in this ashram.

'I established Vatsalya Gram in Vrindavan twenty-four years ago. One hundred and fifty children, girls and women live in about twenty such families. A lot has changed in twenty-four years. In Vatsalya Gram, I have seen an entire generation growing up.' Sadhvi Ritambhara said. Once upon a time, Sadhvi Ritambhara was known for her fast-paced speech, speaking about Hindutva but the establishment of Vatsalya Gram introduced an entirely new facet of her to me. The most special thing about Vatsalya Gram was that in the system set up therein, destitute children got a mother, the destitute mother got children and a house, and destitute older women got families who would love and take care of them.

However, the problem is very big and there is a need for many such Vatsalya Grams in our society. I spent almost a day with these 'families', gathering details about their lives. The children of these families hold a special place in my heart even today.

Experience of spending time with students at Indian Institute of Management, Ahmedabad was pleasant. I was invited to India's number one management Institute to deliver my maiden address to its students on 20 January 2014. The success of the first lecture led Prof Biju Varkkey, who worked on our case study at IIM-A, to invite me again on 17 August 2015. Now, I was featured as an annual guest speaker at this institute. On the same day, I was told that Prof. Ashish Nanda, who joined as Director on 2 September 2013, was meeting industry leaders and he would like to meet me at the earliest. I took Shreyans with me. Nandaji received me with respect and made me feel important. Coming directly to the point he said, 'Sir, my vision for IIM-A is to get associated with leaders of enterprises. I understand you are the leading light of diamond industry in Surat and are giving lectures to the students here. I want to know from you what can be done together.'

I decided to engage in some small talk first, as if buying some time to respond. He took my cue and started sharing his story, 'I was born in New Delhi in a family which had migrated from West Punjab during the Partition, which we call as independence. I am a former student of this Institute and was teaching at Harvard University before coming here as Director. People say that I am the first professor from a foreign school to head an IIM. My wife, Shubha Nanda, is a faculty at Tufts Dental School, Boston. Our son, Pranav, is a neurosurgery resident at Massachusetts General Hospital. So, leaving both behind, I am here to see what difference I can make.'

Not knowing what to say next, I asked Nandaji why he disturbed his family life and quit teaching at Harvard? Nandaji said, 'I received a call from L&T Chief Anil Naik, who is the Chairman of Board of Governors here. You don't say no if someone of that stature calls you for anything.' I liked his transparency and straight talk. 'What can I do for you?' I asked, having no other way to escape. 'I want you to find out ways to get connected so that knowledge from IIM-A can reach the industry and society at large.' When we were leaving, Nandaji said, 'Let us meet again.'

On our way back I discussed with Shreyans what he felt. He said sponsoring industry people to study at IIM-A would not work. He said from his experience of studying at Regent University in London, 'It is like boxing. Education must precede before entering the ring. Once you are in the ring, it is very difficult to come out. Maybe we can work out something.' Then he gave the idea of signing a long-term agreement with IIM-Ahmedabad wherein we would start with sponsoring an expert of global eminence to go to IIM-A for a lecture and honour one faculty member every year. We wrote to Ashish Nandaji, and he immediately agreed. He said, 'I like your idea of long-term. Let us make an agreement for twenty-five years.' I said,

'OK Sir, calculate the amount of the corpus.' He said, 'Give us two crores.' I said, 'Done.'

In October 2015, SRKKF entered a twenty-five-year MoU with IIM-A for the dissemination and the acknowledgement of knowledge and wisdom of individuals from various fields by initiating the Annual Lecture Series, the first of its kind at IIM-A, inviting prominent people to drive debate on significant social issues. The aim of the lecture series was to become an important event on IIM-A's calendar which would encourage students and invitees to enter dialogue—often about difficult subjects—to address the challenges faced by society today.

Sometime in mid-November, Nandaji called me to inform that Dr Raghuram Rajan, Former Governor, Reserve Bank of India, had agreed to deliver a maiden lecture in the lecture series sponsored by us on 9 December 2016 at IIM-A. The lecture was the first of the IIM-A-SRK Lecture series. I sat on the dais with Dr Raghuram Rajan and Prof. Ashish Nanda.

It was a pleasure to meet the handsome and tall Raghuram Rajan, who was now serving as the distinguished service professor of finance at the University of Chicago Booth School of Business. He was head of the Reserve Bank of India under two governments, about eight months in the Congress Government and twenty-six months under the BJP Government

Rajanji spoke most eloquently and received applause from the audience several times. He told the jubilant audience that he had expressed his desire to head the central bank one day decades ago while studying at IIM-A in the late 1980s. Answering a question on corruption during interaction, Rajan noted that it was a complex problem, which was the outcome of a host of factors. Corruption is the result of many complex forces coming together.

Ashish Nanda Arranged a personal meeting with Raghuram Rajan for me. Speaking in Hindi, I asked about his childhood. He enjoyed the question and answered in Hindi, 'I am a Tamil born in Bhopal. My father R. Govindarajan was working at Indian embassies. I studied in Sri Lanka, and then attended a French school in Belgium when my father was posted there. Throughout my childhood, I presumed my father to be a diplomat as we were travelling on diplomatic passports. Only later, I learnt that he was working for the external intelligence unit of the Intelligence Bureau, the dreaded Research and Analysis Wing (RAW).'

After the function, I invited Ashish Nanda home for a meal together. He surprised me by saying that he was stepping down from the post, well before his five-year term that would end later in September 2018. He cited personal reasons. 'Personally, living a long distance from my wife and son has been a challenge. When I joined, I had committed to serving at most one term. It will be four years, to the day since I took charge. It is a good time to step aside and hand over the responsibility and honour of leading the institute to the next, fortunate person.' I felt sad but said nothing.

On 3 March 2017, in order to mark the twenty-fifth year of the V. N. Godhani School, established in memory of my partner Virjibhai Godhani, we deployed a mobile school dedicated exclusively to helping street children and others coming from poor and vulnerable sections of society. These educational materials are designed for mobility, adaptability, durability, and resistance to theft. Close to 3000 parents, Shree Bhupendrasinh Chudasama, Cabinet Minister of Education, Gujarat, Shree Mansukhbhai Mandaviya, State Minister of Road Transport and Chemical, Government of India, Shree Nanubhai Vanani, Minister of State for Education, Gujarat, Smt. Asmitaben Shiroya, Mayor of Surat; Dr Dakshesh Thakar, Vice Chancellor, Vir Narmad South Gujarat University, and Dr U. N. Rathod, District Education Officer graced the event.

On 17 April 2017, Prime Minister Narendrabhai Modi inaugurated Kiran hospital. He had laid foundation stone for this project in 2013 as Chief Minister of Gujarat and was instrumental in allotment of 3.53-acre land by Surat Municipal Corporation for this project. This 550-bed non-profit multi super specialty hospital has been built at a cost of around Rs 500 crores by Samasta Patidar Arogya Trust, having 400+ donors including 200+ Trustees, to serve people from all sections and communities. I was reluctant, but unanimously, I was appointed as its chairman. It was a dream come true for me and my friends especially Mathurbhai Savani, Laljibhai Patel and Dr Jagdishbhai Patel. We always expected that from commonest to richest segment people of Surat, South and Central Gujarat areas, shifting to Mumbai or Ahmedabad for further treatment would one day be a matter of past. Dr Jagdishbhai played a key role during the construction of this hospital and set up its administrative structure in its initial years. Later in the same year Dr Jagdishbhai decorated Mayoral post of the city.

Most donations for this project came from diamond, textiles and real estate businesspersons coming from outside and making Surat as their Karma-bhoomi.[4] It was their way of giving something back to the city that gave them success. Donations were also received from diamond fraternity of Mumbai and Antwerp. Vallabhbhai Lakhani of Kiran Gems donated Rs 65 crores for naming the Hospital in his mother's name. Lavjibhai Daliya, also known as, Lavji 'Badshah' and Jayantibhai Babariya together donated almost Rs 40 crores for putting up the first brick of the building in their name. Including SRK family, Savjibhai Dholakia of Harikrishna Group, the duo of Himmat Sorathiya and Mukesh Patel of Happy Homes and Laljibhai of Dharmanandan Diamond donated between Rs 10 crores and Rs 20 crores. More than 10 individuals gave between Rs 5 crores and Rs 10 crores and fifty persons donated between Rs 1 crore and Rs 5 crores. We used the best available equipment from America and Europe and recruited the best doctors of the country. Before its opening, we kept the hospital building open for 26-days

---

[4] कर्मभूमि, the land where one works, especially when it is different than where one had born.

for a public visit and deployed guides and volunteers on every floor to explain details. On an average 15,000 visitors turned up every day. Their beaming faces were expressing the feeling that it was their own hospital.

On 2 May 2017 Parliamentary Standing Committee on labour visited SRK specially to acknowledge the pioneering initiatives of SRK Institute of Diamonds (SRKID), a first in the Gems & Jewelry Sector under Pradhan Mantri Kaushal Vikas Yojana (PMKVY). It was a great feeling of hosting twenty-two parliamentarians led by young Dr Kirit Somaiya of BJP from Mumbai. When Somaiyaji came to know about the social work we have been doing he opened up to share his 'Yuvak Pratishthan' which has been active for over three decades in taking up several initiatives such as slum rehabilitation, affordable and accessible healthcare for all, and promotion of education and sports.

Like many others, I was shocked and surprised when on 16 June 2017, Chinese soldiers began extending an existing road southward in Doklam, a territory claimed by both China and India's ally Bhutan. It was totally against the spirit of friendship and collaboration I witnessed during President Xi Jinping's visit to Ahmedabad in September 2014 and later in my China visit in 2015. Our soldiers entered Doklam to stop construction by the Chinese. On 15 August 2017, a melee broke out between Indian and Chinese soldiers near Pangong Lake but later both India and China withdrew all their troops from the face-off site in Doklam.

Prime Minister Narendra Modi and Japanese Prime Minister Shinzo Abe laid the foundation stone for the Bullet Train Project in Ahmedabad on 14 September 2017. Expected to be completed by 2022 at an estimated cost of $17 billion, this project provided a station at Surat, connecting DREAM City with Mumbai. Twelve stations have been proposed that include Mumbai, Thane, Virar, Boisar, Vapi, Bilimora, Surat, Bharuch, Vadodara, Anand, Ahmedabad, and Sabarmati. The Ahmedabad-Mumbai will be a 2 to 3 hours journey depending upon at how many of these twelve stations a train would stop. People lined up the streets as the cavalcade of Narendrabhai and Abe pass through Ahmedabad. It was such a pleasant sight to see Japanese Prime minister and his wife wearing Indian attire. Among the top 15 industrialists invited, I was the only person from Surat to remain present in cultural program and dinner hosted in honor of Prime Ministers Narendrabhai and Shinzo Abe.

I was pleasantly surprised to be nominated for the Leadership Award by the U.S. Green Building Council (USGBC). I travelled to Boston, where the annual Greenbuild International Conference and Expo was held that year with the theme 'ALL IN' – which was meant to reinforce the commitment and optimism needed to confront climate change head-on. Shreyans and my grandnephews Dhruval and Utkarsh, studying in London and Nirav Mandir joined me. On 9 November 2017, Mahesh Ramanujam gave me a pleasant surprise by arranging a short meeting with Mr Bill Clinton, Former President of United States and acting as an interpreter.

I was very impressed with the way Maheshji told President Clinton, the handsome man and a personification of luxurious living as I found him after meeting, in a brief time, the manner in which 5000 people worked at SRK Empire building as if a part of the building itself became a part of their being. He especially highlighted our kitchen and dining facility and the elegant uniform of the employees harmoniously blending with the building. Further, I told him that God's will was reflected in a meeting between once all-powerful man in the world and a rustic man having no educational background, hearing this President Clinton, looking directly in my eyes, holding my hand in a warm grip and radiating smile, gave a silent appreciation and patted my shoulder after the handshake. He said, 'The contribution of Indians in making America a great nation is huge.' I felt proud being an Indian.

Later, I received the award, heard President Clinton's Plenary speech which was beyond my head for most of its pep talk, but I got all right when he said that the most successful organisms on earth that collaborate are honeybees, termites, ants, and humans. While there was a lot of work to do, we needed to celebrate the fact that millions of people were cooperating to solve global problems. Scientists, entrepreneurs, teachers, and designers are sharing and collaborating like never. That day, I had a lunch with Herbert Kohler Jr., Executive Chairman of Kohler Company created in 1873 and now run by the third generation of the Kohler family of Wisconsin. Maybe SRK prodigies will follow the Kohler's shining example, I wishfully thought.

Next day, my friend, Prof. Ashish Nanda, who had returned from IIM-A to Harvard, hosted breakfast for all of us, Mahesh Ramanujam deputed his colleague P. Gopalakrishnan for the breakfast. Shree Ashish Nanda came with his wife, Dr Shubha Nanda. After the breakfast, Nandaji gave a 3-hour tour of the Harvard University. It was 35 Fahrenheit, which is 4 degrees Celsius and I was very uncomfortable. In addition, I had never seen this class of landscaping and building producing a surreal environment. In this bitter cold we spent more time in coffee shop than in Harvard campus.

I was especially captivated by the statue of a clergyman John Harvard, who bequeathed US$ 780 in cash and his 400-volume scholar's library that started this institution in 1636. John Harvard had died of tuberculosis, at the young age of thirty. This is how great men become immortal despite their short stay in the world. Even today, I can close my eyes and see in all details—a young clergyman sitting, holding an open book on his knee. Wearing simple clerical garb, low shoes, long, silk hose, loose knee breeches, and a tunic belted at the waist, while a long cloak, thrown back, falls in broad, picturesque folds. When I noticed the shining toe of the left shoe, Nandaji told me, 'Sometime in the 1990s tour guides began encouraging visitors to emulate a 'student tradition'—nonexistent—of rubbing the toe of John Harvard's left shoe for luck, so that while the statue is darkly weathered the toe now gleams bright.' There was another popular superstition. Nandaji told me that though the Harvard University has many gates always open, two gates are kept locked and opened only twice a year. Once to take fresh students in and at another time to walk the graduates out. Shreyans reminisced his stay at Harvard in 2014 for GIA HBS Leadership Program.

Next day, we flew to Washington DC, where Mahesh Ramanujam organized for us a tour of Capitol Hill and the White House, both LEED Certified Platinum Buildings. We stayed at the classy Hotel Washington, also known as the W, opened in 1918. Standing in front of the 500 feet tall Washington Monument and looking at the Capitol Hill can make anyone feel the greatness of the idea of the United States. The White House is in comparison an ordinary building, much smaller and paler than our very own Rashtrapati Bhawan.

While in the White House, I remembered my visit to another famous building, the Edgar Hoover Building, which houses the FBI, like our CBI, at Washington. When my friend and former Commissioner of Police, Surat for the period between 1998 and 2000, Kuldeep Sharma, went for special training on anti-terrorism at FBI in 2003, he invited me to visit him at FBI.

I have come to know about Maharashtra Institute of Technology World Peace University (MIT-WPU) located in Kothrud, Pune by a chance meeting with Nirav, son of my friend Nilesh Mandlewala, who went to MIT-WPU for studying Political Science. I visited MIT-WPU on 23 December 2017 and met Suchitraji, daughter of Dr Vishwanath Karad, the Founder-President of the University, arguably the best private University in India. She told me, 'Govindbhai, like you my father began his life in a rural village.' She fondly spoke of his father's village Headmaster, VenkatraoKulkarni, who conducted his classes out of a cowshed. After the cattle were taken to the fields, all of the children would sweep the floor and remove the dung before sitting on their 'seats' which were nothing more than tattered gunny bags. This inculcated a deep value and reverence for education in Dr Karad. She said with a sense of deep satisfaction, 'My father's dream of value based universal education system is finally coming into reality.'

I later spent good time with the faculty and students. Ms Suchitra introduced an interesting book 'The Once and Future King,' written by Terence Hanbury White, who was born in Bombay, British India. His father, Garrick Hanbury White, a superintendent in the Indian police, was posted in Pune. The book observed that humans were always divided into one wise man, nine knaves, and ninety fools out of every hundred. That is, by an optimistic observer. The nine knaves assemble themselves under the banner of the most knavish among them and become 'politicians'; the wise man stands out, because he knows himself to be hopelessly outnumbered, and devotes himself to poetry, mathematics, or philosophy; while the ninety fools plod off under the banners of the nine villains, according to fancy, into the labyrinths of chicanery, malice, and warfare.

I used this opportunity to visit the Raj Kapoor memorial and their family farm 'Raj Baugh', which is located inside the campus. I was told that Kapoor family sold part of 125 acres farmland to the University and a memorial for the Kapoor family was built on its campus. It was unveiled in 2014 in the presence of Bharat Ratna Lata Mangeshkar and the Kapoor clan. The Kapoor family memorial has seven pagodas showing elements of Raj Kapoor's movies, a museum or viewing gallery that shows family photographs and moments from his movie making.

I have institutionalized 'Santokbaa Manav Ratna Award' by creating a nomination process and a jury to pick up the winners every year. The first person came to my mind was old friend N. Gopalaswami. When I spoke to him, he said, 'Anything for you, more so if your mother is involved.' Then I spoke to Prof. Ashish Nanda, who had gone back to U.S., and he too readily agreed. Lord Bhikhu Parekh, the recipient of 2014 Santokbaa Award also

An interactive dialogue at IIM-A on 9 April 2019 with their PGPX students. On initiative of Prof. Biju Varkkey, I have been addressing the students annually. My maiden experience sharing was on 20 January 2014.

At the library of Harvard University, 10 November 2017. Seen in picture (from left) are Dr Velan Chidambaranathan, Shreyans and Prof. Ashish Nanda. In a freezing cold Prof. Nanda gave guided tour of university to us.

On 17 February 2014, I was invited at Space Applications Centre (SAC), Ahmedabad to share 'spiritual dimension in entrepreneurship' with the scientists. Seen in the picture on my right is Shree Kiran Kumar, then Director, SAC.

On 28 May 2018 two precious 'Diamonds' of India full of humility, humbleness, simplicity and sensitivity, Shree Kailash Satyarthi and Shree Kiran Kumar visited our 'SRK Empire.'

Indus University, Ahmedabad conferred upon me Honorary Doctorate on 18 January 2020.

Shree Satyen 'Sam' Pitroda, Indian telecom engineer, inventor and entrepreneur was awarded first Santokbaa Award on 19 January 2007.

Visited Dr Verghese Kurien at his home in Anand, Gujarat in January 2007. Sitting with him is his wife Susan Molly Peter.

Mathurbhai Savani has been like another brother. We addressed 'Beti Bachao (Save the Girl Child)' rally on 31 October 2008 in Saurashtra.

The 2011 Santokbaa Award was given to legendary agriculture scientist Dr M. S. Swaminathan on 17 June 2013, aptly called 'Father of Green Revolution in India.'

Smt. Sudha Murthy, Chairperson of Infosys Foundation received 'Santokbaa Award' on 8 February 2015.

Tenth 'Santokbaa Award' was conferred upon nonagenarian Jesuit priest and mathematician Father Carlos Valles of Spain for the year 2015 for his work in Gujarati literature and mathematics.

We founded Relief Center in 1999 to provide whatever relief people might require. When in Surat, I would visit Center every morning. This picture is of 21 February 2007.

On 27 August 2017 at medical and health camp in Dang. We organize such camps every year since then.

In Dudhala, with the support of local villagers and some villagers of Dudhala residing in Surat, we constructed 110 channels of check dams. Picture taken on 15 July 2014.

In more than fifty years of our company's history, we have a HR policy of 'No-addiction' and succeeded. On 13 January 2010 we took an oath to abstain from vices in get-together of over 7000 SRK family members.

In early 1980s, mass weddings started with great enthusiasm and sincerity to curb the extravagance of weddings and excessive expenses. On 11 January 2020, we solemnized the marriage of 500 couples.

'Save the Girl Child' was organised on the first day of year 2006.

On 17 April 2017, Prime Minister Modi inaugurated Kiran hospital. He had laid foundation stone for this project in 2013 as Chief Minister of Gujarat.

We thought that instead of perennially lamenting about the pathetic state of sanitation in Surat, why should we not do something. We organized ourselves as the 'Welcome Clearty Club' on 11 July 1993.

consented. To make the jury complete, it was suggested to include a jurist of eminence. My long-lasting friend Ajay Tomar connected me with Justice Chunilal Karsandas (C.K.) Thakker, former Judge of the Supreme Court of India. Thus, we constituted Jury.

I met Prof. Errol D'Souza, the new Director of IIM-A. He was faculty at IIM-A since 2001 and before that the IFCI Chair Professor at the Department of Economics, University of Mumbai and was also a visiting faculty at Columbia University, New York. Prof. D'Souza was aware of SRK-IIMA Lecture Agreement. He quickly organized a lecture by the Nobel Laureate American Economist, Prof. Eric S. Maskin, on 24 February 2018. He would speak on 'Introduction to Mechanism Design.' Prof. D'Souza enthusiastically told me, 'I am getting you a maverick who says that software patents inhibit innovation rather than stimulate progress.' According to him there should not be any patents in software, semiconductor, and computer industries as they reduce overall innovation and social welfare.

His lecture was widely reported in the newspapers. The Times of India wrote, 'Maskin elaborated on his seminal work on mechanism design theory—the engineering side of economic theory. He went on to give the example of how choices were made when it came to fields such as energy and allocation of radio frequencies.

In his concluding remarks, Maskin said that his current research tried to find answers to questions related to real-world issues— including greenhouse gas emissions, prevention of financial crises and improving the system by which Americans elect presidents— based on the theory. 'It is more necessary to intervene in advance to prevent trouble before it happens', he declared.

After the lecture, Prof. D'Souza hosted a lunch for Prof. Maskin, Shreyans and me in his anteroom. Answering to a question of Shreyans, Prof. Maskin said he was born in a small village of a few thousand people called Alpine on the banks of the Hudson River on the New Jersey side. There was no secondary school in Alpine and he used to walk 3 miles up and 3 miles down to Tenafly. He said he was 'lucky' to have good teachers and fondly remembered his teacher, Francis Piers. Transcending the language barrier and education difference, Prof. Maskin made me feel comfortable and put me in high regard. I told him, 'To me being lucky is being blessed by an Almighty.' He smiled in return.

On 23 November 2017, we travelled to Elphinstone Building in Mumbai to confer the 'Santokbaa Manav Ratna Award' upon Shree Ratan Tata. Situated near Horniman Circle, the Bombay House is a four-storied building. There was a Starbucks Coffee Shop, first in India opened on 19 October 2012, on the ground floor and a Croma showroom, both Tata companies. We arrived earlier than the appointed time of 11.30 a.m. and decided to sit in Starbucks. The lift took us to the fourth floor. No security, no layer of secretaries. We were made to sit in a modestly furnished meeting room and Ratan Tata walked in wearing his blue shirt with his hallmark charming smile. His blend of class and simplicity was unbelievable!

He made us comfortable by declaring at the outset that though he could not speak Gujarati fluently, he understood it very well and we could converse with him in Gujarati. I very briefly told him how great we were feeling at that moment and requested him to speak rather than us speaking. He said, 'Govindbhai you are a self-made man. I actually inherited my company.' This was the last thing I expected to hear from the Doyen of Indian industry and the Face of Modern India across the world.

Shree Ratan Tata chose to tell us the great story in the simplest words possible. 'We had been doing business in textiles, hotels, steel and power from Navsari Building since 1904. When it was felt that the various Tata concerns could not be accommodated in Navsari building which they had been occupying since 1904, we bought 2000 square yard plot and constructed Bombay House that was completed in 1924 and has been the Tata Group's headquarters ever since.' After a pause, Ratan Tata added, 'It was from that building that the first Indian airline was conceptualized in 1932 and where the largest global acquisition of Corus, for $13 billion was made in 2007.' He said with his trademark half-smile, 'While the whole world was changing, we decided to remain same here. After I came here in 1991, I retained the set-up of the office left by my predecessor, J.R.D Tata. I can actually feel him right there.'

We were served tea with cookies. I gave a shawl and bestowed Santokbaa Humanitarian Award along with a cheque of Rs 1 crore to Ratan Tataji. He gave me a memento, promise that he would come to Surat, and visit not only our office but also our home. We took photos and an hour had passed as if in few minutes. Ratan Tataescorted us to the lift and wished us well for our return trip. We met in flesh and blood a great man who was willing to be little. Unlike so many businesspersons I met who undermined my ambitions, here was the man who was making me feel great by saying that I have created my company whereas he had inherited his.

On 4 May 2018, Ratan Tata Saheb fulfilled his promise to come to Surat. He flew in from Mumbai in his private Falcon Jet plane. He was wearing a business suit but when he saw me in normal dress, he said, 'I am little over dressed as you all came to my office wearing suits. But if it is OK, I would like to remove the jacket.' He walked to the plane and removed his tie and jacket. Once again, the Master Gentleman was at his best! Then he said, 'Govindbhai, I touched Surat on my way to Navsari almost 20 years ago. It used to have a small runway just enough for Douglas DC-3 Dakota aircraft.' Straight from the aircraft while getting into the Rolls Royce Phantom, the owner of British car manufacturers Jaguar and Land Rover, since 2008 said smilingly, 'I will have a better view of the city of Surat while driving to your place.'

He went through SRK Empire watching the work in progress, stopping here and there, absorbing technological details. I picked up a polished diamond being worked and asked K.D. Bhai a few questions about the angle between different facets. He was deeply pleased experiencing technology at SRK and said,'I am astonished to see the skills of your employees in dealing cutting edge technology despite lacking formal education'.

We arranged a short walk-through for Ratan Tata at the Kiran Hospital, across the road from SRK Empire. From hospital we reached our home. At our Dholakia Farm he saw car collection of family. He toured Dholakia Farm in a golf-car, after freshening-up while having coffee, we sat together on swing. Later he was served Gujarati cuisine during lunch at my home, including Khaman, Patra, Kadhi, Sukhdi and Puran Poli cooked by the women of Dholakia family.

During his 'Fireside Chat' with the around 25 youngsters, Gen Next SRK, he answered many queries raised by the youngsters. Shreyans asked, 'How do you want to be remembered?' Saheb said, 'Shreyans, I want to be remembered as a person who contributed, though little, to create an atmosphere of equality in India.' He further said, 'India's growth story is written by people like your father, who create global businesses with dream and determination, that too with utmost humility.'

While returning on his way to Dumas Airport, we briefly visited the Parsi Agiyari[5], Chintamani Temple and Dutch Road. He also saw the Sir J.J. Parsi School from outside, where Shreyans took his primary education. I told him in 1964 there were 5000+ Parsis that number is now dwindled to 1000. He also saw Surat fort and newly built 'Hope Bridge', now a heritage structure.

On 15 February 2017, I called Shree A.S. Kiran Kumar, the Chairman Indian Space Research Organization (ISRO) and congratulated him when an Indian rocket successfully launched 104 satellites on a single rocket, creating a world record. I had met Kiran Kumarji for the first time on 16 December 2013, when he visited Surat for a lecture at the Southern Gujarat Chamber of Commerce & Industry and at SRK Empire, as Director of Ahmedabad Space

---

[5] पारसी अगियारी, place of worship of Zoroastrians

Applications Centre. Later, when I visited him at ISRO, Ahmedabad on 17 February 2014 with Rahulbhai and Shreyans, he made me address the 110-strong gathering of scientists there. On 14 January 2015, Kiran Kumarji had taken over as Secretary, Department of Space, Chairman, Space Commission and Chairman, ISRO.

Kiran Kumarji told me that he was 'a happy at one place type of a person.' He said, 'I remained in Bangalore throughout my education—National College, Bangalore University and the Indian Institute of Science—and at Ahmedabad joining Space Applications Centre (SAC) in 1975 till today.' I said, with a genuine feeling of admiration of his humility, 'Sir, people move around the earth to succeed, but for people like you, the world moves around you to succeed.' Shreyans qualified my assertion saying, 'Sir, with you at SAC, what can't be achieved with design, development and realization of satellites and application activities of earth observation, communication, navigation, space science and planetary exploration?'

We had been discussing recommending Kailash Satyarthi for 'Santokbaa Manav Ratna Award.' Therefore, when his name was announced for the Nobel Prize in October 2014 for his work against child labour and education of the poor children, I was naturally happy. Born in 1954 in Vidisha, Madhya Pradesh, he had acquired his degree in electrical engineering but decided to be a teacher. In 1980, he left teaching and founded 'Bachpan Bachao Andolan',[6] an organization that worked towards freeing children from slave-like conditions. He had been actively involved in the fight against child labour and children's rights to education in a wide range of other organizations.

When our team met Kailash Satyarthi in Delhi at his residence in Southeast Delhi's Kalkaji area, they found him living in austerity, the rare but surest sign of a crusader. Once he decided to commit his life for his social work, he dropped his surname 'Sharma' to

---

[6] बचपन बचाओ आंदोलन, Save the Children Movement

'Satyarthi', one who embrace the truth as it is. He is one of the tallest leaders and the loudest voice in the global fight against exploitation of children. Not caring even once about the life-threatening attacks that he had survived, Satyarthiji has personally rescued tens of thousands of children from the scourge of slavery. His fearless and unrelenting policy advocacy efforts towards elimination of violence against children have resulted in path-breaking legislations globally.

While the children were being rescued, providing them proper rehabilitation emerged as a major issue. Keeping this in mind Satyarthiji established India's first short-term transit rehabilitation center for rescued children in Delhi named 'Mukti Ashram' in 1991. In 1998, a long-term rehabilitation center 'Bal Ashram' was established at Virat Nagar near Jaipur in India. These rehabilitation centers for children rescued from exploitation, slavery and servitude are ideal and replicable models for childcare institutions. He rose to global fame when in 1998, he conceived and led one of the largest civil society movements 'Global March against Child Labour', traversing across 103 countries covering 80,000 Kms with a demand for an International Law on Worst Forms of Child Labour. This eventually led to the adoption of ILO Convention No. 182 on worst forms of child labour which was formally acclaimed in 1999 and went on to become the fastest ratified convention in the history of ILO. Then came the Nobel Prize in 2014 for 'struggle against the suppression of children and young people and for the right of all children to education.'

Names of Nobel Laureate Kailash Satyarthi and A.S. Kiran Kumar emerged out of extensive deliberations on the 'Santokbaa Manav Ratna Awardees.' The problem was who would present the award to these luminaries? We reasoned that the President of India was the most appropriate person to do this honour. The only problem was that as per the protocol, the President of India had never given away any private award, but I said we must not take it for granted and that traditions were made to be broken someday by someone.

With the help of my young friend, Mansukhbhai Mandaviya, who was the Union Minister of State for Shipping and Union Minister of State for Chemical and Fertilizers, I secured an appointment with President Pranab Mukherjee.

On 22 March 2017, I went to Rashtrapati Bhavan with Rahulbhai and Shreyans to meet President Pranab Mukherjee in a meeting arranged by Union Minister Mansukhbhai Mandaviya. I heard a lot about Bhadra-Lok,[7] the elite of Bengal, but could comprehend its meaning only after meeting Pranab Mukherjee Saheb. While waiting to meet him in the palatial Rashtrapati Bhawan, Mansukhbhai told me that Pranab Babu was born in a political family and was teaching at Vidyanagar College, Kolkata when Smt. Indira Gandhi gave him a break by getting him elected to Rajya Sabha. Somehow, Rajiv Gandhiji never trusted him, but Pranab Babu regained his power by being the principal architect of Smt. Sonia Gandhi's entry into politics and when Manmohan Singh Government took over in 2004, he was considered as number-two in the government and held charge of Defence, Finance, and External Affairs based upon the need of the time.

Rashtrapatiji received us with warmth and heard about Santokbaa Manav Ratna Award and its recipients for whom we were requesting his presence. He expressed his happiness that I had created this award in the memory of my mother and remembered his mother Smt. Rajlakshmi Mukherjee. 'More than a noun, mother is a verb. It is not what you are but what you do. I am convinced that this is the greatest power in the universe. Though I have only three months left here as President of India and my calendar is awfully full, I shall try to accommodate a visit to SRK, Surat.' I was deeply touched by the genuineness of every word he spoke.

President Pranab Mukherjee could not come to Surat, so we prayed to Shree Mansukhbhai Mandaviya for an appointment with

---

[7] भद्रलोक, elite people or first rated citizens

newly elected President Shree Ramnath Kovind on 25th July 2017. We met the President on 19 May 2018 at Rashtrapati Bhavan. And he gladly accepted the invitation to come to Surat. Our joy was unsurpassed.

The day of Santokbaa Award function finally arrived. On 29 May 2018, President Ramnath Kovindji came to Surat for the first time to present the 'Santokbaa Humanitarian Award' instituted by SRK Knowledge Foundation (SRKKF) to Noble Laureate Kailash Satyarthi and former ISRO Chairman A.S. Kiran Kumar. Because of the involvement of the President of India, the event assumed a different dimension. Hordes of security people sanitized the venue, Sanjeev Kumar Auditorium, which occupied 1200 guests coming from various places of the country and overseas. Punctuality is a hallmark of SRK, in tune with that the entire program was conducted, with due consideration to President's protocol. All experienced micro planning carried out for the function.

President Shree Ramnath Kovind arrived with Governor Shree O. P. Kohli and Chief Minister Shree Vijaybhai Rupani, this is what I consider as the highest point of the Santokbaa Manav Ratna Award institution. Both the awardees were presented with rupees one crore along with a statuette of an Award. After conferring the 'Santokbaa Humanitarian Award' to Shree Kailash Satyarthi and Shree A.S. Kiran Kumar, the Hon'ble President admitted that he came to attend the award function by breaking the tradition. The President of India would not attend award functions of private organizations. 'When I learnt that Satyarthi and Kiran Kumar were to be awarded, I said these two are good men. Later, after checking the credentials of the award-giver, I learnt that he is also fine. So, I decided to break the tradition a little bit to felicitate two good people.' the President said. He kept me at par with those two awardees. He said, 'Kailash Satyarthiji, Kiran Kumarji and Govindji are persons of humility, humbleness, simplicity and sensitivity.' He narrated the role of Surat's Vir Kavi Narmad during British regime. He also said, 'Surat is a mini-India, people come for livelihood from across the nation. People of Surat convert adversities into opportunities.' President Kovindji also recalled his visits to Surat in 1970s and shared some personal anecdotes widely reported in the newspaper next day.

He said he would go to railway station early in the morning to get newspaper when halting in Surat. President Kovind described the city of Surat as the city of opportunities.[8] On this occasion a letter received from Prime Minister Narendrabhai Modi was read.

Kailash Satyarthiji donated the award money of Rs 1 crore to Surakshit Bachpan Fund (Safe Childhood Fund).[9] We all knew that earlier Kailash Satyarthiji had given away Rs 50,00,000 he received from Amitabh Bachhan's famous show 'Kaun Banega Crore Pati' and the entire prize money that came with his Nobel Peace.

Kiran Kumarji declared that he was receiving the award not as an individual, but as a representative of the Indian Space Research Organization (ISRO). He remembered Vikram Sarabhai, son of Gujarat, who foresaw space technology to be used in all walks of life in India. Governor Shree O. P. Kohli bowed to Santokbaa's portrait and sought her blessings. Chief Minister Shree Vijaybhai Rupani complimented SRK for bringing jewels of India like Shree Kiran Kumar and Shree Kailash Satyarthi to people at large.

After the function, while the President was walking out, I hesitantly asked him if he could pose with our family members for a photograph. He readily agreed and during the few minutes, it took everybody to assemble in a frame, when I was telling him about our family, Rashtrapatiji said, 'We are also five brothers and two sisters. After my elementary school education, I had to walk each day to Kanpur from my Paraukh village in Kanpur Dehat, 8 km away, to attend junior school, as nobody in the village had a bicycle.' I remembered my going to school at Lathi on bicycle. We organized

---

[8] https://www.deshgujarat.com/2018/05/30/president-kovind-sets-aside-tradition-and-attends-santokba-award-function/. Last accessed on date to October 10, 2021.

[9] सुरक्षित बचपन फंड, safe childhood fund

a separate function just after the Presidential function at a different venue, Science Centre, City Light Road, wherein the Award winners could speak and interact with the audience.

I was very happy to receive an invitation from President Ramnath Kovindji to attend the traditional Independence Day on 15 August 2018 'At Home' in Rashtrapati Bhawan with my wife. We were truly delighted. Mingling with powerful people, leaders, diplomats, and officials, and among the 400 guests, was indeed a dream world. When Prime Minister Narendrabhai saw us, he said in a loud cheerful voice, 'O re Govindbhai, kyaare aavya? (O Govindbhai, when did you arrive?).' By addressing me as O re Govindbhai, Narendrabhai made me feel special in that gathering of greats. When someone likes you, the way they talk about you is different. You feel safe and comfortable.

On 31 October 2018, Prime Minister Narendrabhai unveiled Sardar Patel's 'Statue of Unity' on the banks of the river Narmada in Kevadia. The occasion marked the 143rd birth anniversary of Sardar Patel. The statue has been built using over 70,000 tons of cement, 18,000 tons of reinforcement steel, 6,000 tons of structural steel and 1,700 metric tons of bronze. It was at the cost of about Rs 3,000 crores by over 3,000 workers, including 300 engineers from Larsen & Toubro (L&T). A remarkable sight because of its sheer size, at 182 meters, the statue is 23 meters taller than China's Spring Temple Buddha statue and almost double the 93-meter-tall Statue of Liberty in the U.S. Tears of joy rolled out of my eyes for being the part of this historic day. Forgotten by people at large, who would have imagined that Sardar Patel, who died in December 1950, would ever get such recognition.

In 2011, Narendrabhai created a special purpose vehicle Sardar Vallabhbhai Patel Rashtriya Ekta Trust (SVPRET) to carry out this project in a business-like time-bound manner, he also launched a social movement to collect 129 tons of iron implements from nearly 100 million farmers in 169,000 villages across all states to construct the base of the statue. It was rightly called the 'Loha' campaign. Renowned sculptor, Ram Vanji Sutar, born in 1925 in Dhule district of Maharashtra and decorated with the Padma Shree in 1999 and later Padma Bhushan in 2016, was invited to design the statue. Sutarji had built more than 50 sculptures in his 60-year long career, including the statue of Mahatma Gandhi inside the Parliament. His son Anil is also a sculptor.

Once on a visit to Mauritius, Sachchidanand Swami saw Mangal Mahadev statue, a 33 m (108 feet) tall sculpture of Lord Shiva at the entrance of Crater Lake Ganga Talao and had the idea of setting-up a statue of Sardar Patel in Gujarat. He circulated the idea to construct a statue of Sardar on a small plot of land measuring around 2 acres between Gandhinagar and Ahmedabad. I readily accepted this idea and expressed to support the project financially. When Swamiji asked for an appointment of then Chief Minister Narendra Modi to discuss this project, Narendrabhai surprised Sachchidanand Swami by announcing to construct world's tallest statue of Sardar. Some ideas springs to happen as God's will. Blessed are those who become the medium and instrument in this process.

Sir Parthasarathy Dasgupta, the Frank Ramsey Professor Emeritus of Economics at the University of Cambridge, United Kingdom, gave the third lecture in the IIM-A-SRK Annual Lecture Series on 10 January 2019. I could not attend the function and sent Jayantibhai Narola in my stead. Born in Dhaka and raised mainly in Varanasi after the partition of India, Dasguptaji went to England in 1962 after graduating in Science at Hans Raj College, India. He completed his master's in mathematics at Trinity College, Cambridge, and PhD in Economics at Cambridge. He married Carole, daughter of James Meade, a British economist and winner of the 1977 Nobel Prize in Economic Sciences. Partha Sarathiji taught at the London School of Economics before moving to the University of Cambridge in 1985 as Professor of Economics. Queen Elizabeth II knighted him in 2002.

Sir Partha Dasgupta spoke on 'Human Well-Being and Economic Accounting.' The Press Trust of India reported his speech. 'Indices of human well-being in current use are insensitive to human dependence on the natural environment, both at a moment in time and across generations. By economic growth we should mean growth in the social worth of an economy-not growth in gross domestic product nor the many ad hoc indicators of human development that have been proposed in recent years. The concept of wealth invites us to extend the notion of capital assets and the idea of investment well beyond conventional usage.' He further said, 'by sustainable development we should mean development in which wealth per head, adjusted for its distribution, does not decline. This has radical implications for the way national accounts are prepared and interpreted.'[10]

---

[10] https://www.theweek.in/wire-updates/business/2019/01/11/pwr7--shree   per cent20ramkrishna per cent20knowledge per cent20foundation per cent20(srkkf). amp.html. Last accessed on date to October 10, 2021.

9

New India

मित्राणि धन धान्यानि प्रजानां सम्मतानिव ।
जननी जन्म भूमिश्च स्वर्गादपि गरीयसी ॥

(वाल्मीकि रामायण, युद्ध कांड 6, सर्ग 124, श्लोक 17)

The friends, the riches and the grains are highly honoured in this world. Mother and motherland are far superior to even the heaven.

(Valmiki Ramayana, Yudh Kand 6, Canto 124, Verse 17)

I woke up to the bad news of death of 40 soldiers in Kashmir by a suicide bomber on 14 February 2019. As was later reported, 'a terror attack was carried out in Pulwama in Jammu and Kashmir by a suicide bomber resulting in the death of 40 CRPF personnel. The suicide bomber, identified as Jaish-e-Mohammad's Adil Ahmed Dar, rammed his vehicle into a bus with the CRPF convoy.[1] State

---

[1] https://www.thehindu.com/topic/pulwama-attack-2019/. Last accessed on date to October 10, 2021.

funerals of security personnel killed in the attack were held in their respective native places created widespread outrage throughout the country. Protests, bandhs, and candlelight marches were held across India.

Surprising everybody, India responded by airstrikes on 26 February 2019. Twelve Mirage 2000 jets of the Indian Air Force bombed the biggest JeM terror camp in Balakot, Khyber Pakhtunkhwa deep inside Pakistan. The operation eliminated many JeM terrorists and senior commanders. I felt happy that India could finally decide to punish the perpetrators. On 4 March 2019, speaking at a rally in Ahmedabad Prime Minister Narendrabhai asserted that the terrorists would be hunted even if they hid deep underneath the Earth. 'Chun chun ke hisab lena meri fitrat hai, ghar mein ghus kar marenge (It is in my nature to the settle score, we will go into the houses of terrorists and kill them).'

It is indeed difficult for the current generation to understand the magnitude of Sardar Patel's contribution to independent India. Nevertheless, the 'Statute of Unity' created a new awareness. I organized buses for SRK employees and their families to go there and they returned inspired and informed. Many of them were indeed surprised to know that there was a serious attempt to take away Junagarh from Gujarat. So, let me start this chapter with that story which I had heard from my father. The new is built over the old as the building is made over the foundation and we cannot understand the passion of Narendrabhai Modi to create New India militarily strong and socially aware of their civilization without knowing the horrendous things that had happened to us as a nation in the past.

In the run-up to the Indian Independence 550-odd princely states, another legacy of the British Raj, were being divided up between India and Pakistan. The Nawab of Junagadh was an eccentric character, famously obsessed with dogs. His Diwan carried out the actual governing of the Junagadh. In the last months of

British India, his Diwan was a Muslim League politician named Shah Nawaz Bhutto, the father of future Pakistani Prime Minister Zulfikar and grandfather to Benazir Bhutto. On 15 August, as independence rolled around, Junagadh declared itself acceding to Pakistan.[2]

Sachchidanand Swami narrated once that one of the most potent weapons during the Aarzee Hukumat movement, the campaign against Junagadh Nawab`s decision to merge with Pakistan, was the economic boycott of the state. In fact, special boycott committees were constituted mainly in Mumbai and various other cities across India, which strategically planned the economic collapse of Junagadh state. The Nawab fled to Pakistan, taking all the money in the state treasury, most of his wives and few of his dogs with him. Bhutto was left in charge of the state.

The drama soon ended with an anticlimax. Bhutto kept on asking Pakistan for military and financial assistance, but the help never came. Focused on annexing the Kashmir Valley, Pakistan had nothing to help Junagadh with. Bhutto eventually relented on 8 November, offering India to take over the reins of Junagadh. Government administrator reached Junagadh on 9 November, only to discover that Bhutto had already decamped for Pakistan. At the end, fate of these disputes was sealed by military power. A plebiscite was eventually held to decide what the people wanted. The result was 1,90,870 for India, 91 for Pakistan.[3] Junagadh has come a long way since then.

On 9 March 2019, I attended the wedding of Akash, son of Mukesh Ambani and grandson of Dhirubhai Ambani. Akash Ambani, twin of his sister Isha Ambani, married Shloka Mehta, daughter of Russelbhai Arunbhai Mehta of Rosy Blue, a diamond company. I was there from the bride's side for two days and got

[2] https://revisitingindia.com/2013/08/28/accession-of-junagadh-farce-of-history/. Last accessed on date to October 10, 2021.
[3] Ibid

a chance to meet the family during the surreal wedding at the Jio World Centre in Bandra Kurla Complex. At the beginning of the wedding, the entire family payed respect to Dhirubhai Ambani and Nitaben's father Ravindrabhai Dalal. Shree Ratan Tata was also there. Even in the hustle-bustle of the wedding, the gracious man inquired about by my family recalling his visit last year.

Coming to Vadodara, a princely state ruled by the Gaekwad dynasty of the Maratha Confederacy from its formation in 1721, it remained an island of excellence throughout. Housed in the sprawling 55 acres campus of the Pratap Vilas Palace at Lal Baugh in Vadodara, built by Maharaja Sayaji Rao III for his eldest son Fatehsing Rao, is The National Academy of Indian Railways (NAIR). The palace was leased by the then Bombay Government in 1949 and given to the Railways for their use. In 1964, the Railways purchased the property. I landed there on 10 April 2019 to interact with Officer Trainees inducted into Engineering, Medical and Management Cadre of Indian Railways, at the NAIR. The Academy is the 'Centralized Training Institute' for Officer Trainees assigned to 'Indian Railway Accounts Service', Indian Railway Personnel Service', 'Indian Railway Stores Service' and 'Indian Railway Medical Service' by UPSC.

I was very happy to interact with the young officers. They had reached here by passing through strong competition and sturdy evaluation process. When I told them about my meagre education and succeeding in life by following certain values and methods, they were all ears. Citing teachings of Dongreji Maharaj and adding my practical experience, I asked if they were aware that by joining the Railways, they were indeed joining the task of managing the lifeline of India. Since the origin of railway in 1853, the Indian railway has been one of the most popular mode of transport employed by all classes of people of India. It is interesting to note that railways have done progress in every decade. With the time, railways routes, railway lines from narrow gauge, meter gauge converted to broad gauge and steam engine, diesel engine replaced by electric engine. Moreover, the beauty is, that all this even exists in some or the other form, somewhere in the vast system of Indian Railways.

The first ever train in India ran between Bombay to Thane in 1853 and the second train ran between Howrah and Hubli in 1854. In 1855, the BB&CI (Bombay, Baroda, and Central India) Railway was formed, with a broad gauge from Ankleshwar to Utran on the West Coast and in 1864, within a year, it was extended to Bombay. In 1908, BB&CI Railway opened the Baroda to Mathura line. In 1879, Palanpur to Ahmedabad Meter Gauge (MG) was inaugurated. In 1881, Rajputana State Railway join hands with BB&CI by opening MG line for Ajmer to Ahmedabad. In 1937, a fast train named 'Flying Rani 'was introduced between Surat to Bombay, which leaves Surat every day at 5.25 a.m. for Mumbai even today. In 1948, railways owned by princely states of Bhavnagar, Kathiawad, Dwarka, Gondal, Morbi and Jamnagar merged with BB&CI and soon Gaekwad's Baroda State Railway (GBSR) merged in BB&CI. In November 1951, BB&CI Railway were merged to create Western Railways.

After the lecture, I had a good meeting with Pradeep Kumarji, Director General at NAIR. He had traveled widely over various countries and undergone trainings in High-Speed Rail at Japan, Strategic Management at Carnegie Mellon University, Pittsburgh, USA. I used this opportunity to know about the Bullet Train Project, called the Shinkansen technology. Pradeep Kumarji told me that Shinkansen in Japanese means 'New Trunk Line.' The first Shinkansen train between Tokyo and Shin-Osaka in 1964 ran at 210 kmph. Japan made continuous improvements in this technology and current Shinkansen trains run at a speed up to 320 kmph. Shinkansen technology is the most reliable and with a proven safety record of zero passenger related fatality records in last 54 years. India will have state-of-the-art Shinkansen trains (E5 series).

On 10 May 2019, 130 members of the SRK family went to Spain. We took a flight from Mumbai to Barcelona via Dubai. Barcelona is a big, flourishing city on the coast of northeastern Spain. It is the capital and largest city of the autonomous community of Catalonia, which wants to become an independent country. Barcelona is also the second most populous municipality of Spain. With a population of about 20 lakhs people living within city limits, we found it very lively. Considered a global city, Barcelona is a major cultural, economic, and financial center in southwestern Europe, and the main biotech hub in Spain. We took a cruise in the Balearic Sea and went to see along the coast French city Marseille and Italian cities of Genoa, Naples, Messina, and island country Malta, located in the central Mediterranean Sea, docking at Valletta.

On 23 May 2019, BJP under the leadership of Narendrabhai Modi won majority in Loksabha election. It turned out to be even bigger than the 2014 victory. After dinner our Dholakia family was sitting and talking in our garden at night. Everybody wanted me to speak. I said, 'While this world is changing, India is changing, there are certain things which will never change. They forever remain as unalterable facts. Like Diamonds, they emerge out the great depth of earth and one must find them at great cost and effort. It is important to be aware of these paramount truths.' There was a pin drop silence. No one spoke for a while. Then Champa prodded me to explain what I consider as my 'Triveni of Life.' The three unshakeable facts are: (1) Honesty and ethics are the only valid ways to progress in life; (2) This world is governed by an unseen force, that permeates everything, and nothing can escape that force. God is omnipresent, omnipotent; and (3) Family is a fact of life. You do not choose your family. They are God's gift to you, as you are to them.

I was surprised the way I expressed these facts. If there is one center, around which my mind moves it is Shree Dongreji Maharaj.

By his speech, the listeners become different. Whatever I heard in his voice I took it as my scriptures. Dongreji converted as large a Grantha as Shreemad Bhagwat, into a delicious bowl of Kheer[4] by putting together the milk of Knowledge, energy of Ghee as Vairagya and sugar of devotion. Gyana, Vairagya, and Bhakti[5]-all the three are combined in a wonderful manner in his Kathas.' Shreyans asked curiously, 'Father, can you tell as few teachings of Dongreji Maharaj.' I said, 'Why not?' 'The first teaching I must share is that of a father-son relation.' And I narrated to him the story of Dronacharya and his son Ashwatthama.

Ashwatthama obtained the ultimate weapon, the Narayan-Astra,[6] as a special gift from his father Dronacharya. Though the learned father warned the son never to use the weapon recklessly but as it always happens, the unprepared prodigy never listens to their parents and quickly make a mess of the family fortunes. Ashwatthama attempted to destroy the foetus of the son of Abhimanyu with the Narayan-Astra but failed as Narayana Himself protected the helpless child yet to be born. Now, we all know, this boy, saved in Uttara's womb was Parikshit, the only descendent of the Pandava brothers, who would later die by a snakebite. 'So, know this that no father can give anything to his son and no son must take his fortune as granted. This world is run by God and His Ways are above our knowledge and beyond our understanding.' I told my family members.

To my surprise, Champa chipped in and said as if supplementing my answer, 'Whatever exists belongs to Lord Ram. To serve Lord Ram means to follow his life. If one lives as Lord Ram lived, only that person can be called as learned, only that person can be called a devotee. Lord Ram came to this mortal world in the human form

---

[4] क्षीर, a sweet made of milk and sugar
[5] ज्ञान, वैराग्य और भक्ति Gyana (knowledge), vairagya (renunciation), and bhakti (devotion)
[6] नारायणअस्त्र, The Narayanastra was the personal weapon of Lord Vishnu in his Narayana form. This astra in turn fires a powerful tirade of millions of deadly missiles simultaneously.

to set the supreme example of human conduct. Following example of Lord Ram in every situation of life is the surest way to flourish in this world.'

My nephew Rakeshbhai asked, 'Kakaji, what do we do where there is no example? In the modern world, there are so many situations, which were not there at the time of Lord Ram.' I said, 'There is no situation which is not included in Shree Ram Katha. Outer forms may be different but basic issues are universal and same. Lord Ram followed the orders of his father, which were wrong, but he obeyed. Shree Sitaji followed her husband to the forest even though Lord Ram himself asked her not to. The relationship between brothers is so beautifully explained between Shree Ram, Lakshman, Bharat and Shatrughna. Whatever is the situation, sit quietly and remove the outer layers and you can see it in its true form and then follow the example of Shree Sitaramaji. Not only that you will never regret, but you will also flourish in your life beyond your imagination.'

Therefore, the first principle of Honesty and Ethics I learnt from Dongreji Maharaj was to understand this life as God-directed phenomenon. There is no real problem and therefore there are no real answers. All problems are created before you like questions in an examination. Know this, 'God will not give you any problem ever beyond your capacity of sorting it out.' We are all tested if we would stick to honesty and ethics or succumb to cheating and manipulation. This is the first and foremost principle I learned and followed in my life. One day in Satsang of Indravadanbhai Choksi. The Sanskrit Pandit Dani Dutt Jha recited one Shloka of Adi Shankaracharya:

अविज्ञाते परे तत्त्वे शास्त्राधीतिस्तु निष्फला ।
विज्ञातेऽपि परे तत्त्वे शास्त्राधीतिस्तु निष्फला ॥

(विवेक चूडामणी, श्लोक 61)

The study of the Scriptures is useless so long as the highest Truth is unknown, and it is equally useless when the highest Truth has already been known.

(Vivek Chudamani, Verse 61)

'What is the second principle?' my Bahu,[7] Sweety asked. The second principle that I learned and followed has been that an unseen force governs this world. This also I learnt from Dongreji Maharaj, quite early in my life. One day Dongreji Maharaj said, if you want peace of mind, stop worrying about the world. Make no attempt to change the world, rather change yourself if you want change in world. There was nothing wrong in the world. However, nothing would be right in this world without God. What one likes, loves, appreciates, values today, one may dislike tomorrow. What was useful today can become useless tomorrow. What was attractive can become repulsive. Your mind is ever changing; your attitude also keeps changing, and as per fate life keep on changing. What goes up comes down. Today if you praise someone, you will criticize him tomorrow. Those who praise you today will despise you tomorrow. There is nothing wrong in the world. But nothing is right in this world without God.

King Parikshit knew that end of his life was to come upon him within seven days, according to the curse of the Rishi Shamika's son Sringi, for disrespecting Rishi Shamika. It was at that time, the great Shukdev Maharishi happened to pass that way. Parikshit put a question to the sage that was foremost in his mind: With death staring at him, what is the one good thing he could do? Parikshit was perplexed because with life, the world ends and without the world all pursuits become irrelevant. The answer to this question can only be found by understanding yourself beyond your physical body and beyond the world that our senses present before us. Shukdevji says,

---

[7] बहु, Daughter-in-law

'O king! Do you have any expectations in the end?' The Parikshit says, 'No. I have enjoyed so much happiness in this life. There is no expectation.' Shukdev says, 'I will tell you the Bhagavat Katha in seven days.'

'On the first day I will tell you about the nature of human life. Everyone's life is different. I will tell you how to live in it. Next day I will show you the ways and means for controlling the nature of self. I will tell you how to attain God. On the third day, I will talk about how everyone should try to live with dignity and tolerate humiliation with restraint. On the fourth day I will talk about the relationship between Jiva and Shiva.[8] God dwells in the heart of every human being. I will talk about man's relationship with the world as well as with God. On the fifth day, when a man reaches the peak of ascension and ego comes into him at that time, I will tell the story of how he falls. On the sixth day God is one despite the different forms of God. I will describe how God can be worshiped in any form. On the seventh day man will worship God in any form. Finally, I will say that God is One. God gives every human being a little bit of splendor with birth. To keep God's share from whatever wealth, knowledge, form etc. is obtained, i.e., to set aside a fixed portion and help the needy out of it. Don't just live for yourself, Sacrificing for the sake of others.' – Thus spoke Shukdevji.

In this way Shukdevji helped King Parikshit to explain our true form beyond the physical body and the senses. It is important to understand that just as thousands of fissures in the water of an ocean come in the form of waves, in fact only one basic function remains. Just as the ocean seems to have the same function, so does the universe have the same function. Everything in this world continues to evolve from the lowest to the highest levels of consciousness. That is the only action that keeps happening. All other functions revolve around it.

---

[8] जीव और शीव, Human and God

My nephew Rahulbhai raised a doubt, 'There is a temptation in this world which tells us that there is something here which is good enough and we need not seek another good in some other realm of creation.' I said, our sensory organs create this feel-good. We are caught in the web of sensory activity, attracted to what is pleasant, running away from what is unpleasant. But running always. That which appears to be good now may not be good tomorrow. Some mysterious action is making us run like a person controlling puppets in a puppet show. We see only puppets moving, and we enjoy the play, not knowing that somebody is manipulating strings to control their activity. Likewise, we are not aware of what takes place when we contact things in the world which give us joy, because these are puppet shows.

My younger brother's wife, Sharda asked, 'But Bhai, why does this force simply witness? Why does it not stop wrong things from happening?' I said, 'God has given free will to every human being. He will never take it back. Therefore, whatever human beings do, God does not interfere. But everyone must face the consequences; there also God does not interfere.' In Shreemad Bhagvad Gita, Lord Shree Krishna says:

ये यथा मां प्रपद्यन्ते तांस्तथैव भजाम्यहम् ।
मम वर्मानुवर्तन्ते मनुष्या: पार्थ सर्वश: ॥

(श्रीमद् भगवद् गीता, अध्याय 4, श्लोक 11)

Whoever resort to me in whatever way, in the same manner do I favour them; men experience Me alone in different ways, O Arjuna.

(Shreemad Bhagavad Gita, Chapter 4, Verse 11)

About my third principle of family that it is the biggest truth of one's life also I remembered Dongreji Maharaj. 'Lord Ram is the peerless devotee of His parents. Whoever is devoted to his parents is a beloved of Lord Ram. If you err in your devotion towards God, the God may not mind, but if you err in your devotion to your parents, neglect your duty towards them, do not serve them, God will not like it. God may even reprimand you. Parents are indeed God physically present, right in front of you.'

'But Kakaji, what about Shree Krishna? He left his parents. In fact, he abandoned Mathura altogether and had come to Dwarka.' asked my nephew's wife, Komal. I said, 'In the incarnation of Shree Krishna the God was in the world as God only. The earlier Avatars of Lord Ram was to set an example in terms of the rules and regulations of human society. Lord Krishna came as God. He is not Maryada Purushottam,[9] He is Purna Purushottam.[10] The demonstration of the perfection of human nature is the subject of the Ramayana; and the demonstration of the perfection of God, as He would operate Himself, independently, free from all accessories, is the theme of the life of Lord Krishna. Everything that Shree Krishna did was the opposite of the world, while everything that Lord Ram did was in consonance with the world.' So, the life of Rama is exemplary, and the life of Krishna is contemplative.

I further said, 'When we started our business company, it started in the name of God, Dongreji Maharaj says if you do any work, keep God with you, do it in the name of God, both Rama and Krishna are our liked God, who to leave? So, we kept the names of both and Lakshmi means wealth, so we named the company 'Shree Ramakrishna'. We wanted to create wealth for ourselves and for the

---

[9] मर्यादा पुरुषोत्तम, Maryada Purushottam is a Sanskrit phrase in which 'Maryada' translates to 'honour and righteousness', and 'Purushottam' translates to 'the supreme man.' The phrase when combined refers to 'the man who is supreme in honour.' It also means the best man who practiced righteousness until he perfected it.

[10] पूर्ण पुरुषोत्तम, The notion that God, Purna Purushottam, is the all-doer is a Hindu concept found in the the Bhagvad Gita. For a believer, it is important to understand Purna Purushottam to be the all-doer because that knowledge itself is Moksha; it is the key to salvation.

good of others. We wanted to follow the rules and yet go out of the box. Moreover, we have been right.'

Everyone liked my ideas. 'What about abandoning Mathura and coming to Dwarka?' questioned nephew Prabhubhai, I said Lord Krishna completed one phase of his life entirely before he entered another phase. He finished all the Lilas[11] of childhood before he entered the householder life of Dwarka. The majestic, good man who was the ruler of Dwarka was altogether different from the pranky child in Vrindavan. But he had something else to do. His work was not over merely with the Vrindavan Lila and Dwarka Lila, Shree Krishna then performed Kurukshetra Lila—He became a statesman who saved the country, and what a wondrous message he gave us in the role that he played in the Mahabharata war! My nephew Akshay said joyously, 'So, live as Shree Ram lived and do as Shree Krishna said. This is the third principle of Kakaji's life. He kept the entire family together while expanding our business. Kakaji has taken 1500 odd people in our extended Kanjidada's family on path of growth, no one has ever been left out or felt belittled.'

Everyone was satisfied and happy with this impromptu Satsang except my wife Champa. She kept staring at me except briefly interjecting in the beginning about Shree Sitaramaji. Finally, she asked, 'Why did you not become a Sadhu? Did not you ask Dongreji Maharaj about that?' Everyone cheered at her question. But I turned serious. I said, 'Actually, I had asked Dongreji Maharaj that I want to become a Sadhu. But he said that if you want to be a Sadhu, you do one thing and you will be a Sadhu. Look for good qualities in others and remember your defects. You will become a Sadhu. Train your eyes to see virtues everywhere.'

'Have you succeeded in becoming Sadhu?' grand-nephew Dhruval quipped. I said solemnly, my final words, more as a commandment to the next generations in my family, 'Outwardly, I

---

[11] लीला, divine play

am not Sadhu but have always strived to do good things for all. If a Sadhu, or a poor person comes to your place, even if you don't give him money, always give him respect. What do you lose by giving respect? God is not up there hidden behind in any heaven. He is right here, living inside us, around us, watching every deed and thought, every moment. Don't ever fail him, don't ever invite His displeasure.' My brother Arjanbhai's both sons Ishvar and Akshay enjoyed conversation along with their wives Krishna and Madhavi.

To the fourth generation at SRK I wanted to share unique project initiated in name of my father. 'Laljidada No Vadlo.' This multifarious social service complex at Lathi is providing shelter to many, the way Banyan tree provide to passersby. Younger ones in our family are indeed the peripheral branches of a Grand Banyan Tree, Laljidada. The fourth generation of my family received this message well.

Earlier, when Nimeshbhai Mehta, a friend of Ghanshyam Dholakia from Mumbai, visited Dudhala in May 2016, hundreds of bees stung him. He survived this attack solely due to the immediate medical help available at 'Laljidada No Vadlo.' Inspired by seeing such kind of activities being done at 'Vadlo', he set up a company called Sankalp Safety Solutions, Mumbai that now gives away its entire surplus towards charity.

I was one of the happiest persons when I boarded the first international flight Air India Express IX 172 flight to Sharjah from Surat airport on 16 February 2019. I was happy because Ventura Air Connect started by us in December 2014 stood the test of time to contribute in expanding horizon of Surat.

We first went to Nagaland, in 2010, with V.B. Narola, Dhanjibhai Zadafia, Keshavbhai Goti and others. At Nagaland Mr Pankaj Sinha of RSS, Vidyabharati managing educations, introduced ourselves to others as 'Teachers' fearing that as the 'businessmen' we would be taken away by the Naxalites. At that time, the locals did not identify themselves as Indians, and even identified us as 'these people came from India'. There seemed to be no security or safety at the time. There we met Shree Brahmadevji Sharma 'Bhaiji', he was 75 years old. He was the Chairman of Akhil Bharatiya Shikshan Sansthan, Vidyabharati, which is the education activities division of the RSS. More than 35 lakhs children are getting education in over 28,000 schools of Vidyabharati in India. I felt my impression as a 'Bhagat' reflected in Brahmadevji Sharma - the simplicity of dress, speech, and behavior! He explained to me the importance of education in far-flung backward areas.

I have also met another leader of Nagaland, Padma Shree Awardee Peong Temjen Jamir, a learned Hindi writer. He is almost my age and was born in Mokochung district of Nagaland. He came to Wardha, Maharashtra to learn Hindi and stayed there for four years. From there he started the Rashtrabhasha Hindi Shiksha Sansthan at Dimapur. He believes that by teaching Hindi to the children and youth of Nagaland, they will be oriented towards the spirit of India, which will be to their advantage. And today the result is that Hindi subject has been made compulsory in the curriculum in Nagaland.

In June 2019, I travelled to Nagaland after a gap of some nine years. I could see a great transformation. There were fresh roads connecting the hill villages with each other and this time no one told me that 'I have come from India.'

In 2010 when I had visited Nagaland earlier, I stayed at the Sarasvati Shishu Mandir School, at Dhansiripar, founded by Vidya Bharti. Next day morning, we had to draw water from the nearby well using a torn bucket for our bath. Later, with Kishore Jeedung, we went for tea at local villager Kamleshwar Haflongbar's house. On inquiring about any temple in the village, we found none except one depilated small Shiva temple. That day, I resolved to construct a temple here. I offered to the villagers to collect money from the community and that an equal amount would be contributed by me. Over the next few years, the people could collect only Rs 50,000 and the project, which was conceived in 2010, could not be completed until 2017. At that time, I sent my nephew, Rakeshbhai, to Nagaland and ensured its completion. Engineers and workers travelled from Gujarat to stay at Dimapur for a year until the construction of temple was over. The marble of the temple was brought from Jaipur while expert temple designers, Sompuras, planned the Temple. Shree Ramkrishna Welfare Trust bridged the finances by giving away Rs 75 lakhs. This was the first Lord Shiva temple in the Nagaland State. Lord Shiva is called Sibrai in Nagaland.

It was a great pleasure to meet Shree Padmanabha Balkrishna Acharyaji, the Governor of Nagaland along with my host, Kishore Jeedung, and other members of the community. Acharyaji was just concluding his Governor term. We invited the Governor with his wife, Kavitaji Acharya, to inaugurate the Shiva Mandir at Dhansiripar village near Dimapur. Acharyaji performed the puja by pronouncing Sanskrit Shlokas in the perfect manner. During the inauguration, out of almost 150 people, present 130 were women and only 20 were men. Asking Binita Jigdung, a local housewife, to our surprise we found out those women, who not only managed homes but also earned their family's livelihood while most of menfolk indulged only in drinking, dominated this society doing practically nothing. Acharyaji said, 'Hindutva that has united India despite diversity of language, religion, lifestyle and custom. Hindutva accepts diversity, not divisions. That is why India is a Hindu Rashtra. Today Northeast India far from being called the seven sisters and one brother is called a welcoming NAMASTE, capturing the first word for the states—Nagaland, Assam, Meghalaya-Manipur-Mizoram, Arunachal Pradesh, Sikkim and Tripura.'

Following the day of inauguration, Governor Acharyaji asked us to be his guests at Governor House. V. B. Narola, Ravjibhai Monapara and I joined Governor in his helicopter to reach to Kohima. While at the Governor's residence, I remembered the earlier occupant of Governor House, Shree Ashwani Kumar. Surat

Commissioner of Police. Shree G. C. Raigar introduced me to him in 2006, when he was Deputy Director of the Central Bureau of Investigation (CBI). He had paid a courtesy visit to our factory. During the visit, he told Shreyans, who was studying at IIPM then, 'What you study at IIPM is only 2 per cent of knowledge but other 98 per cent, which is required to make you worldly-wise, is available with your father who is a living University.' Unfortunately, he later ended his life on 7 October 2020 at his residence at Shimla.

Later, we interacted with members of Tribeni Constructions and individuals and groups who had extended their co-operations towards the completion of the temple and had lunch with them. Kishore Jeedung recalled how the construction started on 7 November 2011, after my last visit when I committed to financial support to the project. Jeedung mentioned that it took a lot of patience and hard work. We fondly remembered Kamleshwar Haflongbar, who used to interact with him but could not live to see this day. Lanu Tijir, a local Naga and a volunteer at Vidya Bharti, aptly managed entire logistics during current trip of 30 people.

I visited The National Academy of Indian Railways (NAIR) second time on 17 September 2019. Pradeep Kumarji was going to take over as Member (Signal & Telecom), Railway Board and ex-officio Secretary to Govt. of India. After my lecture to the trainee-officers, he hosted a lunch for me, and I once again used this opportunity to hear from the expert more about our Bullet Train project. Pradeepji told me that through this project a technology revolution was being rolled out.

For the first time in India's railway project, we have done aerial LiDAR (Light Detection and ranging) survey, a technology using Laser mounted on Helicopter was chosen due to its multiple benefits and not just a ground survey. Use of LiDAR technology has allowed survey of the 508-km corridor to be completed with draft reports ready in 3 months against the normal 12 months for traditional survey. In another first, Static refraction technique (SRT) survey was carried out for India's first undersea tunnel to be constructed in Thane Creek area. This was part of geo-technical investigations to assess ground situations in areas where Bullet Train will pass.

On 14 September 2019, Union Defence Minister Rajnath Singh came to Surat to honour the families of 122 army men who laid their lives in the line of duty organized by Bhartiya Veer Jawan Trust. His office told me in advance that he would be visiting our home for dinner, something he promised me during 'Hum Chale to Hindustan Chale' event at Nadabet, in Banaskantha district in June 2016. When he reached, my home turned into a hot spot.

Rajnathji spent good time at my home, interacting freely with the family members. He liked the way we have been living—all brothers together in a joint family, with a central garden, a gaushala and greenery in abundance on the bank of Tapi river. 'This is the way people of New India should live. Parivar ke mulyon par chalne wala aisa bharat banana hai.'[12] he said. Next day Rajnathji called me from Delhi and expressed his happiness and thanked for the good time he had at our place. Rajnath Singhji reminded me a saying, 'being Male is a matter of birth, being a Man is a matter of age, being a Gentleman is a matter of choice.' A perfect human gentleman like Rajnathji came to our house and I was blessed!

Bill & Melinda Gates Foundation honoured Prime Minister Narendrabhai Modi as the 'Global Goalkeeper' for his role in leading India in its wide scale. Narendrabhai launched Swachh Bharat Abhiyan, on Gandhiji's birthday in October 2014 to improve the condition of sanitation in India. After observing nine days fasting of Navratri and completing 17 hours non-stop travel from USA, Narendrabhai went to streets of New Delhi for this mission carrying a broom. Who had ever seen a Prime Minister doing this anywhere in the world? The mission paved the way for the construction of over

---

[12] परिवार के मूल्यों पर चलने वाला ऐसा भारत बनाना है, wish to create an India that is based on family values

11 crores toilets across India. The mission has been most beneficial for the women in the country, especially in rural India. Narendrabhai dedicated the award to those Indians who transformed the Swachh Bharat Abhiyan into a mass movement and made it a part of their daily lives. 'The success of the Swachh Bharat Mission is due to the people of India. They made this their own movement and ensured that the desired results were attained',[13] he posted on Twitter.

After reading in the newspaper that Santokbaa Manav Ratna Awardee Kiran Kumar is involved in Isha Foundation's Rally for Rivers project, with primary focus on enhancing farmers' wealth while simultaneously boosting the flow of the rivers and riverine ecosystems, we went to Coimbatore on 9 October 2019, and met Sadhguru Jaggi Vasudev at the Isha Yoga centre located on the foothills of the Velliangiri Mountains, forty kilometers from the city. I liked Sadhguru's idea of inner engineering way of experiencing joy. I was told that every year an all-night Mahashivarathri is held here, attended by thousands of people. Sadhguru also established a Linga Bhairavi temple in Coimbatore where women conduct the rituals. Spirituality keeps changing its methods as necessitated by the new times. Inspired by Shree Kiran Kumar, we participated in Sadhguru Jaggi Vasudev's 'Kaveri Calling' project by giving a grant of Rs 51 lakhs towards plantation of 1.21 lakhs trees.

On 24 November 2019, the SRK family, this time 1000 people, took a train journey to Haridwar. The happiness was palpable. I took two choppers carrying seven other couples from Rishikesh to Uttarkashi for Ram Katha. After Katha on that day, I called on Morari Bapu, who was in Uttarkashi. He said in a happy voice, 'Sarvabhoot Hitaye, Sarvabhoot Sukhai Aur Sarvabhoot Pritaye (in the welfare of all, for the happiness of all, and pleasing for all). Ram Kinha Chahe So Hoi, Kare Anyatha Nahi Koi (that transpires

---

[13] https://twitter.com/narendramodi/status/1176671806608093186. Last accessed on date to October 10, 2021.

which Ram wills, nothing other than that can happen). Ram does not belong to any one sect or a country. He belongs to the whole world.' Later upon his return to Gujarat, he targeted to mobilize Rs 5 crores for the construction of the Ram Mandir. However, on the Bhoomi Puja Day, August 5, 2020, Morari Bapu contributed Rs 18.61 crores to the Shree Ram Janmabhoomi Teerth Kshetra Trust. I contributed Rs 1 crore on my part, later 15 January 2021 SRK donated additional Rs 11 crore towards this greatest cause of our times.

Upon my return from Haridwar, I found one wedding invitation waiting. My staff told that one woman by name Laliitaben[14] visited multiple times to invite me for her son's wedding. Perplexed and unable to identify her, I asked for more details. I was told that back in May 1993, her husband, an advocate, died in a jeep accident near Palej, Bharuch while returning from Amreli leaving behind his pregnant wife, Lalitaben and a two-year-old son. Nobody including the family supported the young widow except our relief center. We appointed her to take care of the children at nursery in V N Godhani School. Finding her bearings, she ran a kitchen; gave tuitions to raise her two sons well. Later, I appointed her at Prannath Hospital as a supervisor, a job that she did with utmost joy and sincerity. I immediately called Champa, and we both attended her son's wedding in the evening. Folding her hands in disbelief and with tears in her eyes, Lalitaben told Champa, 'I am even more fortunate than Mata Shabri. She received Shree Ram, but I have Sita Mata also coming to my house today.' Nothing more could she speak nothing more were we in a position to listen.

My biggest satisfaction comes from hearing the echoes of good deeds that God carried out through my hand. Parita Mangukia was a first-year student of chemical engineering at SVNIT, Surat when her father died in an accident in 2002. She could continue

---

[14] Name changed to protect her privacy

her study through our relief center. She earned a Gold Medal from University, got a job at L&T on her merit and she is now happily settled in US with her husband. The Deputy Collector of Bharuch District came to repay back a scholarship given to him in 2003. Mohamadd Tausif Ansari, son of a street vendor, wanted to study mechanical engineering. I gave him a scholarship in 2008. Today he is working and settled well at Valsad in a fabrication company. In fact, all these stories make my story worthy of being written and read.

The reward I get in return is much more than any help I offer to individuals who come to me. Never has a request been turned down. I listen to their woes related to health, to their wounds related to education and other social issues. All kinds of problems I hear. Many a times, merely listening resolves their cries. I tell all who come to me, 'I am with you.' These four words act as magic. Many instances, I have acted as an arbitrator. I have judged from my position and my verdict is accepted by warring partners, fighting brothers. Many cases of hostile children and parents are resolved. Lovers eloped from their parent's eyes are brought back only to be happily married. People who were strangled by 'Shylocks' were set free. Couples who came for divorce, went back giving promise to stay together forever. Elderly parents who were abandoned by their wards have been happily received back in homes. Partnerships were made, partnerships were resolved.

The suffering of the people who come to the Relief Center is different. What should my son study? In which college? Who is a best doctor for this ailment? Will you give reference for a job? My partner has HIV, what do I do? Do I put my child in English school or in vernacular language? I have lot of debt, what should I do? How can my son, who is addicted to drugs, be rehabilitated? We want to build a library; can you support us? Will you promote Art that we are practicing? Will you patronise a tradition of singing? Will you support our college annual function? Will you support start-ups? I have come across many such questions daily at Relief Center. By God's grace, I have been successful in reconciling many situations.

On 9 January 2020, Professor Dr Eric Alan Hanushek delivered a talk on 'The Economic Value of School Quality—Knowledge Capital of Nations' as the 4th IIM-A-SRK lecture. Dr Hanushek is a Senior Fellow at Hoover Institution; an American public policy think tank located at Stanford University in California. He said, 'The ambitious Sustainable Development Goals of the United Nations can only be reached if there is sufficient growth in world incomes to support them. Moreover, sufficient growth is dependent upon having quality schools. While most people would agree that quality education is important, most also tend to underestimate the economic value of improved quality of schools.'

We had organized Shree Bhagwat Katha by Rameshbhai Ozaji during that period and therefore none from the family could attend and officials of Shree Ramkrishna Knowledge Foundation did the honours to Prof. Hanushek. Upon their return, they told me an interesting thing about Prof. Hanushek. In the early 1970s, when many people went to court in America to increase school funding based on local property taxes, Hanushek had been called by the U.S. Supreme Court to testify as an expert witness in defense of the state. He testified that the problem with schools was not so much as lack of funds as inefficiency and asserted that increasing funding could be wasteful. The court ruled that attention should be focused on student outcomes rather than on inequalities of spending and other inputs to schools.

I found Prof. Hanushek's view reflecting the ideology of Brahamdeoji Sharma. Vidya Bharti Schools are not greatly funded but their outcomes are much better than many expensive schools. Besides, they were fighting an ideological battle against mindset that perceive India as a fragmented group of different people ever fighting against each other and never as a nation. Prof. Hanushek was indeed validating the Vidya Bharti approach of Indianisation, nationalization and spiritualization of education. In the areas of study that are peripheral to the core curriculum, as physical education, music, and cultural education, indeed lie the seeds of complete human personality. I called Prof. D'Souza over phone and thanked him for bringing such an eminent educationalist to India.

When I came to office on 13 February 2020, I was not even aware that I would be meeting the all-powerful Public Accounts Committee (PAC). Brought in by Member of Parliament of Surat, Darshanaben Jardosh, as the parliament embodies the will of the people, this 22-member committee, 15 from Lok Sabha and 7 from Rajya Sabha, headed by the leader of opposition, check parliamentary exercises over the executive by ascertaining whether the money granted by Parliament has been spent by government within the scope of the demand. Committee was headed by Shree Adhir Ranjanji Chowdhary of Indian National Congress (INC) elected from Baharampur (West Bengal) to the 17th Lok Sabha for which elections were held in 2019.

After lunch, I decided to escort them through our factory and explain the finer points of the work going on. Adhir Ranjanji was all ears and made me comfortable by speaking simple words in Hindi. I told him that we not only convert people doing manual work (Kamdar) into artisans (Karigars), but we also encourage them to become artists (Kalakaars). One graduates from being a worker to artisan by applying intellect and training his mind. The transformation of artisans into artists happens with the involvement of the heart and putting creative emotions into the work. I suggested to Adhir Ranjanji that he ask from the people at work about how much they were earning working here and he did ask. He was visibly shocked when he got replies in upward of Rs 1,00,000. Then he asked about educational qualifications. Most of them were simple matriculates and some of them even school dropouts.

After the factory visit, we sat in the conference room and Adhir Ranjanji took over the talking. 'In my entire political career and visits I have never seen this kind of rewarding skill generation. You are not only working on diamond roughs and making them precious gems, but you are also doing a peerless human resource development exercise unparalleled anywhere in India. I have never seen a school dropout earning Rs 1 lakh a month simply by working.' Other parliamentarians were also visibly pleased. Then, Adhir Ranjanji turned to his wife and said something in Bengali. He then turned to the members and said, 'Pure emotions are best expressed in mother tongue. He said that 'Gurudev Rabindranath Tagore had said that If you divide happiness then you will get two things, one is Knowledge and another is Love' – 'Ānandakē bhāga karalē duṭi jinisa pā'ōyā yāẏa; ēkaṭi hacchē jñāna ēbaṁ aparaṭi hacchē prēma'[15] – but here these people are mixing knowledge and love and creating happiness for themselves, for their employer and also for the economy of the country'.

Adhir Ranjanji called me next day after reaching Delhi. He said, 'I will never forget what I saw yesterday at your factory. You have indeed discovered that the biggest value addition in life is love. By taking care of your people well, treating them with respect, teaching them, skilling them with tender care and strict discipline, you have created not only wealth but also human wealth.' I was deeply touched by the openhearted appreciation from a man I hardly knew a day before. It was yet another example of an unseen force driving this world, making people meet and depart, to a design none of us have any clue. I felt as if God sent a message to me that my enterprise and effort of lifetime was a job well done. I am merely an instrument, used by divine force as per His wish. I am not a poet but that day I remembered one popular line:

---

[15] আনন্দকে ভাগ করলে দুটি জিনিস পাওয়া যায়; একটি হচ্ছে জ্ঞান এবং অপরটি হচ্ছে পেরম

जे गमे जगत गुरु देव जगदीशने, ते तणो खरखरो फोक करवो ।
जेहनां भाग्यमां जे समे जे लख्युं, तेहने ते समे ते ज पहोंचे ॥

(नरसिंह महेता रचित, किर्तन मुक्तावली 1-557)

Je game jagata guru deva jagadisane, te tano kharakharo phoka karavo.

Jehana bhagyama je same je lakhyum, tehane te same te ja pahonce

Whatever the Almighty does; Never despise,

Whatever He wrote in one's destiny; It reaches at defined moment.

(Narasimha Mehta, Kirtan Muktavali 1-557)

I thanked Darshanaben Jardosh, our Member of Parliament, for bringing the PAC to SRK Empire. A member of the Bhartiya Janata Party, she was elected to Lok Sabha in 2009, 2014 and 2019. Her margin of victory 5.47 lakhs votes in 2019 was the highest lead by any woman MP in Indian Electoral History after Smt. Indira Gandhi.

I was deeply saddened when my political idol, Keshubhai Patel, passed away on 29 October 2020. I saw in him, the tallest figure after Sardar Patel and must mention that his departure was the ending of an era in Gujarat politics that saw farmers of Saurashtra emerge out of the poverty of their arid lands and by their intense entrepreneurial energy, make a name for their community not only in Gujarat but also in the world. There was a rule in Gujarat that no one can buy agriculture land beyond 8 km from his place of birth. The idea was to keep the farmers pinned in their poverty. However, Keshubhai had done away with a regressive land law that prevented farmers from purchasing land outside 8 km of their place of habitation. It is because of repealing of that law that the Saurashtra farmers like me have been able to venture out and get into other vocations to become prosperous.

10

Go Win

उत्तिष्ठत जाग्रत प्राप्य वरान्निबोधत ।
क्षुरस्य धारा निशिता दुरत्यया दुर्गं पथस्तत्कवयो वदन्ति ॥

(कठोपनिषद्, अध्याय 1, वल्ली 3, श्लोक 14)

Arise, awake; having reached the great, learn; the edge of a razor
is sharp and impassable; that path, the intelligent say, is hard to
go by.

(Katha Upanishad, Chapter 1, Valli 3, Verse 14)

On 18 January 2020, the Indus University conferred upon me the
Honorary Doctorate Degree in Philosophy (D. Phil.). I had been
giving lectures to the students at Indus University and when Dr
Nagesh Bhandari first time broached this idea of giving me this
honour, I was little hesitant. I said, 'Nageshji, you know I got no
formal education.' He disarmed me by saying, 'Govind Kaka, your
personal philosophy 'Problem is Progress' is the foundation on

which SRK stands on humbly yet proudly, and Indus University reflects it in every sense. I attended your lecture, given here in my university on 22 August 2018. We discussed this matter at length in our Academic Council. You may have got no formal education, but your experiences and life principles are priceless lessons that sets examples for all of us to achieve beyond the ordinary. The University would indeed be honoured by bestowing this degree upon you.'

Upon my return to Surat, I showed the degree to Champa. She held it with utmost respect and kept it in the Puja Room. Next day morning when I sat for my puja, I saw the degree along with the other pictures kept there. There are five framed pictures and two idols in my Ghar-Mandir:[1] An idol of Shree Lakshmi Narayan, in marble and the Padmanabhan[2] form, is my principal deity. By its side is an idol of Shree Bal Krishna and pictures of Shree Sita Ram Darbar, Shree Radha-Krishna, Shree Vishnu giving Darshan to Dhruva and Bhagwan Swaminarayan. Then there is a small metallic framed picture of Shree Ram. In 1971, Champa's brother Limbabhai used to stay with us, and he brought this Shree Ram picture and kept in his room. Later in 1973, he left for his own home after marriage but asked me to keep worshipping Shree Ram. Since then, so many houses have changed but this picture remained with me. Therefore, sitting there, that day in front of various forms of God, who have been the faculty, I wondered how God gave me education in the University of Success.

Now my attention shifted to the next idol of Bal Krishna, one in the center of the upper row in my Ghar-Mandir. This picture Champa brought from Haridwar in 1976. There is a secret embedded in Krishna's playful activities in Gokul, where he grew up in a foster home. The first part of the Tenth Skandha of the Shreemad Bhagwat

---

[1] घर-मंदिर, temple in individual home
[2] पद्मनाभम्, Lord Vishnu is represented in the reclining form lying on Adishesha and Brahma the creator, seated on a lotus that stems from the navel of Lord Vishnu. Mother Lakshmi is attending to Lord's feet.

occupies itself with these pranks of the child Krishna. Dongreji Maharaj had said, 'This body is Mathura, and the heart is Gokul. Install Bal-Krishna in your heart. If you safeguard your heart from worldly attachments, then only will your body become Madhura and the heart Gokul. Madhura and Mathura are same. Sensual pleasures and wealth bring drunkenness (Mada). You must safeguard yourself from two varieties of drunkenness then only your body will be healthy (Madhura). Nevertheless, your heart is caught between these two—Sensual pleasures and wealth—if you refrain your body from these two but crave them in the heart that is hypocrisy. Both are engines of Maya. You must save yourself from them from being rolled over. God has created these two very attractive—wealth and woman. Both create drunkenness. You must save yourself from them. Saving your heart from these two in presence of wealth, strength and availability is the real discipline.' Else:

पूर्वे वयसि यः शान्तः स शान्त इति मे मतिः ।
धातुषु क्षीयमाणेषु शमः कस्य न जायते? ॥

(पंचतंत्र, मित्रभेद 1, श्लोक 176)

Only a person who is peaceful at young age can really be called as a 'peace and calm.' What is the big deal in being calm and peaceful when your body has weakened?

(Panchatantra, Mitrabheda 1, Shlok 176)

One who can control his heart in youth is only wise. In old age, when eyes lose sight, if one stops going to cinema what is great about it. Do not debase your youth in sensory pleasures. I followed this principle almost throughout my life and my health, peace, prosperity, and tranquility in my advanced age are due to the wisdom I received from Dongreji Maharaj.

Second picture is of Shree Sita Ram Darbar. In Dudhala village, there was Atmaram Bapu, a Bawaji who lived like Sudama. There were no belongings in his small house. He used to worship until afternoon and eat light food. He used to speak only 'Sita Ram' and no other word. One day, I insisted that he tell me something and he gave me my first lesson. Atmaram Bapu said, 'I am convinced that life is just a game, here on Earth, a game where none is a loser, no matter what his plight or condition may be. Everyone is a winner here who has understood this world as a game—Lila of Sita Ram.'

He further said, 'Our real job here is to live. Mother Sita and Shree Ram have created all of us noble, and all possess the same array of potential virtues. Because of this inherent nobility, we never have the right to belittle anyone. Poverty and wealth are temporary conditions, limited to the boundaries of this material world. Born here in the arid land of Saurashtra in the house of a Bawaji, I could have become an agricultural laborer, or a teacher in a school, but I chose to live like a destitute and chant the name of Sita-Ram, daily. Every night I sleep, I do not know if I will wake up in the morning. Everybody knows this, but they pretend and create lot of security around them—big houses, servants, relatives, and friends—but one day they all leave this world—leaving behind everything and everyone. I do not pretend that way. The real live by a day. Eat little to keep my body moving, worship God and sleep as if there is no tomorrow.'

Atmaram Bapu never left me. Many years later, after I had left Dudhala and was struggling in Surat, I would find time to attend Satsang in Indravadanbhai Choksi's house, who was living like an ascetic. He lived five or six months in Surat. Rest of the time he spent in Vrindavan, Haridwar and in the Himalayas. He so soulfully sang one evening Shree Shankaracharya's Bhajan:

भज गोविन्दं भज गोविन्दं
भज गोविन्दं मूढमते ।

सम्प्राप्ते सन्निहिते काले
नहि- नहि रक्षति डुकृञ्करणे ॥

(चर्पट पञ्जरिका स्तोत्रम्, ध्रुवपद)

Worship Govinda, worship Govinda,
Worship Govinda, oh deluded mind!
At the time of your death,
Rules of grammar will not save you.

(Charpat Panjarika Stotram, Dhruvapad)

Indravadanbhai said, 'When Gyan[3] matures and lodges securely in the heart, it becomes Vigyan[4]. A medical student becomes a doctor, a clerk becomes an accountant, and a lawyer becomes a judge. When that Vigyan is integrated with life and issues out in self-less action, it becomes Bhakti.[5] Gyan upon maturing is spoken of as Bhakti. If it is not transformed into bhakti, such Gyan is useless decoration. So, I spend more of my time in Bhakti.' Sachchidanand Swami once told me, 'Govindbhai, you live like King Janak, तेन त्यक्तेन भुञ्जीथा मा गृधः कस्यस्विद्धनम्, having renounced the unreal, enjoy the Real. Do not covet the wealth of any man.).' Despite all the wealth that I earned, I never let Atmaram Bapu, happily living in poverty, and Indravadanbhai willingly living an ascetic life in Bhakti, go out of my mind.

The third picture in my Ghar-Mandir is that of Shree Radha-Krishna. Like Sita-Ram, the combined forms of feminine as well as the masculine realities of God are embedded in Radha-Krishna. It is believed that Krishna enchants the world, but Radha enchants even Him. Therefore, she is the supreme Goddess, and Radha-Krishna is indeed one word and not two. Man is one form of spirit; woman

[3] ज्ञान, knowledge
[4] विज्ञान, science
[5] भक्ति, devotion

is another, each one having its own strength and weakness. Man as man and woman as woman can never realize God unless they transcendence their gender limitations. When man becomes more than a man—kind compassionate—and woman more than a woman does—brave and daring—they attain the perfection of spirit, which is Radha-Krishna.

Dongreji Maharaj said, 'Satsang leads to successful family-life. What bliss a yogi gets in Samadhi; no lesser bliss is available in the house where both husband-and-wife worships Shree Krishna in their privacy. Householder life is acclaimed in our scriptures. What is censured is indulgence in sexuality. No man or woman is indeed bad, it is the lust hidden in the heart that is bad. Seers have even declared bliss of a householder superior to their own bliss. The house of Kashyap-Aditi was superior and divine. That is why God decided to take birth in their bloodline. Even today if a woman lives like Aditi and her husband lives like Kashyap, God is ready to bless them with God-like children.' Champa and I have followed this principle and are blessed by three children. We very thoughtfully named our two grandsons as Ish and Aan as our belief in their arrival in our home as God's blessings.

Now, I come to the fourth picture of Dhruva getting Darshan of Lord Vishnu. The story of Dhruva is well known. However, here it is sufficient only to mention that insulted by his stepmother, the five-year old child took severe penance as advised by his biological mother, forcing Lord Vishnu to appear before him. I received two learnings from Dongreji Maharaj from Dhruva, included in the fourth Skandha of Shreemad Bhagwat and share them here.

Dongreji Maharaj had said, 'Parents are responsible for the misfortune of their children. A child grows up characterless because of mother's faults, stupid because of father's fault, coward because of faults of ancestry, and destitute because of his own fault.'

मातृ दोषेण दुःशीलो, पितृ दोषेण मूर्खता ।
कार्पण्यं वंश दोषेण, स्वदोषेण दरिद्रता ॥

The second learning is by unwavering resolve most difficult tasks also get accomplished. The resolve should be:

देहं वा पातयामि कार्यं वा साधयामि ।

('अम्बिकादत्त व्यास रचित, शिवराज विजय, चतुर्थ निश्वास)

Either I will succeed or give up this life.

(Ambika Dutt, Shivraj Vijay, Nisvasa 4)

I imbibed these principles in my son Shreyans and my brothers' sons Rahulbhai, Rakeshbhai, Akshaybhai, Ishvarbhai, Prabhubhai, Dineshbhai and Vishnubhai and my sisters' sons Dineshbhai, Jayantibhai, Kantibhai, Chandreshbhai and Pareshbhai right from their childhood. Their children have absorbed it also. Dongreji Maharaj cautioned, 'Those who seek God right from their childhood they only get Him. People who start seeking God later in their lives may improve their next births. If you seek God in this very life, devotion must start in childhood. Learnings of childhood remain active throughout lifetime.'

The fifth picture in my Ghar-Mandir is of Bhagwan Swaminarayan. Shree Sahajanand Swami founded the Swaminarayan movement in 1802. Swamiji was later known as Swaminarayan after the mantra he taught. Under the visionary leadership of Shree Swaminarayan Maharaj, the sect spread all over Gujarat, mainly Saurashtra and central Gujarat. He convinced people to abandon the cruel practices of Sati[6], female foeticide and dowry and inspired people to give up their addictions to tobacco, alcohol, gambling, and other vices. The Swaminarayan influence spread through all strata of

---

[6] सति, Historical Indian practice in which widow sacrificed herself in deceased Husband's funeral pyre.

Gujarati society, from the elite classes to the lower classes, inspiring them to forsake their wayward lifestyles and adopt a morally pure, God-centric life.

व्यभिचारो न कर्तव्यः पुम्भिः स्त्रीभिश्च मां श्रितैः ।
द्यूतादि व्यसनं त्याज्यं नाद्यं भङ्गादिमादकम् ॥

(शिक्षापत्री, श्लोक 18)

All my followers, males, and females, shall never practice adultery and/or gambling and such other bad habits, nor shall eat or drink intoxicants like hemp, opium etc.

(Shikshapatri, Shloka 18)

In more than 50-years history of our company, we had a HR policy of No-addiction and succeeded. Either quit addiction or leave Company. Today, each one of the 5000 and more SRK family members live a happy and addiction free life. Dongreji Maharaj said, 'One who practices only has a right to preach.' Not only my next generation, but also even the current younger generation of my family or my partners' families have remained away from any addiction. Therefore, I tried to learn not from the books but from the life around Satsang and me. I tried to learn by doing what I undertook as my livelihood while giving my best effort and living a pious life. When I sit for puja in my house, I reiterate these principles and live every day in a self-imposed conformity. It is my belief that a glorious New India will emerge out of practice of these timeless principles and will be built by its enlightened citizenry.

At this juxtapose, I must wind up my story. Living my seventh decade of life, creating a rag to riches example, and having lived a family life entranced in devotion of God, I have been a keen observer of this world. I have visited more than 80 countries and some 1000 places, seen different cultures, and spent thousands of hours in the company of realized souls. The Kathas of Dongreji Maharaj, Morari Bapu, Rameshbhai Oza, Sachchidanand Swami, Akhandanand Swami and Satsang of Indravadanbhai Choksi, Atmendraji helped me expand my consciousness. I was greatly influenced by Baba Ramdev and Dr A.P.J. Abdul Kalam. I have seen the historic rise of Narendrabhai Modi and how he became one of the most powerful leaders of the modern world. I have witnessed Parshottambhai Rupala, Mansukhbhai Mandaviya, Vijaybhai Rupani, Nitinbhai Patel and others attaining peaks in their careers.

I have seen the transformation of Surat City from the days of the pneumonic plague to an excellent DREAM City competing with Antwerp. I have seen how Anandiben Patel, on 5 August 2020, sat in the Bhoomi Puja of Lord Shree Ram Mandir in Ayodhya. Who could imagine that a girl born in Mehsana Gujarat would be there as the Governor of Uttar Pradesh? It is all God's Lila[7] of putting people through a great grinding machine called Karma. No one is ever abandoned, no one is ever forsaken!

In the previous chapter, I shared the three streams through which my life progressed—(1) Honesty and ethics; (2) An unseen force, and (3) Family as the foundation of life. In this concluding chapter, I will attempt to present my understanding of this world and how I visualize our younger generations to win the place that India deserves in the global community. I will be sharing with you five sutras, or aphorisms, that have emerged out of my pithy observation and contains a general truth, validated by my first-hand experience. It is indeed true that this world is a stage and life is indeed a game and to be in this game, one must follow certain rules so that the mysterious force that runs this world does not become a head wind and that we do not find travelling on the wrong side of the road facing incoming traffic every moment. I will call these five

---

[7] लीला, God's desire

Sutras[8] collectively as that Go-Win Sutras, declaring the purpose of life as taking the living conditions of the people of the family you are born into at a superior level of living.

Let me name these five 'Go-Win Sutras' as

(1) Burn your bad seeds
(2) Harness your mine
(3) Cut, polish, mount
(4) Build your Hiranyagarbha
(5) Become the Instrument of God

These five Sutras are put in this sequence considering the phases of life. Over the following pages, I will be explaining each of the Sutras in the light of what I learnt in my Satsang and experiences in life.

(1) Burn your bad seeds

Let us begin with 'Burn your bad seeds.' In childhood, if the vigilant parents or primary school teachers with discipline and self-example do not burn the bad seeds in a child's mind, during the hormonal flooding in adolescence it is inevitable that the bad seeds will sprout. In addition, once that happens, it becomes extremely difficult, and I would say impossible to stop them from becoming a tree bigger than even the life of the person itself.

As each person has unique fingerprints, no two people have the identical brains, the neuro circuits connecting different muscles of brain differ significantly in configuration and triggering pathways. This uniqueness is both by birth and due to individual life experiences. However, even unique than that is a person's temperament. Each child comes into the world with a set of inborn traits that organize the child's approach to the world. Success and life's blessings are

---

[8] सूत्र,Principles

based on our nature, temperament, as much as on the efforts. Each one of us is born with propensities from numerous past lives—hundreds, maybe thousands—it is important to burn the bad seeds brought into this life; else they will surely sprout as and when they find favourable conditions.

While staying with Akhandanand Swami, in Vrindavan, I learnt about the three bodies: Karya Sharira[9], Sukshma Sharira[10], and Karana Sharira[11]. These three bodies are connected, and a person functions best when they are in harmony with one another. The soul wandering in and out of the physicality of the world, under fate and Karma.

The Atma[12] is covered under five sheaths (Koshas[13]) namely, Annamay Kosha, Pranamaya Kosha, Manomaya Kosha, Vignanamaya Kosha and Anandmaya Kosha.

Karya Sharira or outer body which makes our identity, is made of food that converts a 3 kg newly born to a 70 kg man. It is aptly called the Annamaya Kosha.

The next three inner sheaths, namely Pranayama Kosha (vital life breath), Manomaya Kosha (mind) and Vignanamaya Kosha (intellect) together makes Sukshma Sharira or Subtle Body. It includes the five organs of sense (touch, sight, hearing, smell, and taste), the organs of action (genitals, anus, hands, legs and speech), the five vital breaths (Prana, Apana, Samana, Udana, and Vyana), as well as wisdom and intellect.

So far so good. However, the fifth sheath is Anandmaya Kosha, which is called causal body and it is attached to the soul as dust upon the mirror—not connected to the mirror but goes with it. On the other hand, fragrance in the air, not mixing with

---

[9] कार्य शरीर, outer body
[10] सुक्ष्म शरीर, subtle body
[11] कारण शरीर, casual body
[12] आत्मा, soul
[13] कोष, sheaths

air but carried away. Every soul enters the world with the Karana Sharira.

Lord Shree Krishna very clearly declares in Shreemad Bhagvad Gita:

ईश्वरः सर्वभूतानां हृद्देशेऽर्जुन तिष्ठति ।
भ्रामयन्सर्वभूतानि यन्त्रारूढानि मायया ॥

(श्रीमद् भगवद् गीता, अध्याय 18, श्लोक 61)

O Arjuna, the Lord resides in the region of the heart of all creatures, revolving through Maya all the creatures (as though) mounted on a machine!

(Shreemad Bhagvad Gita, Chapter 18, Verse 61)

Nature is created by God. He has made my nature very good, which is why I have a full life. I am bestowed with a happy family, treasured friends, wealth, happiness, respect, and love. At the root of all this is my nature, my temperament, there is nothing for me to be proud of. Because I did not create this nature, God created it. God has instilled total acceptance in my nature. Life has been based on 'will do, will suit, will like.' I have always been satisfied with what all I ever received; and adapted myself to whatever situation fell upon me; hence, I have remained happy through the journey so far.

Why did God make me like that? God is not partial to anyone. All the good and bad things that happen to us are the results of past actions. Like the dust on the mirror, the fragrance in the air, it travels with the soul from one Jiva[14] to another. On a larger scale, Karma determines where a person will be reborn and their status in their next life. Good Karma can result in being born in one of

---

[14] जीव—creature

the heavenly realms. Bad karma can cause rebirth as an animal, or torment in a hell realm. In addition, each life presents an opportunity to get rid of it, to burn the bad seeds, so that they do not sprout ever again. Morari Bapu sings from Shreemad Ramcharit Manas:

सो तनु धरि हरि भजहिं न जे नर l
होहिं बिषय रत मंद मंद तर ll
काँच किरिच बदलें ते लेहीं l
कर ते डारि परस मनि देहीं ll

(श्रीरामचरितमानस, उत्तरकांड, दोहा 121, चौपाई 11, 12)

Men who fail to adore God even after obtaining this body, and wallow in the basest pleasures of sense, throw away the Paras Mani in their hand to pick up bits of shining glass in exchange for the same.

(Shree Ramcharit Manas, Uttar Kanda,
Doha 121, Chaupai 11, 12)

An addiction free life is impossible without bad seeds -the Vyasanas-[15] being burnt. How can they be burnt? By mindfulness, by being always on guard where the mind is leading you to. The easiest way I found was the company of pious and devoted people and friends with no addiction of any kind. I have remained free from any addictions in my life. While reading Gandhiji's autobiography 'My Experiments with Truth', I realized that when he went to London for higher studies, he promised his mother that he will remain always away from maas, madiraa and mohini (non-vegetarian food, wine and women). This sentence has been ingrained within me and I have survived because of that sentence.

---

[15] व्यसन, addiction of vices

Dongreji Maharaj also said, 'One who wants happiness will have to give up meat, alcohol, women and gambling.' This sentence is also become my lighthouse in the unchartered sea of this world. I have been to Las Vegas, a global gambling den, many a times, since the Diamond Fair is held every year there. I have been there some twenty odd times but so far, I have not gambled even a single dollar, God forbid. When I first went on tour with my family in Las Vegas in 1989, there were only 3 hotels, and only 30 flights to the airport, which today has transformed to around 400 flights, and the largest 8500-room hotel in the world, testifying that not many people are able to burn their bad seeds.

(2) Harness your mine

Harnessing your mine is all about education. The grown-up child must be exposed to the education—the rules of life—by which things happen around him and everybody must act accordingly—following them and not running away from them or violating them.

'Harness your mine' is all about using your body-mind system to tap power from the universe. Many of us spend our lives searching for success when it is usually so close that we can reach out and touch it. When I was working as a diamond-polisher, I realized that only if I can buy a rough diamond, polish it and sell it back as a gem, am I going to make money. No one told me this; I saw it happening around me. Then the day I could pool savings from my daily wages to Rs 500, I paddled my bicycle to the office of Babubhai Doshi to buy a rough. When I was told that roughs are sold in a minimum lot of 10 carats of Rs 500, which would be Rs 910 and a brokerage of Rs 10 had to be added, I did not walk out. Instead, I approached Virjibhai, who handed me Rs 220 he had and borrowed another Rs 200 from his neighbor. Our success was sown that day.

Many years later, when I visit new places, I never hurry up my schedule. I arrive a day earlier than necessary. I walk around as a 'nobody' and meet ordinary people. I drink tea at a roadside stall, find out the rates in the vegetable market, visit, if possible, some factories, stores, and a hospital, and talk to people some small talk about 'how is life.' Moreover, I tell you within hours I know what opportunities that town or city has, and what they have failed to do—and then the next day when I go to my business meeting, I know every lever in the cockpit. The truth of life is that everyone, everywhere, can make 'more of himself' in his own environment 'then and there' with his own energy, and with his own friends.

Why most of the people fail to do so is because they secretly enjoy the comfort and coziness of their present life. Even if it is bad, they do not want to change it. If one needs progress, one needs to go out of his comfort zone. Somehow, they like their prison; the idea of freedom scares them. Even if an idea comes to them, someone tells them and guides them; they may never act on the cue. Adi Shankaracharya writes in Vivek Chudamani:

आप्तोक्तिं खननं तथोपरिशिलाद्युत्कर्षणं स्वीकृतिं
निक्षेपः समपेक्षते नहि बहिः शब्दैस्तु निर्गच्छति ।
तद्ब्रह्मविदोपदेशमननध्यानादिभिर्लभ्यते
मायाकार्यतिरोहितं स्वममलं तत्त्वं न दुर्युक्तिभिः ॥

(आदि शंकराचार्य रचित, विवेक चूडामणी, श्लोक 67)

As competent instruction for its extraction, excavation, the removal of stones and other such things lying above it and finally grasping, a treasure hidden underground never comes out by being merely called out by its name, so too through the instructions of a knower of Brahman, followed by reflection, meditation and so forth, is to be attained the transparent Truth of the self, which is hidden by Maya and its effects but not through perverted arguments.

(Adi Shankar, Vivek Chudamani, 67)

When I went to Botswana in 2014, I arrived early as per my policy and hung around to have a feel of the place. You just step out of the Gaborone City and nothing you would find of human effort and enterprise. Mostly, the unexplored desert area divided between several ethnic Chiefdoms who co-existed in relative peace. When Europeans arrived in Africa, Britain was consolidating its military and economic strength as a major colonial power in Southern Africa but at the same time, Dutch settlers and German settlers were pushing northwards and westwards, annexing more and more lands. Defeating them, the British in 1885, carved out Bechuanaland Protectorate that after 80 years attained independence in 1965 and named itself Botswana. Within a year, a huge diamond mine was discovered in a remote area called Orapa, about 250 miles from the capital city of Gaborone by De Beers, the dominant seller of 'rough stones' in the world. What had happened suddenly?

The next day after concluding my business, I visited Maru-a-Pula School. The Principal, Mr Andy Taylor, was away. We paid our respects to his deputy, Ms Tebogo George, and took her permission to go around the school, which she gladly gave. Going around the well-kept campus, my first question was about the name of the school. What is meant by Maru-a-Pula? Ms Tebogo George told me 'Rain is a great blessing in Botswana, and you wish a person well by saying to them, 'Pula.' Therefore, Maru-a-Pula means the 'rainclouds' conveying the promise of blessing.' I was stunned by the profound answer I received. Rarely are schools so aptly named.

What I will never forget from that day came from Mr Munyaradzi Magate, a teacher of History in the school. I asked why De Beers had found Diamond Mines in Botswana within a year it gained independence from Britain and not earlier during the 80-year long British rule there. Mr Magate very wisely avoided any direct answer. Later, he explained me by a story that it was, 'A typical tale of family discord, where three brothers—broke away from their father, Chief Malope, to establish their own followings. Realistically, these fractures probably occurred in response to drought and expanding population eager to strike out in search of new pastures and arable land.'[16]

There once lived not far from the Molopo River, an ancient Khoikhoi[17] known as Bathoen. He owned a very large tract of land. He was indeed a wealthy and contended man. He was content because he was wealthy and wealthy because he was content. One day, an old Khoikhoi Priest visited him. His body was covered with a mere sheet of saffron cloth, and he was wandering barefooted unafraid of beasts and snakes. He sat down by the river and told Bathoen how this world was made. The Almighty God stirred the dense fog into a ball of fire. The ball of fire went rolling through the universe, burning its way through other banks of fog, condensed the moisture without, until it fell in floods of rain upon a hot surface, and cooled the outward crust. The flames upon cooling down became uneven surface of the earth—the mountains and valleys and beneath the surface different minerals—granite, copper, silver, gold and deepest of all the original sunlight was frozen as diamonds. Then the priest was gone without a trace.

Now possessed by the dream of having found a diamond, Bathoen sold his land, collected his money, left his family in care of a neighbor, and away he went in search of diamonds. He wandered through the continent, indeed crossed it over, and at last when his money was all spent and he was in rags, wretchedness, and poverty, he stood on the shore of Dar-es-Salam, when a great tidal wave came rolling. The poor, afflicted, suffering, dying Bathoen could not resist the awful temptation to cast himself into the incoming tide, and he sank beneath its foaming crest, never to rise in this life again.

The man who purchased Bathoen's land one day noticed a curious flash of light from the white sands under the shallow water

---

[16] https://www.lonelyplanet.com/botswana/history. Last accessed on date to October 10, 2021.

[17] Khoikhoi are the traditionally nomadic pastoralist indigenous population of southwestern Africa

of a narrow brook, the only source of water in that area. He took the pebble into the house, put it on the mantel, and forgot all about it. A few months, or may be a year later, the same old Khoikhoi priest came to visit Bathoen's successor, and the moment he opened the door he saw that flash of light on the mantle, and he rushed up to it, and shouted: 'Here is a diamond! Had Bathoen returned?' Then together they rushed into that brook, stirred up the white sands to find many diamonds buried there.

Had Bathoen remained at home and dug his own land, silted out the little brook, instead of wretchedness, starvation, and death by suicide in a strange land, he would have his diamond mine. When Mr Magate completed the story, I knew what the wise man told me without even saying it. He who would be great anywhere must be great in his own house, in his own community, in his own city, in his country.

Had Bathoen not abandoned his family, sold his land, and left to search the diamond alone, his life would have turned out differently. Such many people ignore this simple, straight, and apparent truth, repeatedly. Having given the will power, freedom to choose our actions, God does not interfere beyond this. In addition, as I said earlier, our temperament is our own creation of earlier births, carried forward as a debt to be discharged. Goswami Tulsidas says this through Sage Brihaspati to Indra.

करम प्रधान बिस्व करि राखा ।
जो जस करइ सो तस फल चाखा ।।

(श्रीरामचरितमानस, अयोध्याकांड, दोहा 219, चौपाई 4)

He [Lord Shree Ram] has made Karma the ruling factor in this world, so that one reaps what one sows.

(Shree Ramcharit Manas, Ayodhya Kanda,
Doha 219, Chaupai 4)

Dongreji Maharaj explained, 'What you send out returns to you.' In addition, it is not merely limited to the materialistic and physical efforts like business enterprise. It is true even for feelings and emotions. If you respect others, you will be respected. Dongreji Maharaj explained with an example of hearing back of echo in midst of mountains. I have implemented it by respecting everyone since I was seventeen, including young and elders alike. I started addressing everyone with respect. As a result, I received much respect from this world, and no one insulted me. Hence, my life is blessed. Respecting others has brought me great benefits. For example, everyone in the family is lovingly attached with me. In the same way, the workers, managers, key persons, all staff, and suppliers in the factory began to respect me in return. The buyers started giving me first preference while doing business transaction. All of this led to an ever-expanding business, wealth, and prestige.

(3) Cut, polish, mount

Cut, polish and mount, are the terms of diamond industry. It is all about professional life—how far you are going to grow in your chosen field of activity. Thousands of doctors become graduates every year but only few hundreds from amongst them become specialists and only a select few can reach the Super-specialist stature. Furthermore, very rarely does a super-specialist practice without regard of money that is involved in their situations.

'Cut, polish, mount' is from a lifetime of my work in the diamond industry. We buy roughs that are sold by companies like De Beers, Alrosa and from there onwards, the burden of value addition lies with us. Most of the time, the rough is divided into two or more pieces through a process that involves both science and art and a sense of what is valued in the market at that point of time. I have narrated how we erred when we started working with bigger roughs. But for the honest commitment of

Ashitbhai 'Munnabhai' Mehta, who returned two crores of losses as promised –'Try big roughs, Govindbhai, profit will be yours, but loss will be mine.' There was no written contract, not even a witness. I learned from this incidence that the truth needs no witness. Truth has its own enormous power. Munnabhai held his word, as I was holding to my word, thanks to my grounding in Shreemad Bhagvad Gita and Shreemad Bhagwat and the Satsang of realized souls that never left me to my great fortune. I have never had to resort to lies, and I have never had to lie to gain money or prestige. The policy of never giving up my honesty has proved true and valid. By God's grace, my mind did not succumb to doing clever things for small profits and success remained attached to me as my shadow. I am citing here the Twin-Verses with which Buddha's Dhammapada starts.

मनःपूर्वङ्गमा धर्मा मनः श्रेष्ठा मनोमयाः ।
मनसा चेत्प्रदुष्टेन भाषते वा करोति वा ।
ततो एनं दुःखमन्वेति चक्रमिव वहतः पदम् ॥१॥

(धम्मपद, अध्याय 1, श्लोक 1)

मनःपूर्वङ्गमा धर्मा मनःश्रेष्ठा मनोमयाः ।
मनसा चेत्प्रसन्नेन भाषते वा करोति वा ।
ततो एनं सुखमन्वेति छायेवानपायिनी ॥२॥

(धम्मपद, अध्याय 1, श्लोक 2)

All that we are is the result of what we have thought: it is founded on our thoughts; it is made up of our thoughts. If a man speaks or acts with an evil thought, pain follows him, as the wheel follows the foot of the ox that draws the carriage.

(Dhammapada, Chapter 1, Verse 1)

All that we are is the result of what we have thought: it is founded on our thoughts; it is made up of our thoughts. If a man speaks or acts with a pure thought, happiness follows him, like a shadow that never leaves him.

(Dhammapada, Chapter 1, Verse 2)

Now, going a little deeper in this Sutra, we need to visualize the best scenario of what is in our hand, what is our situation, what is that which needs to be done here and now. When I hold a rough in my hand, I concentrate only on that. I don't clutter my mind with what if this rough could have been 'that' instead of 'this.' What a waste of time this kind of mental work is! Yet, so many people do it as an obsession. Once the diamond is cut, the process is over. Even if a wrong cut is made, we cannot make the pieces whole again. Therefore, equally foolish is to lament and brood over the wrong or sub-optimal decisions. Like water flowing in a river, time passes by like an arrow, only forward, never backwards. Even if you want to make a second attempt, all the other things have already changed, as when you re-enter into the river for a bath, you find new water.

Therefore, think, plan, and take advice of those who have already done, which you are trying to do, and then do it with complete faith and confidence. What I think is a wrong cut by the present trend in the market may very well turn out to fetch me double the price by the time 'that only' shape and size of the gem is 'needed at any cost' by someone, somewhere, and people come searching for it. I repeat— think, plan, and take the advice of those who have already done that which you are trying to do, and then do it with complete faith and confidence, and after that, throw it out of your mind. The gem will find its own value and customer. This is not a philosophy but my own experiential learning of five decades and you can take it as true.

After a rough is cut, and the diamond is split, the separated rough stones are ground against each other. This process is called girdling in the industry. In this process, I see the real process of education. A Guru and Shishya[18] grind together their minds. The worthy Shishya is necessary to make a good teacher great. There is no Shreemad Bhagvad Gita without Arjuna. Shukdevji needs Parikshit to extol Shreemad Bhagwat. So, have a teacher in your life, as early as possible. I did not go to formal education, but I found my teacher first in Dongreji Maharaj, then in Indravadanbhai Choksi and later in Shantibhai Mehta.

In my case, Morari Bapu, Rameshbhai Oza and Swami Sachchidanandji did this for me. Morari Bapu did most of the blocking and Rameshbhai brillianteering. Now, when these great souls read this, they will laugh their hearts out and disown this acknowledgement. But what I feel must be expressed. Diamonds are forever. They come from the deepest depths of earth along with molten lava and are brought forth from the earth at great effort and cost. Transforming my life from that of an uneducated daily wage earner to a billionaire with an Honorary Doctorate would not have been possible without the combined efforts of all my teachers who worked on me as a diamond.

It is interesting to know that as in the year 2021, almost all rough diamonds pass through different hands in the world and out of these rough stones that are traded, 92 per cent of them will end up in India and are cut in Surat. When I came to Surat in 1964, not more than 20 per cent diamonds came to India, today value-wise, India now owns 80 per cent of the global diamond business and once the long-awaited Surat Diamond Bourse (SDB) in Diamond REsearch And Mercantile (DREAM) city is operational, Surat will become a global diamond business hub.

The final process of mounting the diamond gives it the ultimate stature. Like the Koh-i-noor Diamond that was mounted in the Crown of Maharaja Ranjit Singh was further cut, polished, and

---

[18] गुरु-शिष्य, Teacher and Pupil

mounted in the Crown of Queen Elizabeth II. To me, the best mounting of a human being is in his or her family. Remember that your family is not some biological accident; it is a crucial station in the journey of the soul. Like when you board a train from Surat to go to Mumbai, whichever train you take will pass through Navsari, Bilimora, Valsad, and Vapi. The soul is separated from the Supreme Soul to experience physicality to return to it. In this long journey besides being a mineral to millions of life forms, one finally gets human birth. Soul gains all around experience of the world and realizing its identity that is of a fragment of God and meeting its destiny to merge into One Consciousness. As Dongreji Maharaj said, 'One who can control his heart in youth is only wise.' and emphasize the need to be more watchful and cautious in early years of life.

(4) Build your Hiranyagarbha

Hiranyagarbha is the source of the creation of universe or the manifested cosmos in Vedic philosophy, as well as an Avatar[19] of Vishnu in the Bhagwat. In the worldly sense, it is about building your family and organization for the future generations. I came to Surat as a daily wage earner. I did not get even a rupee during my apprenticeship of six months. I could create a Hiranyagarbha—my extended family and a billion-dollar business where thousands of people are working.

'Hiranyagarbha' is all about family, a close-knit family. Your success must be shared by the family and not separate you from your family. Like birth to a particular parent, marriage is also fated. There is no other way that two people are married outside the cosmic design. It is also said that marriages are made for seven lifetimes. Both embodied souls swap their genders to experience each other and then the world together akin to the process of girdling. I pity people

---

[19] अवतार, reincarnation

who go for divorce, extra marital affairs and spread complications in the society by failing in their marriages. Total dedication and acceptance play a vital role in a marriage. Character and nature of an individual should take precedence over the outer beauty of a person while choosing a life partner. According to me, the ideal age for marriage for girls should not be more than 21 years while that for boys should not be more than 24 years, as with the advanced age, total dedication, and acceptance between two individuals diminishes. My marriage with Champa would be fifty years old soon, on 31 January 2021. I was twenty-one at the time of my wedding, Champa was sixteen, and our marriage was considered 'just-in-time.' We have not quarreled even once; never ever resented. But for Champa, I could not have developed our joint family.

Dongreji Maharaj said, 'One who does not see God in his brother cannot perform service of Nation or God. If he forgets his brother and does service to God, it is not his Bhakti[20] but is an illusion.' We were seventeen cousin brothers, children of our parents' siblings, including 5 siblings and thirteen cousin sisters including two siblings. All thirty cousins together in a campaign from 1977 worked for each other, ensuring that each one of us had their own businesses, their own houses, and their own cars. Six generations from our Kanjidada family, now numbering more than 1,500 meets annually during Navratri time to commemorate our union that further strengthens family ties.

This is the meaning of our lives. It was possible because we have always maintained an open mind and generous heart. This openness has kept our family and friends connected. Our life experiences fulfilment out of this union. History remembers generosity not greed. Money is valuable, but relationships are priceless. This is how most of our money is spent, and relationships are nurtured. In this process, many a times, one is willingly victimized, but we ensured that

---

[20] भक्ति, devotion

the relationship is not spoiled. We created, operated, and expanded business as one entity where wealth was created for the bigger and overall good of everyone involved. This has kept friends, relatives and even employees and their families connected and flourishing. I name this idea of my business enterprise as Hiranyagarbha.

To put things in perspective for my younger readers, In the Hiranyagarbha Sukta of the Rigveda it is declared that God manifested Himself in the beginning as the Creator of the Universe, encompassing all things, including everything within Himself, the collective totality, as it were, of the whole of creation, animating it as the Supreme Intelligence.

हिरण्यगर्भः समवर्तताग्रे भूतस्य जातः पतिरेक आसीत् ।

(ऋग्वेद, मंडल 10. सूक्त 121, पंक्ति 1)

Hiranyagarbha was present at the beginning; when born, he was sole lord of created beings.

(Rig Veda, Mandala 10. Sukta 121, Line 1)

I see the Tata Group as the ultimate Hiranyagarbha of modern India. It is important to know, why I say that, to comprehend this Sutra. The beginning of the Tatas was with the birth of Jamsetji Tata in 1839 in Navsari. Jamsetji wanted to emulate the roaring English textile industry in India. He took the bold decision to step out of the business zone of Bombay to save cost to move to Nagpur and have ready access to raw cotton production, a bustling railway junction and an abundant supply of fuel and water. This decision ultimately led to his success.

Jamsetji really cared about his workers. He started several initiatives to ensure the standard of living provided to the labourers. Jamsetji was one of the first people of his time to introduce the concept of a provident fund. He set up four goals in his life: an iron and steel company, an excellent educational institute, a hydroelectric plant and a five-star hotel. He could only complete the spectacular Taj Mahal Hotel in Bombay, but his son realized the remaining dreams to completion. That is the first characteristic of Hiranyagarbha. It is bigger than an individual is and transcends time as well as generations of people involved.

In 1907, Jamsetji's son Dorabji established the Tata Iron and Steel Company in Sakchi. In 1909, he inaugurated the Indian Institute of Science. In 1915, he established India's first hydroelectric plant at Khopoli. Dorabji also completed his father's vision of an entire township surrounding the Tata steel plant. This township was to provide comfortable accommodation for the workers along with provisions for relaxation and entertainment such as lawns, gardens, places of worship, etc. He named the township Jamshedpur to honour his father's memory. That is the second characteristic of Hiranyagarbha. He also established the Tata Institute of Social Sciences in 1936. Pioneers are respected and their work expanded giving them the credit of the beginning they had made and not to what is built over it.

After Dorabji's death, Jehangir Ratanji Dadabhoy (JRD) Tata started Tata Airlines in 1932 and flew the inaugural flight from Karachi to Bombay himself to become the first Indian pilot. He took over as the Chairman of the Tata group in 1938. As goes the legend, 'Under JRD's leadership, the total assets of the Tata Group grew from $100 million to over $5 billion.

When he retired from the company in 1991, the family business had grown to a conglomerate of 95 companies. Some of his most noteworthy contributions include Tata Chemical, Tata Tea, Tata Motor (TELCO) and TCS.[21] With regard to his philanthropic

---

[21] ttps://www.finnovationz.com/blog/tata-vs-ambani. Last accessed on date to October 10, 2021.

contributions, he started the Tata Memorial Hospital in 1941 for not only affordable but the most advanced cancer treatment. That is the third characteristic of Hiranyagarbha, you grow and make society grow along with you.

In 1991, Ratan Tata, the son of Naval Tata who was born in Surat, succeeded JRD Tata.[22] Ratan Tata expanded the business rapidly and ensured that revenues earned by the Tata Group grew over 40 times and the profit earned grew fifty-fold. Ratan Tata broke new grounds when he acquired famous British companies Tetley, Jaguar Land Rover and Corus. These acquisitions made Tata a global business, with 65 per cent of its revenues coming from outside India. Ratan Tata continues to head the main two Tata trusts—Sir Dorabji Tata Trust and Sir Ratan Tata Trust and their allied trusts, with a combined stake of 66 per cent in Tata Sons, Tata group's holding company. That is the fourth and final characteristic of Hiranyagarbha, transcending boundaries.

We have Reliance as another Hiranyagarbha in the making. Founded by Dhirubhai Ambani, born in Gujarat in 1932. He created history with an IPO for Reliance in 1977-78 that was oversubscribed seven-fold. In fact, I consider that as the original birth of New India. Dhirubhai aimed for the Stars. In 1985 itself, he changed the name of his company from Reliance Textile to Reliance Industries. In an incredible example of backward integration, he kept on acquiring the raw material source of his product going up to petroleum refinery waste. Reliance was the first Indian company to be included in the Fortune 500 companies list.

When the Reliance IPO was launched in 1977, the annual revenue of the company was in the region of US$ 85 million. In 2002, when Dhirubhai passed away, the annual revenue of the company was over US$ 16.3 billion. Mukesh Ambani took over the control of Reliance Industries Limited. One of his most successful

---

[22] https://en.wikipedia.org/wiki/Naval_Tata. Last accessed on date to October 10, 2021.

endeavors in recent times is Reliance Jio. His net worth, which was about US$ 49 billion in 2007, has now grown to US$ 80 billion as in July 2020, making him the richest man in India, and the fifth richest person in the world. In terms of market capitalization, Reliance Industries is in the region of US$ 135 billion. Why do I call Reliance as another Hiranyagarbha in the making is due to its 'work in progress' on transcending boundaries which would be complete when Reliance Jio brings 5G technology to Indian households!

My first 25 years of business were most happily spent with Bhagwanbhai and Virjibhai. Eternal design brings people together and separates them. Though separated in business in 1995, the families of three partners stand united even today. But that separation transformed SRK and today I can see Hiranyagarbha of SRK. Sustaining a family business is a challenge especially when younger generations enter the arena. Balance between performance and equity was never a trial for me. Back in 1995, I restructured SRK by inducting Rahulbhai, Jayantibhai, Dineshbhai and Arjanbhai as partners. Results are evident that a US$ 15 million company is now roaring at US$ 1.3 billion in 25 years. Collective clarity of vision, followed by actions of individuals who form a brilliant team with no competition amongst themselves, working without an iota of ego or lethargy has taken SRK where it is today.

The third generation at SRK consists of Shreyans, Akshay, Nirav, Arpit and Brijesh. They are fully trained and have made their individual mark in business. Their association in the company has brought many new ideas and innovations with technology and modern principles of management. Now coming in business, the fourth generation taking training in the company at various stages are also following footsteps of their elders. Kevin, Utkarsh, Darshil, Dhruval, Tej, Dhruv and Raj are the rising stars. They are equipped with good education; having experience of faraway lands and are now rearing to go. Like their fathers, this young lot have no addiction

and possess a religious bent of mind. More than a coincidence, I
see it as Providence that Gyanvatsal Swami, my friend since 2007,
Adhyatma Swarup Swami and other saints are close to Shreyans and
the young generation. They talk with them on varieties of subjects
including stress management, ethics in profession, attitude, work-
life balance, and more. It is beyond doubt that SRK will continue
holding its flag high in a business when the world would enter the
22nd Century.

(5) Become the Instrument of God

And finally, becoming an instrument of God is the ultimate message
of Shreemad Bhagvad Gita—Arjuna is despondent, unable to stand
up for a battle which he had been trained for his entire life, his love
for his brothers and uncles, though they are wrong was not allowing
him to slay them—but Lord Shree Krishna told him to fight and
remove them from the earth as a task of God and not his personal
enterprise.

The fifth and final Sutra is, 'To become the Instrument of God.'
Unwavering faith in God that you will get according to your destiny
is very important. Many people said it in so many ways, but I liked
most this expression of my friend, police officer, Ajay Tomar, 'Live
in a state of acceptance. The effort is yours, but an outcome depends
on so many factors including some uncontrollable, hence never
blame anyone else for your failures.' This can become a fatalistic
attitude that can lead to defeatist and resigned mindset. I consider
that the following shloka from the Shreemad Bhagvad Gita should
be mandatorily displayed in all workplaces:

कर्मण्येवाधिकारस्ते, मा फलेषु कदाचन ।
मा कर्मफलहेतुर्भूर्मा ते सङ्गोऽस्त्वकर्मणि ॥

(श्रीमद् भगवद् गीता, अध्याय 2, श्लोक 47)

Your right is for action alone, never for the results. Do not become the agent of the results of action. May you not have any inclination for inaction.

(Shreemad Bhagavad Gita, Chapter 2, Verse 47)

Sachchidanand Swami explained to me that there are four commandments given in this shloka. The first commandment is कर्मण्येवाधिकारस्ते -You have a right to perform your prescribed duties. Not doing it is dereliction, the shameful failure to fulfill one's obligations. The second commandment is मा फलेषु कदाचन - you are not entitled to the fruits of your actions. When you eat your food, look at your Thali.[23] Imagine the complex supply chains converging there. Salt from the sea, oil from the groundnuts grown in Gujarat, roti from the wheat grown in Punjab, mango in the pickle from Andhra Pradesh. Feel grateful while consuming all this, not great that you have paid for it. Because in that case, you must remember who is paying for you.

The third commandment is मा ते सङ्गोऽस्त्वाकर्मणयेणि ll - Never consider yourself the cause of the results of your activities. Each action depends upon so many factors, how would you read this book, if I do not write it, if it is not published, if you don't buy it, buy it but don't read it, and finally read it but reject it.

Finally, मा ते सङ्गोऽस्त्वाकर्मणयेणि ll - Never be attached to inaction as a bicycle is balanced only while moving and being paddled. If you are alive, you must work. Each breath inhaled must be accounted for in doing something purposeful. In addition, if it can be service to others, it is wonderful.

It is indeed the doctrine of work. You are born, provided circumstances for training, given the right to perform with duties prescribed. Fruits of your actions are based on a bigger game, which

---

[23] थाली, dish

is beyond your comprehension. You are not the actual doer anyway as work is done through you and any claim is therefore bogus. Being attached to your achievement by thinking that you are the doer, you are the cause, and therefore entitled for the fruit of effort is therefore delusion. Attachment to inaction is an even bigger stupidity, outrageous waste of life.

Sheer out of experience and self-realisation I utter that 'Human effort united with God's grace' is the most accurate definition of Karma Yoga. One needs to work with body-heart-mind. I worked relentlessly for at-least 14 hours for almost fifty years. Even now, having crossed 70, I work 10 to 12 hours a day.

Wealth and progeny are subject to destiny; you need to endeavour for the same but never commit wrong to achieve them. Neither do I remember the past nor do I worry about the future but always strive to live in the present. Whatever wrong, stupid, I might have done in the past, here I am safe and sound. I firmly believe that the better the present, better will be the future. The power of this 'Let go' attitude comes from having faith in destiny and God. In addition, the ability to let go brings happiness, peace, and prosperity in life. During my entire life, till date I have never quarreled with anyone, never insulted anyone. Anything and everything that happens in the world is as per God's wish. I keep saying that I am a doer, but I am merely a puppet. Man proposes and God disposes. We must dance as per His wish. I also firmly believe that if things happen the way I desire, it is God's Grace, and if things happen the way I do not desire, it is God's Will. This reduces grief and unrest. God is the giver of Wisdom. Shreemad Bhagvad Gita declares:

तेषां सततयुक्तानां भजतां प्रीतिपूर्वकम् ।
ददामि बुद्धियोगं तं येन मामुपयान्ति ते ॥

(श्रीमद् भगवद् गीता, अध्याय 10, श्लोक 10)

To those, who are ceaselessly united with Me [Shree Krishna] and who worship Me with immense love, I lovingly grant that mental disposition (Intelligence) by which they come to Me.

(Shreemad Bhagvad Gita, Chapter 10, Verse 10)

So, where is the place for pride? This book project comes to an end now. I could recall my journey from Dudhala to the finest places in the world, from an impoverished rural life to the riches of life in the city, from a seeker to a provider. In the next few paragraphs, I present the gist of the book, as Morari Bapu repeats the theme of his Katha in the last few minutes of his every discourse.

In the ten chapters of this book, you can see a progression, an expansion of consciousness, from darkness to light तमसो मा ज्योतिर्गमय l (बृहदारण्यकोपनिषद् अध्याय 1, वल्ली 3, श्लोक 28). It is my journey towards brilliance.

In the first chapter, 'Activation', I narrated how I migrated from Saurashtra to Surat in 1964 as a teenage school dropout and started our company in 1970. Adi Shankaracharya's shloka from Vivek Chudamani is used as an epigraph reflecting this 6-years-long period as a process of excavation that involved a resolve, guidance, effort, tools and means, and above all persistence—a determination to keep trying until success was achieved. Staying with my elder brother Bhimjibhai, I was trained as an apprentice by Arvindbhai at Gordhanbhai Khadsaliya's diamond factory. In 1968, during the Diwali vacation, I visited Bombay with my friends. I had my first glimpse of the power and wealth there. Then, Sant Shree Ramchandra Dongreji Maharaj entered my life. I was like a moth attracted to a flame. But the flame of wisdom and compassion in Dongreji Maharaj illuminated me instead of scorching me. I call these two events of 1968—my going to Bombay and meeting Dongreji Maharaj at Surat as the first real turning points of my life. Thousands of young men reach Surat every year and are assimilated in the city as nobodies.

That I had the resolve to become somebody was important. It came from outer exposure to Bombay and my inner connection through Dongreji Maharaj.

The second chapter, called 'Enterprise', captures the eight years of my initial growth in business. It is like building up a critical mass. If you do not reach a particular size, a certain scale of operations, a certain turnover, you forever remain stuck there. Shantibhai Mehta and Navinbhai Mehta held my hand while I was making those transitory moves. I had two extensive tours with other friends and their families covering North India first in 1976 and South India later in 1977 by road in a Matador. This followed my trip to Antwerp, Belgium with Dilipbhai Mehta from Bombay and our decision to buy rough diamonds directly from there. It was an opportunity that changed my league in the business. This success led diamond businessmen from Kathiawar to migrate to Antwerp. Mohanbhai Dhameliya, Nanubhai Surani, and Arvindbhai Mavani became pioneers of this new stream. I have made self-reliance as the theme of this chapter beautifully captured in Manusmiriti as सर्वं परवशं दुःखं सर्वमात्मवशं सुखम् । (मनुस्मृति, अध्याय 4, श्लोक 160) All that is dependent on others is painful; all that is dependent on oneself is pleasing. If I did not expand my vision and take a plunge in buying roughs directly in the Antwerp market, I would not have entered the big league.

'Edification' is the title of third chapter that captured a twelve-year period including the entire decade of 1980s and conveyed the Upanishadic wisdom of मनो हि द्विविधं प्रोक्तं शुद्धं चाशुद्धमेव च । (ब्रह्मबिन्दु उपनिषद्, श्लोक 1)—the twofold nature of mind—pure and impure—generating desires and emancipation. My family was completed with three children—two daughters and son, I built my house in Surat, and started my business internationally—Hong Kong, New York, Antwerp, and Tel Aviv. My entry in the Israeli market is narrated where I met the doyen of Indian diamond industry, Kirtilal Manilal Mehta, and his son, Rashmibhai Mehta. I have shared in this chapter my spiritual growth facilitated and guided by some enlightened people, namely, Indravadanbhai Choksi, an original Surti, who held Satsang in his house, Atmendraji, who had been the Collector of Ahmedabad, and who later spent his life in renunciation and Dani Dutt Jha, a teacher of Sanskrit Paathshala in Surat. They helped me to remain grounded in spiritual values while I was succeeding in the physical world.

In the fourth chapter 'Power Plays', I shared my insights about how this world works. I remembered three great leaders—Dalsukhbhai Godhani, Chimanbhai Patel, and Keshubhai Patel whom I saw relentlessly fighting for their people, whatever be the odds and mentioned Dalsukhbhai as my role model in politics for his social service. I have made न कश्चित् कस्यचिन् मित्रं न कश्चित् कस्यचिद् रिपुः । (हितोपदेश, मित्रलाभ 1, श्लोक 71) as theme of this chapter—No one is the friend of anyone, no one is the enemy of anyone—the drama of this world makes us take sides and conduct ourselves in certain ways. In this chapter I also mentioned meeting with Morarjibhai Desai, economic reforms in country, political upheavals, silver jubilee of my partnership, emergence of plague in Surat and my tryst with bigger diamonds.

The fifth chapter 'Ascend', covering period up to 2005, celebrates my business success. I expanded my factory into a three-story building and upgraded the technology with laser machines and computer-based management systems, started working with roughs from Russia, Australia and Canada, and my next generation in nephews Jayantibhai, Rahulbhai and Dineshbhai joined business holding key positions. I married both my daughters off in families working in the diamond business, and I was felicitated with the best businessperson award by The Southern Gujarat Chamber of Commerce and Industries (SGCCI) and the unique citizen 'Suryapur Ratna' Award by the Surat Municipal Corporation. With the theme of नाभिषेको न संस्कारः सिंहस्य क्रियते मृगैः । (हितोपदेश, सुहृद्भेद, भाग 2, श्लोक 19) There is no official coronation ceremony held or ritual performed to declare that

Lion is the king of jungle, this chapter also captured Narendrabhai Modi becoming the Chief Minister of Gujarat.

The sixth chapter 'Human Gems' celebrates the human excellence defining it in living for the others and the rarity of such lives – दाता भवति वा न वा ॥ (व्याससृति, अध्याय 4, श्लोक 58) This chapter, covering the period of 2005 to 2011, narrates the institutionalisation of the Santokbaa Humanitarian Award presented in the memory of my mother, and my involvement with the Jaldhara and Beti Bachao movement, and how we handled the 2008 Financial crises without any job cuts and includes the creation of SRK Empire, a LEEDS Gold Rated building inaugurated by Varda Shine, Managing Director, Diamond Trading Company (DTC), the parent company of De Beers, and upgraded to Platinum Rated building in 2019. This chapter also celebrates the convergence of excellent human beings—Sam Pitroda, Narayanbhai Desai, Sachchidanand Swami, Morari Bapu, Rameshbhai Oza, Dr Verghese Kurien, Dr H. L. Trivedi, Poornimaben Pakvasa, and Dr M.S. Swaminathan—by giving or receiving Santokbaa Manav Ratna Award.

'Higher Orbits' is the seventh chapter with पालत्वात् धनमाप्रोति धनात् धर्मं ततः सुखम् ॥ (हितोपदेश, मित्रलाभ 1 श्लोक 6)—from wealth one does good deeds, from which comes bliss—as this theme captures the period of 2010s till August 2016. Vikram Sarabhai's son, Kartikeya Sarabhai, and Dr APJ Abdul Kalam enter therein, imparting an equation: Creativity + Courage + Purity of Character = Knowledge to SRK family and defining the higher form of human life. Fifty years of my coming to Surat was celebrated with the who's who of the Indian diamond industry in attendance. Narendrabhai Modi led BJP to election victory and becomes the Prime Minister of India. I go to China with Chief Minister Anandiben Patel and top officials to be with PM Narendrabhai Modi at the Great Hall of People in Beijing. I started going to IIM-A to share my knowledge and experience with their students. We began inclusion of third generation at SRK—Shreyans, Akshay, Nirav, Arpit and Brijesh. It also introduces the

We start Ventura Air Connect Ltd., connecting Surat with other cities. Dalai Lama, Lord Bhikhu Parekh, Sudha Murthy and Father Valles were awarded with Santokbaa Humanitarian Award. Chapter concluded with formation of SRK Knowledge Foundation.

In the eighth chapter, called 'Rainbow People', setting-up of Kiran Hospital incessantly providing treatment in today's times of Covid-19, beginning of DREAM City is described that would house Surat Diamond Bourse and replicate Antwerp here. I consider this project the acme of my dream—जयोऽस्मि व्यवसायोऽस्मि सत्त्वं सत्त्ववतामहम् ॥ (श्रीमद् भगवद् गीता, अध्याय 10, श्लोक 36) - the victory of the victorious, the resolve of the resolute, and the virtue of the virtuous. The doyen of Indian Industry Shree Ratan Tata, Nobel Laureate Kailash Satyarthi and ISRO Chairman Kiran Kumar received the Santokbaa Award. The Hon'ble President of India, Ramnath Kovindji, come to Surat to give away the award while breaking his official governmental protocol. The SRK Knowledge Foundation was created, which entered a 25-year cooperation with IIM-Ahmedabad to bring the best in the world there for annual lectures and this arrangement saw Raghuram Rajan, Nobel Laureate Eric S. Maskin, Sir Parthasarathy Dasgupta, and Eric Alan Hanushek coming to Ahmedabad and interacting with the students.

In the ninth chapter, 'New India', I expand my vision further from social to national. Written on the theme जननी जन्म भूमिश्च स्वर्गादपि गरीयसी ॥ (वाल्मीकि रामायण, युद्ध कांड 6, सर्ग 124, श्लोक 17)—Mother and motherland are far superior to even the heaven—I share my interactions with the officer's trainees inducted into the Engineering, Medical and the Management Cadre of Indian Railways, at the National Academy of Indian Railways (NAIR) in Vadodara. Narendrabhai Modi won the 2019 elections with even bigger majority, Evening with my family that turned into an impromptu Satsang. I said, as Diamonds emerge out from the great depth of earth and one must find them at great cost and effort, certain truths have emerged in 5000-years old Indian civilization. Then, I shared the three truths that I consider as my own 'Triveni of Life', namely, (1) Honesty and ethics are the only valid ways to progress in life; (2) This world is governed by an unseen force; and (3) Family as the existential fact of life. I encouraged each in the family to participate and the narrative is shared in this chapter.

Then comes this final chapter, 'Go Win', I conveyed about Indus University conferring upon me the Honorary Doctorate Degree in Philosophy (D. Phil.). I mentioned the Upanishadic call for youth to arise and awake—उत्तिष्ठत जाग्रत प्राप्य वरान्निबोधत । (कठोपनिषद्, अध्याय 1, वल्ली 3, श्लोक 14) – where I shared five Sutras as my final gift to posterity. These five Sutras have emerged out of my experience in life—from the churning of events, some good, some bad—and I have offered them as what I see as successful strategies: (1) Burn your bad seeds; (2) Harness your mine; (3) Cut, polish, mount; (4) Build your Hiranyagarbha; and (5) Become the Instrument of God. As God has given the great gift of 'free will' to each human being and He will never take it back, one is free not to burn one's bad seeds but then they will sure sprout and become weeds. One can always choose to live a life in poverty and scarcity or can take one's chances and venture out, as my mother would say in Gujarati—Je Fare, Te Chare![24] Cut, polish is how diamond roughs are converted in to gems and then mounted in the jewellery—big diamonds are mounted on the crowns. I hailed Tatas and Reliance as Hiranyagarbha—the golden egg of the Great Golden Bird India of the lore. Finally, the secret of knowing that we are in this world for a purpose and this world is not to work according to our little minds, whims, and fancies. Know your duty in every situation and at every moment and do what is needed from you—like giving someone a glass of water; or saying thank you for all that we have been receiving from the moment of our birth.

I have no qualms about giving advice in politics, but my prayer is that God has given power and wisdom to all at helm of affairs. If it is not exercised prudently, millions of rupees may go down the drain because of a single inappropriate action. We are not immortal in this

---

[24] जे फरे ते चरे, The one who moves grazes

world. Why indulge in wrong practices when we are not going to live in this world for more than a hundred years?

खोटुं लेवुं, खोटु करवुं, जीवन आखु खोटाडुं ।
अणसमजणना अंधारामां क्यांथी आवे अजवाळुं?

Khotu levu, khotu karvu. Jīvana akhu khotadu,
Anasamajanana andharama kyanthi ave ajavalu?
Incorrect preaching, wrong practices, when life is based on immorality. From where the light will come from, in the darkness of misunderstanding.

I conclude my story here as all stories must conclude. I have lived a healthy and purposeful life and may hang around in the world for some more time, maybe a few years; it may be. It really does not matter. Once you bow out of the stage, you mingle with a thousand people watching those who are under the spotlight, saying their lines. With this book, I have said my lines, and perhaps more. Therefore, I must now stop. Nevertheless, before that, I must share a deep sense of anxiety that has entered my mind.

So many Indians live in our villages, mostly in poverty, in deprivation and fighting with diseases and debts of all sorts. Some of them make early bold moves. They migrate out to cities, even go abroad, depending upon the size of the canvas they could manage to paint their pictures. I consider myself in the category of the second type of people. Together with Devchandbhai, Nakubhai Jodhani, Karamshibhai Malaviya and Ravjibhai Radadiya as if I have brought Dudhala to Surat. Over the last 50 years, we have shared each other's pains and pleasures and brought good name to our little village. In fact, Ravjibhai is called 'Dudhala Naresh'[25] while Gordhanbhai Khadsalia was known as 'Dudhala no Darwajo'.[26]

---

[25] King of Dudhala village
[26] Door of Dudhala village

I went out of my country and did business with the best in the Diamond World but never a thought crossed my mind that I could ever leave my country and live in a foreign land. Wherever I went, Dudhala never left me, Saurashtra never left me and the only business I diversified into was starting Air Connect so that hours on road could be saved by minutes of air travel by many businesspeople travelling every day and so that people living in Surat away from their families back in Saurashtra could meet them at will very conveniently in few hours' time. All remaining fortune is for the family—the people who were born in the bloodline, and people who joined my company and various other enterprises.

My life is transparent. It is stored in an archive, containing primary source documents that have accumulated over the course of my lifetime and—thousands of letters, hundreds of thousand photographs, daily diaries, recorded speeches, mementos, and press cuttings—showing how I lived. I tried to experiment with Mahatma Gandhiji's teaching—Truth never damages a cause that is just—and found it a great truth. Do not hide, if the facts spoil deals, relations, reputation, so it be. All these things are transitory, ephemeral. However, if you hide, you are staining your consciousness in this life and smearing your soul for the future birth.

Every story must have a title, as every person must carry a name. As in Shreemad Bhagvad Gita, Lord Shree Krishna told Arjuna that we are not the bodies we are right now living but the immortal souls on a sojourn in this world, I call this story as Diamonds are forever, so are Morals. From my childhood discovery of my ability to recite Shreemad Bhagvad Gita with ease and later memorize it completely rather instinctively than by effort, I always considered myself unique, if not special. There is something in me that propelled me to take challenges, be it selling balloons during Janmashtami in Dudhala, or climbing upstairs to the office of Babubhai Doshi to buy my first rough diamond, or taking a flight to Antwerp with Dilipbhai, doubts never infested my consciousness.

There are some cherished memories but all of them are bereft of the involvement of money. Morari Bapu doing Ram Katha at our house attracting 8,00,000 people, Chief Minister Narendrabhai Modi attending Shreyans' wedding and later as Prime Minister pulling me by the arm to stand by his side during the inauguration of Kiran Hospital, the President of India coming to give away the Santokbaa Award in my mother's name, visit of APJ Abdul Kalam at my office and Ratan Tata dining at my home, sharing a meal at my home. All these events happened in different times, different places, at different stages of my life, but I can feel them every moment as a long yarn held as ball on a spindle—all the past experiences alive just below the present moment. More especially, I can feel the blind woman Rajuma eating sugar for the first time in her life and blessing my mother profusely that her prodigy will forever live in affluence, even now and consider her blessings as the reason for my wealth and comforts that have been brought to me and my family.

I can hear the words spoken by Dongreji Maharaj when I was a teenager as clearly and loud as if he is speaking now. He said then, 'What you send out will return, like echo of your voice in the mountains.' I not only did not send any unpleasant, unwholesome, unworthy thought, voice, or deed but also, I tried to hear if any old deed of my ancestor is returning for me to hear. My experiences of Dudhala, Shreemad Bhagvad Gita written on my unconscious mind as if, set their seal on the events that came my way and assumed importance for me in youth and later. My parting advice to my reader is this: when you hear no from the voice inside, no answer comes out from within to the problems and oddities of life you are facing, do not do anything. Like clouds, your problems will disperse. Do not react to everything that happens to you in life. Do not answer every question that is hurled at you. Respond if it is coming from inside or let it pass. Your real self is your inner world, keep it pure and clean and follow your inner voice.

Though occasionally there is smooth sailing, I have observed that life is occupied with challenges, conflicts, and crises that can leave one feeling disturbed, disordered, and unaided. Knowing what to do in complex periods can be tough and this is the emphasis of the classical yogic text, the Bhagvad Gita, my saviour.

The Gita has motivated many persons, from freedom fighters like Lala Lajpat Rai, Bal Gangadhar Tilak, Bankim Chandra Chattopadhyay, Mahatma Gandhi and Vinoba Bhave to intellectuals like Swami Vivekananda, TS Eliot, Herman Hesse, Ralph Waldo Emerson, Albert Einstein and APJ Abdul Kalam. Shreemad Bhagvad Gita is indeed a way of my life—it taught me better concentration, overcoming anger, self-control, the art of right action, true happiness, devotion and so on.

My livelihood has revolved around diamonds—from polishing roughs to creating facilities to cut and polish them and trading them as gems, I treated diamonds as my God in the physical form— pure, unblemished, transparent, and forever. From the hundreds of kilometers depth in the netherworld to the roughs and finally as glittering gems, as fireballs of trapped lights by its multiple facets inside the pure carbon lattice structure, mounted on crowns, and jewellery, diamonds never get altered, like human soul, that remains untouched by any human act:

नैनं छिन्दन्ति शस्त्राणि नैनं दहति पावक: ।
न चैनं क्लेदयन्त्यापो न शोषयति मारूत: ॥

(श्रीमद् भगवद् गीता, अध्याय 2, श्लोक 23)

Weapons cut It not, fire burns It not, water wets It not, wind dries It not.[27]

(Shreemad Bhagvad Gita, Chapter 2, Verse 23)

---

[27] https://www.gitasupersite.iitk.ac.in/srimad?language=dv&field_chapter_value=2&field_nsutra_value=23&etsiva=1&choose=1. Last accessed on date to October 10, 2021.

So, remain forever unchanged the morals in life. A good life is all about living by one's morals. What better could be a way to conclude than this shloka of Shreemad Bhagwat that I learned from Dongreji Maharaj:

अणिमा महिमा मूर्तेर्लघिमा प्राप्तिरिन्द्रियै: ।
प्राकाम्यं श्रुतदृष्टेषु शक्तिप्रेरणमीशिता ॥
गुणेष्वसङ्गो वशिता यत्कामस्तदवस्यति ।
एता मे सिद्धय: सौम्य अष्टावौत्पत्तिका मता: ॥

(श्रीमद् भागवतम् पुराण, स्कन्ध 11, अध्याय 15, श्लोक 4-5)

Shree Krishna says, Among the eight primary mystic perfections, the three by which one transforms one's own body are animā, becoming smaller than the smallest; mahimā, becoming greater than the greatest; and laghimā, becoming lighter than the lightest. Through the perfection of prāpti, one acquires whatever one desires, and through parākāmya-siddhi, one experiences any enjoyable object, either in this world or in the next. Through īśitā-siddhi one can manipulate the sub potencies of māyā, and through the controlling potency called vaśitā-siddhi one is unimpeded by the three modes of nature. One who has acquired kāmāvasāyitā-siddhi can obtain anything from anywhere, to the highest possible limit. My dear gentle [Uddhav], these eight mystic perfections are naturally existing and unexcelled within this world.[28]

(Shreemad Bhagavatam Purana,
Skandha 11, Adhyay 15, Shlok 4-5)

These eight mystic perfections, Asht-Siddhis, are naturally existing and unexcelled within this world. Siddhi is a Sanskrit noun that

---

[28] https://vedabase.io/en/library/sb/11/15/4-5/. Last accessed on date to October 10, 2021.

can be translated as 'perfection', 'accomplishment', 'attainment', or 'success.' The attainment of eight siddhis leads to one becoming rid of pain-causing ignorance, gaining knowledge, and experiencing bliss. The path to attain Siddhis is very difficult. Nothing is ever achieved with ease and not to deviate from this path has been my journey so far.

Looking back, I am satisfied with the way my life evolved. I took my chances and the odds favoured me. Good things kept happening and the chances I took turned out in my favour. Many things worked out as I planned them to, naturally and by destiny. Much might have been different had I been different. However, it was as if it had to be like that only. I have no judgment about my life and myself. There is nothing I am quite sure about, except that more than I was living my life, life was living through me. God is clear and only man's mind is clouded. I kept attending to little responsibilities that came my way and God never failed me. You are nothing but you can do anything. Mantra stands written at SRK – 'I am nothing, but I can do anything.'